Henry Fanshawe Tozer

Turkish Armenia and eastern Asia Minor

Henry Fanshawe Tozer

Turkish Armenia and eastern Asia Minor

ISBN/EAN: 9783743316423

Manufactured in Europe, USA, Canada, Australia, Japa

Cover: Foto ©ninafisch / pixelio.de

Manufactured and distributed by brebook publishing software (www.brebook.com)

Henry Fanshawe Tozer

Turkish Armenia and eastern Asia Minor

TURKISH ARMENIA

AND

EASTERN ASIA MINOR

BY THE

REV. HENRY FANSHAWE TOZER, M.A., F.R.G.S.

TUTOR AND LATE FELLOW OF EXETER COLLEGE, OXFORD
AUTHOR OF 'RESEARCHES IN THE HIGHLANDS OF TURKEY' ETC.

LONDON
LONGMANS, GREEN, AND CO.
1881

All rights reserved

TURKISH ARMENIA
&c.

LONDON: PRINTED BY
SPOTTISWOODE AND CO., NEW-STREET SQUARE
AND PARLIAMENT STREET

TO

MY BELOVED WIFE

I DEDICATE THIS BOOK

PREFACE.

THE JOURNEY which is here described was the execution of a plan conceived many years before. My original intention was to explore the interior of Asia Minor; but this was interfered with by the great famine which visited that country in 1874. By this, travelling was rendered difficult, or at all events so painful to the feelings that no one would have wished to undertake it except in the character of an agent of relief. This circumstance turned my thoughts towards Armenia, and before long I was seized with a strong desire to see that land, and especially to visit the upper waters of the Euphrates and Tigris; but this plan again was for the time overthrown by the war between Russia and Turkey, so that it was not until 1879 that it became practicable. In the interval those regions and their inhabitants had acquired an additional interest, owing to the campaign itself and the negotiations which followed. In that year I was fortunate enough to accomplish the journey, and to combine with the circuit of Turkish Armenia a visit to the objects of greatest interest in the east of Asia Minor.

My best thanks are due to the Rev. R. ST JOHN TYRWHITT for the care and skill with which he has made from my pencil sketches the water-colour drawings from which the illustrations are taken; and to my companion, Mr. CROWDER, without whose vigorous co-operation the journey could not have been carried through.

H. F. T.

CONTENTS.

CHAPTER I.

ACROSS PONTUS.

Constantinople—The Bosphorus—Southern coast of the Black Sea—Sinope—Samsoun—Discouraging prospects—The Circassians—Banking in the interior—Leave Samsoun—Turkish graveyards—Chakalli Khan—Solitary road—The Kara Dagh—Geographical features of Asia Minor—Ladik—Blessing the harvest—The Ak Dagh—Descent to Amasia—Position of Amasia .   1

CHAPTER II.

AMASIA TO EUYUK.

Amasia—The English military consuls—The ancient walls—The Tombs of the Kings—Cave of the Mirror—Dat of the sepulchres—The German consul—State of the country—Political feeling—The postal system—Leave Amasia—Ancient aqueduct—Roads to Yeuzgatt—Turkish village of Koyounjak—The travellers' outfit—Provisions—Travelling in Turkey—Kara Hadjip—The central plateau—Aladjah   29

CHAPTER III.

PRIMITIVE ANTIQUITIES.

Arrival at Euyuk—Products of the country—Ancient building at Euyuk—Bas-reliefs on the front—The entrance—The sphinxes—Assyrian features—Origin of the sphinxes—Boghaz-keui—A native meal—The Yazili Kaya—Description of the bas-reliefs on the rocks—Figures in neighbouring cleft—Ancient palace at Boghaz-keui—Origin of these monuments—Meaning of the bas-reliefs—Views of Barth, Hamilton, Texier, and Perrot—Similar sculptures found elsewhere—The Hittites 55

CHAPTER IV.

YEUZGATT TO KAISERIEH.

The Boghaz—The Cabak Tepe—Yeuzgatt—Family of Tchapan Oglou—The Angora goat—Causes of the depopulation of Asia Minor—The Tekieh of Osman Pasha—Bread in Asia Minor—The famine of 1874—Its causes—First view of Mount Argaeus—Unwonted reception—Armenian village of Tchakmak—Contrast of Armenians and Turks—Approach to the Halys—The 'Bridge of the numerous eyes'—Rock chambers near the river—Plain of Kaiserieh—Arrival at Kaiserieh 79

CHAPTER V.

MOUNT ARGAEUS.

Kaiserieh: History of the city—Arrival of the British consuls—Mosque and tomb of Houen—Start for Argaeus—Cross the ridge of the mountain—Village of Everek—Hospitality in Turkey—Native visitors—Preparations for the ascent—Gum tragacanth—Bivouac on the mountain—Moonlight start—Steep climbing—Summit of Argaeus—View from the summit—Ancient habitations in the rocks—Return to Everek—Former ascents—Volcanic character of the mountain 106

CHAPTER VI.

THE LAND OF ROCK-DWELLINGS.

Leave Everek—Threshing—Village of Basch-keui—Obelisks of tufa—Native views of politics—Urgub—A Greek entertainer—Valley of Gueremeh—Caves and niches—A refectory—Rock-hewn churches—Byzantine frescoes—Ancient monastic community—St. Basil, Bishop of Caesareia—System of St. Basil—His retreat in Pontus—Severe climate of Gueremeh—Earlier inhabitants—The horseshoe arch—Departure from Urgub—Indje-su—Broad-tailed sheep—Completion of the circuit of Argaeus . 132

CHAPTER VII.

KAISERIEH TO SIVAS.

Weather prospects—Leave Kaiserieh—Seljouk tombs—Monastery of Surp Garabed—Importance of St. John the Baptist in the Armenian Church—The church of Surp Garabed—Salt lake—Sultan-khané—Clearness of the air—Turkish matrons—Oppressive taxation—Houses in Asia Minor—Sivas—A Dere-bey—Position and history of Sivas—Student-interpreters—Relations of Mahometans and Christians—Condition of the country—Future prospects 158

CHAPTER VIII.

ANTI-TAURUS AND EUPHRATES.

Armenia—Its geographical features—Sketch of its history—The Armenian Church—Influence of the Armenians—Guide-book for Armenia—Departure from Sivas—Pass of Delik Tasch—Visit of Count von Moltke—Village of Allaja Khan—Hekim Khan—Character of the Anti-Taurus—First view of the Euphrates—Ferry at Keban Maden—Two streams of the Euphrates—Its lower course—The Euphrates in history—Village and mine of Keban Maden—Arrival at Mezireh . . 187

CHAPTER IX.

KHARPUT AND THE WESTERN TIGRIS.

Town and castle of Kharput—Crusaders confined in the castle—Position and history of Kharput—The Jacobites—Origin and fortunes of the sect—Armenia College—Its students—Course of study pursued—Relations with the Mahometans—A summer retreat—Armenian grievances—The girls' school—Estimate of the American missions—Plain of Mezireh—Lake Gheuljik—Construction of a dike—Head waters of the Tigris—No connection between the Euphrates and Tigris 217

CHAPTER X.

THE KURD COUNTRY.

Valley of the Murad or Eastern Euphrates—Town and castle of Palu—Cuneiform inscription—St. Mezrop's dwelling-place—

Effects of the Ramazan—The Dersim Kurds—Kurdish village of Grolla—The Kurdish race—Their religion—Kizilbashes—Wild mountain road—Chevli—Birds in Armenia—Terbassan—Kurd physiognomy—Manna—Changeli, or Surp Garabed of Mush—The church—Manuscript of King Hatoum—Ziaret—A Hindoo colony—Zenobius's account of it—St. Gregory the Illuminator—Conversion of the Hindoos 247

CHAPTER XI.

BITLIS AND THE EASTERN TIGRIS.

Town of Mush—State of the neighbouring population—Quartering of Kurds on Armenians—Plain of Mush—Armenian villages—The Kara-su—French-speaking natives—Trials of a loyal Turk—Pass into Kurdistan—The watershed—Eastern source of the Tigris—Accounts of Strabo and Pliny—Communication with the Euphrates—Xenophon's route—Bitlis—A retreat in Kurdistan—Mode of collecting manna—Castle of Bitlis—First view of the lake of Van 282

CHAPTER XII.

THE LAKE OF VAN.

Remarkable character of the lake—Village of Tadvan—Shores of Lake Van—Powdery volcanic soil—Akhlat—The Kharabasheher, or 'ruined city'—The castle of Akhlat—Dust storm—The upper valley—History of Akhlat—Tunuz—Adeljivas—Ascent of Mount Sipan—Village of Norshunjuk—The crater—View from the ridge—Summits of Sipan—Height of the mountain—Legends relating to it—Walls of Adeljivas—Circassian colonies—Boats on Lake Van—Crossing the lake—Armenian sailors—Landing-place of Avanz 311

CHAPTER XIII.

VAN.

Situation of Van—Its appearance and population—The great inscription—Telegrams in Turkey—A Christian assistant-governor

CONTENTS. xiii

—Castle of Van—Naphtha well—View from the summit—Excavated chambers—The caves of Khorkhor—The cuneiform inscriptions—Object of the rock chambers—Unhealthiness of Van—History of the city—Moses of Chorene's account of its foundation—Legends of Semiramis—Assyrian influence—Later history—Timour's siege—Difficulty in obtaining horses—Armenian ponies—Lake of Artschag—Karakenduz—First view of Ararat—Head of Lake Van—Pergri 343

CHAPTER XIV.

THE HIGHEST UPLANDS.

The Bende-Mahi-su—A friendly warning—The nomad Kurds—Kurdish encampment—Description of the tents—Lofty ridge—Grand view of Ararat—Noticeable points respecting it—Village of Diyadin—The roof of Western Asia—Head waters of the Murad—Geography of the district—Sketch of the Russo-Turkish campaign—Monastery of Utch Keliseh: its church—Persian villages—Description of native dwellings—The Turkish currency—Plain of Alashgerd—Pass of Delibaba—Meeting with Englishmen—Battles in the pass—The Persian traffic—The Araxes—Plain of Pasin—Deveh Boyoun—Arrival at Erzeroum . . 372

CHAPTER XV.

ERZEROUM AND BAIBURT.

Erzeroum: its history—The Persian quarter—Principal buildings of the city—The castle—Prospects of famine—Consular reports on the country—Possible remedies for its disorders—Warm springs of Ilidja—The Frat, or Western Euphrates—Pass of the Kop Dagh—River Tchoruk—Baiburt: its castle—Ancient buildings at Varzahan—Armenian architecture—Intricate passes—'Thalatta! Thalatta!'—Route of the Ten Thousand . . . 410

CHAPTER XVI.

SUMELAS AND TREBIZOND.

Valley of Sumelas—Extraordinary position of the monastery—Rich vegetation—Approach to Sumelas—The interior—Its foundation—Story of Sultan Murad IV.—The church—Bull of Alexius III.—Firman of Mahomet II.—The refectory and library—Rhododendrons and azaleas—Exquisite scenery—Greek characteristics among the people—First view of Trebizond—Position of the mediæval city: its history—Court of the Grand Comneni—Antiquities of Trebizond—The great siege—Mediæval game of polo—Church of Haghia Sophia—Destruction of ancient monuments—Conclusion of the journey 434

LIST OF ILLUSTRATIONS.

MONASTIC ROCK CHAMBERS AT GUEREMEH . . .	*Frontispiece*
PINNACLES OF MOUNT ARGAEUS	*To face p.* 125
THE EUPHRATES AT KEBAN MADEN .	,, 205
MOUNT SIPAN AND LAKE VAN . . .	,, 317
THE MONASTERY OF SUMELAS	,, 435

TURKISH ARMENIA

AND

EASTERN ASIA MINOR.

CHAPTER I.

ACROSS PONTUS.

Constantinople—The Bosphorus—Southern coast of the Black Sea—Sinope—Samsoun—Discouraging prospects—The Circassians—Banking in the interior—Leave Samsoun—Turkish graveyards—Chakalli Khan—Solitary road—The Kara Dagh—Geographical features of Asia Minor—Ladik—Blessing the harvest—The Ak Dagh—Descent to Amasia—Position of Amasia.

In the afternoon of July 14, 1879, I embarked on board the French steamer 'Méandre,' which was lying in the harbour of Constantinople at the meeting-point of the Bosphorus and the Golden Horn, in readiness to start for the ports of the southern coast of the Black Sea. My companion was Mr. T. M. Crowder, Bursar of Corpus Christi College, Oxford, and Major in the Oxfordshire Militia, with whom it had been my good fortune to make four previous journeys in Greece and European Turkey at intervals during the preceding twenty-seven years, and our destination was the port of Samsoun, which lies rather less than two-thirds of the way along that coast, between Sinope and Trebizond, whence we intended to penetrate into the eastern part of Asia Minor. We had arrived from Marseilles three days before, after touching at Naples and the Piræus, and by great good fortune a rapid passage had brought us a day in advance of our time, so that we were able to complete our preparations, and proceed on our onward voyage without delay. During the interval we had obtained a dragoman, a Greek of Mitylene, who had just returned from the service of some of the English commissioners for settling the limits of Bulgaria—a rough and far from first-rate travelling-servant, but hardy and healthy, which is the first consideration in journeying in remote districts, capable of doing much work, a good plain cook, and possessing a thorough knowledge of Turkish, which language, in fact, he spoke like his mother tongue. Anyhow he was the best we could get, though we had made enquiries beforehand, for the more experienced dragomans are somewhat unwilling to undertake these hard journeys; but the result was that much of what is ordinarily done by the servant fell to the lot of his employers. We had also purchased Turkish saddles in the bazaars, shaped as nearly as possible like English saddles, but less hard, and for that reason preferable, because they are less liable to gall the horses' backs in a long continuous journey. Stirrups and stirrup-leathers we had brought from England, as those of the country are untrustworthy and uncomfortable. To this must be added a small and simple *batterie de cuisine*, and a few other necessary articles. Last, not least, we had provided ourselves with a supply of the money of the country. We were fortified by a firman of the Sultan, which through the kindness of the Foreign Office had been forwarded to us before we left England—a document of the first importance to the traveller, as it not only ensures respect on the part of the local authorities, and enables the bearer to claim hospitality, if necessary, and the means of transport, when that is difficult to obtain, but also guarantees admission to places which it might otherwise be impossible to visit.

While our vessel was taking in merchandise, we had time to survey the scene around us and on board. On one side was Galata with its massive Genoese tower, and the more aristocratic Pera on the hills above; on the other the Seraglio point, with its gardens and quaint buildings, behind which rose the gilded dome of St. Sophia, and the line of mosques and minarets which crown the successive heights of Stamboul; while on the Asiatic side lay Scutari, surmounted by the dark cypress-grove of its vast cemetery. In the foreground of this unrivalled view, which from its steep yet graceful ascents, the combination of conspicuous edifices, irregular wooden buildings, and numerous trees, and the variety of colour which it presents, combines every element of picturesqueness, lay numerous vessels, principally French, Austrian, and Russian steamers, occupying the space between us and the sea of Marmora. A fresh north-east wind had set the blue water dancing, and crested it with white, and in the midst of this boats darted in all directions, some of them being gilded caïques, the gondolas of the Bosphorus, though far more elegant in shape and gayer in colour than their Venetian cousins. So numerous were they that it seemed as if they must come into collision with one another or with the buoys to which the vessels were moored; indeed, such casualties were not wholly avoided, and when they occurred, or were on the eve of occurring, they occasioned wild and polyglot exclamations. Our vessel was crowded with deck-passengers—Armenians, Turks, and Persians with tall black caps, lying about on carpets and rugs, and closely packed together. The cabin was raised above the deck, and behind this, in the stern, the whole space was occupied by the ladies and children of a harem, who reclined on mattresses and bundles of various colours, few of them being veiled and fewer good-looking. The cabin passengers were not numerous, the principal being an old Russian lady, a vigorous smoker of cigarettes, who was on her way to visit a married daughter at Samsoun, together with her two sons.

At six o'clock we loosed our moorings and proceeded up the Bosphorus. We were both of us heartily glad to leave the city, for on no occasion had we been so much impressed by the contrast between the beauty of its appearance from without and the repulsiveness of the interior. We had been prepared to find considerable improvements introduced since our last visit, but in reality the change seemed to us to be rather for the worse. There is now, it is true, a tramway across Stamboul, and a railway runs along the sea-wall in the direction of St. Stephano, if these are to be regarded as advantages, but one did not then see extravagant Parisian costumes side by side with loathsome squalor; and certainly at the present time the streets of Galata are not less filthy than formerly, nor the pavements of Pera less rugged, nor the scavenger dogs less numerous or less noisy. But the shores of the Bosphorus had lost none of their charm. First we passed along the magnificent palaces on the European shore, which represent the extravagance of successive Sultans and the money of ruined bondholders; and afterwards between villas and villages on both banks, sometimes lining the shore, sometimes creeping up the hillsides, and interspersed with abundant vegetation in the cypress-groves and gardens, though here and there ruin defaced the scene in the shape of handsome wooden houses deserted and falling into decay. As the evening advanced it rendered the scene doubly beautiful, throwing the Asiatic shore into light in contrast with the dark shade opposite, until we passed between the castles of Europe and Asia on corresponding promontories, and finally reached the lordly villages of Therapia and Buyukdere, the summer resorts of ambassadors and wealthy Greek and Armenian merchants. Night had fallen before we issued from the narrow strait, but we discovered that we had entered the Black Sea from the plunging of the vessel, owing to the long waves that were brought down by the wind.

On coming on deck the next morning we found that we were out of sight of land, for the coast in this part forms a considerable bay, before it begins to project northward and form that remarkable hump in the outline of the country, as seen on the map, which in ancient times represented the district of Paphlagonia. After midday, however, we neared the shore, at a point not far from Amastra, the ancient Amastris, and from this time onward continued to follow the coast.

The ground in this part rises immediately from the sea, sometimes more and sometimes less steeply, and though most of it was uncultivated, yet at intervals there were extensive clearings where corn was grown. Behind, at a few miles' distance off, ran a range of mountains parallel to the shore, of considerable height and fine outline, while below the ridge precipices of limestone made their appearance. The rest was clothed with dense forests, reminding us that this entire region furnished a large supply of timber to the Romans. One part of the range bore the name of Cytorus, and is spoken of both by Catullus and Virgil as famous for its box trees;[1] and Horace, on the one occasion when he employs allegory, in speaking of the Roman state under the image of a storm-tossed vessel, addresses it as 'a pine from the Pontus, daughter of a forest of fame.'[2] The richest scenery along this southern coast of the Black Sea, however, is further east, between Samsoun and Trebizond, as we discovered on our return journey from the last-named city. The country in that part is well cultivated and beautifully wooded, and owing to its humid climate retains its freshness all the year. As you pass it in the steamer, the numerous well-built villages and the gracefulness of the mountain outlines might make you think you were following the shore of one of the Italian lakes.

At 8 A.M. on the 16th we were off Sinope. This famous place, the most important of all the Greek

[1] Catull. iv. 13: Amastri Pontica et Cytore buxifer. Virg. *Georg.* ii. 437: Juvat undantem buxo spectare Cytorum.
[2] Hor. *Od.* i. 14. 11, 12:
> Pontica pinus,
> Silvæ filia nobilis.

colonies on the Euxine, which was at a later period the birthplace and capital of Mithridates the Great, derived its greatness chiefly from its geographical situation, as it occupies a central position in the projection of the coast which I have just noticed, and thus commands the two great reaches on either side, for from this point the land begins to trend towards the south-east. In this respect it may be compared to Carthage in ancient, and Tunis in modern times, the site of which cities similarly holds the key of the two basins of the Mediterranean and of the communication between them. The situation of the town itself is striking, as it occupies the narrow isthmus which joins a triangular peninsula to the mainland, and consequently has two sea-faces. It is enclosed by massive walls, with towers, which follow the shore and run across from the sea to the harbour; and on the side towards the mainland there is a large castle. The peninsula spreads, and rises steeply towards the sea, where the ground which forms the base of the triangle falls in precipices. This promontory is called Boz Tepe, or the Gray Cape. After passing it we obtained a view of the harbour which it shelters from the north; this was the scene of the burning of the Turkish fleet by the Russians in November 1853, shortly before the commencement of the Crimean war. It is probably to the injury done to the town at that time that its decline in prosperity is to be attributed. Texier speaks of it as the principal station for the steamers in the Black Sea, but now they have ceased to call there, as its commerce does not repay them. In bad weather, however, they are glad to take refuge there, as it affords the best, and almost the only good harbourage on the south of the Euxine, the other harbours being hardly more than open roadsteads; and the storms, as more than one of the captains of these vessels assured us, are as terrific as of yore.

Between Sinope and Samsoun a promontory intervenes, which though it forms a conspicuous object on the map, from the deck of a steamer might almost escape observation until you are close to it, for the mountain line, which has hitherto followed the coast, here runs a long way inland, and the intervening ground is so low, that except for the trees and bushes that grow upon it, it reaches little above the sea-level. This is the delta of the Halys (Kizil Irmak), the largest river of Asia Minor, of which we shall have frequently to speak in the course of our wanderings. The amount of alluvium here brought down testifies to the size of the stream, but throughout its course its water is very turbid, containing a large quantity of deposit. It was about 2 P.M. when we reached the apex of the delta, and we found the sea at this point much discoloured by the sediment carried down into it. As we approached Samsoun the number of villages increased, and the hillsides were covered with cornfields and other kinds of cultivation. Passing a lighthouse at the angle of the bay, we entered the harbour, which, however, is not only fully exposed to the north wind, but owing to continual neglect is so shallow that a steamer cannot approach within half a mile of the shore. Accordingly our vessel was soon surrounded by a small fleet of boats, and in one of these we and our effects were deposited. We had heard beforehand of the badness of the landing when there is any sea running, owing to the breakers at the landing-place, so we considered ourselves fortunate in having tolerably calm water; and, as it was, only one wave broke over us, as we approached the pier near the custom-house station. After a certain detention at this point, more from hopes of *bakshish* on the part of the officials than from any real examination of our luggage, we were again rowed out in the direction of a *locanda* which stood on the shore at some little distance off, and finally were landed on the shoulders of a Turk.

The town of Samsoun, though it is the residence of a pasha, owing to its commercial importance as the outlet of almost all the trade of north-eastern Asia Minor, is inconsiderable in size, and by no means imposing in appearance. The greater part of it skirts the shore on the western side of the harbour, but some of the better houses run up the hills behind. There are few minarets, and the most conspicuous building is a Greek church of recent construction. The place has a bad name for dangerous fevers during the summer, and this was confirmed to us by those of the inhabitants with whom we conversed. They are attributed chiefly to the extensive marshes on the eastern side of the bay, where the river Iris forms a considerable delta, and from the middle of July onwards, few of the residents wholly escape them. The ancient Greek city of Amisus, which at one time was only second in importance to Sinope, did not occupy the site of the modern town, but was built at a distance of about a mile and a half to the north, nearer the entrance of the bay. The ruins were described to me by one who had visited them as being a confused mass of débris. It is a curious fact that though, as I suppose, the name Samsoun is a corruption of Amisus, yet the two towns subsisted side by side for some time during the Middle Ages. The one was the Turkish, the other the Greek settlement; and as early as the beginning of the thirteenth century we find the two in alliance with one another, the walled town of Samsoun being the emporium, in the warehouses of which was stored merchandise of immense value which had been transmitted from the interior, while the Greeks of Amisus provided the capital and the ships by means of which it was distributed through Russia and western Europe. Amongst the articles of commerce thus put in circulation were cloth of hair and wool, and variegated carpets, the manufactures of the nomad races, the copper of Tocat, and the brilliant dye-stuffs of Cæsareia.[1]

When our passports were demanded at the landing-place, we had shown our firman; but the officials, who were extremely uncivil, demanded a separate passport for our dragoman, contrary to all custom, for in such cases the travelling servant is supposed to be included. However, there was no help for it, and he had to be despatched to the pasha to give an account of himself. As it was long before he returned, and the keeper of the *locanda* maintained that if the pasha had left his office and gone to his country house, he might be detained for the night, we thought it as well to pay a visit to the French consul, who was acting as the representative of England also, hoping at the same time to obtain some information about horses for our journey. When we reached his

[1] See Finlay, *History of Greece*, vol. iv. p. 322 (new ed.).

house, we were shown into his bedroom, where we found him laid up with a broken leg, the result of an accident at Constantinople. We apologised for our intrusion; but he kindly requested us to stay, and desired the dragoman of the Consulate to arrange matters for us. Before long, however, we found that our servant had had an interview with the pasha, who at once decided that a passport was unnecessary.

The account which the consul gave us of the state of things in the interior, and the view he took of the prospects of our journey, were in the highest degree discouraging. 'You must not think of starting,' he said, 'for several days; you must wait till a caravan is formed, for no one travels now with less than a company of twenty persons. The roads are thoroughly unsafe, owing to the Circassians and other brigands.' When I asked whether it was only in this neighbourhood that danger was to be apprehended from the Circassians, 'Oh, no,' he replied, 'they are everywhere in the interior; we are constantly hearing of their robberies.' This intelligence was certainly not reassuring. We knew how to discount the consul's statements, for we had learnt from former experience what exaggerated ideas prevail in the seaport towns, especially among persons engaged in trade, on the subject of the dangers of the interior. At the same time we were aware that these stories about Circassians were not wholly fiction, for our dragoman, when travelling with two Englishmen in the west of Asia Minor, on the road between Scutari and Angora, in the previous year, had twice been robbed by brigands of that race, and the same thing had happened to an American party in the same district.

Still, our experience of travelling in the wilder parts of European Turkey suggested that the chances were in our favour, and we had great confidence in the unwonted appearance of our European costume, for the idea prevails that the Frank, like the porcupine, is an unsafe animal to meddle with, and that if he is molested, the fact will not be left unnoticed. As an American resident in the interior sententiously remarked, ' The shape of your hats will protect you.'

The next question was that of getting horses, and on this point also the consul had little encouragement to give us. Our object was to hire them as far as Amasia, three days' journey, for though some experienced travellers advocate buying horses and taking them through the whole journey, we have no hesitation in pronouncing against that plan. It is true that in this way you save yourself the trouble of frequently changing your horses and making a fresh bargain; but on the other hand, if the horses are your own, you are liable to detention from one of them falling lame, getting a sore back, or otherwise knocking up; and besides, if you travel at the rate of about eight hours a day, which is not unreasonable, your horses cannot go on for more than five or six days without a long rest, and this the traveller who is limited in time cannot afford. But when we asked about hiring horses, we were told that it would certainly take us several days to get them, and the consul added, amongst other corroborative facts, that not long before this the post from Bagdad, which passes this way, had been detained because no horses could be found to bring it on. He led us to suppose that the same difficulty would be found throughout the country, as horses had been very scarce ever since the Russian war; and this, if true, would have been a serious impediment to our progress. We could not help hoping, however, that our representative's state of health had made him unnecessarily despondent.

At the little *restaurant* where we took our meals, we found the same views to prevail among the *habitués* of the place with regard to the risks of travelling in the interior, especially on account of the Circassians. These people have immigrated into Turkey at intervals during the last half century, according as their native country has been brought into subjection by the Russians. Allotments of land have been assigned to them by the Government, and many of them have settled down on these and become peaceable folk; but not a few, on the other hand, have preferred a marauding life, and are now the terror of the inhabitants. A fatal mistake was made when they were allowed to enter the country fully armed, for coming amongst a population either unarmed or carrying only very rude weapons, they soon found that they commanded the situation; besides which, their daring and resolute character rendered them much more formidable than the ordinary *mauvais sujets* who are wont to appear when a country is disorganised. We heard a good deal also of a new scourge that was beginning to infest the neighbourhood of Samsoun, viz. the Lazes, who have emigrated from Batoum since the Russian occupation of that place, and have landed on this coast. The authorities proposed to send them also into the interior; but up to this time they had refused to move, and resisted when any attempt was made to force them. Under these circumstances, we thought it desirable to take guards, and this we continued to do, generally being accompanied by two, sometimes by one only, throughout the whole of our journey. The advantages of this we found to be very great; for besides serving as a protection, they were frequently well acquainted with the roads, and could give information about objects in the neighbourhood, and also might be made serviceable in loading and unloading baggage, finding a night's lodging, and various other forms of usefulness. The local authorities are bound to provide them, free of charge, to one who bears a firman, the traveller only paying a voluntary remuneration—we found the average payment to be a shilling a day for each guard—in case he is satisfied. They are picked men, and generally are well mounted and well armed, most of them carrying breechloaders, and some even repeating rifles. We also usually found them good-natured and willing fellows. In case of a serious attack, they would probably not be of much service, as they would be overpowered by numbers; but, anyhow, their presence is an evidence that the party they escort travels under the auspices of the Government.

It may also be worth while to mention before starting what arrangements we had made for obtaining money on our journey, for it need hardly be said that when the country is at all disturbed it is well to carry as little coin as possible. Now in many of the large towns of the interior of Asia Minor and Armenia there are American Protestant missionaries settled, and by good fortune before we left England my companion learnt from an acquaintance who travelled in these parts some years ago, that he had been allowed to employ these gentlemen as a banking agency. Accordingly, when we arrived at Constantinople we visited their central office or 'Bible House,' as it is called, in Stamboul, and enquired whether we might be allowed the same privilege. To this their secretary, Mr. Baldwin, kindly replied without any hesitation in the affirmative, and on our depositing a sum of money with him, gave us a circular letter for that amount addressed to the various missionaries, and from them we obtained from time to time a sufficient sum to carry us to our next stage, reckoned according to the current rate of exchange. In default of a regular system of banking in these countries it is possible to negotiate bills of exchange by taking them into the bazaars and offering them to the highest bidder, and so great is the confidence reposed in a piece of paper with an European signature, that I have known a draft to be cashed, when the receiver could not read a word of it, and had no guarantee beyond the presence of the person who drew it. But the method which we adopted is far more secure, and we found it answer admirably.

Of course, when such exaggerated notions prevailed with regard to the difficulty of travelling, we were not surprised to find that the object of our journey was interpreted in various ways. Subsequently, at more than one place we found that we were supposed to be surveying for a railway. But about one thing every one was agreed, and that was that we must have some more definite purpose than merely seeing the country, for it was ridiculous to suppose that any one would go there unless he was obliged. Mr. Baldwin at Constantinople evidently shared this view, for, to our great amusement, his first question was, 'Are you Government agents, or newspaper correspondents?' And at our dirty *locanda* at Samsoun, when the usual enquiries were made, and we replied that we were travelling for pleasure, the only comment that was returned was a laugh of incredulity.

The books that we carried with us to give information on this part of our route were—Texier's 'Asie Mineure,' the smaller work of that name in one volume, published in Didot's series 'L'Univers;' Hamilton's 'Researches in Asia Minor,' 2 vols. 1842; and Van Lennep's 'Travels in Asia Minor,' 2 vols. 1869. The first of these works is the most complete and exhaustive; the second is distinguished by the author's classical research and geological knowledge, and is a model of an accurate book of travels; while the third gives the experience of one who had long resided in the country, and is a careful observer and excellent draughtsman. Our map was Kiepert's invaluable one of Asiatic Turkey.

But enough of preliminaries, let us start for the interior; and certainly the stifling heat of the night at Samsoun, and the filthiness of the accommodation, did not dispose us to linger beyond what was necessary. When the morning came, and we set ourselves to work in earnest to get horses, our difficulties began to disappear. There did not seem for the moment to be any lack of horses, though the prices asked for their hire were utterly unreasonable. Hour after hour was spent in fruitless negotiations, until, in despair of making any agreement with a *katirji* or carrier, we obtained horses from the *menzil* or Turkish post, though we had reason to believe that the arrangement was a private speculation on the part of the postmaster, and the rate of payment was far higher than is usual in this service. However, at last five horses were forthcoming, three for ourselves and our servant, one for the baggage, and one for the *suridji* or postboy, whose office it was to look after the animals and bring them back at the end of the journey; and at 3 P.M. we started, accompanied by two guards, who had been provided by the pasha at the request of the dragoman of the Consulate. One of these was a good-looking young Turk, with wonderful matted locks of hair hanging down behind; the other was a Circassian, dressed in the costume of his nation, who was supposed to be likely to have influence with the robbers of his race, in case we should fall in with them. As we mounted steeply to the top of the hill behind the town, we passed large patches of tobacco, and a number of olive-trees, the last specimens of that tree that we should see before returning again to the coast of the Black Sea, for the climate of the interior of Asia Minor and Armenia is too cold to admit of their cultivation. From the level summit we descended again to a valley, at the further end of which the sea was visible away to the north. In one part of this was a small Turkish cemetery, half ruined, the graves being enclosed by slabs and marked by headstones. In the course of our subsequent journey we must have seen more than fifty similar ones, and the solitude of these rustic graveyards would be impressive—for they are almost always at a distance from human habitations—were it not that their uncared-for state suggests a feeling of dreariness and melancholy.

At this point we commenced a steady ascent towards the ridge of the mountains that lie at the back of Samsoun, which we accomplished at a good pace in three hours. In the stubble-fields by the roadside were numerous herds of buffaloes, and from time to time we met trains of peasants from the interior, bringing grain for exportation in sacks which were packed on the carts of the country. These were extremely primitive contrivances, having two solid wooden wheels each, the surface of which was rudely carved in rather graceful patterns. Here and there harvesting was going on, though on the high ground it had not yet been begun ; and in one place we found the reapers working to the sound of a drum and bagpipe. Gradually the views became very extensive, though one would rather call them spacious than grand ; on our left lay a deep valley in which flowed the stream of Samsoun, and beyond this spread lofty sloping mountains, while behind us was a wide expanse of sea. About our route on the higher ground there was much undergrowth, including juniper bushes, and trees resembling our hazel, oak, and beech, though they were not the same ; but there was no fine timber, and we were disappointed at not finding the same rich vegetation which grows elsewhere in the neighbourhood of the coast. From the summit of the ridge we obtained views over the uplands of the interior, but shortly after we began to descend on the other side the sun set, and the evening rapidly closed in. The road now became so steep and rough that it was necessary for us to get off and lead our horses ; it is the high road from the Black Sea into Eastern Asia Minor and Southern Armenia, but notwithstanding this, the occurrence of such rugged and broken pieces as what we met with here evidently renders it impracticable for carriages. At this time it was very dusty, but from the clayey nature of the soil it must be extremely muddy in wet weather. It was dark before we reached Chakalli Khan, or the Jackal Tavern, which was to be our resting-place for the night. It was a country inn, such as we had been accustomed to in European Turkey, in which less provision is made for 'man' than for his 'beast'; but we had no reason to complain, for there was an empty room upstairs in which our camp-beds could be placed, and, if there was no lack of vermin, they were at all events not as plentiful as at Samsoun. Of the surroundings of the place we could form no idea, only we knew there must be water near from the croaking of the frogs. Its height above the sea was 1,100 feet.

The arrival of daylight showed us that we were in a valley surrounded by hills, through which flowed a small stream, a tributary of the river of Samsoun. A few houses on its banks formed a village, and hard by was a massive stone structure with a pointed arch over its entrance-gate, called the Old Chakalli Khan, which is now disused. From this point we ascended through country resembling that of the previous evening, only the undergrowth was thicker, and the traveller's joy which trailed in profuse luxuriance over the bushes reminded us of the hedgerows of England. Our attention was also attracted by the beautiful birds, especially the hoopoes with wings barred with white, which spread their brown crests as they alight on the roadside in front of the traveller. These and the ringdoves were the commonest birds in the country, and we met with them throughout our whole journey; the magpies also were very numerous, especially in the neighbourhood of habitations. When we reached a height of somewhat more than 2,000 feet we obtained our last view of the sea towards the north; in the opposite direction was a succession of rolling hills, the most definitely marked of which was the line of the Kara Dagh or Black Mountain, while the horizon was bounded by the loftier Ak Dagh or White Mountain, a fine range, though with no very marked outline. The summits of this were grey and bare of trees, and in the winter would be covered with snow, from which feature the name is probably derived; but the Turkish nomenclature of places is singularly limited. Our road in this part was very solitary, for we met but few people, and as we passed through a wood we noticed the skeleton of a horse which had been left to its fate, a sign of barbarism which is not commonly seen in European Turkey, except in the wilder parts of Albania; in Asia, however, we soon became familiarised to carcases and skeletons. In both countries the skulls of horses and oxen are placed on poles in the fields as a charm to avert the influence of the evil eye. We descended to the village of Cavak, which we reached after two hours and a quarter's riding from the khan; it was a poor place, with one rickety wooden minaret, and, as it lies under a projecting crust of rock on the hillside, it is hardly seen from above until you descend into it. Here we were to change our guards, and while our fresh escort was being obtained we spent an hour at the house of the chief of the police, in a balcony overlooking a tangled garden.

Our direction from Samsoun had so far been due south-west; we now struck into a long valley among pretty wooded hills leading rather west than south, which was called Ak Su Deresi, or the Vale of the White River, from a muddy stream which intersected it; but all water is valuable in these parts, for the soil is dry and there are few springs. When we had nearly reached the head of this, we turned southwards and ascended the flank of the Kara Dagh, passing a village which takes its name from it, Karadagh-keui. The summit, which is about 2,900 feet high, is covered with beech-woods. The flowers that I noticed on these mountain ranges closely resemble those that are found on the lower slopes of the Alps— small yellow foxgloves, tall pinks, a variety of campanulas, the yellow salvia, and dwarf broom. There was also one kind of gentian, a rather scrubby plant with a pale-blue flower (*gentiana cruciata*), and of the orchid tribe I saw but a single specimen, a dull-red epipactis (*epipactis rubiginosa*). We descended to a wide level, whence a conspicuous mountain, the Taoutschan Dagh, was seen far away to the west, and then crossing another range about 3,000 feet high and also wooded, we reached the elevated plain of Ladik, which was covered with rich crops of hay, barley, and oats. Throughout this region we were struck by the general appearance of prosperity, and the cultivation of cereals appeared to be very extensive.

I have described in some detail the features of the country through which we have hitherto passed, because they may serve to introduce the reader to the general geography of Asia Minor, which is very remarkable, especially in respect of the elevation of the interior. The determining feature of this great peninsula is to be found in the mountain chains, which run from east to west parallel to the two seas—the Taurus to the Mediterranean, and to the Euxine the successive ranges called Olympus, distinguished as the Galatian, Bithynian, &c., according to the districts they pass through. The countries which form the sea-slopes of these are warm in temperature, those towards the north being temperate, those towards the south almost tropical; but the great area of the interior which they enclose between them is a series of irregular plateaux of great elevation, containing numerous salt lakes, and exposed to great extremes of heat and cold, being scorched by the sun during the summer months, and frequently covered with snow during the winter. The ranges which we are now crossing—for we have already passed three reaching nearly 3,000 feet in height since leaving Samsoun, and another has to be crossed before reaching Amasia—are a part of the Olympus chain, or rather of the mountains which join it to the Anti-Taurus, and which here are somewhat irregularly broken. At Amasia we reach a lower level, though that place is still more than 1,100 feet above the sea; but after that we rise gradually to an average level, first of 3,000 and then of 4,000 feet, until at last in the extreme east, where Asia Minor abuts on Armenia, the plains are 5,000 feet high. The courses of the rivers are hardly less remarkable. The largest of these, the Halys, rising in the north-east part of the country, flows at first in a south-westerly direction until it reaches the neighbourhood of Kaiserieh, and then, making a great sweep towards the north, falls into the sea, where we have already seen its delta, between Sinope and Samsoun. Within this great arc a lesser arc is formed by the course of the Iris, which flows by Amasia, and below that place is joined by another considerable stream, the Lycus, which rises at the back of Trebizond. It is over these uplands of the interior, and for the most part within or near the arc of the Halys, that our route for some time to come will lie.

The town of Ladik lies at the edge of the plain, backed by a range of hills, behind which again rises the lofty Ak Dagh. Its situation is picturesque, as it occupies an angle, round which stand wooded heights in numerous folds. It occupies the site of an ancient city called Laodicea, one of some half-dozen in Asia which bore that name; of this its modern name is a corruption, and the same change has taken place elsewhere, for Laodicea Combusta in the south of the country, near Iconium, is now also called Ladik. It does not appear to have had any history in ancient times, and it is a poor place at the present day. It possesses, however, a fine mosque, conspicuous from its two tall minarets of rich brown stone. The mosque itself, which is domed, is built in alternate courses of brick and stone, and has a handsome portico supported by pillars with capitals ornamented in Saracenic honeycomb-work. The khan, at which we passed the night, looked out on the main square, in the midst of which was a fountain playing into a large basin, with a *kiosk* or summer-house. A trough for horses outside it is flanked by two drums of columns, which are probably a remnant of the ancient city. The groups of people that assembled here in the morning formed a gay scene, as they wore turbans, shirts, and waistcoats of every conceivable colour. In the neighbourhood of Ladik we saw storks for the first time on this journey.

The following morning our route continued for some distance along the slopes and valleys to the west of Ladik. At one place, as we rode by a field where the corn was being cut, one of the reapers came running towards us carrying a handful of the ears, with the object of requesting a present from the passing travellers. This custom, which we found to prevail in most parts of this country and Armenia, is probably a very ancient one, and is thought to have been originally a mode of asking for a blessing on the harvest. In that case it may be the same which is referred to in Psalm cxxix. 7 : 'Wherewith the mower filleth not his hand, nor he that bindeth sheaves his bosom ; neither do they which go by say, The blessing of the Lord be upon you : we bless you in the name of the Lord.'[1] At the present day, however, it is regarded merely as a means of obtaining *bakshish*. We met with many more streams in this part than we had hitherto seen, for the Ak Dagh is a parent of waters ; and along the courses of these the tall spikes of the purple loosestrife, which is so great an ornament to our ditches in England, were growing abundantly. After two hours and a half we made a short halt at a large khan in a very pretty valley, where a rapid stream called Dereniz was spanned by a bridge. At this point began the real ascent of the Ak Dagh, and

[1] See Ritter's *Erdkunde*, x. 296.

as we proceeded we found the slopes clothed with numerous pines, of which trees we had only seen a few specimens hitherto; their aromatic scent, drawn out by the heat of the sun, now filled the air. The great mallows too, which might almost be described as half-brothers to hollyhocks, gave evidence that we were approaching a hotter region. Up to this time since leaving Samsoun we had had cool and cloudy weather, and as we crossed the plain of Ladik there was even a slight scud of rain; but this day the sky was clear, and the heat of the sun, though tolerable on the higher ground, became scorching as we descended. When we reached the shoulder of the mountain we looked down on the great and fertile plain of Marsovan, which presented for the most part a bare appearance, from the crops having been removed; and when we reached the highest point of the pass we obtained still more extensive views over successive mountain ranges towards the south and west in the direction of Kaiserieh and Yeuzgatt. The summit of the pass measured 3,200 feet by the aneroid, and was consequently the greatest elevation we had yet reached; but the highest points of the Ak Dagh, which appeared away to our left, could not have been much less than 2,000 feet above us. Some of the precipices on the mountain sides in that direction were finely coloured with purple and red. The descent was long and steep, so that during part of the way we dismounted and left our horses to follow us; the ground, too, was bare, except where it was thinly clothed with the prickly bushes of the heat-loving palluria, for the southern side of the mountains in these parts has usually less vegetation than the northern owing to its exposure to the sun. At last we reached the valley, just where the Marsovan plain forms an angle, and the river that drains it flows out on its way to join the Iris. Here we found the best piece of road we had ever seen in Turkey, wide and well macadamised, forming part of an intended road from Samsoun to Amasia; but like most of such schemes, the greater part of this only exists on paper. The valley gradually becomes almost a gorge from the steepness with which the rocks rise on both sides; but in the neighbourhood of the stream it is filled with the brightest vegetation, vines, walnuts, poplars, and mulberries, the last-named tree being cultivated for the sake of the silk, which, though on a smaller scale than formerly, is still produced in Amasia.

When looking from the mountain heights above, we had noticed below us, to the south, what appeared like a meeting of narrow gorges; and here, we were told, was the site of Amasia. It was this point that we were now approaching; and as the river we were following drew near to its junction with the Iris, the valley opened out, so as to form a small triangular plain, which was irrigated and carefully cultivated. As we skirted this, there rose above us, on our right, a mass of steep rock, surmounted by the walls and bastions of a mediæval castle; and when we had proceeded a little further we caught our first glimpse of the town, a portion of which is seen running up the slopes on the opposite side of the Iris. We then crossed this river, by a stone bridge, and followed its right bank upwards through the town, passing numerous large wheels which are turned by the current, and are employed to irrigate the neighbouring gardens. By these, our thoughts were carried back to Verona and the waterwheels in the Adige, only those in this place are on a much larger scale. The Iris here is about sixty yards broad, and though the water was low at that time, owing to the unusual heat of the season, yet it seemed to be of some little depth, for, in one place, we saw horses swimming in it, and a man following them who was also swimming. Its current is turbid, and of a dull whitish colour, so that its Turkish name of Yeshil Irmak, or the Green River, is not inappropriate.

The khan at which we took up our abode—an oblong structure, built round an interior court, with stables below, and a gallery above, giving access to numerous chambers—opened out on the quay, and directly faced the famous 'Tombs of the Kings,' which were the principal object of our visit. At this point the river runs nearly due east and west, but before it reaches the bridge by which we entered it makes a considerable bend towards the north. The rocks, which are composed of red and grey limestone, rise to a great height on both sides ; those towards the south are the loftier, reaching perhaps 2,000 feet, but are less precipitous ; and on their lower slopes the greater part of the town is built, presenting a picturesque appearance from the numerous trees that are interspersed among the houses. On the opposite side, the cliffs—in the face of which the 'Tombs' are excavated—rise with extreme steepness, until their summits are crowned by the castle which we have already seen from the back ; this seems to occupy two separate heights, which are joined by a ridge. Near our khan, the river was crossed by another bridge, built of wood, but the substructions are of stone, resting on round arches, which, from their massiveness, appear to be of the Roman period; these emerge but little from the surface of the water, and at most seasons of the year must be covered; but from between the arches there rise piers, which, though now broken, must evidently have served to support an upper bridge. Some distance above this, the gorge opens out towards another small plain, through which the river passes before reaching the city. It is a magnificent position, and reminded us of that of Berat in Albania, which lies in a similar ravine, with a river flowing through it, between an upper and a lower plain, and surmounted by a steep castle-rock on its northern side. But Amasia suffers greatly, as might be supposed, from extremes of temperature, and in summer resembles a furnace, so that the heat would be intolerable, were it not moderated towards evening by the breeze that draws up the valley. The population of the place is estimated at 20,000.

CHAPTER II.

AMASIA TO EUYUK.

Amasia—The English Military Consuls—The Ançient Walls—The Tombs of the Kings—Cave of the Mirror—Date of the Sepulchres—The German Consul—State of the Country—Political feeling—The Postal System—Leave Amasia—Ancient Aqueduct—Roads to Yeuzgatt—Turkish Village of Koyounjak—The Travellers' Outfit—Provisions—Travelling in Turkey—Kara Hadjip—The Central Plateau—Aladjah.

THE next day (July 20) was devoted to the sights of Amasia; but, as it was a primary consideration to make provision for our onward journey, we determined first to pay a visit to the pasha, in order to secure horses. His official residence lay at a little distance off on the other side of the stream: as we proceeded thither, numerous vultures—the scavengers of the town—were wheeling over our heads. These were splendid birds, totally unlike the repulsive specimens of that tribe to which persons have a traditional dislike, and far handsomer than eagles, as we subsequently discovered by frequent comparison in the wilder parts of Armenia, where vultures and eagles were among the commonest birds. These scavenger vultures are said only to eat carrion, so that there is no fear of their carrying off chickens and lambs; in fact, were this not so, they could hardly be tolerated in oriental cities. The wild vultures in the mountains, on the other hand, we were told, commit great depredations in these parts, especially among the goats, which they watch until they have reached a projecting rock, and then, swooping down, strike them a heavy blow, by which they are thrown over the precipice. We found the *konak* to be a spacious building with large cool rooms, and here his Excellency received us with much friendliness. In the course of conversation—for we were delayed a long time, while inquiry was being made about horses, and about the most desirable route to Yeuzgatt, allowing for our visiting some important antiquities on the way —the pasha informed us that four years before this, in the month of March, a great flood of the Iris occurred, when the river overflowed its banks, which here are fifteen feet above the water, and cased with stone, and carried away half of a wooden bridge which spanned the river at this point. The ruins of this were still visible, for it had never been repaired. When I asked about the effects of the Russian war on the population of this district, he answered that 15,000 men had gone to the war from the *sandjak* of Amasia, but of these only one in ten had returned. The loss to the industry of the country was consequently very great.

From the pasha we first heard of the despatch of consuls from England to Asia Minor and Armenia; he said he understood that representatives were coming to all the great towns of the interior, though they had not yet arrived. We afterwards found that most of them had preceded us by a few weeks, and we had the opportunity of visiting several in their new spheres of office. The system under which they were appointed was in some respects a novel one, for their place of residence was not fixed in any one city, as was the case with the old consuls, but each of them had a sort of roving commission within a certain area, so that he might move from place to place, and reside for a limited period in different towns, in order to collect information, and exercise that undefined influence which attaches to the consular office. They were also universally military men, chosen from different branches of the service. What may have been the reason for appointing officers in the army I do not know, but I can honestly say that I do not think a better choice could have been made. We found them to be not only capable, prudent, and energetic men, but open-minded and free from prejudice, prepared to sift impartially the evidence that came before them, and neither to exaggerate complaints nor to palliate abuses. Such men must always be of service in a country like Turkey, for their presence is a protest against wrongdoing, and they are feared for their uprightness and their power of reporting misdeeds at headquarters. The only misfortune connected with their appointment was the circumstances under which it was made, for, following as it did in the wake of the assumption by England of a protectorate of the Asiatic provinces of Turkey, it gave rise to the most exaggerated expectations on the part of the natives. Everywhere we found the idea to prevail that the English had come to govern the country; and everywhere, at least in Asia Minor, the report was hailed with satisfaction. Thus at Sivas we were told that, a fortnight after the arrival of Colonel Wilson, the consul-general, at that place, a peasant was heard to say that 'the Inghiliz pasha must be an extremely good-natured man, for everybody knew that he was ruling the country, and that all the power was in his hands, and yet he allowed the Turkish pasha to retain his position and title.' Abuses, it was thought, were soon to come to an end, and a period of prosperity to begin. Of course these hopes were doomed to disappointment as soon as it was found that the English officials had no administrative functions whatsoever.

We requested the pasha to provide us with a zaptieh, who might act as our guide in visiting the antiquities, and at the appointed time in the afternoon this functionary presented himself at the khan. He was a fine-looking man, with an agreeable countenance, and as he was intelligent, and being a native of the place was familiar with the various sites, he proved a pleasant and serviceable companion. Crossing the wooden bridge in the neighbourhood of our dwelling, we ascended through the narrow streets of that part of the town which lies at the foot of the castle-hill, by a flight of stone stairs, which by the use of the familiar oriental round number are spoken of as 40. Emerging from among the buildings, we reached a line of old walls, partly of the time of the kingdom of Pontus, partly mediæval—Saracenic or Seljoukian—at a point where a passage has been broken through them. Some of the towers belonging to them are fine, and in one I counted as many as thirty-three layers of ancient masonry. These are the walls mentioned by Strabo[1] as enclosing the palace and the royal tombs, and they

[1] Strabo, xii. p. 561.

served the further purpose of commanding the approach to a steep and narrow gully, by which there is a practicable ascent to the citadel above. The lines of fortifications which descend from this acropolis on the two sides, are only carried along those parts of the cliffs where it is possible to scale them. I may notice in passing with regard to the history of this citadel, that its walls were destroyed by Pompey when he captured the city in the Mithridatic war, and that it subsequently resisted the great Timour during a seven months' siege, after he had defeated the Sultan Bajazet at the battle of Angora.

The palace stood on a level platform, which is made at this point by a projection of the rocks, in a fine position overlooking the river and the city. The Tombs of the Kings are five in number, forming two groups, separated by the gully, and several hundred yards from one another. As seen from a distance, their  appearance is that of great ovens formed by some giant's hand, while a nearer inspection suggests a resemblance to huge sarcophagi rounded off at the top. They are all carved out in the perpendicular cliffs, and present for the most part the same features. The approach is formed by a number of broad steps, generally from three to six; then succeeds a rectangular vestibule, receding with a vaulted roof into the rock, on the inner side of which is a smooth face of stone forming the front of the tomb; and in the middle of this face, at a considerable elevation from the ground, sometimes as much as halfway from top to bottom, is a square-headed doorway through which was the entrance. Within is a chamber of moderate size, with a low stone seat or divan running round it. The length of the front, roughly speaking, is from 25 to 35 feet, while the height of the roof is usually about three-quarters of the length. All these which have been described is hewn out of the solid stone, but they have the further peculiarity of being detached all round—at the sides, behind and above— so that they only touch the rock at their base. Of some this is true without qualification, but others are in part connected with the stone above them. The object of this seems to have been to prevent the damp caused by moisture filtering through; and at the same time, as M. Perrot, the greatest authority on these monuments, suggests,[1] the sort of frame thus formed serves to increase the effect from a distance. They are at present almost devoid of ornament, and though several explorers speak of having found pieces of carved stone in the débris below some of them, they never could have had much architectural decoration. The holes, however, which are seen at regular intervals along the fronts, are a pretty clear evidence that they were covered, either wholly or in part, with metal plates.

By clambering up some broken steps behind the site of the royal palace, we reached the nearest group of tombs. They are three in number, and of these the first stands on a somewhat lower level, while the two others, which are side by side, seem to form a pair. All of them are less perfect in their execution than those which we saw subsequently, and the first two are not entirely detached from the surrounding rock.

[1] *Exploration archéologique de la Galatie, &c.*, i. p. 367.

After examining these we scrambled down to the gully by a steep path, and crossing this, ascended again along the cliff to a more elevated point where two others form a second group. The further of these is the higher of the two, and the communication between them is by a flight of steep and slippery steps cut in the face of the rock, which is so precipitous that in one part the passage is scooped out in the cliff, with the protection of a parapet on the outer side. These two stand at least 300 feet above the river, and the view of the gorge that they command is very striking. They are on a larger scale than the three of the former group, and are distinguished by the finish of their execution.

Returning to the bridge, we noticed opposite our khan another tomb in the cliffs, smaller and lower down than the tombs of the kings, and after passing this we made our way through the town, following the river bank, by the same route by which we had entered. At one point we stopped to examine a handsome building of the Seljoukian period, with a beautiful Saracenic portal, which our zaptieh called by the name of Timour-khané. The door of entrance was closed, but through it we could see that there was a central court within and on either side of it rows of pillars, which together with the outer walls supported an upper storey, an arrangement which we several times afterwards met with in buildings in this style in Asia Minor. It appears to have been intended for an hospital. We then recrossed the river by the stone bridge, and proceeded for some distance through mulberry plantations, which afforded a grateful shade from the scorching heat of the sun, until we reached the tributary which descends from the plain of Marsovan. Following the road thence to a place where lofty rocks approach the stream of the Iris, about two miles from the town, we came to the largest of all the tombs, which stands by the roadside, excavated in the same manner as the others, and constructed on the same plan. The execution of this is extremely perfect, and the walls of the passage that runs round the sides and back of the sepulchral chamber, are so highly polished as to present an almost glassy surface, from which circumstance it has obtained from the natives the name of 'The Cave of the Mirror.' Alone of all these monuments it bears an inscription, for above the entrance door, which here stands higher than the centre of the wall, is carved in large letters:

ΓΗΣ
ΑΡΧΙ
ΙΕΡΕΤΣ

i.e. 'Chief-priest of Mother Earth,' the tomb having apparently been erected to the head of one of those important priesthoods, of whom Strabo speaks as having existed in this part of Pontus.[1] On the face of this wall also there were traces of Byzantine frescoes, for within the letters of the old inscription a head of a saint with a golden nimbus was visible, and below this stood a full-length figure. Whatever the date of these may be, they must certainly be anterior to the Mahometan conquest of the country, for the representation of such objects would not have been tolerated subsequently to that time.

---

[1] Strabo, xii. pp. 557, 559. See Perrot, *Exploration archéologique,* i. p. 372.

The question now presents itself, to what period do these remarkable monuments belong? Strabo speaks of those within the wall expressly as 'the tombs of the kings;' and the princes here referred to—as the expression comes from a writer of the Augustan age, who was born at Amasia and lived there, and as the palace is mentioned in the same sentence—can hardly be any others than those of the historic line of the kings of Pontus. Relying chiefly on this authority, M. Perrot refers them to this dynasty, and he draws attention to the fact that the number of the tombs corresponds to the five princes who ruled at Amasia before the seat of government was transferred to Sinope.[1] As the kingdom was founded by Ariobarzanes in B.C. 363, and Sinope was captured by Pharnaces I. in B.C. 183, this would place their date between the middle of the fourth and the beginning of the second century before our era. Dr. Barth adopts the latter date for the two westernmost tombs; but regards the three which form the other group, on account of the simplicity of their construction, as not later than the fifth century, thus making them anterior to the kingdom.[2] This view differs little from that of Ker Porter, the first traveller who seems to have drawn attention to the antiquities of Amasia. He notices their resemblance to the early places of interment which he had seen in Persia, and remarking that this region formed part of the third satrapy of Darius Hystaspis, gives it as his opinion that the simpler tombs were introduced from Persia, while the later were imitated from them by the princes of the

---

[1] Perrot, *Exploration*, pp. 370, 371.
[2] Barth, *Reise von Trapezunt nach Skutari*, pp. 32, 33.

line of Mithridates.[1] M. Texier refrains from speculations on the question, owing to the absence of any characteristic features in their construction which might help to determine it.[2] For my own part, I should be disposed to refer them to a still higher antiquity, especially after having seen the chambers in the castle-rock of Van in Armenia, on account of their extreme simplicity and freedom from the influence of any style of art, were it not for the Greek inscription on the chief-priest's tomb. But this, which, it can hardly be doubted, is of the same age as the monument itself, is evidently of a late date, from there being no sign of archaism in the letters; and it is singularly improbable that such a work as the tomb should then have been executed in imitation of objects the history of which was lost. This evidence, taken in connection with that of Strabo, seems almost to settle the question; at the same time the conjecture that the idea of these rock-tombs came from Persia appears highly probable.

Having mentioned the name of Strabo, I cannot refrain in this his native city from paying my tribute of homage to that great writer, to whom everyone who is interested in ancient geography is so much indebted. This is not the place to speak of his writings in general; but I may at least draw attention to the excellence of his description of Amasia. It is a model of conciseness, where the temptation was to enlarge upon objects with which he was so familiar, and at the same time it is so clear and accurate, that almost everything that he mentions can be easily identified.

---

[1] Ker Porter, *Travels in Georgia*, &c., ii. p. 711.
[2] Texier, *Asie Mineure*, p. 604.

In returning from the Cave of the Mirror, we crossed the Iris at a point where a dam has been carried for a considerable distance across the stream. Our zaptich, who conducted us by this way, must have had some confidence in our powers of scrambling, for the latter part of the passage was made along an inclined plane composed of poles overhanging the water, where a slip would have been unpleasant. Between this and the city he showed us an old fountain by the roadside, into the walls of which several ancient Greek bas-reliefs, representing hunting scenes, had been built, but with so little regard to what was represented on them, that one had been set up on end. We also passed two more tombs, resembling the others; but small, and not detached from the rock. Just before entering the town, we turned to the left, and mounted the hill opposite the castle-rock, our object being to visit the German consul, Mr. Krug, whose house occupies an elevated position in the outskirts. As we were ascending, we heard the sound of a vigorous hymn proceeding from a neighbouring building, and this on inquiry we found to be a church belonging to a body of Armenian Protestants, who are in connection with an American Mission established at Marsovan, and have a native pastor. They are one hundred in number; and early the next morning a deputation of eight of their chief men waited on us to express their gratification at our visit to Amasia. They said they understood we were surveying for a railway, which would connect them with the sea, and would be a great advantage to their trade.

The consul's house is an airy mansion, agreeably

furnished, and from its high position and northern aspect less exposed to heat than the residences in the town. Here he was living with his younger brother and his sisters. Their father, who is now dead, settled as a merchant in Amasia many years ago, and established a prosperous business, especially in the silk trade. His sons have now succeeded him; and though the cultivation of silk in these parts has greatly declined of late, owing to a disease among the silkworms, they have made for themselves openings in other branches of trade, as, for instance, the manufacture of lucifer matches, which they have just established. Their appearance was much more English than German; and when we remarked this, they told us that they were of Swiss extraction. Both of them were born here, and were educated in Germany; the elder only spoke German; but the younger, who had resided some time in India, spoke English also. Neither of them appeared more than thirty years of age. We were surprised at seeing a pianoforte in their house, and still more so when we learnt that this had been transported entire from Samsoun; but the East has always been a land of carriers; and later on in our journey, at Bitlis on the frontier of Armenia and Kurdistan, we saw a harmonium which had been brought there from the Mediterranean through Mesopotamia, by way of Aleppo and Diarbekir. From these gentlemen we obtained much information about the country, which it may be worth while now to communicate.

We inquired first about the inhabitants of the district that we had been passing through since leaving Samsoun, remarking that we were unable to distinguish between the Christians and Mahometans. This, they replied, was not surprising, as they wore the same dress, including the turban, though colours which had a special significance, such as green and white, were forbidden to the Christians. The Turks, however, might generally be distinguished as having fuller and rounder, the Christians more attenuated, faces. These latter are Greeks, that is to say, members of the Greek Church, though their language is Turkish, and they are under the Bishop of Samsoun, who is subordinate to the Patriarch of Constantinople. There are but few Armenians in these parts. The Greeks carry arms as much as the Turks, and are, if anything, the fiercer of the two. When we said that we were surprised at seeing no churches in any of the villages, they said they existed, though they were very insignificant buildings; but until five years ago, to have built a conspicuous church would have raised a persecution at once; now, however, matters were on a different footing. They corroborated what we had noticed with regard to the fertility of the soil and the fineness of the crops; it was quite a mistake to think that there was misery and want in the country, the necessaries of life were much too cheap for that. Anatolia was a very rich and productive land, and almost anything might be made of it under a good government. No doubt, at the time of the famine, five years before, the people had suffered greatly, especially in the neighbourhood of Yeuzgatt, but the effects of that had now passed away. As to justice, that, no doubt, was venal, but then the decisions went to the highest bidder, and as the Christians were the wealthier, they had the better chance of obtaining them in their favour, for the Turks were everywhere declining, and, owing to this, the equality of the races was increasing. Of the administration they spoke in terms of strong condemnation. The taxes were heavy, and the pashas usually corrupt; these governors were being constantly changed, as their offices were purchased from the Grand Vizier; sometimes there were even three in one year; and on one occasion a person was sent to Amasia who could neither read nor write, having been appointed by court favour. Yet this *sandjak* was one of the most important in Turkey. The present pasha they spoke of as a fairly good ruler. The whole population was now thoroughly disgusted with the government, so much so that all of them, the Turks included, would gladly welcome any European Power that would step in. Towards Russia, in particular, there was an excellent feeling, mainly owing to the favourable treatment of the Turkish prisoners during their detention in that country. Those who returned said: 'The Russians fed us well, and gave us good clothes and boots; they are the very people to suit us as governors.' Were it not for a long-standing feeling of goodwill towards England, they would all go over to the side of Russia. I give this information as the result of the observation of intelligent residents. Part of it we had afterwards, in some degree, to correct, and the condition of the people was certainly represented in too favourable colours; but, on the other hand, some of its most startling statements we had occasion ourselves to verify.

When we had visited the pasha during the morning, we inquired from him about the post, with a view to sending letters to Samsoun. He informed us, in reply, after making inquiry from his attendants, that it went twice a week, and mentioned the days. We were amused after this to hear from Mr. Krug that there was no regular post at all, notwithstanding the importance of this line of communication, but that the letters were often handed over by the authorities to a common carrier, who might happen to be journeying in the direction by which they were to go, with orders that he should take them to the next station—say, Ladik; thence, again, they had to take their chance of getting on by a similar 'occasion.' He added, however, that they almost always reached their destination at last. We found that this strange and casual system prevailed throughout a great part of the country.

As we were leaving Mr. Krug's house, we stopped to admire the magnificent view, the finest that can be obtained from anywhere, of the position of Amasia. From this point are seen the town, lying beneath you, with its trees and minarets, the river, spanned by several bridges, the rocky heights on both sides—especially the steep cliffs of the castle-rock, crowned by the walls of the citadel—and the two rich plains above and below. All these objects, at this moment, were mellowed and irradiated by the light of the evening sun, which was descending opposite to us, at the further end of the gorge. On our way down, we were met by two hearty-looking men, whose features and complexions proclaimed them unmistakably Germans, even before a ringing 'Guten Abend' escaped from their lips. We found that they were living here, in the employ of the Messrs. Krug.

We left Amasia, on the morning of the 21st, at half-past seven, having been delayed by the non-appearance of the promised post-horses. These had been engaged to take us as far as Yeuzgatt, our next stage, which lies to the south-west of this place. As we emerged from the town, we met numerous Turkish women, mounted on horses or donkeys, and riding astride, probably on their way to market. Others, who were on foot, presented a ghost-like appearance, from the long white veils in which they were enveloped. But the veil in these parts, and elsewhere in the Asiatic provinces, is something very different from that of Constantinople, for in addition to the ordinary *yashmak* a dark handkerchief is drawn over the face, so that it is difficult to understand how the wearers see through it. To this rigid concealment corresponds an extraordinary avoidance of the gaze of the male sex. Of this we had a curious instance as we approached the town from Samsoun, for three women, who were coming in the opposite direction, turned their faces towards the ditch, in order to escape the eyes of the strangers; but after they had passed, curiosity prevailed, and they were caught staring at them with all their eyes.

We were now in the upper valley of the Iris, which is bright with abundant vegetation, being irrigated by waterwheels, like the gardens in the city, and thus forms a marked contrast to the barren rocks which flank its sides. At two miles' distance from Amasia, we came on one of the most interesting pieces of antiquity in this neighbourhood—the remains of an aqueduct cut in the rock on the left hand of the road, which here approaches the right bank of the stream. This must have served in ancient times to supply the city with water. It was here about fifteen feet above the road, and, on scrambling up to it, we found it to be a yard wide and two feet deep; but further on, where a projecting point of rock stands out from the cliffs, it is excavated to a great depth. The traces of it appeared at intervals, as we skirted the rocks, for two miles further. Thus far our road had been equally good with that by which we had entered Amasia, but shortly after leaving the aqueduct, we crossed to the left bank of the Iris by a bridge, and began to follow a country track. The course of the river, above this, lies through a gorge, to the south, after which it bends away eastward, in the direction of Tocat. We, on the other hand, entered a wide plain, resembling the Campagna of Rome in its general features, on the south side of which flows a tributary of the Iris, and it is intersected by smaller muddy streams, in which the buffaloes, as is their wont, rejoice to wallow. Towards the north, where the ground slightly rises, much corn had been grown, which was now stacked; but the middle of the plain, to judge from its appearance, must be marshy in the winter. Here, extensive herds were pasturing, and storks, at intervals, were searching for food. The ground was covered with some aromatic plant, which, though it was not wormwood, had a similar bracing scent.

As the direction we were now following was slightly south of west, we began to be in doubt about the route we were taking. There are two roads from Amasia to Yeuzgatt: the one tolerably direct, which however we avoided, because it is far removed from the antiquities which we desired to visit on the way; the other, by the town of Tchorum, which makes a considerable détour to the north, but afterwards passes those ancient sites. The intervening country is almost a vacant space on Kiepert's map, and Mr. Krug told us that no traveller had passed by that way, and, though it might save us time, recommended us not to try it, as the inhabitants were reported to be a wild set. Accordingly, we made our contract to go by Tchorum. After this, it was with some surprise and amusement that we learnt, on inquiry, that we were being conducted by this intermediate route—an arrangement which we supposed was contrived by our *suridji* (postboy), in order to economise distance and thereby money; but it suited us also, and had, moreover, the charm of novelty. We soon discovered, however, that none of our company knew anything of the way; so much so, that when I asked one of our zaptiehs—a languid fellow—what was the name of the river, he answered—with that curious mixture of indolence and courtesy which makes a Turk prefer to give a wrong reply to no reply at all—' Kizil Irmak '—*i.e.* the Halys! We learnt from the natives that it is called Tchekarek. Still, it was clear that the land was not wholly unexplored, for a line of telegraph wires stretched right in front of us, and as long as we followed these we felt tolerably safe. At last the plain contracted into a broad valley; and here, as we had been riding six hours, and had eaten nothing since a very early breakfast, we proposed to rest, for there was a village hard by on the hillside; but our zaptieh emphatically said, ' No; that is a Circassian village, and the Circassians are a bad lot.' A little further on was a steep bank, overlooking the river, on the side of which a flock of goats—some of them magnificent patriarchs, with long horns and silky white hair—had taken refuge from the sun: these we expelled; and, having established ourselves in their place, waited for our baggage and our other attendants, who were far behind. The heat was overpowering; and between three and four in the afternoon we found it to be 92° in the shade. When the rest of our company arrived, we partook of a meal; and then continued for two hours, until we reached a Turkish village called Koyounjak, which seemed a convenient resting-place for the night. It was situated at some distance above the road, and, as we rode through the fields towards it, we found the stacks of newly-reaped barley defended against the depredations of animals —perhaps of men also—by branches of the prickly palluria, which were arranged all round them. It was noticeable that throughout our whole day's journey we had not passed a single house or khan by the roadside.

The village of Koyounjak was a larger place than it had appeared at first sight, and though its houses were of one story, flat-roofed, and built of sun-dried bricks, it had a general appearance of prosperity. Around it willows and mulberry trees were growing, and in the centre was a fountain of good water, issuing from under an arch ornamented in the style of the Seljouks, which showed that this was an old station. The surroundings were pretty, for the hills on both sides sloped towards the river, and their upper parts were clothed with dwarf pines. The inhabitants received us with much friendliness, and as we wandered among the houses were at great pains to keep off the savage dogs that were ever ready to attack us. We were the first Europeans they had ever seen, and while our tent was being pitched in the middle of the village, a great part of the population assembled to watch the process, and the neighbouring windows and house roofs were crowded with children, though a prolonged look from either of the travellers was sufficient to make them disperse. The type of face was certainly different from that of the Turks of Constantinople, and yet their features were more prominent than one would expect from primitive Turkish peasants; it was only among the children that I observed round faces and flat noses, and the eyes of these, though more usually dark, were sometimes blue. Towards evening, when the cattle came home they formed a long train of goats, asses, cows, and buffaloes, which gazed with large eyes of wonder at our unwonted habitation as they passed it. At sunset an Imam mounted on to a wall, in default of a minaret, and gave the call to prayers, whereupon about twelve persons assembled in a court in front of the humble mosque, and turning their faces to Mecca, chanted the prayers with a nasal intonation. Not far off two women were pounding corn with large wooden mallets in a mortar of white marble, about three feet high and two broad; this is to make a sort of *polenta* or corn pudding, of which the inhabitants throughout the country are fond. There was something very pleasing about the simple primitive life of these people, and it seemed to realise the favourable account we had before received of the Turkish peasantry in

Asia Minor. The climate must be severe in winter, for they told us that snow often lies two feet deep on the ground.

As our tent has now been pitched for the first time, it may be well here to say a few words about our outfit. To begin with, there was this small gipsy tent, just large enough to contain two beds, and weighing fifty pounds. We used it only when necessary, preferring usually, both in order to save trouble and to obtain information, to stop in the houses of the natives; but in the remoter parts of Armenia we found it indispensable. The beds were military camp beds, of wood, and folding, so that they packed into a very small compass, and weighed only fifteen pounds each. They were provided with sacking, and this together with a railway rug rendered a mattress unnecessary. Then, in addition to a few cooking utensils, already noticed, and that greatest of luxuries a portable india-rubber bath, there was a box containing provisions—half a dozen bottles of brandy, which lasted us through the journey and was perhaps the most valuable article we carried; a little tea, though this was not of great importance, as the coffee is everywhere good; and preserved meats, in the form of 'soup-squares,' and essence of beef in skins, which contain much nutriment in a small compass and are not injured by changes of climate. We also had each of us a bag for our personal effects. All this luggage together did not amount to more than the ordinary load of a horse in these parts, though a portion of it for convenience was sometimes transferred to the horse ridden by the *suridji*. Rugs, waterproofs, and other wraps, when strapped tightly

E

together, were fastened behind our saddles, for which arrangement provision is always made in the Turkish saddle; and across the pommel in front were holsters, or rather military wallets, to contain books of reference on the country, a sketch-book or book for drying flowers, a flask, &c.

In reality, the hardships of travelling in Asiatic Turkey did not appear to us to be very severe. A former traveller in this country, to whom I applied for information before starting, said to me,—'You will find less to eat than in European Turkey, and more things that will eat you.' Our experience, I must say, was the reverse of this. One advantage we certainly had, namely, that our travelling servant, among many deficiencies, possessed the merit of being a good judge of a tender fowl, which is no slight gain where *toujours poulet* is the order of the day. Before I reached Asia Minor I was aware that *horos* in Turkish meant 'cock,' and *tavouk* 'fowl,' but I observed that when our man was catering for us, while *horos* was used as a term of strong objurgation, and *tavouk* of very qualified approbation, the word he usually employed was *pilidj*, which I naturally concluded to mean 'chicken.' The result of this was that, though our fowls were generally killed less than two hours before we ate them, our dinners were palatable. But independently of this, and without taking into account what we brought with us from England, we found no lack of good provision, for bread, eggs, and milk were everywhere obtainable in the country districts, and there was plenty of meat to be had in the towns. Vegetables and fruit were the scarcest articles, and wine we only met with at four places in the course of our whole journey. As to vermin—certainly there was no lack, but I do not think they appeared as numerous or as objectionable as in some parts of Turkey in Europe. Of sleeplessness I have said nothing; and truly it is difficult to sleep when, as is constantly the case, your tent in the villages or your house in the towns is visited at intervals during the night by fighting and howling dogs. From this I suffered greatly, but it is perhaps too much a matter of individual temperament to be taken into account.

Our course the next morning continued to follow the valley of the Tchekarek, preserving a south-westerly direction, over ground but little cultivated and often bare, the principal vegetation consisting of juniper bushes. The river flows in numerous windings, and a rude attempt at irrigation has been made by means of dikes, which enable the water to be turned over the reclaimed land at the side of the stream. Behind us the Ak Dagh in the neighbourhood of Amasia, which had been visible all the previous day, continued still in view. After riding for three hours and a half we reached a pleasant spot, where the bank was shaded by willows and plane-trees, and as the heat was already very great, and we did not know how soon we might reach a village, we stopped there to bathe and breakfast, and reposed for three hours. About six miles further on we took leave of the river, which here emerges from a deep rocky gorge towards the south, while we maintained our previous direction, following the telegraph wires, for the road became an insignificant track. We gradually ascended into the mountains, the surface of which is a sort of moorland, but after rather more than four hours from our resting-place our eyes were delighted by a scene of lovely vegetation, where a hillside for nearly half a mile was clothed with magnificent walnuts and poplars, interspersed with well-cultivated vineyards. Passing through this we skirted an extensive cemetery with rude headstones scattered over it, above which stands the village of Kara Hadjip, a much more considerable place than our last night's abode. The first natives that we met were two Circassians, and for the moment I supposed that we had reached a Circassian colony; but this was impossible, for the growth of the trees and the care that had been bestowed on the husbandry proved that it was no new settlement. We found that, like Koyounjak, it was inhabited by Turks, and that the vines were grown for their fruit, and not for making wine. We were welcomed by some of the chief men, and in their company we proceeded to the upper part of the village, where our tent was pitched on a flat housetop in front of the dwelling of our entertainer; for the houses here are so arranged one above another, that a man walks out on to his neighbour's roof and looks down his chimney. These chimneys, which are little more than holes in the roof, are awkward places to stumble into in the dark, and at all times care is required in walking near them. For many reasons we should have preferred to bivouac outside the village, but we were warned against this because of the danger of attacks from prowling dogs and human marauders; and besides, our difficulties would have been greatly increased in the matter of catering and cooking. We now began to feel that we were really in the heart of Asia Minor.

On leaving this place we quitted the line of telegraph, which here diverges towards the south, and ascended steeply over the mountains towards the south-west, from which we obtained extensive views over irregular upland plains, and chains of hills rising one behind another, for a long distance into the interior. The mountain sides were but little cultivated, though the soil is good, and corn might be grown almost everywhere. We now began to notice the absence of trees, which is so remarkable a feature of the interior of Asia Minor and of Armenia; indeed we found that until we approached the coast at Trebizond, after making the circuit of both those countries, we never saw a full-grown tree, except in the neighbourhood of the towns and villages, where they were planted by the hand of man. Up to Amasia, as we have seen, this is not the case, but the greater verdure of the northern region is owing to the humid climate of the neighbourhood of the Black Sea. The ridge which we are now crossing forms the watershed between the tributaries of the Iris and Halys in this part, for the streams on the further side of it, contrary to what is given on the maps, at once begin to flow towards the north. We descended slightly into more level lands, and after seven hot hours, during which we felt sure that we were making a long détour, for we were conducted first for some distance towards the south-west, and afterwards towards the north-west, we reached the small town of Aladjah. This was a poor place, though superior to most of the villages, and the size of the cemetery in its neighbourhood suggested that it once contained a more numerous population. It possesses a large mosque and tall minaret, which were picturesque objects in the evening, as seen from the house where we lodged, with the crescent moon above them, and the sunset light behind, against which stood out the figures of twenty storks that were perched upon the roof. Among the inhabitants were a few Armenians, but the rest were Turks, and the same is the case with most of the villages in this part. Though standing in the middle of a plain Aladjah was by the aneroid 2,700 feet above the sea, so that here we have reached the central elevated plateau. The only fruit to be obtained were very common pears and apples.

CHAPTER III.

PRIMITIVE ANTIQUITIES.

Arrival at Euyuk—Products of the country—Ancient building at Euyuk—Bas-reliefs on the front—The entrance—The Sphinxes—Assyrian features—Origin of the Sphinxes—Boghaz-keui—A native meal—The Yazili Kaya—Description of the bas-reliefs on the rocks—Figures in neighbouring cleft—Ancient palace at Boghaz-keui—Origin of these monuments—Meaning of the bas-reliefs—Views of Barth, Hamilton, Texier, and Perrot—Similar sculptures found elsewhere—The Hittites.

WE had now arrived at the neighbourhood of the antiquities we were in search of, those of Euyuk and Boghaz-keui, which are probably the most ancient remains in Asia Minor. As we found that these two places form a triangle with Aladjah, we determined to send our baggage, under the escort of one of our zaptiehs, to the latter of these two places, where we intended to pass the following night, as it was on the road to Yeuzgatt, while we ourselves proceeded to Euyuk. It took us somewhat less than three hours to reach that place, over undulating country, gently rising towards the north-west. We had passed several other villages on the way, and I was unaware that we were approaching it, when suddenly on the side of a large, low flattened hillock, the top of which was occupied by a village, I saw facing me two uprights of massive stone, on the front of which two figures of sphinxes were carved. Though I was acquainted with their appearance from the engraving in Dr. Van Lennep's ' Travels in Asia

Minor,' and M. Perrot's elaborate photographs,[1] yet it was impossible not to feel astonishment at these strange objects standing in so remote a place. A nearer view showed us numerous other large blocks, some in their original position, forming the walls of the building to which the sphinxes belonged, some displaced and lying about in various directions, in different parts of the village. In the neighbourhood of the sphinxes was a copious fountain, the water from which was carried to a washing place, attached to one part of the ruins, and covered in at the sides and above. The stork whose nest, built over the head of one of the sphinxes, forms such a conspicuous object in Van Lennep's and Perrot's views, has now removed elsewhere, and the nest has disappeared. The impression conveyed by these remains is that they formed the entrance, and a portion of the façade, of a vast edifice, which once may have occupied the whole of the area covered by the hill. Very little now remains, but the wonder perhaps is, that after the lapse of so many ages so much has been spared: possibly excavation might reveal much more, but that would involve the removal of the village. After taking this passing glance at what we had come so far to see, we proceeded onwards in order to establish ourselves in a lodging where we might rest during the hottest hours of the day; and then devoted part of the morning to a minute examination of the antiquities, which we also revisited in the afternoon. We selected a house with a wooden divan open to the air, in the further part of the village, and in doing

---

[1] In vol. i. of his *Exploration archéologique*: I ought perhaps rather to call them those of his *collaborateur*, M. Delbet.

so seemed to have lighted on a favourite abode of antiquarians, for our host assured us that he had entertained several Europeans before; but those he remembered best were an Englishman and a Frenchman together, who remained six days and took photographs. The Frenchman, no doubt, was M. Perrot. The honour of having first discovered these antiquities belongs to Hamilton.

Having noticed, *en route*, the fineness of the harvest that was being gathered in, and the large amount of corn that was grown, we asked whether any of it was exported. Our host answered that much more corn was grown than they could consume, for the country is sparsely populated, and that the peasants sent it to Tchorum and other towns, whence it was carried to Samsoun. A subsequent remark of his showed us that there are firmer bonds of union between Asia Minor and England than can be secured by treaty; speaking of the wool of the goats in these parts—these are the Angora goats, the first specimens of which we saw later in the day—he said, 'The English are the only people who make use of the wool we grow; if it were not for the English we could not get on.' Being anxious to verify my observations about the watershed in this neighbourhood, I enquired what course was taken by the stream that rises in the open valley in which Euyuk lies. His reply was that it runs to join another stream which comes from Boghaz-keui, and that their combined waters flow into the Kizil Irmak (Halys). As to the climate, he said that snow often falls in the winter, but seldom lies more than a foot deep. The previous winter had been singularly mild throughout Anatolia, but five years before (this was the year of the famine), the cold had been extreme, and the snow lay so deep that it was impossible to pass from one village to another.

In examining the antiquities we took Van Lennep for our guide, for I had compared his engravings with Perrot's photographs in England, and had found them trustworthy. They also stood the test of comparison with the originals, and are even of service in elucidating the photographs, for the latter mode of representation, as it depends on the effect of light at the moment, of necessity often loses part of the outline, and this can be rendered by the pencil. In some few points we were able to correct him, but on the whole he has accomplished with success the difficult task of faithfully interpreting lines some of which at first sight are by no means clear. My own object is to give the reader a general idea of the place, and of the character of its ornaments—not to dwell at length on the details, for a delineation of which he is referred to the works just mentioned.

I have said that the portion of the building that remains *in situ* appears to be part of the front and vestibule of some extensive edifice, and I feel little doubt that this was a palace. Though time has spared us but little of the walls of the façade, yet by good fortune what is still standing is remarkably precious, as it mainly consists of a line of bas-reliefs, each on the face of a single block, which form a continuous series on either side of the entrance, just above the present level of the soil. At the entrance the walls turn at right angles and run inward for a short distance, until a high stone step is reached, on either side of which rise to a height of about 16 feet the huge monolithic uprights that bear the sphinx-like figures on their outer face. Here was the first gateway, and within this again the walls can be traced along the same line until the area is crossed by a similar step, marking the position of a second door, so that the space between the two formed a vestibule or entrance-hall. The material of which these walls are composed is a grey granite, and the hardness of this accounts for the sharpness of the outlines of the figures after so many centuries of exposure to the atmosphere. This stone must have been brought from a considerable distance, for it is not found anywhere in the neighbourhood.

Let us now notice the bas-reliefs of the front, beginning from the further end of the wall on our left as we face the entrance. On the first block is the figure of a bull rudely carved, with a circular object like a ring lying in front of it, and on its back a square box. On the next to the right are two men, one of whom carries a sort of guitar, the other a tailed animal resembling a monkey. Beyond them, on the third block, is a group of three, one mounting a ladder, one standing at the foot of it, and the third blowing a horn. These are preceded by three priests, distinguished by long robes with full sleeves. Then come a number of horned sheep, admirably executed, before which a priest is leading an ibex which he holds by its horn. In front of them, on the sixth block, are a female leaning on a staff, with a striped dress, and the hair hanging down in a long plait behind ; a priestly figure, with one hand uplifted in prayer, while the other carries a crook or pastoral staff, which seems to mark him as the high priest ;

and before him an altar. On the last block a bull is represented, standing on a pedestal, and facing the other figures. The general effect is that of a religious procession, while the bull is the object of worship, and the introduction of the ladder suggests a reference to the construction of the building.

On the right hand side of the entrance only two carved blocks are visible on the front, the first bearing a female figure seated on a chair or throne, the second, which is much defaced, representing three men approaching her. Beyond comes the wash-house, which it was impossible to enter, as it was occupied by women washing clothes; M. Perrot here represents a bull with his head down, as if charging. But one large block, which is set up on end, and occupies one angle of this structure, is a remarkable piece of sculpture, for the greater part of it is carved into the figure of a lion, strangely idealised, with a ram under its fore-paws. It has a curious appearance in its present position, for the face gazes straight up into the sky, and as you stand on the roof of the wash-house you can look down upon it.

We will now return to the entrance and proceed inward towards the gateway. Here on the left hand wall we first see two men facing one another and holding a staff between them, and on the same block a priest with a rod or weapon in his hand, and a smaller figure, naked, in front of him. Further in we come to a fallen block, on which are six men, exactly like one another in appearance and attitude, walking in procession, with the left hand uplifted in salutation or adoration. Opposite these the right hand wall was no doubt ornamented with corresponding sculptures, but its ruinous condition does not enable us to learn anything about them. With regard to the dress of the persons represented throughout the whole series, we may remark that with the exception of the priests they wear a close-fitting garment, fastened by a belt at the waist, and reaching in the form of a kilt or short trousers to a little above the knee ; that they either wear close-fitting caps or are bareheaded with shaven heads ; that their shoes are usually turned up at the toe, and that they all wear ear-rings.

And this brings us to the sphinxes. Certainly they are weird-looking objects, as they gaze down upon us from their hollow eyeless sockets, with broad bland faces, and head-dresses resembling the wig of an English judge. In some parts the execution is elaborate, especially in the collar or ornament round the neck, and the pendants hanging from it on either side ; in others it is slight and apparently careless, for the bodies, or the lines that represent them, are hardly traceable, and in the case of one of them the right foot has four, the left five toes. But the hand that executed them, though rude, was that of no despicable workman, for the design is bold and the effect imposing ; and though he was following in the lines of earlier art, his work is nowhere mechanical, for the two sphinxes differ in many points from one another. It remains to mention one other figure, which surprises us by its presence hardly less than these—a two-headed eagle, with outspread wings, which is carved in low relief on the inner face of the stone which bears the right-hand sphinx. There are traces of a similar one which faced it on the opposite side of the gateway, but this has been almost obliterated. Dr. Van Lennep thinks that these last-named figures, a similar one to which is also found at Boghaz-keui, were added at a later period; but their execution is the same as that of the other bas-reliefs, and there is every reason to believe that they belonged to the original work.

The resemblance between much of what we have described and the Assyrian monuments is very striking, and has been noticed by most of the travellers who have visited the spot. In the first place the position of the building and its arrangement, as far as we can judge of it—its occupying a hillock rising out of a plain, the entrance flanked by two colossal figures, the corridor leading from this into the interior, and the bas-reliefs with which the walls are faced—at once recall the great structures of Assyria. The same thing is traceable in the ornamentation. The execution of the lion on the block which I have described as being set on end, partly full sculpture, partly bas-relief; the position and movement of some of the animals; the attitude of the sitting figure of the queen; the man carrying the monkey, the procession of sheep for sacrifice, and the ibex—all these suggest a relationship to the art of that country.[1] But what are we to say to the sphinxes? Allowing for some minor differences of treatment, they are thoroughly and unmistakably Egyptian. We need not enter into the question whether the sphinx as an emblem was developed elsewhere than in Egypt, for the likeness of these to the familiar type of that figure which is seen in that country, especially in respect of the peculiar head-

---

[1] For other points of resemblance, see Perrot, i. 346.

dress, is so strong as not to admit of any doubt. For this reason, and also because of certain Egyptian features which he traces in the bas-reliefs, Dr. Van Lennep concludes that the building is of Egyptian origin,[1] and he is confirmed in this view by resemblances to these figures which are traceable in the figure of a warrior cut on the rocks at Nymphio, near Smyrna, which is undoubtedly the same that Herodotus attributed to Sesostris.[2] But here he is on slippery ground, for the last-named figure, as I shall show further on, is almost certainly not Egyptian, and his suggestion that the Egyptians for once adopted the Assyrian mode of building can hardly be considered satisfactory. But if we allow that these sphinxes are Egyptian, how are we to account for their presence here? To this question it is impossible in the present state of our knowledge to give a certain answer, but more than one explanation may be suggested. They may have come by way of Phœnicia, a country which adopted many elements of Egyptian art, and in which this emblem has been discovered.[3] We know that the Phœnicians extensively influenced the south and south-west of Asia Minor, and it is possible that ideas borrowed from them may have penetrated into the interior of the country. But as the sphinx in its purely Egyptian form is found in Assyria,[4] it seems more probable that it was brought hither together with other emblems from that land.

[1] *Travels in Asia Minor*, ii. 147.
[2] Herod. ii. 106.
[3] Examples will be found in M. Renan's *Mission de Phénicie*.
[4] See Rawlinson's *Ancient Monarchies*, i. 458. The Assyrian sphinx may be seen in Layard's *Nineveh and its Remains*, p. 251 (abridged edition); the treatment is quite unlike that at Euyuk.

We left Euyuk in the course of the afternoon, and rode southward over hill and valley, amid extensive corn-lands, in the direction of Boghaz-keui. In one place I noticed twenty camels standing on the ridge of a hill among the corn. As we were not accompanied by our baggage, we were able to ride faster than usual, and in four hours and a half reached our destination, which lies at the foot of a mountain range in the midst of much vegetation between two streams that flow from different valleys behind the village. By the side of one of these streams I noticed a man washing some fish, and, with the catering instinct which becomes second nature to the traveller, at once desired our servant to bargain for them. The man seemed astonished—more perhaps at the sudden appearance of Europeans than at the request to surrender what was probably his supper—but the agreement was soon made, and they proved to be excellent mountain trout. As we were approaching, we had noticed a conspicuous house on the hillside, which seemed inviting for a night's lodging, and on arriving at Boghaz-keui we found that our effects had already been conducted thither, and that we were to be entertained by its owner, a hospitable Turk called Khalil Bey. He was an extensive landed proprietor, and owned patriarchal possessions in the form of horses, twenty in number, cows, and Angora goats. For the accommodation of these there was a large yard in front with sheds round it, and the house itself, which commanded an extensive view towards the north, contained spacious and airy rooms.

At nightfall we took supper with the Bey and his

son, and this I may as well describe as a specimen of a native meal. When we had taken our seats, partly at the corner of the divan and partly on cushions spread on the floor, a small low circular table was placed in the middle between us, and round this a long narrow napkin, resembling a scarf, was thrown so as to fall on the knees of the guests, to wipe the fingers on between the courses. Numerous servants stood by, bearing the successive dishes, which were placed one at a time on the table; from these the company helped themselves, stretching out their hands, for they were within reach of all. First came a milk-soup mixed with meal and some fragrant herb, then the trout, which were our contribution, and after them a dish intermediate between pudding and pancake. Next followed eggs fried with onions, stewed cucumbers, beans, and finally the pilaf of rice which announces the conclusion of a Turkish meal. The cooking was good, as it ordinarily is unless too much butter is used, for a maxim prevails which is too often put in practice—'the more grease the more honour.' There was no meat, but this was easily dispensed with; it seemed strange though, that nothing was provided to drink, but the people in these parts rarely drink during their meals, and we were obliged to ask for water. We ate with our fingers, a process not wholly easy to the uninitiated. Under such circumstances I am reminded of the remark of some Arabs, who entertained a party of Englishmen for the first time—I met with it, I think, in 'Irby and Mangles' Travels'—and on seeing their difficulties in eating rice with their fingers, while they themselves were shovelling it in handfuls down their throats, exclaimed with a mixture of pity and contempt—'Look at these poor ignorant people; they do not know even how to eat!' Our host, however, was much too polite to betray any such feeling, even if he entertained it. Breakfast the next morning consisted of similar viands, but with the addition of a dish of delicious *kaimak*, a sort of Devonshire cream, only less rich. Khalil Bey informed us that a large number of the male population here had gone to the war, and that some had returned after being prisoners, but of others they had received no tidings, though they hoped they were living and might still be restored to them.

Early the next morning we started in the company of a guide from the village to see the rock-carvings which form the attraction of this place. These are called by the natives Yazili Kaya, or 'The Inscribed Rock,' and lie on the mountain side about two miles east of the village. We were surprised to find them so high up, for we had to ascend at least 500 feet by a steep and rugged path before we reached them. Their existence was first discovered by M. Texier, and their position is so well concealed that we cannot wonder that they remained unknown for so long. Here, almost among the mountain tops, is an opening in the grey limestone cliffs, where a cleft runs in towards the NNE., about 100 feet in length, and varying from 50 to 25 feet in width, and ends in a *cul-de-sac*. The rocks on the two sides are hard and rough, and rise to the height of 50 or 60 feet, and the surface of the ground between them is nearly a level sward. The course of the cleft is slightly winding, but still from the further end you can look out through the entrance, and the broken slopes beyond and the more distant mountains form a graceful picture when set in this massive frame. All round the sides of this, following the irregularities of the cliffs, and elevated a few feet above the soil, runs a long series of bas-reliefs, the general resemblance of which to those of Euyuk is quite unmistakable. Here, however, the material on which they are executed is not granite, but the native limestone, which though hard is of course less durable; and they are somewhat roughly wrought, so that the face of the rock in places is not even smoothed, but some figures lie back, while others stand forward on projecting pieces. All along the left-hand side as you pass inwards a sort of stone seat or bench runs under the bas-reliefs.

The figures on the two sides form two long processions facing in the same direction, and leading up to a central group, which occupies the cross-piece of rock that makes the *cul-de-sac* at the further end. As this group is evidently the key to the whole representation, it may be well to describe it first. In the centre of it stand two figures, male and female, facing one another, and holding out peculiar emblems with one hand. The male figure, who is on the left, is evidently a king, for he carries a sceptre; his dress resembles what we have seen at Euyuk, consisting of a tight-fitting garment, short trousers, and turned-up shoes; but in addition to this he has a tall conical cap on his head. His feet rest on what M. Perrot interprets to be the bended necks of two men, and behind him are two smaller male figures dressed exactly like him, and in the same position, with the left hand extended, but only the foremost of the two bears a sceptre. The female figure, whom we may suppose to be a queen, wears a full jacket and striped skirt; on her head is a high tiara like the mural crown which we are accustomed to see on the head of Cybele; and her hair, like that of the women represented at Euyuk, hangs down behind in a long plait. She is standing on a leopard, and is followed by three figures—first a diminutive male figure, also on a leopard, and dressed like the men opposite, and behind him two women in all points resembling the queen, only smaller, beneath whose feet reappears that wonderful symbol, the double-headed eagle. The largest of the figures is less than life-size.

Let us now turn to the bas-reliefs on the two sides which lead up to this. On the cliffs towards the west, or left hand, stand forty figures, all but two of which are male, and they are dressed with few exceptions like those already mentioned, the peaked caps being especially noticeable. Their faces are seen in profile, as they walk in single file with the left hand forward; but they carry nothing. Two, however, the twenty-ninth and thirtieth in order from the entrance, front the spectator, and support on their uplifted hands what may be a boat, or possibly two crescents, one above the other; and the last six nearest to the central group (though this part is much defaced) are evidently important personages, two of them being apparently women, and a third a priest, who has the long robe, curved wand, and close-fitting cap, and above his head a large pair of wings. The opposite cliffs bear seventeen figures, all female and dressed like the queen, and walking also with extended hands; but beyond these towards the entrance, where there is a return of the rock, stands the figure of a high priest, very large, and the best preserved of all. He also is dressed like the similar figure at Euyuk, but with his right hand he supports an emblem of great size overshadowed by wings. His feet rest on two pyramidal masses which look like pine-cones, but may perhaps be intended to represent mountains. In those instances where it is possible to distinguish the faces, a difference of physiognomy is traceable on the two sides, those on the right hand being the more delicate; this might be thought to signify a distinction of race, but perhaps may only serve to indicate the sex. So too, as the youth who accompanies the queen wears a peaked cap, the head-dresses can hardly represent nationality. The effect which the whole scene produces on the mind is that of a great marriage ceremony, or possibly of the ratification of a compact between a king and queen.

But we have not yet exhausted the wonders of this strange locality. By making a circuit of the neighbouring rocks we found our way to the back of the *cul-de-sac* already mentioned, and from thence penetrated into a narrower cleft, flanked by perpendicular cliffs running parallel to one another, which follows the same direction as the former gully, but lies to the SSE. of it. The figures in this part are even more weird than those just described, but, unlike those, they have no unity of design, and appear almost like an after-thought. On the eastern or left-hand wall of rock stands a tall figure of a divinity, mounted on a pedestal, his body fronting the spectator, but his face seen in profile—a repulsive object, with a pointed cap and grim features, his shoulders formed by lions' or leopards' heads, his sides and legs by similar animals placed head downwards and ending just above the waist in what appeared to me, as they did to Dr. Van Lennep, to be fish's tails. Approaching him, but on a lower level, is a kingly figure, dressed like the chief personage in the great group, and having behind his head the same winged emblem which there distinguishes the high priest. His outstretched right arm supports an object which may perhaps be a naked child, while the left arm is passed, as if in protection, round the neck of a smaller figure with priestly robe and cap and wand. On the opposite rock, near the entrance, is a line of twelve soldiers marching, with the same dress and action as the men in the procession, only they carry sickle-shaped swords in their hands, and are coarser both in type and execution. All the figures in this part wear ear-rings, an ornament which I could only trace on the females in the other ravine, though probably they were once to be seen on the men's faces also, as they are at Euyuk. About half way through the cleft are three hollows or niches scooped out in the rock, two on one side and one on the other; they were probably intended for tombs, and the largest of them is about a yard in length, but only the upper part was visible, for the whole place has been much filled in with stones and earth. It is a romantic spot, and bright with the foliage of the walnut-trees which grow hard by.

In returning to the village our guide conducted

us downwards by a steeper way, where we had to dismount and lead our horses, in order to show us a curious cave which penetrated at one point through the rocks; this, however, was unconnected with the antiquities. Thence we descended into the Boghaz or defile, a deep gorge from which the place receives its name, and having crossed the stream that flows through it, mounted on the opposite side to a sort of platform, on which are the remains of the principal ancient building in this neighbourhood. These stand at some distance above Boghaz-keui towards the south-east, and as you approach from that village you mount by a flight of steps, passing successively two terraced levels, which belonged to the *enceinte*, and were originally encompassed by walls. The building thus enclosed, which ran from south-west to north-east, was finely placed, as it commanded both the lower country through which we had approached the previous evening, and the course of the stream and valley close below. Its outline and dimensions are not unlike those of a Greek temple, though its width is greater in proportion to its length than is generally found in those structures. There is also a rectangular inner enclosure or hall somewhat corresponding in its position to a *cella*, but here the resemblance ceases; for the space between this and the outer walls is occupied by chambers of various sizes, thirty in number, which were approached by means of corridors that skirt this hall. The main entrance was at the south-west end. The material employed in its construction was limestone, except at the north-east end, where a black basalt was used—probably to increase the effect of the building in this part, as the principal chambers are here. One or two courses of masonry generally remain throughout, and these are composed of enormous blocks, which might rival in size almost any in Greece, and are higher than any I remember to have seen. In many of them are artificial holes, which were apparently intended for clamping them together. I saw no signs of columns anywhere, and the architecture in many ways was unlike that of Greece or Rome. The arrangement of the interior suggests that it was not a temple but a palace, and this is the opinion advocated by Dr. Barth and M. Perrot. The former of these authorities traces a marked resemblance to the north-west palace at Nimrud, as described by Layard in his 'Nineveh and Babylon.'[1] This edifice belonged to a city of considerable size and importance, as is shown by the extensive ancient walls and strongly built forts which have been traced on the heights behind. It was only to be expected that such a position should be strongly occupied, as the pass which it commands is the most important in this part of Asia Minor. Nor are we left in doubt about its name. It was Pteria or Pterium, the place which, as Herodotus tells us, Crœsus destroyed on the eve of his final overthrow;[2] and therefore it was

[1] Barth, *Reise von Trapezunt*, p. 48.
[2] Herod. i. 76. I do not discuss this point, as I think it may be considered settled on the authority of Texier, Barth, and Perrot. See especially Perrot, *Exploration*, i. 322. The difficulty which Hamilton felt (*Researches in Asia Minor*, i. 395) on the ground that Herodotus described Pteria as being 'over against Sinope' (κατὰ Σινώπην) is really no objection. That expression does not signify 'near Sinope,' but was the historian's way, in default of lines of longitude, of describing the site of an inland town by its position relatively to a town on the coast. Considered thus, it is an excellent description of the position

MEANING OF THE BAS-RELIEFS. 73

in this neighbourhood that the great battle was fought for the supremacy between that sovereign and Cyrus, by which the response of the Delphic oracle was fulfilled, that Crœsus having crossed the Halys should destroy a great empire.

Having thus concluded this slight survey of the chief monuments in this neighbourhood, we may now proceed to enquire briefly whether anything can be learned of their origin. The reader will hardly have failed to gather from what has been remarked incidentally, both about this place and Euyuk, that opinion inclines towards looking to Assyria as the source of the art here represented. The plan of the buildings in the two places, and both the mode of ornamentation and the nature and treatment of the objects introduced, seem to point in that direction. But if this is so, we must ask further, When and how did Assyrian art find its way hither? And, as a preliminary question which cannot be wholly dissociated from this, can any reasonable interpretation be found of the series of bas-reliefs of the Yazili Kaya?

Let us take Dr. Barth's view first, for, whether right or wrong, it has the merit of being at once complete and interesting.[1] I have already mentioned that the impression left on my mind by the sculptured figures was that it represented a marriage ceremony, or the ratification of a contract, between two royal personages, and anyhow it appeared to me to commemorate some definite historical event. Dr. Barth, whose views I was unacquainted with at the time of

---

of Boghaz-keui. Tavium, which Hamilton would place there, is to be found at Nefez-keui, a village not very far off to the south.

[1] Barth, as above, pp. 45, 46.

my visit, was led to the same conclusion, and the incident which he believes to be here portrayed is the ratification of the marriage contract between Astyages, the son of Cyaxares the Mede, and Aryenis, the daughter of Alyattes, King of Lydia, and the accompanying treaty between those princes. The story of this is related in a few forcible sentences by Herodotus, and from him we learn that in the sixth year of an indecisive war between the Medes and Lydians, an eclipse of the sun took place during a great battle, and so frightened the combatants that they ceased from fighting; whereupon peace was concluded between them, and the royal union negotiated.[1] Dr. Barth even finds an emblematical representation of the eclipse in the two figures which break the line of the left-hand procession, and which support an object not unlike a double crescent, signifying the sun and moon in contact; these he regards as demons of darkness; and though this interpretation may be fanciful, yet certainly these beings with their big ears have a very uncanny look, and the position which they occupy marks them as forming a peculiar feature in the subject treated of. The battle, he conjectures, took place not far from this neighbourhood. He further argues that as Sinope was an important station for the trade from Central Asia, and as Cyaxares was the first ruler who had given the line of communication thither a more westerly direction, it having previously passed by way of Amasia, it is probable that the stronghold of Pteria was founded by him to command the chief pass leading to that place. According to this theory, the

---

[1] Herod. i. 74.

Assyrian style of art and mode of building having been adopted by the Medes, was introduced here by them; and while the palace, of which the ruins remain at Boghaz-keui, was the usual residence of the ruler of Cappadocia, that at Euyuk, being 1,000 feet lower, and therefore warmer, was that to which he migrated for the winter.[1] This last point, I must remark, is based on a mistake, for we found by the aneroid that the height of these two buildings is very nearly the same, viz. about 3,200 feet above the sea. The Greek name of the place, Pteria, Dr. Barth thinks, was connected with the symbol of the double eagle with expanded wings (πτερόν), which he regards as characteristic of this neighbourhood.

Hamilton also is disposed to regard the sculptures as referring to a historical event, and suggests that the chief figures may be the kings of Lydia and Persia, and the rest their attendants, not having sufficiently noticed, apparently, the points which almost certainly distinguish those in the right-hand procession as women.[2] On the other hand, Texier and Perrot both believe them to have a religious signification. According to the former of these writers, they represent the introduction into Cappadocia from the East of the worship of Anaïtis, the great goddess of the Medes, which is known to have been subsequently paramount in that country.[3] M. Perrot would regard the ravine of the Yazili Kaya as a Cappadocian religious sanctuary, and certainly no fitter spot could have been selected for a 'high place'

[1] Barth, p. 43.
[2] Hamilton, i. p. 394.
[3] Texier, *Asie Mineure*, pp. 614, 615.

for purposes of worship. Referring to the Semitic element in the population of these parts, he would regard the divinities honoured here as corresponding to some of those of Phœnicia, and he considers that the mandrake occupies a prominent position among the emblems.[1] This religious character he also attributes to the sculptures at Euyuk. If I pass by these views rapidly, it is not from want of respect, but owing to the difficulty of discussing questions of mythological interpretation. In respect of the origin of the art employed, and of the destination of the buildings, M. Perrot does not differ materially from Barth.

There is, however, a further view to be considered, which introduces another element into the question. M. Perrot has noticed that these sculptures do not stand alone, but require to be considered in connection with two other monuments in Asia Minor, viz. the rock-carvings at Giaour-kalessi in Phrygia, which he was the first to discover, colossal in size, and representing two men almost identically the same in dress and attitude as those who form these processions; and the so-called Sesostris monument near Smyrna, already mentioned, which likewise presents similar features.[2] A third, in which there is a more strongly marked Assyrian element, has been found by Mr. Davis at Ibreez in Lycaonia.[3] But they are not confined to this peninsula, for a figure, somewhat of the same kind, existed at Biredjik, near the Euphrates, where it was built into the walls of

---

[1] Perrot, i. p. 332 foll.
[2] Perrot, i. p. 349; and compare Plate X. in his second volume.
[3] Davis, *Life in Asiatic Turkey*, p. 253.

the castle; and others have been discovered at Jerablus (Hierapolis), the ancient Carchemish, on the banks of the same river.[1] The turned-up shoes, in particular, are found in all these. Besides this, further evidence on the subject has lately been brought to light. Any one who studies the Boghaz-keui bas-reliefs will see that between or about the figures there are peculiar characters, resembling hieroglyphics; and though none of these, as far as I am aware, are found at Euyuk, yet most of the other monuments I have mentioned, and in particular the pseudo-Sesostris, bear similar ones. Now my friend Professor Sayce, who has devoted much study to the subject, pronounces these characters to be the same as those of the inscriptions found at Hamah, the ancient Hamath, in the north of Syria; and from this he concludes that the presence of some one people who employed them is traceable wherever they, or the sculptures with which they are associated, occur.[2] Who were this people?

The answer that Professor Sayce returns to this question is, the Hittites. This race, which is familiar to us as a small Canaanitish tribe, seems, like the Hellenes in Greece and the Osmanlis in Asia Minor, to have eliminated itself by some process of natural selection from among its neighbours, and risen to be a great power; for from the Egyptian annals we learn

---

[1] I first became aware of the existence of the figure at Biredjik from a plate in Dr. Badger's *Nestorians and their Rituals,* i. p. 352. Both this and those from Jerablus are now in the British Museum.

[2] See his Essay entitled *The Hamathite Inscriptions,* reprinted from the 'Transactions of the Society of Biblical Archæology,' vol. v. pt. i. 1876; and compare his letters in the *Academy* for August 16, 1879, p. 124, and for Oct. 18, 1879, p. 289.

that they formed a powerful confederacy in the valley of the Orontes about B.C. 1340; and if, as is most probable, they are the same persons as the Khatti of the Assyrian inscriptions, their empire must have extended to the Euphrates, for the people that bore that name had their capital on that river, and ruled the greater part of Northern Syria from B.C. 1130 to B.C. 850.[1] As it is within this area that a number of the inscriptions we have spoken of occur, it is not unreasonable to attribute them to this race; and since others of the same kind are found, as we have seen, at intervals, as far as the neighbourhood of Smyrna, the conclusion drawn is that the Hittites must at one time have ruled from the Euphrates to the Ægean, and have left these traces of their art, which, as might be expected, bears evident marks of Assyrian influence, throughout that region. I do not myself possess sufficient special knowledge of these points to be able to give a decided opinion on the subject; but as far as I can judge, this view of the origin of the rock-carvings we are speaking of is highly probable. If so, we must assign them a much higher antiquity than has hitherto been supposed, for Professor Sayce regards the era of Hittite conquest as about B.C. 1200.

[1] Sayce, *The Hamathite Inscriptions*, pp. 7, 8; and Smith's *Dictionary of the Bible*, arts. HITTITE and CARCHEMISH. This kingdom seems to be alluded to in 1 Kings x. 29 and 2 Kings vii. 6, which passages imply that it was very important.

CHAPTER IV.

YEUZGATT TO KAISERIEH.

The Boghaz—The Cabak Tepe—Yeuzgatt—Family of Tchapan Oglou—
The Angora goat—Causes of the depopulation of Asia Minor—The
Tekieh of Osman Pasha—Bread in Asia Minor—The famine of
1874—Its causes—First view of Mount Argaeus—Unwonted reception—Armenian village of Tchakmak—Contrast of Armenians
and Turks—Approach to the Halys—The 'Bridge of the Numerous
Eyes'—Rock chambers near the river—Plain of Kaiserieh—
Arrival at Kaiserieh.

It took us six hours to ride from Boghaz-keui to Yeuzgatt, which lies beyond a range of mountains to the south-east. Our road led through the Boghaz or defile which we had crossed in returning from the Yazili Kaya ; through it runs a stream, which has but little water in the summer, but in the winter must be a rushing torrent. Shortly after we enter, the rocks on the two sides close in and form a deep ravine, the scenery of which has a certain wild grandeur, but the pass generally might be described as rather rough than beautiful. It might easily be defended by a small body of men against a large invading force. After ascending for two hours, we reach the watershed, and then descend again into a less rugged valley, the waters from which flow off westwards, to find their way into the Halys. In this part we had ample evidence of the great heat of the season from the state of the vegetation; for whereas Dr. Van Lennep, who passed by here at the beginning of August, describes 'a charming valley full of flowers and fresh green grass,' we, though ten days earlier in the year, found nothing corresponding to this, and the surface of the ground was burnt and bare. But the inhabitants throughout the country declared that no summer as hot as this had been known within the memory of man. In Yeuzgatt we afterwards heard that there had been no rain for three months, and they were in fear lest their wells should run dry. This was all the more strange, because we had left behind us in England a singularly cold and wet season, which continued into the autumn.

At last, after mounting again a long distance by a winding road, we found ourselves on open uplands at a great elevation, whence the eye ranges far away over similar country, with hardly a sign of cultivation. The district to the west of this is the ancient Galatia; in fact we have now for a few days penetrated into that province, for both Boghaz-keui and Yeuzgatt lie within its limits on the confines of Cappadocia. The highest point of these uplands, which is called the Cabak Tepe, reaches the height of 4,850 feet, and the snow, we were told, lies so deep there in the winter that persons are frequently lost in it. From the steep declivities on the further side of this we obtained our first view of Yeuzgatt, lying below us in an open valley between two ranges of hills, up the sides of which the houses partly climbed. As seen from this point it seemed a mass of brown houses, minarets, and poplars, among which one newly built mosque was especially conspicuous. Its appearance was in many respects different from that of the other towns we had seen in Asia Minor, for while it presented many of the familiar features of Turkish cities, in other points it resembled the Anatolian villages, from the clay walls of the houses, and the flat roofs with protruding chimneys, and from the dwellings in the upper quarters being half built into the hillsides. It is estimated to contain about 3,000 families, 50 of whom are Greek, 1,000 Armenian, and the rest Turkish. The importance of its position will at once be seen when we consider that it stands at the meeting-point of two great lines of road, from north to south, and from west to east—from Amasia to Kaiserieh on the one hand, and from Angora to Tokat and Sivas on the other. It is on this circumstance that it depends for its prosperity, for it has no manufactures.

On entering we were struck by the unusual cleanliness of the place, which is probably attributable to its recent origin, as the streets have had less time to fall into ruin, and to accumulate the traditional filth of oriental cities. Our arrival evidently caused great astonishment to the inhabitants, some of whom came rushing out to see us, and we heard exclamations of 'Inghiliz! Inghiliz!' behind us. Threading our way through the winding streets and the rude but picturesque bazaar, we rode straight to the pasha's *konak*, at the further end of the town, being anxious to obtain from him a decent lodging, and information about horses to convey us to Kaiserieh. We found him a lively, cheery man, somewhat sparely made, and therefore a great contrast to the solemn obesity of the ordinary pasha. All that we desired in the way of accommodation was a single clean room, better than what we should find in a khan; but he immediately sent word to a Mahometan gentleman who lived not far off, asking him to receive us in his house, and thither after a short interval we were conducted. We found it a commodious building, and the room which was assigned to us commanded a pretty view over the town and the heights beyond. Our host, whom from the number of retainers that crowded his hall we concluded to be a person of importance, was a man of remarkable appearance, with a type of features such as I have never seen elsewhere in the East. His figure was tall and slight, his complexion very dark, his hair smooth and coal-black, and he had a narrow hatchet face and prominent Roman nose. When we heard his name, we recognised in it that of the great family by whom Yeuzgatt was founded. The following notice of their history is taken from M. Texier.

'In one of these valleys there was a simple Turcoman village where the Yuruks (pastoral nomad tribe) dwelt during the summer; in this was born Achmet Pasha, of the family of the Tchapan Oglou. When he arrived at power, he conceived the idea of founding a town on the site formerly occupied by his summer encampment. It is thus that the town of Yeuzgatt was created towards the end of the last century. Achmet's son, the famous Tchapan Oglou, was one of the last Dere-beys or independent princes of Asia Minor; he exercised the sovereignty during his whole life, and his power reached as far as Kaiserieh, and northward as far as Amasia. He was intelligent enough to attract a number of inhabitants to his new city, without distinction of creed, and the population rapidly increased to the number of fifteen thousand. At his death, which took place about 1805, his power was inherited by his brother and the rest of his family, who continued to induce Greek and Armenian colonists to settle in their province. When Sultan Mahmoud formed the plan of overthrowing the power of the Dere-beys, or 'lords of the valleys,' Tchapan Oglou was the first object of the attacks of the government of the Porte, which excited against him the pashas in his neighbourhood by holding out to them the hope of sharing his wealth. The revenues of the Bey amounted to twelve million francs, and scarcely a fourth part of this found its way to the exchequer.'[1] Of these Dere-beys we shall hear more further on; in the present instance the struggle ended in the downfall of the local ruler, though his descendants have been allowed to live in affluence on the spot. The present representative of the family is Tchapan Oglou Devrish Bey, with whom we were now lodging.

Our host entertained us with much courtesy and hospitality, usually leaving us to ourselves, but joining us at our meals. He provided us with the wine of the country, though as a Mahometan he did not himself partake of it; it seemed wholesome, and was fairly palatable, with an astringent taste, and had a pale golden colour, like manzanilla, but was not clear. We were surprised at finding that wine was made here, for Yeuzgatt is not far from 4,000 feet above the sea; on the following day, however, we noticed some vineyards in the neighbourhood. With re-

[1] Texier, *Asie Mineure*, p. 532.

ference to the cheapness of provisions in these parts, Tchapan Oglou told us that, having a large establishment to provide for, he was accustomed to contract for the usual articles of consumption, and that bread cost him about a halfpenny a pound, and mutton about twopence a pound. Barley also is very cheap, so that the horses throughout these parts are largely fed upon it, that and chopped straw being their only food; in consequence of this they are able to do a large amount of work without fatigue. They are a small breed, but very strong, and not unworthy successors of those which Strabo praises in his time. The chief source of income to the inhabitants is the wool of the Angora goat, or *teftik*, as it is called in the country, which is exported from Yeuzgatt in large quantities. The area over which these goats are bred would seem to have extended itself during the last forty years, for before that time travellers speak only of finding them to the west of the Halys.[1] Their number, however, was greatly reduced at the time of the famine, and they are only being replaced very gradually. I have spoken throughout of their hair as wool, because it is usually so called in England from the extremely silky texture of its fibre. Angora is the only place in the country where it is manufactured into stuffs. During our stay in this house we received numerous visits from the natives, and among others one from the friendly pasha.

Early in the afternoon of the 26th, we started from Yeuzgatt on the way to Kaiserieh, a journey which was to occupy four days. We emerged from the town at its south-west angle, and as we mounted

---

[1] See the notices in Texier, *Asie Mineure*, p. 459.

the hills in that direction, we turned to look back on its striking position at the meeting of valleys and roads, the place itself lying in a hollow, where the ground slopes upward towards it from the west, and rises again behind it to the east. The country as we advanced was solitary, brown, and uncultivated, though here and there little oases could be seen in retired nooks, where a few houses, and a group of poplars and willows, were clustered together, with one or two fields in their neighbourhood. Certainly there are ample openings for colonisation in the interior of Asia Minor, though the new element introduced should be composed of industrious agriculturists, and not of idle and warlike bodies of men, like the Circassians. But though the depopulation of these districts, and the consequent diminution of agriculture, has no doubt increased in modern times, yet it is not in the main of recent growth, but dates from the heart of the Middle Ages. The absence of trees, indeed, which we have before noticed, seems to have been always a characteristic feature, for Strabo remarks upon it as prevailing throughout the interior of the eastern part of the peninsula;[1] but it appears to have produced much corn and wine, and both under the Romans, and during the early period of the Byzantine empire, was a most flourishing and populous province. Its ruin is attributable to two causes, the accumulation of land by the Byzantine nobles, and the inroads of the Seljouk Turks. During the tenth and eleventh centuries A.D. the rapacity of the nobles—who were distinguished both by the virtues and vices of a great aristocracy, personal prowess and

[1] Strabo, xii. p. 538.

chivalrous feeling combined with haughtiness and greed—destroyed the small holdings throughout the country, by gradually getting into their own hands the properties, which they thenceforth cultivated by means of serfs or slaves. The result of this was the destruction of the class of small free proprietors, who before that time had always shown themselves ready to defend the country, and who would have been more than a match for any barbarian invaders. Accordingly, when in the eleventh century the Seljouks began to attack this portion of the empire, they met with no power that could resist them, and their mode of proceeding in establishing themselves there soon converted the greater part of a fruitful land into a wilderness. Being at that time a pastoral race, their only object was to obtain feeding-ground for their flocks, and thus they found that their easiest mode of conquest was to ravage the country and destroy the inhabitants by incursions on a large scale, and subsequently to occupy the territories thus laid open by their own nomad tribes. No more complete method could have been devised for permanently ruining a land. Finlay remarks on these events—'History records few periods in which so large a portion of the human race was in so short a period reduced from an industrious and flourishing condition to helplessness and poverty.'[1] From the wounds inflicted at that time Asia Minor has never recovered.

When we had crossed the heights in the neighbourhood of Yeuzgatt, our road turned towards the south-east, which direction it continued generally to maintain the whole way to Kaiserieh. As we de-

[1] Finlay, *History of Greece* (new ed.), iii. 87.

scended, a flat valley was gradually formed, with a rivulet running through it, and sloping ground at the sides. This we followed until late in the afternoon, when we left the high-road and struck over the hills, which commanded a wonderful view over innumerable undulations, brown and monotonous, where corn seemed to be everywhere grown. Towards sunset we reached a village called the Tekieh of Osman Pasha, from an institution, half religious, half charitable, founded here by a person of that name—one of many such that exist in Turkey—partly for the maintenance of a mosque which he built, and partly for the entertainment of passing strangers and similar benevolent purposes, to keep up which the neighbouring villages are charged with a perpetual payment. The houses, as in most of these upland villages, were built of sun-dried bricks. That to which we were conducted belonged to an old, green-turbaned Turk, called Abdullah, who told us that he had lived his whole life in the place. When dinner-time came he dined with us, and provided us with an excellent meal; but we were a little provoked to find that the Pasha of Yeuzgatt, in his politeness, had sent word beforehand that we were to be expected. The bread that we ate here is of a nature to surprise an unaccustomed traveller, but it is found not only in this country but throughout Armenia also. It consists of large thin round cakes, about eighteen inches in diameter, flat like oatcake, but soft and flabby like a pancake. At the commencement of a meal, one of these, folded up, is thrown down on the table, like a damp napkin, in front of each guest. Great was our amusement the first time that we saw a man returning from the bazaars wrap up in his bread, as if it were in a sheet of paper, the meat that he had bought. The natives are fond of folding it round a flake of onion or a piece of strong cheese, and then munching it. It is made of different thicknesses, and varies much in quality. You like it at first, but soon get tired of it. Hamilton describes the process of baking as laying the flattened dough on the bottom of a large cauldron, under which is a small fire; here it is only left a few minutes, and is in fact merely dried.[1] In the Armenian villages I have seen a number of them clapped on to the clay sides of a small round pit, at the bottom of which were the hot embers; there they stuck until they were sufficiently baked. Another kind of bread, which we less frequently met with, but found convenient for carrying on a journey, is a kind of crusty roll, several of which are carried together, with a string passed through them; they are very hard, and require to be moistened in water before eating. We saw too here for the first time, plastered against the house-fronts, where they were drying, the cakes of prepared dung which, in default of natural fuel, is used for making fires. This is the *tezek*, of which we shall so often hear in Armenia. We found a small quantity of it burning in our room on our arrival, and it emitted no unpleasant smell. Our old host also showed us some bunches of opium, as a specimen of one of the products of this neighbourhood.

It was at this place that we first began to have ocular evidence of the results of the famine of 1874. Seeing a number of the houses in the village in ruins,

[1] Hamilton, *Researches,* i. 301.

we enquired the cause of it, and were informed that their desertion, and the extinction of the families that occupied them, dated from that time, and that whereas before that date there were 110 inhabited dwellings, there were now only 80. Abdullah described how both this place and all the neighbouring villages had been blocked with snow, so that their occupants were unable to escape, and great numbers of them died of hunger. The magnitude of this disaster has hardly been fully appreciated in England. It began with a failure of the crops in 1873, in consequence of a great drought. Then came a deluge of rain, in the following November and December, and in January and February the great snow-fall, of which we so often heard in the course of our journey. The towns suffered severely, at this time, but it was on the villages that the misfortune fell heaviest. There the reserves of food were small, and when, at last, the grain which had been spared for the sowing of the next year had been consumed, and nothing remained, the barrier of snow that cut them off from one another, and from the towns, rendered starvation inevitable. Even the thaw did not bring immediate relief, for the swelling of the streams, combined with the scarcity of bridges, broke up the country—as it usually does during the winter time—into a number of separate districts, and prevented communication with the coast. It was not until the month of April that the condition of things in Asia Minor began to be suspected at Constantinople. Immediately that the truth began to be realised, benevolent people in that city, aided by subscriptions from England, set to work to organise schemes of relief, and residents in the country, especially the American missionaries, devoted themselves to the work of distributing food. At last the Turkish Government, which began by discrediting the rumours, was persuaded of their truth, and afforded aid to the best of their ability. Heartrending accounts reached us at that time of the scenes in the towns, to which the emaciated peasants often with difficulty dragged themselves; some lying about the streets in the last stages of exhaustion, while others, when they reached the place of relief, were unable to swallow, and died in spite of all the efforts that could be made to save them. The number of human beings that died during this winter was estimated at 150,000; and the loss of property was enormous, for about 100,000 head of cattle perished, and the number of sheep and goats was reduced 60 per cent. But the evil, as might be expected, did not end here. Though the harvest of 1874 was good in quality, it was very deficient in quantity; for the seed-corn, as we have seen, had been consumed, and the oxen destroyed; and the population were too enfeebled and disheartened to be able properly to till the soil. The result was that, notwithstanding the efforts that were made to check it, famine and accompanying sickness prevailed during the following winter also; and the total number of their victims, from first to last, is computed, I believe, at over a quarter of a million souls.

If it be asked how it came to pass that the failure of a year's crop, followed by a bad winter, reduced a province with such capabilities to a condition of famine, the explanation is to be found in two principal causes. In the first place, the change in the mode of administration which has been introduced within the last sixty years has tended more and more to impoverish the country, and render it powerless to resist a strain on its resources. Before that time large districts had been in the hands of local governors, called Dere-beys, who, like the hereditary pashas in European Turkey, exercised a kind of feudal rule under the Porte. But when Sultan Mahmoud found it necessary to his reforms to centralise the power of the empire in his own hands, he made it his first aim to put down these semi-independent chieftains, who, to say the truth, were apt to be somewhat turbulent and troublesome vassals. His object was attained, but at the same time the country suffered. For notwithstanding the hard-handed and often rapacious dealings of these men, they had an interest in the prosperity of their subjects, and under them the native manufactures flourished in various branches. But when the system of centralisation was introduced, no further thought was bestowed on these interests, and a ruinous system of irregular taxation for some time prevailed, until the capital invested in them was exhausted. Then followed commercial treaties with foreign countries, which introduced articles inferior perhaps, but much cheaper, until at the present day the native manufactures have been almost destroyed, and the income derived from them has been lost to the inhabitants. Latterly also the agricultural interest has suffered in a similar way. The taxes on the produce, in themselves considerable, have become doubly oppressive from the mode of their collection, and other portions of the community having ceased to be able to contribute, additional charges have fallen on the land. The result has been that many of the cultivators are reduced to borrowing from usurers, and all have to be content with obtaining their bare bread from the soil. No margin exists anywhere, and consequently there is no means of meeting an emergency.

The second cause of the calamity being on so great a scale was the supineness of the Turkish Government at the time when it might have been checked. As early as July 1873 warning was sent to Constantinople that the harvest had failed, and that unless liberal aid were sent there must be great distress during the winter. Then followed a bread riot at Yeuzgatt; and subsequently similar indications of the approaching evil came from different parts of the country. But of all this no notice was taken. It is also hard to explain how, even when the interior was blocked with snow or isolated by swollen rivers, the state of things could have failed to be known at the Porte, since telegraphic communication exists between Constantinople and most of the chief towns of Anatolia. It seems at first sight to imply culpable negligence, either on the part of the local authorities in not sending the information, or on that of the Government in not acting upon it ; but it may partly, perhaps, be explained by the isolation of the villages on account of the snow, so that the worst of the suffering was not known, even on the spot. At a later time, as I have observed, the Porte exerted itself to provide relief. Nothing however can palliate the collection of the taxes from the surviving population during the following spring ; and notwithstanding orders to the contrary that were subsequently issued from Constantinople, we find this going on even into the autumn. In places this intolerable treatment was followed by an attempt at emigration. We cannot wonder that the country has still only partially recovered, and it will be long before the injurious effects of so disastrous a time will have wholly passed away.[1]

The next morning, as we left the village of Tekieh, we noticed that the rocks in the neighbourhood were composed of grey granite, and blocks of the same kind of stone were to be seen in the place itself. Our attention was attracted to this, because the palace at Euyuk was built of this material, though it is not found near that place. It may have come from here, but I am not certain that it is of exactly the same sort. When we rejoined the main road we found ourselves on the bank of a river called Kanak, which at that time was a small stream, but according to our suridji brings down a great volume of water in the winter. This accounts for the existence of a well-built stone bridge with three pointed arches which we reached shortly afterwards. Here we left the valley, and after four hours arrived at the large Armenian village of Keler; an hour more brings us to Sarikaya, or 'Yellow Rock,' a Turkish village with vineyards, willows, and fruit-trees, under which we rested to lunch. The neighbouring country on all sides was dreary, but relief awaited us; for as we proceeded, in the middle of the afternoon, crossing some low

[1] See on this subject a pamphlet published at Constantinople in 1875, entitled *The Famine in Asia Minor; its history, compiled from the pages of the Levant Herald.* It is to a great extent composed of letters from residents in Asia Minor who were engaged in the work of relief.

hills, I suddenly caught sight of a very distant mountain peak, which was appearing above the horizon almost due south of us, with a large mass of snow on one side. I pointed it out to my companion, and exclaimed: 'Surely that can be nothing but Argaeus.' One of our guards overhearing this, cried, 'Erjäus! Erjäus! that is it!' So closely has the ancient form been retained at the present day! We heard the name constantly afterwards in the mouths both of Turks and Armenians, and it always took this form. Gradually, as the mountain rose, a second and lower peak appeared to the right of the former one; both were beautifully cut, and a large snow-bed lay in the hollow between them. When at last the whole was revealed, it reminded both of us of the peak of Mount Athos, as seen from its eastern side. We knew it to be a volcano, and yet it had none of the rounded forms that such mountains usually have, but showed the sharp and pointed outline of an alp. It was here more than fifty miles distant in a direct line. This was our first view of a mountain, the highest in Asia Minor, with which we were afterwards to make very intimate acquaintance.

Later in the day, as we were pursuing our way through the solitary country, we saw three men on horseback, two of whom were armed, approaching across the fields to our right. The suddenness of their appearance, where no human habitation was in sight, and the fact that they were making straight for us, seemed strange at first, and my companion, I believe, began to feel for a small revolver which he carried, though it was seldom loaded, in his holsters. However, it soon appeared that their message was one of peace, for their leader, who rode between the other two, informed one of our guards who went to meet them that they had heard of our coming, and were anxious that we should pass the night at their village, a place called Tchakmak, which was not far off. Now our intention had been to reach a village two hours further on, for the evening was the pleasantest part of the day for travelling; but anticipating an agreeable entertainment, such as we had received on several previous occasions, we agreed to change our plans, and rode off in their company through the stubble. A mystery still hung over the whole proceeding, for we had no idea who they were, or how they knew anything of us. A little further on, three other men, also mounted and armed, saluted us and joined our escort; and again three more in the same manner came and 'turned behind' us, until at last we formed an imposing cavalcade. This brought us to the foot of a slight hill, where we found a number of men and boys drawn up on the two sides of the path, and these, immediately we came near them, began singing hymns lustily in the Armenian tongue to tunes which are popularly associated in England with the names of Moody and Sankey. Thus we went in procession up the hill, and again at the top of it met another crowd, headed by some Armenian priests. The village was hard by, and we found that it was inhabited entirely by Armenians, the greater number of whom belonged to the Armenian Church, while a minority, including the chief man who had first met us, were Protestants, having been under the influence, apparently, of the American missionaries in Kaiserich. Their only place of worship was Armenian, but a Protestant church was in course of erection. It appeared that the Pasha of Yeuzgatt had telegraphed our approach (for there is a line of telegraph here) to some *kaimakam* in the neighbourhood, and he had sent word to our present entertainers.

So far everything had been agreeable and complimentary; not so what followed. When we entered the village, we were conducted to a small room, which was immediately crowded with people, the priests and chief men occupying the divan. Little conversation passed, and we got but brief replies to our questions; the one idea of all present seemed to be to stare at us to their hearts' content, and talk to one another about us. At last the stifling heat and dust became insupportable, and we begged for permission to escape into the fresh air. Even then we were not left to ourselves, but were pursued through the village by a gaping crowd. When we returned to the room, it was still full, so in despair of finding any resting-place elsewhere we asked leave to pitch our tent in a neighbouring garden. Our host entertained us at dinner in the course of the evening; but even then we met with rather scant courtesy. I was surprised at the openness with which he animadverted on the Government, considering that our zaptiehs were not very far off. He told us he was anxious that the English should know how discontented they were with the existing state of things, and especially with the administration of justice, for it was impossible to get any suit settled without bribing the officials heavily all round. This was a complaint which we now frequently heard.

Our treatment on this occasion leads me to notice one marked trait of the Armenians—their great curiosity. I never met with so inquisitive a people. We did not experience this again in quite so unpleasant a form, but after making the circuit of Armenia later in the summer we almost came to the conclusion that it was their most characteristic quality. No doubt this has its favourable as well as its unfavourable side. To the traveller it is naturally unpleasant; and though it was explained to us that they felt they would be slighting those who come from a far country to visit them if they did not show interest in them and what belongs to them, yet this does not represent the whole of the case. On the other hand, when regarded as a sign of national character, it contains a hopeful element, for the interest in things and desire for knowledge, of which it is an exaggeration, are qualities which belong to a progressive people. This feature makes all the more impression, because of the strong contrast it presents to the polite indifference of the Turk. But this also can be regarded from two points of view. It is graceful in itself, and has a large element of Oriental courtesy, but at the same time it is closely connected with the feeling of pride and superiority to others, which is usually found among Mahometan peoples. It is a part also of that mental apathy which declines to assimilate anything that is new. This contrast may perhaps be regarded as symptomatic of the present position of the two races, the one being undeveloped but progressive, while the other inherits features of traditional culture, but is stationary in ideas and declining in prosperity. These are general statements, to which of course there are exceptions. I should be sorry, in making such criticisms as are almost unavoidable in giving an account of a country, to appear wanting in gratitude for the kind and generous entertainment which we received from persons of both these nationalities.

The people of this village had a healthy look and appeared well fed; but we remarked here, as we had throughout on our way from Yeuzgatt, both among Christians and Mahometans, that their clothing was very tattered, and we heard much of the famine and the numerous deaths that then occurred. They said there was still much poverty among them, though things were on the whole restored. It was cold at night in our tent, for a strong east wind was blowing, and the elevation was not under 4,000 feet above the sea. It is this freshness of the nights which renders travelling possible in Asia Minor and Armenia during the summer months, for even after the hottest days the temperature falls considerably a few hours after sunset. Thus the body is re-invigorated during the night, and able to bear fatigue and exposure to the sun during the day, which it could not do if exhausted by the continuance of a lesser degree of heat. The air too here is very clear and exhilarating, so that however warm it may become it has a tonic effect on the system. In other respects also this is a very healthy region, from the absence of malaria and other forms of miasma.

When we left Tchakmak, our entertainer and two other farmers accompanied us on horseback for some miles until we rejoined the mainroad to Kaiserieh at a Turkish village called Yon Hissar; and after three hours we reached Boaslian, the largest village of these parts, though its low cottages of sun-dried bricks gave it as wretched an appearance as any of them. Here we called on the kaimakam, a rather feeble-looking young man, from whom we had already received pressing invitations to stay with him through our host of the previous night. He was very anxious that we should at least breakfast with him, but we were forced to excuse ourselves from want of time and the need of making the most of the early hours of the day. The bareness of this treeless region at this season of the year is quite extraordinary, so that were it not for the stubble it would resemble one vast burnt steppe. All this district was at one time a great resort for the nomad Kurds, and in like manner at Amasia we were told that they were to be found between that city and Aladjah, but either they have retired from this part of the country or the heat of the season had driven them away, for we saw none anywhere. After proceeding over this for three hours more we rested for some time at a village, and then mounted gradually to the Dervend, or pass, where a small khan or guardhouse marks the highest point of this part of the road. We were now all anxiety to arrive at the Halys the same evening, for we knew our route must ere long cross that river, which not far from here reaches the southernmost point of the great arc it describes in the direction of Kaiserieh in the middle of its course. Our suridji, however, and our zaptiehs were unable to tell us whether any accommodation was to be obtained there, for though this is a high-road between two important cities, it is very little travelled. In descending from the Dervend, the path winds through a rough and stony defile, and when this opened out, the rocks, from being of a clayey nature before, became basaltic, showing us that we were approaching a volcanic region. The view of Argaeus from here was splendid, and now that we had come nearer to it we could see numerous smaller craters on its flanks, and others again were revealed by the shadows they cast as the evening advanced.

For some time we had seen before us a sort of deep cut in the nearer mountains, with cliffs of basalt on the further side of it, and at last a turn of the road brought us in sight of the Halys, which runs through it.[1] The river is here spanned by a highly picturesque bridge of fifteen round arches of various sizes, rising irregularly towards the middle, from which it obtains its name of Tchok Gheuz Kiuprisi, or the 'Bridge of the numerous eyes.' The width of the stream may be somewhat over 100 feet, but both the length of the bridge and the immense bed of shingle along its right bank give evidence of the size to which it is swollen in winter. To resist its force the piers which support the arches are strengthened by large buttresses. A little way below the bridge the river turns at right angles, where a steep face of tufa rock rises to some height above the water, pierced by numerous caves which when seen from a distance resemble large pigeon-holes. Beyond this again the precipitous cliffs of tufa and basalt close in on either side. Some of these caves are inhabited, and from their occupants, who form a small community, our attendants were able to obtain corn for their horses, and either coverlets or some rude accommodation

---

[1] The depth of the depression in which the Halys here flows is shown by its being 800 feet below Tchakmak, and 150 below Kaiserieh.

for themselves. After pitching our tent in the shingle we proceeded to bathe, and in doing so soon discovered why the Turks have given the Halys the name of the Red River (Kizil Irmak), for the water was filled with a thick red deposit, and the mud at the sides was of a most adhesive nature. This accounts for the formation of the great delta at its mouth, which we had seen from the sea between Sinope and Samsoun. Near the bridge the water was deep enough to allow of swimming, but lower down the current became rapid and apparently shallow. Towards nightfall the scene was pretty and pastoral, for a flock of Angora goats was browsing close to the old bridge, and a herd of bullocks was collected close by, while the moon, which was now gathering light, rose above all.

The next morning we visited those of the caves that were inhabited. These run along at some little height above the stream, though the people told us there were traditions of a great flood in which the Kizil Irmak had risen to their level. They form a sort of corridor within the face of the cliff, as they open into one another, with windows at intervals pierced in the rock, so that one might almost compare them to the triforium of a cathedral. These chambers —for they are evidently artificial, and not merely natural caves, since the signs of the chisel are everywhere visible—are of very various form, and sometimes inner chambers are excavated within these again. Their average height is six feet. Here and there niches are to be seen in the walls, and a sort of low seat or divan, hewn in the stone, runs round. We went along, stooping our heads as we traversed the low passages, until after about sixty feet this series of chambers comes to an end. To reach the others, which are visible in all directions, we were told that we must climb the rocks behind, and then clamber down to them. There was no ornament or sign of architecture in those that we saw, and the people said there were no inscriptions anywhere. Of the great antiquity of these rock habitations there can be no doubt; perhaps they were the work of the earliest settlers in the country; but probably also, as this neighbourhood was a great monastic centre, they were at a later period the abodes of anchorites. We were glad to escape when we had examined them, for the heat within them was stifling, and they were alive with fleas.

We then commenced our last day's journey to Kaiserieh. When we had crossed the stream, we ascended the basalt rocks on the opposite side by a winding path, and looking back took a farewell view of the valley, where the river, the quaint bridge, and the fantastic rocks formed a picturesque scene. Our road lay over dusty volcanic hills, where the heat appeared to us greater than on any previous day; but this was no matter for surprise, for besides the cindery nature of the soil, and its being still the height of summer, we had journeyed far to the south, being now between half and two-thirds of the distance from the Black Sea to the Mediterranean. On the way, one of our zaptiehs, who as we afterwards discovered had been feeling unwell for some days, fell ill from the effect of the sun; and at his request we left him at a village together with his companion, whom we charged to take care of him and accompany him back to Yeuzgatt when he was recovered. At length we began to ascend somewhat rapidly, and after a brief halt under some fruit trees near a hamlet in a sequestered upland valley, reached the brow of a high hill from which Kaiserieh was visible. At our feet lay an extensive plain, perfectly level, and light-brown in colour, and at the further end of this, about eight miles off, at the edge of the lowest spurs of Argaeus, appeared what looked like a dark carpet outspread upon it—for we could hardly believe it to be a city, since neither minarets, nor trees, nor other individual objects, could yet be distinguished. Argaeus itself, which we now saw for the first time in its full proportions from base to summit, was a most imposing object, with its snows and the numerous cones about its flanks and base. Hence we descended by a steep path, having on our left the large Armenian village of Erkilet, the houses of which climb up the abrupt hillside, while its plantations and vineyards extend below in a long sweep of green. It took us still an hour and a half to ride across the plain, in the middle of which we crossed a small stream that runs through it, which has always borne the name of the Black River— Kara Su now, and Melas in antiquity; it is a tributary of the Halys.[1] The plain was covered with volcanic stones and powder, and exactly corresponds to what Strabo describes it to have been in his time; he adds that it was unproductive and uncultivated.[2] The ground in places was quite mined by a kind of rat, resembling a weasel without a tail, many of which

---

[1] Strabo by a curious mistake makes it flow into the Euphrates; xii. pp. 538, 539.
[2] Strabo, xii. p. 538.

we saw running about, though they were shy of anyone approaching them. Hamilton, who met with this animal in several parts of Asia Minor, calls it the *rat des steppes*, and says they abound in the southern provinces of Russia.[1] We also noticed numerous *tourbillons* of dust, rising in tall columns resembling waterspouts at different points in the plain.

When we reached the city, we went first to the pasha's residence, but were informed that that dignitary had betaken himself to the country for the sake of fresh air, and that a vice-pasha reigned in his stead. When we were admitted to his room, we found with him a native Armenian Protestant pastor, Mr. Keropé Yakobian, who spoke English, having been educated for the ministry in Scotland, where he had resided two years. This gentleman at once offered to entertain us, and when we reached his house, which is at the further end of the city towards the south-west, in the Armenian quarter, we found it to be a fine stone-built mansion with spacious and airy rooms. Hard by, in the garden, is a large Presbyterian church, which was built by the subscriptions of friends and sympathisers in Scotland. Here he preaches, though he ministers also in the villages in various parts of the surrounding country. We were introduced to his wife, but she did not appear again until the time of our departure. Female seclusion is practised by the Christians in this country almost as strictly as by the Mahometans; indeed, except when we visited American families, throughout our journey, the female sex may be said not to have existed for us at

---

[1] Hamilton, *Researches*, ii. 189.

all. The views from this house were very extensive. From the front, where a large central hall on the first floor opened on to a balcony, the eye ranged over the roofs of the city, with minarets and tall poplar trees at intervals; but in the opposite direction Argaeus and his outliers, stretching in a long line close at hand from east to west, formed a magnificent spectacle. The great mountain itself, which stands a little west of south, shows a large snowfield just below its summit, and then descends, first steeply, and afterwards more gently, until its last slopes approach closely to this quarter of Kaiserieh. On the left hand rises directly from the plain a tall cone with striking outline, which evidently was once a crater, the Ali Dagh; and on the right, away to the south-west, the Yilanli Dagh, or Serpent Mountain, the sinuous form of which projects northwards, with the appearance of a crawling monster.

CHAPTER V.

MOUNT ARGAEUS.

Kaiserieh : History of the city—Arrival of the British consuls—Mosque and tomb of Houen—Start for Argaeus—Cross the ridge of the mountain—Village of Everek—Hospitality in Turkey—Native visitors—Preparations for the ascent—Gum tragacanth—Bivouac on the mountain—Moonlight start—Steep climbing—Summit of Argaeus —View from the summit—Ancient habitations in the rocks—Return to Everek—Former ascents—Volcanic character of the mountain.

WE had heard much of the greatness of Kaiserieh—our suridji from Samsoun to Amasia, for instance, came from here, and highly extolled its magnificence—and we were consequently disappointed. On entering the city we had passed many ruined houses, and there seemed to be a general look of dilapidation about the place, though the bazaars were extensive, and appeared to be provided with good articles. Its healthiness is said to depend in great measure on the neighbourhood of Argaeus, for the heat would be very oppressive were it not for the breezes that blow from that mountain. Its height above the sea has been very variously estimated. Ainsworth makes it only 3,236 feet, but Hamilton as much as 4,200 feet. Our estimate was 3,300, but I have every reason to believe that the aneroid marked low throughout this part of our journey; and Colonel Wilson, who had acquired great experience in the measurement of heights on the Palestine Survey, told us at Sivas that he had found the neighbouring village of Talas, by careful observation, both with the aneroid and the mercurial barometer, to be 4,355 feet; and this cannot be more than 300 feet above the city. Its comparative nearness to the Mediterranean is shown by the greater part of the merchandise that is exported going by way of Mersina, the port of Tarsus. The present population amounts to 60,000 souls, of whom 16,000 are Armenians, 4,000 Greeks, and the rest mainly Turks. The Armenians in the town speak Turkish, even in their families, but in the villages Armenian is generally spoken. As illustrating this, our host told us that he preaches in Turkish here, but in Armenian in the country. The Greeks also until quite lately spoke Turkish as their native tongue; but now, we were informed, some of them were returning to the use of Greek, owing to the spread of national feeling. The teacher from whom I learnt Turkish in London was born in this district, and from him I heard the story which is current to account for the loss of their original language, namely, that the Turks at one time cut out the tongues of all the Greek children in order to exterminate that speech.

The earliest name of this place was Mazaca, but Strabo, who is the first writer that mentions it,[1] says that it was also called Eusebeia by Argaeus, the latter part of this title being added to distinguish it from other places of the same name. It was Tiberius who bestowed upon it the name of Caesarea at the time when he made Cappadocia a Roman province; this it ever afterwards retained, and its

[1] Strabo, xii. p. 538.

Turkish name is a very slight corruption of it. It was unwalled, as it is at the present day, but the ancient city did not occupy exactly the same position as the modern, being situated a little to the west of it, and closer to the buttresses of Argaeus, so that it could be defended by forts erected on the heights behind.[1] It does not, however, come prominently into notice in history until the time of the later Roman empire, when its situation rendered it a point of attack to invaders coming from the East. After the defeat of Valerian by Sapor in 268, Caesareia was attacked by the Persian monarch, and after sustaining a long siege, during which it was bravely defended by one of its citizens called Demosthenes, who had been appointed governor by the Romans, it was captured and pillaged, and a great number of the inhabitants were massacred. At this time the population is said to have amounted to 400,000 persons. Justinian repaired its fortifications, but narrowed the line of defence, which he found to be too wide, for the remains of one of the forts is to be seen even as far out as the Ali Dagh.[2] He also built a castle within the city to receive a garrison. During the Middle Ages, Caesareia followed the fortunes of the Byzantine Empire, but after Asia Minor fell a prey to the Seljouks, it was eclipsed in splendour by the neighbouring Konieh (Iconium), which became the capital of that people.

The next morning we received a visit from our vice-consul, Captain Harry Cooper, one of those whom I have already spoken of as having been lately de-

---

[1] Strabo, xii. p. 539.
[2] Texier, *Asie Mineure*, p. 541.

spatched to this country by the British Government. He had heard of us the day before from a peasant in the country, who told him that two Englishmen had arrived who were surveying for a railway—the old story, only this time it was from Kaiserieh to Sivas. He had himself reached this place about ten days before, having ridden in the company of Colonel Wilson, the consul-general for Anatolia, from Smyrna to Angora, and thence to Kaiserieh through Karaman on the northern side of the Taurus chain. During the latter part of their journey they had suffered much from the heat, as might be expected in such a season, for Karaman is a very hot country. As the average number of Europeans that visit Kaiserieh is estimated to be one in two years, the arrival of two parties of Englishmen from different quarters within such a short time caused no small stir. Captain Cooper had the vilayets of Angora and Adana assigned to him, that is, the greater part of Central and South-Eastern Asia Minor, and about this he was commissioned to move at will, though he intended to make Kaiserieh and Adana in Cilicia his chief head-quarters. His instructions, he said, were in the first place to look out for British interests, commercial and otherwise, and at the same time to gather information as to the state of the country. As to the latter of these two functions—he seemed to be occupied all day and every day in investigating cases, for all kinds of grievances, whether real or imaginary, were submitted to him. As to the former—well, I believe we were the only British interest in Kaiserieh for the moment, and he certainly took very kind care of us.

In his company, and that of our host Mr. Keropé,

we went to visit what is the most interesting object in this city, the mosque and tomb of a Mahometan saint called Houen (pronounced by the natives *Hwant*). On our way, as we were passing through the bazaars, we met Dr. Farnsworth, the American missionary, who has resided twenty-five years in this place. It was a great pleasure to me to make the acquaintance of this excellent man, many of whose letters I had read during the famine, and who had saved hundreds of lives by his exertions at that time. He was bald, and worn in the face, but seemed full of vigour. Speaking of the famine, he mentioned especially the losses the people had sustained in sheep and goats; there was hardly one now where there were four before. His great satisfaction was that he had been instrumental by what he had written in forcing the Government to acknowledge the reality of the calamity, and to contribute largely to its relief. Of the work of these missions I will speak further on; suffice it to say here, that besides the higher knowledge that is diffused by their schools, they have benefited the people much by teaching them medicine and improvements in various branches of handicraft. Formerly the mission station was in Kaiserieh itself, but lately it has been removed to the village of Talas, about two hours distant towards the east. Another of the missionaries, Mr. Staver, pressed us much to stay with them there, but this we were obliged to decline from want of time. Dr. Farnsworth himself was encamped just then, together with the ladies of his family and thirty native girls belonging to his school, in tents on the summit of the Ali Dagh, in order to avoid the heat and obtain fresher air. It is one of those curious contrasts which constantly present themselves in this country that, whereas in the city these persons were liable to have stones and dirt flung at them, they were able to occupy so solitary a spot without fear of molestation. The entire number of Protestants in this district is 2,500. When I asked our entertainer what sort of relations existed between them and the members of the Armenian Church, he answered that they were friendly now, and that the latter send their children to the mission schools, though sometimes, as was natural, a good deal of jealousy was shown by the priests.

Before reaching the mosque, we saw the walls of the old castle, the foundations of which are composed of large blocks of stone, the remains of Justinian's building, while the walls themselves were the work of the Seljouks, and contain large picturesque towers, on which numerous storks have built their nests. Adjoining this is a more extensive wall of the same date, which incloses a portion of the city. At the entrance of the precincts of the mosque is a portal with beautiful honeycombed work over it, through which we passed into a court with curious outbuildings, resembling an extensive cloister, the arches of which are slightly bent into the horse-shoe form. On the right-hand side stands the mosque, which is almost devoid of ornament, and most peculiar in plan, for its width is much greater than its length, and the lines of the arches run from side to side, and not lengthways, so that the building seems to be composed of three transverse aisles. Each of these has seven arches, and the passage from the entrance-door to the holy place at the further end is through the line of the central arches. It dates from the fourteenth century, and was built by Houen on his return from a pilgrimage to Mecca—a circumstance which coincides with M. Texier's remark that, whereas there is nothing corresponding to it in Asia Minor, it bears a strong resemblance to edifices of the kind in Egypt and Arabia.[1]

The tomb occupies the angle of the court on the left-hand side of the entrance, and is an octagonal building of tufa, richly ornamented, and sloping upwards to a point at the top, while below it is supported on an elegant base of white marble, receding inwards underneath with elaborate honeycomb patterns. We were anxious to see the interior, but this was not so easy a matter to accomplish. The key had been lost, and when a locksmith was sent for to force the lock, none could be found. A lost key so frequently in the East means unwillingness to show some treasure, as we had found ere this in the libraries of the Greek monasteries, that after waiting some time we were going away in despair, when suddenly we were recalled by the news that a smith had appeared. When we entered, we found a chamber containing three marble tombs of different shapes, standing side by side, which we were informed contained the bones of Houen, of his sister, and of his maid-servant. But the whole place, tombs and all, was thickly littered with leaves of books in Arabic, which our Turkish guide said it would be sacrilege to destroy. It was in fact a sort of mausoleum for old sacred books, and a more dismal spectacle it would be hard to conceive. From near the entrance to the tomb a gateway leads into an old *medressé* or college, built round a quad-

[1] Texier, *Asie Mineure*, p. 544.

rangle, with a regular cloister, and cells for students opening out from it. It is still used, but as it was vacation time the rooms were unoccupied. The old professor, however, was there, and asked us to rest awhile in his apartment; he was pleased to hear that I pursued the same calling in England as he did in Kaiserieh.

In the evening we dined with Captain Cooper, who had established himself in a house in the Armenian quarter, close to where we were staying. It was a truly Oriental dwelling; the rooms, which were on the ground floor, opening out of a cool central hall, surmounted by a sort of lantern canopy. At his table we tasted some excellent wine of the country, which came from Indje-su, a town at the foot of Argaeus, some hours distant to the west, which contains a considerable Greek population.

Our object now was to make the circuit and, as we hoped, the ascent of Mount Argaeus. Having hired horses for the number of days this excursion was likely to occupy, we started early in the morning of the last day of July for the village of Everek, on the southern side of the mountain, that being generally considered the most favourable point of attack. Our way lay over a shoulder of the mountain, but before we reached its outliers it was necessary to ride for nearly an hour over the dusty plain, where we met numerous men of all classes mounted on donkeys, on their way to the bazaars; for during the summer the merchants of Kaiserieh, great and small, when the business of the day is over, retire from the city to their cottages, with which the hill-sides are studded. We passed the double cone of the Ali Dagh on our left, and then commenced a steep ascent over lava and basalt, until we reached a plateau of no great width, covered with gardens, vineyards, and plantations. Among these lay some of the humble summer retreats. Again we mount, and again we find a similar level, bright like the former one with artificial vegetation. From this, looking back, the eye ranges over a number of craters that stand about the base or on the flanks of the mountain, beyond which Kaiserieh appears, outspread upon the level ground. Then follows another long ascent, overlooking a rocky valley, until after four hours an extensive stony upland appears, between six and seven thousand feet above the sea, the dreariness of which is only relieved in places by a clear trout-stream which hurries through it. From this point the snow-fields on the eastern side of Argaeus are finely seen; but as I looked at them, misgivings about our ascent began to creep into my mind, for whereas the mountain had been cloudless up to this time ever since we first saw it, now wreaths of vapour began to gather about the summits, and other clouds were drifting up from the south, as if portending a change of weather. I could not help fearing the same fate as Hamilton experienced, who after a fortnight of clear sky saw similar clouds appear as he started for the ascent, and was enveloped in mists and drizzling rain before he reached the top.

Here we found a *yaila*, or summer encampment, of Turkish shepherds, whose flocks were cropping the scanty herbage. The covering of their tents was black, but the sides were composed of common brown cloth. They brought out carpets and bedding for us to rest on, and we found them clean ; the fact of their possessing them was a sufficient evidence that they were not poor. After a pleasant *siesta* at this spot we proceeded to the top of the pass, and as we descended on the other side, caught sight of other craters still more definitely marked, which, from their shape and number, carried our thoughts back to the volcanic region of Auvergne. Beyond these, as we looked through a fold in the nearer hills, appeared a lake that occupied the centre of a plain, and on the further side of it a succession of mountain chains. The descent to Everek was long and wearisome, all the more so because we knew that the further we went the hotter our resting place would be, and the greater the distance that would separate us from the higher parts of Argaeus. We ultimately found that that place is only a few hundred feet higher than Kaiserieh, and being situated on the southern side of the mountain, would naturally be hotter, were it not for the abundant vegetation in the midst of which it lies. That it is cooler was shown by the Pasha of Kaiserieh having made the place his summer quarters. The source of all this freshness is found in a copious spring of limpid water—almost a small river at its birth—which wells out into an extensive stone basin or reservoir at the entrance of the village. In this the boys of Everek are fond of bathing, so that, as the water supply of the place comes from here, the natives have the unusual arrangement of washing in the water first, and drinking it afterwards. The stream however is divided into numerous channels, and consequently, as you look down from above, the plain in this part seems to be inundated with a sea of verdure.

The village itself, which is built on lava, has an imposing look from outside, but within presents an irregular and somewhat ruinous appearance.

The kaimakam, to whom we addressed ourselves with our usual modest request for a clean room, immediately sent us to what we had now learned to be our regular destination under the circumstances, the best house in the place. This belonged to a well-to-do Armenian, who received us with every token of hearty goodwill. Throughout this journey we were surprised by the evident pleasure manifested by our entertainers at a visit from an European. In our former travels in Turkey we had always abstained from obtaining accommodation in private houses for fear of being burdensome to the people; but in Anatolia, where the *khans* are few and bad, we were forced to change our resolve, and certainly we did not repent doing so. Sometimes our wishes were forestalled by some native who saw us enter his town or village offering us hospitality, and when this happened, it was natural to suppose that we should be welcome. But when we were, to speak plainly, quartered on a private family, there was good reason to fear that it might be otherwise. But in no single instance did we find this to be so. The persons selected to entertain us, whether Christian or Mahometan, were generally people on good terms with the authorities, and regarded it as a compliment. It was only in the poorer houses that we were allowed to make any payment in money, though, as a matter of fact, the necessary presents to the servants of our wealthier hosts rendered visits to them the more expensive of the two. Our present abode was a good-sized dwelling, standing in a garden, which was surrounded by a high stone wall. We were established in a large *kiosk*, or summer-house, built against the south wall of the garden, which proved a delightful abode, both by night and day, as it was sheltered from the sun and open to the air. The garden was planted partly with flowers and partly with vegetables, and at the further end of it lived a number of fowls, distinguished by a peculiar loud cry of ' Abarak! abarak! abarak!' which they repeated at frequent intervals.

We remained at Everek until the following afternoon, for there seemed to be no object in making an early start for the ascent of Argaeus, as it would be necessary anyhow to pass the night on the mountain side. During our stay we received numerous visits in our summer-house. One of these was from a Greek, who, though a native of this country, spoke Greek, having learnt it at Constantinople. He assured us that there are some places in these parts where that language has been spoken all along without intermission, and I afterwards heard the same thing affirmed by others; but considering how utterly it has perished elsewhere in Asia Minor, except on the sea-coast, I have difficulty in believing it without further evidence. It is well also that we should understand what is meant by Greeks in this country. They are in reality the descendants of the early inhabitants of the land, with some slight admixture, perhaps, of Hellenic blood, derived from Greek traders settled in the cities and from the Greek colonies which were introduced by Alexander and his successors. Their forefathers became Greeks, as being subjects of the Byzantine Empire and members of the Eastern Church, and it is this latter bond which is still the real test of their nationality. We must not therefore expect to find in them those Hellenic traits of character which are still so strikingly marked in the inhabitants of the kingdom of Greece. We were especially impressed with this contrast when we reached the neighbourhood of Trebizond, where the people have all the characteristics of true Greeks.

Another of our visitors was a Vartabed, or superior monk, from the monastery of Surp Garabed (St. John the Baptist) on the further side of Kaiserieh. Before beginning a conversation he apologised to us through our dragoman for not addressing us in English, for he said he had forgotten that language, though he once knew it ; and then he went on to give us a specimen of it by repeating several times, 'Golgota very good! Golgota very good!' As might be supposed, we were not a little perplexed as to the meaning of this expression ; but shortly afterwards we discovered that he had been in India, and then it flashed upon our minds that 'Golgota' was his pronunciation of Calcutta, and that he had been expressing his admiration of that city. He had lived there fifteen years, he told us, in connection with the Armenian community in that place. A third visitor was an Armenian Protestant, who seemed to be on very intimate terms with our host. As the latter belonged to the Armenian Church, I took the opportunity afterwards of asking him about the relations in which the two bodies stood to one another, and he replied that no diminution of friendliness arose from the difference in their religious opinions.

Our first care on reaching Everek had been to

inquire about a guide for Argaeus, and the kaimakam recommended to us an Armenian named Stephan, who was reputed to have made the ascent several times. Others also whom we consulted believed that he knew more about the mountain than anyone else. When he had been fetched he proved to be an old man, and though he appeared still vigorous, we felt somewhat doubtful whether he would reach the summit. However, we engaged him, and he presented himself in readiness about noon, which was the time we had fixed for starting. Our company, who were all mounted, consisted of our two selves and this guide, our servant, one of the zaptiehs who had accompanied us from Kaiserieh, and two men to whom our horses belonged. A baggage horse carried the tent, our camp beds, and some provisions. It was a festival day, and as we rode through the village, we noticed what we had also seen in Kaiserieh, that the younger women, who were dressed in holiday attire, wore pretty frontlets of small circular gold ornaments, resembling thin coins, hanging from their fez caps. When we reached the open country the view of the mountain was very striking, for its peaks look sharper from here than they do from the northern side, though there is less snow upon them. The clouds which had caused me misgivings the day before had now dispersed, and all the summits were perfectly clear. Our course lay towards the north, and after retracing our steps along the plain by the same road by which we had approached Everek, we began to ascend between some of the lower craters, first gradually, and then more steeply, in the direction of the highest peak. After two hours we arrived at a copious spring which gushes out into a trough, and as this was the last water we should meet with on the mountain, we gave our horses a long drink and took a supply for ourselves.

At this spring we found three Turkish women washing their clothes. One of them was old and rather handsome, and as she stood there smoking a cigarette in a holder would have made a good portrait of a witch. The story of the two younger women was a sad one. Their husbands had gone with the Turkish army to the Russian war, and had not returned, nor had any tidings come of them. Having now no means of subsistence, the wives, in order to gain a livelihood, had come in the company of the old woman to gather gum from the bushes on the mountain side. This is the gum tragacanth, which exudes from the shrub called goat's-thorn (*Astragalus verus*), and is sold in large quantities in the bazaars of Kaiserieh, and is also exported to England, where it is used mostly for medicinal purposes. We saw these bushes frequently in Armenia; at this time the gum adhered to the stems and branches, looking from a distance almost like down, but later in the season it usually had fallen off, so that the ground below was strewn with it. The common way of obtaining it, however, is to cut the plant and leave it to bleed; after some days, when the gum has exuded and hardened, those who collect it return and gather it. The ordinary price that is paid here to those who collect it is a medjidie for an oke (about 3s. 6d. for 2½ lbs.). We then continued to mount until the slopes became so steep that we wondered how our baggage-horse could manage to struggle up them, and after two hours from the spring halted on the mountain side at a height of between 8,000 and 9,000 feet above the sea. Here we determined to pass the night, for the rocks afforded shelter for our attendants, and the dry stems of the dwarf juniper, large patches of which covered the ground, provided fuel to make a fire. While I was wandering about amongst these, I put up a fine hare. There are no forest-trees now on Argaeus, though Strabo speaks of extensive groves as covering its sides in his time, thus forming a contrast to the bareness of the rest of Cappadocia.[1] The principal flowers that we saw on our way up were a phlomis and a kind of cushion-pink or lychnis, but almost all were now past. The stillness at this spot was something extraordinary.

We pitched our tent, and proceeded to make preparations for an early start on the morrow. We had brought with us from England an alpenstock and ice-axe, with a view to any possible mountain excursions, and both these had to be fitted together, for they had been made in separate pieces for convenience in travelling. The alpenstock was a good piece of ash, which I had brought from Switzerland the year before; and this I had had cut in two, and the ends sheathed with brass ferules, so that the upper piece should fit closely into the lower, and be fastened by a strong screw holding the two together. In this way the strain was taken off the screw by the ferules, and the stick, though somewhat heavy, was sound and trustworthy. The ice-axe was made with a

[1] Strabo, xii. p. 538.

moveable head, which was fixed into the metal-work at the top of the pole, and secured by a steel screw passing diagonally through both. This, no doubt, was not as strong as if it had been in one piece, but it would have required a very unusual strain to break it. The usefulness—I might almost say, necessity—of these contrivances will be obvious to anyone who is accustomed to Eastern travel, for a pole of any length, or a crooked object like an axe, is almost certain to be broken when packed on a baggage-horse—either from a collision with another laden animal, or from striking against a rock by the road-side, or finally from one of those capsizes of the luggage which periodically happen. It was only by constant watchfulness that even our short implements were preserved intact, for the suridjis, if left to themselves, would always fasten them on the outside of the baggage, where a crash was only a question of time. As it was, they travelled through with us nearly the whole way, but owing to bad packing, just at the end of our journey one half of the alpenstock was lost between Erzeroum and Trebizond. As to provisions, we determined to take as little as possible, for our old guide could not be expected to carry anything. We therefore contented ourselves with a piece of meat and some bread each, and a small flask of brandy; this, together with the aneroid and a map and compass, formed the whole of our equipment.

The next morning (August 2) we were off—that is, Mr. Crowder, Stephan, and myself—at 2 A.M., after a cup of hot coffee, which was welcome, for the thermometer had gone down to 25°. By good luck the moon was at the full, for without her brilliant light it would have been impossible to commence the ascent by night, owing to the extreme roughness of the mountain sides. Illuminated by this, the wild solitudes in front of us, and the lower craters and the indistinct expanse of plain and mountains behind, formed a very impressive scene. In the plain the lake was visible, which we had seen in descending the pass from Kaiserieh. Our guide set off at much too fast a pace, which we in vain endeavoured to check, and the natural result was that he had to rest frequently, and showed signs of fatigue when we reached the steeper ground. Our way lay up a gully, which comes down from the higher peaks, and may at one time in its upper part have formed a portion of a crater. After two hours of moderately rapid ascent, we reached the first patch of snow, and here began a climb of sixteen hundred feet, which occupied two hours more, and was as hard a piece of work as either of us had ever experienced, for the angle was extremely steep, and the face of the mountain was covered with loose stones, and masses of fallen rock equally untrustworthy to the foot. When we were in the middle of this climb the first rays of the sun fell on the porphyry rocks above us, and produced a splendid effect by turning them to a bright crimson. After a time we took to the rocks at the side of this talus, thinking to find a firmer footing on them, but these were of such a friable nature that they gave way even when grasped with the hand, so that it was a choice of evils between this and the screes we had left. In an ordinary season, so our guide afterwards told us, this gully would be half full of snow, but the great heat of this summer had caused it almost entirely to disappear. In this way we escaped the only real danger which attends this expedition. Both Hamilton and Tchihatcheff, the two travellers who had ascended Argaeus before us, and whose visits took place about the same time of year as our own, the one in the end of July, and the other in the middle of August, speak of the risk arising from falling stones in this part. The latter of these two writers, whose account throughout is somewhat rhapsodical, speaks of daybreak being announced by detonations followed by a hail of blocks of stone in all directions; and the more cautious Hamilton describes these at sunrise as 'rushing past at a rapid rate, and making the ascent in some places a work of toil and hazard.'[1] In consequence of this, by the advice of his guides, he descended by a different route. The explanation of this phenomenon is that masses which have fallen from the cliffs above lie embedded during the night in the hardened snow, and when this is softened by the heat of the sun they are detached and shoot down. As there was no snow here when we passed, we neither saw nor heard anything of such avalanches of stones. It is clear also that Hamilton was mistaken in speaking of glaciers as existing here; there are none, in fact, on either side of the mountain.

At last, at about 6 o'clock, we reached the ridge, where there is a long *arête* of snow, joining two sets of summits, at the head of a vast snow-slope on the north side which forms a conspicuous object when

[1] Tchihatcheff, *Asie Mineure*, i. 445, 446; Hamilton, *Researches*, ii. 278.

1.

PINNACLES OF MOUNT ARGAEUS.

seen from Kaiserieh. Our guide was now an hour or more behind, and as the cliffs on our left, away from the *arête*, were quite precipitous, we thought at first that we had reached the highest attainable point. However, we discovered a way by which it was possible to scramble round the foot of these, cutting a few steps in the frozen snow, and thus reached a point some 200 feet higher, at the base of the final peak, which rises about 50 feet above, and is perpendicular and wholly impracticable—if, indeed, at the present day anything can be pronounced impracticable. The view was quite clear and very extensive, including the long line of the Anti-Taurus to the east, the Allah Dagh and other mountains that run down towards Lycaonia to the south-west, and to the north the vast undulating plains of the interior which we had crossed in coming from Yeuzgatt. One or two small lakes were visible, both that which we had seen at starting, and another towards the north-east, which we afterwards found to be covered with a salt incrustation; this circumstance would account for its being so clearly seen. We could also trace the depression in which the Halys runs, though the river itself was not in sight. Kaiserieh lay below us, as it appeared when first we saw it, like a dark carpet spread on the bare plain. But far the most remarkable feature was the mountain itself, for the lofty pinnacles of red porphyritic rock, rising from among the snows around and beneath us, veritable *aiguilles*, were as wonderful a sight as can well be conceived. The crater or craters, which once occupied the summit, are too much broken away to be easily traceable, the best-marked being that which faces east; but below, all round the base of the mountain, is a belt of volcanic cones. The idea that prevailed among the ancients, that on clear days both the Euxine and the Mediterranean were visible from here,[1] is wholly impossible on account of the distance, and the height of the intervening mountains.

We remained an hour and a half on and about the summit, during which time we breakfasted and made some observations. Before this time had expired our old guide had made his way up to us, much to the credit of his pluck. The aneroid gave the elevation as 9,100 feet above Kaiserieh, and if we take 4,050 feet as our estimate of the height of that place, this will give a total of 13,150 feet as the height of Argaeus above the sea—an estimate which nearly corresponds with that of Hamilton, who puts it at about 13,000 feet.[2] I was much disappointed at the absence of flowers, but even at this altitude the great heat had left but few remaining, whereas Hamilton speaks of the ground as being enamelled with them even lower down than the spot where we had encamped. The flora of a lofty mountain in this position, on the confines of Europe and Asia, ought to be highly interesting. As we were climbing about the rocks close

---

[1] Strabo, xii. p. 538.

[2] Hamilton, ii. p. 279. Three weeks after our visit Argaeus was again ascended by Captain Cooper and Dr. Farnsworth. Captain Cooper found the elevation by the boiling point a little way below the place where our measurement was taken to be 13,024 feet, and estimated the height of the summit at 13,100 feet. He adds: 'I fancy if any men want to follow your example another year, they could not do better than choose your time. Earlier than the middle of July they tell me there would be too much snow in ordinary years, and after the middle of August the weather in the higher regions is not to be trusted.' Tchihatcheff makes the height of Argaeus 3,841 mètres, which would be some 500 feet lower than our measurement.

by, we found to our great surprise that in places they were perforated with ancient human habitations. One of these wound inwards to a considerable depth with rude niches hollowed in the sides like those which we had seen on the banks of the Halys. We knew already that Cappadocia was a land of rock dwellings, but it seemed none the less strange that any should be met with here. Who was it that made for himself this aerial abode? Was it one of the primæval inhabitants? But in those days when stores of food were scanty, what was the inducement for anyone to occupy so inhospitable a spot? Was it a goatherd, who was accustomed to seek refuge here from stress of weather? But where was the herbage on these barren rocks, which should tempt him to climb to such a height? And besides, the labour required for such a work was not likely to have been expended by a casual visitor. Or was it a hermit? If so, he was a Stylite indeed, for he had elevated himself on the highest rocky column in the country. Anyhow there was no question of their being artificial abodes, for besides the niches, the marks of some hard instrument were evident on the roof and sides.

Our descent was uneventful. At first we took a somewhat more direct course than that by which we had ascended, and then struck into our former route, and thus reached our encampment in rather over two hours. There we reposed agreeably for some time, and during the afternoon returned to Everek, where we were welcomed once more by our kind Armenian host.

It now remains to say a word about former ascents

of this mountain. It seems to have been ascended even in ancient times, for Strabo mentions this, adding at the same time that few attempted it.[1] Possibly this may have been connected, as was the case on high mountains in Greece, with some act of worship, for another author tells us that the summit was believed to be the abode of a god.[2] The first ascent on record in modern times may fairly be considered mythical. The story runs as follows. 'A traveller once came from Frangistan, in search of a rare plant which grew only on the summit of Argaeus, having ten leaves round its stalk and a flower in the centre. Here it was said to be guarded by a watchful serpent, which only slept one hour out of the four-and-twenty. The traveller in vain tried to persuade some of the natives to accompany him, and point out the way; none of them would venture, and at length he made the ascent alone. Failing, however, in his attempt to surprise the dragon, he was himself destroyed. The story adds that he was afterwards discovered, transformed into a book, which was taken to Caesareia, and thence found its way back into Frangistan.'[3] Another attempt, if attempt it can be called, was historical, and unfortunately had a fatal ending. This was made by an American missionary, who lies buried at Kaiserieh, where there are various versions of his story. The following account is given by the writer just quoted, though he says that even in his time it was difficult to ascertain the truth. 'The unfortunate traveller ascended the mountain from Hissarjik, on the north side, not intending or expecting to reach

---

[1] Strabo, xii. p. 538.   [2] Solinus, xlv. 4.
[3] Hamilton, ii. 275.

the top; but on reaching the snow, which appeared hard and easy of ascent, he determined, notwithstanding the advice of his guide, who refused to accompany him any further, to make the attempt alone. After a time, finding it impossible to get on, he sat down, in an almost exhausted state, and rolled to the bottom, where he lay for half an hour, wet and shivering in the snow. On recovering a little, he drank some cold water, rode home four hours in a heavy rain, and ate a great quantity of fruit. It was during the month of October, and he caught the fever of the season, but still intended to attempt the ascent again from the other side when he should recover. However, he got worse, and expired in a fortnight. One account says that he died in six days, another in two; while some assert that his death was occasioned by the wounds he received in his fall.'[1]

We now come to the real ascents, those of Hamilton and Tchihatcheff. The former of these travellers, who was the pioneer of all future explorers of the mountain, started from Everek on July 29, 1837, with several guides and a body of guards, and rode a good distance further up the mountain than we did on the first day. He was unlucky enough, however, to be caught in drizzling rain, and having no tent, was forced to bivouac on a carpet under a large stone. The next morning he took the same course as we did, except that he kept more to the left in ascending the side of the gully, and mounting for a considerable distance over the snow, which then covered the detritus and fallen rocks, made his way straight to the

[1] Hamilton, ii. 266.

summit, or rather the rocks immediately below the summit, without approaching the *arête*. The sky here was clear above him, but the view was almost entirely intercepted by a sea of clouds below. M. de Tchihatcheff, the Russian *savant*, also devoted two days to the ascent, and followed much the same route; but I am unable to discover from his account whether what he calls the highest attainable point is that which Hamilton and we ourselves reached, or whether it is only the *arête*. What makes it probable that it was the latter is that he computes the height of the summit above this as 100 mètres, an estimate which it seems hardly possible for anyone to arrive at who had reached the higher point. His ascent was made on August 15 and 16, 1848.

The interest which attaches to Argaeus arises partly from its being considerably the highest mountain in Asia Minor, and still more from its being the second in importance of the remarkable extinct volcanoes which form a line through that country and Armenia. This commences in the Burnt Country, as it was called in ancient times (Κατακεκαυμένη) in the west of Phrygia; where the surface of the land over a wide area is covered with well-marked craters; then it rises in Argaeus; afterwards reappears in the centre of Armenia, where the massive Bingheul Dagh stands, two or three days' journey to the south of Erzeroum, and the loftier Sipan Dagh above the lake of Van; until it reaches its final point and greatest elevation in Ararat. No eruption of Argaeus has occurred within the historic period, but Strabo mentions that in his time flames used to burst out of fissures around its base. As might be expected, the neighbouring country is much exposed to earthquakes, and that of 1835, in particular, did much damage and destroyed many lives in Kaiserieh. It will be seen from the account that I have given that there is no real difficulty in the ascent.

CHAPTER VI.

THE LAND OF ROCK-DWELLINGS.

Leave Everek—Threshing—Village of Basch-keui—Obelisks of tufa—Native views of politics—Urgub—A Greek entertainer—Valley of Gueremeh—Caves and niches—A refectory—Rock-hewn churches—Byzantine frescoes—Ancient monastic community—St. Basil, Bishop of Caesareia—System of St. Basil—His retreat in Pontus—Severe climate of Gueremeh—Earlier inhabitants—The horseshoe arch—Departure from Urgub—Indje-su—Broad-tailed sheep—Completion of the circuit of Argaeus.

WE left Everek the following morning, our next object being to visit Urgub and the district in its neighbourhood to the west of Argaeus, which is famed for its rock-dwellings. The road by which that town is usually reached passes by Karahissar, to the south of the lake which we have before noticed in the plain; but we could see by the map that this involved a long détour, and conjectured that the preference given to it must arise from the ground nearer to the mountain being marshy, an objection which would not be likely to have any force in this season. We inquired accordingly for a more direct route, and discovered that there was one, but it had a bad name for robberies, and no one in Everek—still less any of our attendants —knew anything about it, except that we must pass by a place called Basch-keui. However we determined to take it, and inquire our way as we went, so we rode north-westwards over a bare plain at the foot of the outliers of Argaeus, from which we obtained very striking views of its summits. Threshing was now going on by the roadside in places, the operation being performed by horses or oxen pulling a sort of frame of flat boards over the corn which is strewn on the threshing-floor. This is armed with numerous sharp flints inserted on the under side, and effects the double process of separating the grain from the ear, and cutting the straw small, after which it is used for feeding cattle. A boy stands on the drag as it goes round, to give additional weight. This process is at once classical and Oriental. The instrument is exactly the *tribulum* of Roman husbandry, and is probably also the 'sharp threshing instrument having teeth,' which is mentioned in Isaiah.[1] At last we pass on our right hand a small lake encrusted with salt, and then at the end of six hours reach the foot of the hills which bound the plain to the west. In the side of these a narrow winding valley is here scooped out, and near the head of it we found, what we had long been on the look-out for in this thirsty land, a copious spring. Of this the natives have made the most, for the water, which gushes out into a basin, is conducted from it into a succession of stone troughs, twenty-five in number, which stand side by side, one slightly below the other. In this way a large number of cattle can drink at the same time. The weather had now changed and become sensibly cooler, and at this point the clouds began to gather—the first that we had seen in any considerable numbers for a fortnight. We could not help congratulating ourselves, both on our having obtained a

[1] Isaiah xli. 15.

clear view from Argaeus the day before, and on the prospect of a more moderate temperature in the district we were going to, which from all accounts was a natural furnace.

When we had crossed the hills at the back of the spring by a gradually ascending path, we suddenly came in sight of Basch-keui. Its position was most striking, and foreshortened as it here was, with its houses clustered together, it at once recalled to my mind David Roberts's view of the convent of Mar Saba near the Dead Sea. It seemed to cling on to the edge and face of the cliffs, which here fall away and form a narrow valley. But as we approached nearer a strong point of contrast appeared. For when we could see the bottom of the valley, we found it to be filled with the richest vegetation—vines, apricot trees, poplars, and willows; and after it has been joined opposite the village by another valley, and becomes wider and deeper, a great stream of green, including vegetable gardens and cornfields, appears—a most refreshing sight in so dreary a volcanic land. In the rocks which face Basch-keui numerous caves were visible, and when my companion visited these, he found some of them hewn at the sides into numerous niches, exactly like a Roman *columbarium*. The village itself was highly curious, for the flat-roofed houses, which rose steeply one above another, were partly excavated out of the tufa, and partly built of blocks of the same material, while the fronts of some were rather elaborately carved. We were conducted to one of these in an elevated position, and established ourselves in a good room with a barrel roof of stone and ornamented fireplace. The absence of fuel in the neighbourhood, notwithstanding the numerous orchards and plantations below, was shown by the cakes of *tezek* or prepared dung, which were plastered against the walls. Still larger masses of a coarser kind were lying about on the ground, in shape like Brobdingnagian gun-wads a foot in diameter. We were much struck by the absence of young men among the inhabitants, indeed there were but few men at all. When we asked the reason of this, we were told that whereas two hundred went to the war from here, only twenty had returned. Indeed, from information which we obtained on this point in various places, it seemed that the average of those who had come back was one in ten.

The valley of Basch-keui continues to descend gradually for about fourteen miles below that place, until it reaches the more level ground, on the further side of which is the town of Urgub. The path leads along the lower edge of the hills, just above the watercourses by which it is irrigated, and as we passed down it the next day, we noticed numerous villages on the declivities or in small retired valleys, some occupying steep positions like our last night's resting-place; others lower down, but conspicuous from the pointed cones and obelisks of tufa which stood up in the middle of them, pierced and honeycombed with chambers. The effect of these was very singular, but the whole of the region we are now approaching is so extraordinary, that I can hardly hope to give the reader a faithful impression of it. In one part of the valley I had ridden on in front of my company, when I was overtaken by an old green-turbaned Turk, stout himself and riding a stout horse, and looking the very reverse of a malcontent. As we stopped to water our horses at the same spring, we got into a conversation, which turned first on two Circassians, whom we had passed shortly before, standing by their horses at the side of the road; these he remarked were bad fellows and notorious brigands. Notwithstanding the ominous warnings we had received at Samsoun, these were the first *mauvais sujets* of that race whom we had met with, though we used to hear of their depredations. Our host at Everek had been loud in his complaints because a horse worth 100*l.* (Turkish) had been stolen from him by one of them, and though he had set the police on his track it had not yet been recovered. These fellows were well clothed and armed, and provided with good horses, so that they seemed favourable specimens of the Dick Turpin of the country. My new companion soon got on the subject of politics. When I complimented him on the beauty of the district he inhabited, he replied that the soil was good enough, but it was impossible to make anything of it under so bad a government. He was anxious to know whether an English consul had not lately arrived at Kaiserieh, and whether he was to stay there. When I said that he would remain four months, and then go to Adana, he inquired about the prospect of his return. He then went on to speak of England and Russia, but by this time I had stuck fast in my Turkish, and had to await the arrival of our dragoman before I could learn more. I found he was saying that he was glad the English had come, and would be pleased at their undertaking the administration, for at present nothing could be done, and no justice obtained, without the payment of large sums of money. But if they could not have England, he would be glad to see Russia here, for anything was better than the present Ottoman Government. This seemed an amazing speech, considering the quarter from which it came, but I remembered that it exactly corresponded to what Mr. Krug had told us at Amasia.

As we approached the end of the valley, Urgub came in view, but before we reached it we passed an extraordinary rock, called Sivli Tasch, which rises out of the level plain, quite solitary, and presents altogether a most grotesque appearance. Though the mass of it is no doubt natural, yet it might easily be supposed to have been shaped throughout by the hand of man; and whether to compare it to a house or a hayrick I do not know. It stands about 150 feet high, and has a flat ridge at the top and sloping roof, from which the sides descend, sometimes sheer, sometimes more gradually, to a massive base. In many parts, both above and below, the entrances to rock habitations can be seen, and here and there the surface has been smoothed into large plates, in which numerous niches are scooped out. Behind this, at a little distance off, the town rises steeply, first in terraced gardens, and then in lines of houses, placed one above another at various levels, with conspicuous colonnaded balconies in front, while above all stand cliffs of white tufa, excavated like those of Basch-keui, and supporting at one point a row of natural obelisks, which contrast curiously with a tall minaret close by. It seemed a strange medley of card-houses, pigeon-holes, rocks, caves, and niches, all in one view. When we entered, we were surprised to find it so large and important a place, for it covers a considerable area, and the houses of the wealthier inhabitants are on an imposing scale, and the fronts of many of them are sculptured with tasteful ornament. For this the softness of the stone affords great facilities, and wherever such decoration is found it is an adaptation of the Saracenic style. The Greeks, of whom there are five hundred families here, seem to form the most prosperous part of the population.

Our reception here illustrates the liberal hospitality of the country, and the off-hand way in which travellers are expected to avail themselves of it. Before leaving Everek, we heard our Armenian host discussing with some of his intimates what house we should be recommended to go to in Urgub, and it was agreed that we should find none so comfortable as that of a Greek gentleman, called Capitan Oglou. So we were advised to betake ourselves to his house without further ceremony ; and this accordingly we did, though prepared, I fancy, as a matter of form, to ask if he could find us a lodging. We discovered that he lived in the upper part of the town, but when we had made our way to his dwelling through the steep and tortuous streets, he proved to be for the moment in the bazaars. His family, however, immediately sent word to him and requested us to enter, shortly after which he arrived in hot haste, and expressed great satisfaction at having the opportunity of entertaining us. Like other Greek residents in these parts he only spoke Turkish, and his Turkish name, which would have appeared, I suppose, as Capitanopoulos in Greece, shows how much his family had been under the influence of the dominant race. His house was entered through a courtyard, in which were the stables, and on the first floor, where we were lodged, was a large central room, or furnished vestibule, from which the others opened out; this is a common arrangement in houses of this class, and contributes much to coolness and airiness in the summer, but we were led to believe that all but the ground floor is almost uninhabited during the winter. In this room hung a large glass chandelier, and on the walls were a variety of pictures, English, Russian, and German, which formed a curious mixture. One of these, which seemed to be a favourite in these parts, for we met with it in one or two other places in the course of our journey, represented the crowned heads of Europe, and was distinguished both by catholicity and gallantry; for the central figure was the Pope, with Victoria of England on his right hand, and on his left Isabella of Spain: from this it will be seen that it was not a work of very modern date. Our host himself, be it remembered, was of the Greek Church. Another picture represented the arrival of Sultan Abdul Aziz at Windsor Castle, and as a pendant to it on the opposite wall—no doubt by accident—was the Queen of Sheba visiting Solomon.

As we had arrived early, Capitan Oglou proposed after breakfast to act as our guide to the valley of Guercmeh, where the most remarkable of the rock-dwellings in this neighbourhood were to be seen. He accompanied us on horseback, and brought with him a servant, also mounted, to hold our horses, as there was a prospect of much climbing among the rocks. Our path rose above the town, and we soon emerged on to an extensive plateau, which ascends gradually the whole way to Gueremeh. In a short time we entered a valley, which for want of a better name I might call the Valley of Headstones. All about it stood pinnacles of white tufa, each surmounted by a large cap of stone, the remains of some harder stratum which had lain there superimposed before the process of abrasion commenced by which they were formed. These made them resemble the headstones that are seen in Turkish cemeteries. The day was what a medical man would call 'a very dangerous day,' for on the exposed uplands a chill and penetrating northwest wind met us, and in contrast to this, in any depression where the path led through the white rocks, the heat was like that of an oven. It was well, however, that we had escaped the temperature of the previous days. Our direction was nearly due west, and at the end of four miles we reached a point where the eye rested on a most extraordinary sight. Below us lay a valley, perhaps three-quarters of a mile in length and three hundred yards across, which had been scooped out to a depth of some five hundred feet by the action of water or some other natural force. The cliffs fell steeply on both sides, sometimes with a sheer descent, sometimes in a succession of precipices with terraces or irregular levels between them, and about these terraces, and sometimes attached to the cliffs, were pinnacles, obelisks, pyramids, and broken towers of the tufa, presenting the wildest scene of confusion. At the bottom of the valley, which was more or less level, were numerous fruit trees, and these, together with the deep tints of the distant mountains, which were purpled by the shadows of the clouds, formed a welcome relief to the glare of the nearer objects. It was a strange and beautiful sight, but the real wonder of the place has yet to be told, for both on the face of the cliffs and on the detached masses appeared caves and niches, all of them the work of human hands, which seemed more numerous the more the place was surveyed from different points of view ; and a nearer inspection showed, not only that these had been the habitations of men, but that the whole valley had once been the abode of a vast monastic community. At the present time they are completely deserted.

Our Greek host here proved of the greatest service to us, for he was well acquainted with the locality, and was able to conduct us to the objects of greatest interest, which, without his guidance, we should never have discovered. We rode downwards for a little distance by a sloping path, at a point where the cliffs had broken away, until we reached the first level. Here we dismounted, and began to wander about, for our curiosity was too great at first to allow of our adhering to any other person's programme. What especially attracted our attention was the great difficulty—in some cases impossibility —of access to these habitations. Here and there they may have been reached by a passage on the inside, for in one place we saw a staircase running up into the rock, though to the foot of this, strange to say, there was no approach ; but in most instances the entrances to the caves were far out of reach, and in precipitous places.[1] Similarly the niches, which were especially conspicuous on the opposite side of the valley, where they sometimes formed six tiers, one above another, had been hollowed out on the

[1] See the Frontispiece.

steep face of the cliffs. At first we conjectured that the rock must have fallen away, and destroyed the means of access which once existed; but a nearer examination overthrew this supposition, for there was no sign of fracture, and wherever there was carving or architectural decoration it had remained intact. The most probable idea that suggested itself was that they had been reached by ladders or scaffoldings attached to the rocks, which may have been movable, as is the case in some Greek monasteries at the present day, with a view to greater security. The desire of concealment was clearly an influential motive with those who dwelt here, for in the places nearer to the ground which we entered, the passages were sometimes not more than three feet high, and the staircases were very narrow and winding.

The first chamber to which we were conducted had evidently been a refectory. It was oblong in shape, and excavated to some depth; and in the walls at various points were niches, intended apparently to receive lamps, which must have been frequently needed, for the light only entered through the door. On the left-hand side, running nearly the whole length of the room, was a narrow stone table, hewn out of the rock, and detached everywhere except at its base; it was rounded at the inner end, where seemed to be the seat of honour. A stone bench ran all round it, which equally formed part of the native rock. The roof was flat, and about fifteen feet high. I say 'the roof,' but in describing any of these objects one is hampered in the use of terms derived from architecture and building, for there is neither the one nor the other throughout—no construction, that is to say, but only excavation, whether in doorways or arches or groinings or pillars. Passing on from this we came to a church, which was entered by a vestibule, vaulted above, and decorated half-way up the side walls with a blind arcade of horseshoe arches. At the further end of this there is a narrow passage, leading by a winding flight of stairs into the church, which is twenty-four feet long, and quite concealed in the bowels of the rock. The arrangement of this church, and of all the others we visited, and to a great extent their architecture, was thoroughly Byzantine, for the form was that of a Greek cross, and it had two cupolas, supported on six columns, two of which were engaged in the wall of the *iconostasis*, or altar-screen, which in places of worship of the Greek Church separates the sanctuary from the rest of the building. On the front of the screen were two seats, and another within it as well as the altar. Four columns had been knocked away, but their capitals remained, all cut out of the tufa; and here too the arches were horseshoed, as indeed we found them to be almost universally in these structures. The whole place was covered with frescoes in the Byzantine style, and these were in the main well preserved, owing to the dryness of the air, though many had been intentionally defaced, probably by the Mahometans. The execution was good for Byzantine paintings, and often more spirited and original than what is usually found in that style.

We next scrambled down by a steep way among the rocks—following our Greek friend, and admiring the activity with which he scuttled over them in his slippers—to a place where we should never have expected to find the entrance to a building, for the approach was concealed by rose bushes and prickly shrubs. Here was a second church, the plan of which resembled that of the former, except that it had in addition semi-cupolas at the two sides. It likewise was decorated with frescoes, among which I noticed the head of the Saviour, in its usual position in the central cupola; and on the side walls, among other scenes, representations of the triumphal entry into Jerusalem, and the crucifixion, and also figures of saints of the Old and New Testaments, including David, Solomon, and Daniel. Leaving this, we gave a passing look to two refectories, arranged in the same manner as that I have described, and then made our way into another chapel, which was rougher, both in architecture and painting, than the former two. On one of the side walls were figured two of the military saints, St. Theodore and St. George, on horseback; the drawing of these was clumsy, but not destitute of force. At last we reached a fourth, which was the largest that we saw; to penetrate into this it is necessary to descend considerably, and the entrance has evidently been filled up by fallen masses of rock and deposit brought down by the rain. The vestibule, which is long and has a round vault, is covered in every part with frescoes; within this are transepts to right and left, ornamented with arcades at the sides, one of which is an open arcade, with a chapel beyond it. Behind the altar in the apse is what appears to have been a seat for the bishop. Finally, as we returned, we examined a sepulchral chamber, in the floor of which were six or eight hollows, in the shape of coffins, which apparently served for sarcophagi, though some were only large enough to receive the bodies of infants. They must once have been covered with lids, for a ledge had been made to support these. From the back of this chamber again a door leads into an inner chapel.

It is not too much to say that the sides of this long valley are filled with similar traces of its former occupants. The entire region may be described as one sepult monastic dwelling-place—a Byzantine Pompeii. And after seeing it we are naturally led to inquire what period it dates from, and what was the history of its inhabitants. But here we are left almost entirely to conjecture, for there are no documents relating to it, no annalists that mention its existence,[1] and no inscriptions on its walls. There is one name, however, from which it seems difficult wholly to dissociate it, that of St. Basil. That eminent saint, who was born at the neighbouring Caesareia, and at one time of his life taught rhetoric there, and finally became bishop of that see, has been always regarded by the monks of the Eastern Church, and is still regarded by them, as the founder

[1] I ought not, however, to pass over wholly unnoticed the passage in Leo Diaconus, the Byzantine writer of the tenth century, which almost certainly relates to this neighbourhood. Speaking of one of the campaigns of Nicephorus Phocas, in which he passed through Cappadocia, Leo remarks of the inhabitants of that country—'This race was formerly called Troglodytes, because they burrowed in holes and clefts and labyrinths, as it were in dens and lurking-places' (iii. 1. p. 35, edit. Bonn. See Barth, *Reise*, p. 65). The passage, though curious as an evidence that the existence of these places was known in early times, seems to be merely a piece of antiquarianism on the writer's part (it is introduced in a parenthesis), and does not show that Leo and his contemporaries had any knowledge of their state at that time.

of their rule. Living as he did in the middle of the fourth century A.D., in the ecclesiastical affairs of which period he played a prominent part, he was a great man in a great age; and it is no slight glory to Cappadocia that it should have produced in one generation three such distinguished persons as him and his brother, Gregory of Nyssa, and his friend, Gregory of Nazianzus. He was at once strong and tender; a learned divine, and at the same time a vigorous administrator; and notwithstanding the weakness of his health throughout his life, he both practised severe asceticism and exercised a powerful influence over his contemporaries. He seems to have been impressed with the evils attendant on the hermit life, which up to that time had been the regular form of monasticism, and accordingly he instituted the coenobite system, or organisation of monks in communities. On this subject he writes: 'The eremitical life conflicts with the essential character of Christian love, since here each individual is concerned only for what pertains to his own good; while the essence of Christian love prompts each to seek, not alone what serves for his own advantage, but also the good of others. Neither will such a person find it easy to come to the knowledge of his failings and deficiencies; since he has no one to correct him with love and gentleness. What is written in Ecclesiastes (iv. 10) applies to the case of such a person: "Woe to him that is alone when he falleth, for he hath not another to help him up." In a society many can work together, so as to fulfil the divine commands on different sides. But he who lives alone is ever confined to one single work;

and while this is being done other works must be neglected.'¹ The principle here stated, though of course strongly opposed by the hermits, met with a wide acceptance, and before long monasteries with a rule of common life became numerous in the Eastern Church. In a place so well fitted for the purpose as this valley, and so near Caesarea, the dwelling-place of the originator of the system, it seems highly probable that such a community should have been established; and the primitive character of the dwellings and of the mode of life implied by them points also to an early date. In that case neither the architecture nor the painting was anything like coeval with the foundation of the societies. Of the precise date of Byzantine paintings it is always difficult to speak, because of the uniformity of type and treatment which has been maintained in the Greek Church. To me these frescoes do not appear to be very early.

The life of these monks of Gueremeh must have been a severe one—very different from that which St. Basil himself experienced. The letter of Basil to his friend Gregory, in which he extols the delights of his monastic abode in the neighbourhood of the Iris, in Pontus, is well known. He says: 'It is a lofty mountain, clothed with a dense forest, and irrigated on its northern face with cool transparent streams. At the foot of this lies outspread a level plain, ever enriched by the waters that descend from the mountain. Round this plain grows a natural grove, composed of a variety of trees of all kinds,

---

[1] S. Basilius, *Regulae fusius tractatae*, No. vii.; quoted by Neander, *Church History*, iii. 340 (Bohn's edit.).

which serves almost as a fence to it, so that in comparison of it, even Calypso's isle would be insignificant, which Homer seems to have admired above all others for its beauty. For it is not far removed from being an island, because it is inclosed by boundaries all round. On two sides of it lie deep abrupt gorges, and the river, which skirts it in a precipitous course, itself forms a continuous and impracticable wall; and as the mountain extends opposite to this, and makes curved bends where it joins the gorges, it cuts off the accessible parts of the lower slopes. To these there is a single access, of which I have the command. Then after the dwelling-house comes another neck of land, which throws up a lofty ridge at the summit, in such a way that this level lies extended to the view, and it is possible from that elevation even to see the river flowing round it.'[1] He then goes on to praise the clearness and rapidity of the stream, the profusion of flowers and number of singing-birds, and above all the tranquillity which such a retreat afforded him. Notwithstanding this highly coloured description, neither the ruggedness of the spot nor the severity of the life seems to have been agreeable to Gregory, to judge from two letters which he addressed to his entertainer after his return from a visit to this retreat.[2] They are couched in a tone of banter, and in a third letter the writer half apologises by laying stress on the delights of the spiritual exercises they there enjoyed; but there is sufficient evidence in them that the hardships had made a strong impres-

---

[1] S. Basil, *Epist.* xiv.
[2] S. Gregory Nazianzen, *Epp.* iv. v.

sion on his mind. But anyhow there was a great difference in this matter between Pontus and Cappadocia; for the latter country was not only bare of trees while Pontus was wooded, but it was also, as Strabo remarks, the colder of the two, notwithstanding its lying further to the south.[1] Basil had good reason to know it, for at the commencement of his episcopate, writing from Caesareia to Eusebius, to apologise for a long silence, he tells him that he had been unable to send a letter on account of the severity of the weather, which had such an effect on his people that they would hardly put their heads outside their doors; and he adds that the snowfall had been so great, that for two months they had been covered by it, houses and all, and seemed to be lurking in dens.[2] Now this valley is 1,000 feet higher than Kaiserieh, being not less than 5,000 feet above the sea. When we add to this the rudeness of the dwellings and the difficulty of obtaining fuel, we may easily judge that a spirit of self-mortification was required to induce men to dwell here. It was a very different thing from a life, however ascetic, in the genial climate of the Thebaid in Egypt.

A further question arises, whether these monks were the first inhabitants of these dwellings. It seems probable enough that before monastic communities were established the place was the residence of hermits; but the original formation of these rockchambers may date from a much earlier period still; in fact, from the first occupation of the country by settlers. The neighbouring Phrygians, as we learn from Vitruvius, used to construct their abodes much

---

[1] Strabo, xii. p. 539.   [2] S. Basil, *Epist.* xlviii.

in the same way as the Armenian villagers did in Xenophon's time, and do at the present day; that is to say, they burrowed into the hillsides, and after roofing over the hollow thus made with trunks and branches of trees, piled earth over the whole.[1] But in this country, where there was no timber, such a mode of construction would be impossible, and consequently the early inhabitants must almost certainly have been Troglodytes in one form or another. For this kind of life the soft tufa would offer most attractive facilities, and there is a further point which leads us to suppose that this region was occupied by cave-dwellers in pre-Christian times. For whereas some of the burial-places are arranged, like the one I have described, with a view to the interment of bodies, the numerous niches which appear on the rocks, and still more those which are arranged all round the interior of chambers, could hardly have served any other purpose than that of sepulture, and this implies the process of cremation. But cremation does not seem to have been practised by the early Christians, and consequently we are led to the conclusion that these niches were the work of heathens. Their number is very great, and it is quite conceivable that the dwellings in their neighbourhood may have been occupied almost without intermission from the earliest period.

One more point of interest remains to be noticed, and that is the recurrence of the horseshoe arch in the ornamentation of these structures. This is to me, I confess, a very puzzling phenomenon. The origin of this form of arch is in itself a curious and

---

[1] Vitruv., *De Architectura*, i. 2.

difficult question, for we must remember that the horseshoe is of no use constructively, but must always have a working arch inside it, and therefore, if it was not introduced simply for effect, we must suppose that it possessed some significance or symbolism. Now the fact that it is principally found in early periods of art—in Spain, for instance, where we are most familiar with it, it prevails much more in the early and simple Moorish buildings, such as the Mosque of Cordova, than in the later, such as the Alhambra—seems to be against the supposition that it is purely ornamentative; but what significance it may have had, or what could have suggested it, I have never seen explained. The idea, however, which has commonly prevailed, that the Arabs were its inventors, is certainly erroneous. If the buildings of which we are now speaking do not sufficiently disprove it, there is the further evidence of the church of Dana, near the Euphrates, which exhibits the horseshoe arch, and which is stated by an inscription to have been founded in 540 A.D.;[1] and the same feature is seen in another church of later date, but still as early as the ninth century, that of Dighour in Armenia.[2] The Arabs would rather seem to have borrowed it from the Byzantines. Still, ordinary Byzantine architecture, while it affects the stilted arch, has not the horseshoe arch as one of its features; and therefore it is all the more striking to find it here, when the other characteristics of the structures so nearly resemble what we find in later Byzantine buildings. It should be remarked also that the

---

[1] Texier and Pullan, *Byzantine Architecture*, p. 174, and plate lix.
[2] Texier, *L'Arménie et la Perse*, i., plates xxv., xxvii.

architecture which we see here cannot be regarded as in any degree original. As it was not used for constructive purposes—for we have already seen that every part, both of the chapels and dwellings, is excavated—it can only have been intended to assimilate these subterranean chambers to the style of building that existed at the time. We thus seem to be led to the conclusion that the use of the horseshoe arch must once have prevailed extensively in this part of Asia, and that what we find in the sixth century in the church of Dana was perpetuated in this district to a later period. It is also not improbable, as Dr. Barth remarks, that different buildings here may be of different dates.[1]

We rode back to Urgub with our thoughts full of these extraordinary objects, and at the entrance of the town passed a large Greek church appropriately dedicated to St. Basil. Otherwise, the memory of this saint did not appear to us to be celebrated in these parts in proportion to his greatness, though the Ali Dagh at Kaiserieh is also called the Hill of St. Basil. Our host had invited a Greek, who lived in the neighbourhood and spoke Greek and French, to meet us at dinner; but his French turned out to be poor stuff, and was frequently interlarded with '*vous savez*,' '*par exemple*,' and similar expressions which serve to conceal ignorance. He had learned it at Constantinople, and had travelled much, apparently as a merchant, having visited Bagdad, Nineveh, and Babylon. Though Capitan Oglou, as I have said, only spoke Turkish, this visitor assured me that some of the Greeks in the neighbourhood spoke Greek. Our

---

[1] Barth, *Reise von Trapezunt*, p. 65.

entertainer seemed much impressed by his friend's knowledge, but not so the domestics, who were evidently under the impression that he was something of an impostor. On one occasion, when he was brought to a stop by not knowing a French word, one of them suggested to him in Turkish, 'Try Greek;' and when he did so, and we told him the French for it, there was a gentle triumph among the attendants, and an expression of 'I thought so' upon their faces. He was a fat, good-natured fellow, and I have no doubt was much relieved when his task was over, for when he and our host had retired, we heard him talking vigorously downstairs. At nightfall the effect of moonrise on the weird rocks above the town was very beautiful, and their appearance was hardly less strange and impressive the next morning under the growing light of dawn.

At an early hour we took a warm farewell of our most considerate entertainer, who had gone so far in his hospitality as to issue injunctions to his servants that they were not to accept any present from us. We started at six, and after threading our way through the lower part of the town, and passing the bazaars, crossed once more the valley by which we had approached, and ascended the hills opposite, in a direction somewhat north of our former route. The ridge of these commanded a striking view over Urgub and the extensive low plateau behind it, the sides of which were broken into white precipices, at the edges of wide valleys that were scooped out at intervals. In the opposite direction, and directly in front of us, rose Argaeus, which is better seen, perhaps, from this point than from any other, for its snowfields are very conspicuous, and the mountain itself, from being seen in profile, assumes a pyramidal shape. For several hours after this we were crossing a stony desert, in which we met very few human beings, and there were hardly any signs of cultivation ; the wind that swept over it was keen and chill. At last we descended into a valley, where a copious stream rises, and flows along together with an accompanying belt of vegetation between steep broken cliffs of red porphyry, in which the entrances to rock-hewn chambers appear here and there. After we had followed it for half an hour, a sudden bend brings us in sight of Indje-su, a town of considerable size, principally situated on a hillside which rises beyond the stream. The houses are well and massively built of stone, and a large number of the inhabitants are Greeks, who are said to form a thriving community. It is owing to them that the good white wine is produced, which we had already tasted at Kaiserieh.

It is a ride of six hours from Indje-su to Kaiserieh, and the track between the two places partly skirts and partly crosses the last outlying spurs of Argaeus, which is in view almost the whole way. Shortly after leaving the town, where we only allowed ourselves a brief halt, we saw one of the tourbillons of dust, which I have already noticed in the plain of Kaiserieh, and which are common throughout this part of Asia Minor, in process of formation. Just in front of us a cloud of dust was suddenly caught up by the wind from a neighbouring field, and after having been whirled round with great violence and borne away to a considerable distance, was finally formed into a spiral about a hundred yards high. It continued thus for some time, until it gradually dispersed. At first our road lay through a narrow plain between volcanic hills, and this gradually opened out into a wider plain, parts of which were occupied even at this time of year by green marshes. In these the Indje-su stream seems to be lost, and we must have crossed it without knowing it at this point, for lower down it joins the Kara-su, the river of the plain of Kaiserieh, before it flows into the Halys. The dikes in the neighbourhood of the marshes require to be forded with care, as both the banks and the bed are rotten, and a horse may easily lose his footing and sink in. A little way beyond this a rather ludicrous incident occurred. A kind of rocky pass is here formed between two sections of the plain, where one of the mountain-spurs descends to the level ground and then springs again into a high hill; from this, as we approached, two old peasants emerged, mounted on asses, and on seeing us they stopped short, and then suddenly faced round and returned on their steps with all speed. When we came out on the other side of the pass, we found that they had left the road and slunk away under the rocks to a considerable distance off, whence they were watching us. When we had well passed, they returned to the road again and resumed their journey. We have often since laughed at the remembrance of this, for there was no ignoring the fact that they suspected us of being highwaymen. It had not occurred to us before that there was anything aggressive in our appearance, but *omne ignotum pro mirifico*, and it was evident that our Frank costumes had inspired them with fear. It was just so far interesting that, as Captain Cooper afterwards observed, the possibility of such a thing happening showed that the insecurity of the country is no fiction.

The sheep that we saw feeding in these plains were of the same kind which we met with in great numbers in Armenia, being distinguished by their wide fleshy tails, which appear to be composed of three lobes, but the middle one is in reality the bone, while those at the side are appendages of fat. This tail is an encumbrance to the animal, and at first sight seems useless, but in reality the extreme delicacy of the fat causes it to be used on a large scale in the country in the place of butter; and owing to this, and also to the excellence both of the mutton and the wool, these sheep are an extremely valuable breed.[1] The corn was being carried on the peculiar carts, which we had seen throughout this part of Asia Minor, composed of a triangular frame of simple construction, supported on two wheels, and very wide, so that it projects both over these and over the heads of the oxen; in this way it is capable of containing a great quantity. About two hours' distance from the city, as we were crossing some uplands, we noticed two men reclining on the ground, the shape of whose hats showed that they had come from Western Europe. When we came up to them, they proved to be two Germans, whose story we had already heard in part at Kaiserieh. They were mechanics, who had come to Constantinople by way of Belgrade during the previous spring in hopes of getting employment, either as engineers on railways or in some other line. Finding no occupation there, they had pursued their jour-

---

[1] See Van Lennep's *Travels in Asia Minor*, ii. 242, where a figure of this sheep is given.

ney on foot through Asia Minor without knowing a word of the language, until they had spent all their money. At last they arrived at Kaiserieh, ill and destitute, and were found there by Captain Cooper, who put them in hospital and took care of them. After they were recovered, however, he found them in the bazaars in a tipsy condition. They were now on their way to Mersina, the port on the Mediterranean, whence they hoped to get a passage back to Europe. After leaving them, we had to cross the neck of the Yilanli Dagh, which here intervenes in the direction of Kaiserieh. From this we descended on foot, owing to the steepness of the path, through clouds of dust, and then rode across the plain towards the city. Night had already fallen before we reached it, and lights were beginning to twinkle from the buildings. On entering, we made our way at once to Mr. Keropé Yacobian's house, where we received a friendly welcome.

CHAPTER VII.

KAISERIEH TO SIVAS.

Weather prospects—Leave Kaiserieh—Seljouk tombs—Monastery of Surp Garabed—Importance of St. John the Baptist in the Armenian Church—The church of Surp Garabed—Salt lake—Sultan-khané—Clearness of the air—Turkish matrons—Oppressive taxation—Houses in Asia Minor—Sivas—A Dere-bey—Position and history of Sivas—Student-interpreters—Relations of Mahometans and Christians—Condition of the country—Future prospects.

HAVING thus accomplished the circuit of Argaeus, we now prepared to continue our onward journey. The following day (Aug. 6) we were entertained by Captain Cooper in his hospitable abode, and during the morning received a visit from Dr. Farnsworth, who was accompanied by Dr. Thom, a medical man from the American mission station at Mardin, near Diarbekir. The latter of these two gentlemen, who was a wiry, vigorous-looking man, had lately arrived, partly on a visit, and partly because his medical aid was required. Dr. Farnsworth had now returned from his encampment on the Ali Dagh, much invigorated by the fresh air. On the morning of our ascent of Argaeus he had still been on that mountain, and had speculated on our being then on the summit; and he remarked (so he told us) that that day had been the clearest and best of the whole season for a distant view.

When we inquired from Dr. Thom about our weather prospects in Armenia, he replied that that country was hot, no doubt, throughout the summer, and that if we descended the Tigris to Diarbekir, we should suffer a good deal ; but if, as our intention was, we should keep to the highlands, on the northern side of the range which separates Armenia from Mesopotamia and Kurdistan, there was nothing to fear, and anyhow there was no prospect of the fine weather breaking up before the autumn arrived. This was satisfactory intelligence, because some travellers' accounts had greatly exaggerated the heat, while others spoke of frequent storms and unfavourable weather during the summer months, which, in fact, would not be a matter for surprise in so mountainous a country. In an ordinary season, the great heat of the summer is regarded as being over throughout all these regions after the middle of August.

We hired fresh horses, and the same afternoon started for Sivas, which lies to the north-east of this place, about four days' journey distant, and is the frontier town of Asia Minor on the borders of Armenia, close under the flank of the Anti-Taurus range. The road between the two places, which is very little travelled, is nearly parallel to the course of the Halys, but does not touch that stream, or the valley in which it runs, until close to Sivas. We had arranged, however, to make a slight détour at the commencement of our journey, in order to visit the monastery of Surp Garabed—one of the most famous of the Armenian convents—which lies to the east of this route, about four hours from Kaiserieh. For the first few miles Captain Cooper and Mr. Keropé accompanied us on horseback, for the old custom is still maintained in this country of speeding the parting guest by escorting him for a certain distance on his way. As we crossed the plain we noticed a number of Seljouk tombs, mostly in a half-ruined state, placed at intervals at some distance from one another. These are octagonal buildings with a pyramidal roof, somewhat on the type of that of Houen in the city, which I have already described, but without either the basement or the elaborate decoration of that fine work of architecture. They belong to a style which at one time must have prevailed extensively, for we afterwards found similar ones at Erzeroum. The village of Talas appeared to our right, occupying a steep position on the face of the hills which here descend abruptly to the plain; and when we reached these, we found two other large and flourishing villages, the churches of which, surmounted by cupolas, showed that they were inhabited by Christians. The higher ground forms an undulating level, bleak and rocky, and in many respects similar to that between Urgub and Indje-su; the evening began to close in as we crossed it, and the wind that swept over it was so cold that we were glad to put on extra clothing. Shortly before nightfall we again approached the edge of the plateau, and at last caught sight of the monastery. It is built against the cliffs, just where they are broken by a gorge, and stands several hundred feet above the plain, which in this part is covered with rich verdure, owing to the fertilising waters of a stream which here bursts out from the rock. As we approached we noticed a number of caves on our right hand, but by far the most prominent objects were three fine poplar trees, which rise below and immediately in front of the building. The position is magnificent, but the monastery itself can hardly be called imposing, for the most conspicuous part of it is a new wing, almost entirely destitute of architectural features, and the lofty walls, which inclose the courts at the back, are bald and bare.

The gate of entrance stands in the middle of the front, where a long terrace overlooks the steep slopes below. Here we found the monks and a number of the other occupants of the monastery waiting to welcome us, for one of our zaptiehs had ridden on and given notice of our coming. By them we were conducted to the guest-chamber, a good-sized room with a divan running round three sides of it, and a large airy window occupying the whole of the front, and commanding a superb view. The community at present is a very small one, consisting only of four monks and a superior, and as one of the monks was the man whom we met at Everek, there were only three at present in the building. But, notwithstanding this, it is a very important society, and in Armenia we heard it spoken of as ranking probably third among the conventual establishments of the Armenian Church, those of Etchmiadzin in Russian Armenia and of Jerusalem being the two first. The superior is always an archbishop, and is appointed by the Armenian patriarch of Constantinople, who has the superintendence of the Armenian churches in Turkey; and is confirmed by the patriarch of Etchmiadzin, who is the head of the whole Armenian community throughout the world. The present superior had returned a month before from Etchmiadzin, where he had been conferring with the patriarch, having gone thither by the way of Samsoun and Poti. In the course of the evening he paid us a visit. His personal appearance was most extraordinary, for though not a tall man, he was immensely broad, having big limbs, a vast grey beard, and the largest head I have ever seen on human shoulders, with huge features. His countenance certainly was not pleasing. We found both him and the other monks wonderfully ignorant, especially about the antiquities of their own monastery and its neighbourhood. In particular they could tell us nothing of the chapels in the rocks close by, of which Texier speaks, and which, if he has rightly described them, ought to be highly interesting. Before the superior left he reminded us of the clause in the Treaty of Berlin specially providing for the amelioration of the condition of the Armenians, and urged us to remember, and to let it be known, that their hopes were now wholly fixed on England; and he spoke in strong terms of the sufferings to which they were exposed in these parts. I requested him to specify what these were, but failed to elicit anything beyond generalities. We told him, as we had been commissioned to do, that the English vice-consul from Kaiserieh was intending to visit them before long, and at this he expressed great satisfaction, for he observed that we were the first Englishmen who had come to the monastery for five-and-twenty years.

At our supper some of the wine of the monastery was brought to us, which had been grown on their farms on the banks of the Halys, but I am afraid we were unable to pronounce it palatable, in spite of its classical associations. After the moon rose, the appearance of the plain below our windows, with the long shadows of the poplars thrown over it, was very impressive. During the night we heard the noise of the *semantron*, a wooden board, grasped in the middle by the left hand, and repeatedly struck with a mallet—by which here, as in the Greek Church, the brethren are summoned to prayers; and again, at an early hour of the morning, the sound of chanting proceeded from the church, boys' voices being distinctly audible among the others.

The name of this monastery, Surp Garabed, means St. John the Baptist, or rather 'The Forerunner,' by which title that saint is known in the Armenian Church, just as he is ὁ ἅγιος Πρόδρομος amongst the Greeks. Judging from the number of convents that are dedicated to him, he must be a very popular saint in Armenia, probably in consequence of the early period at which his supposed relics were introduced into the country; and Garabed is frequently found as a Christian name among the Armenians. Surp Garabed of Kaiserieh, as it is called by way of distinction, is said to possess the head of the saint, but the monks did not show us any of their relics. Tradition says that it was founded by St. Gregory the Illuminator, the apostle of the Armenians, and the monks told us that St. Basil used to live here sometimes, when he was at Kaiserieh; but the foundation of the present monastery is of a much later date. The buildings, which we visited the following morning, are of stone, very massive and very irregular, rising one above another at various angles. There was hardly any pretence of architecture, and none of the picturesque appearance which is so characteristic of

Greek monasteries. The new part, which we first saw as we approached, is principally occupied by families from Kaiserieh, who come here for change of air during the summer months; and at the time of our arrival we saw numerous women looking out of the windows. Formerly this monastery used to be a great place of pilgrimage, but for some years past, probably since the disturbances caused by the war, the country being unsafe, but few pilgrims have come. In one narrow court, at the angle formed by a passage, we saw four alabaster tombs of former superiors, with inscriptions in Armenian, and mitres resembling those with which we are familiar in the Western Church. There is no refectory, and when we asked for the library, we were taken to a small case in a room at the top of the building with a glass front, which no one seemed to know how to open. When at last it was unlocked, we found it to contain a number of books from Venice and Vienna, but only one manuscript, as far as we saw, which was a Commentary on the Scriptures in Armenian, and not very old. In this part there was also a small school for children.

It remains to speak of the church, which is the most important structure, though the general effect of it is certainly not imposing, and like all the other buildings, it has a cold and gloomy appearance. It is entered by an ante-chapel, and composed of a nave and aisles with barrel roofs, and the arches which separate these are pointed, though those that are found in the rest of the building are round. The feature which most attracts the eye is the covering of blue and white encaustic tiles, with which the pillars are encased up to their capitals, and the side walls also up to the same height. The effect produced is rather what one expects in a Turkish bath than in an ecclesiastical edifice, and these tiles are believed to have come from Moudania, the port of Broussa on the Sea of Marmora, where there was a manufactory of such things some centuries ago, and where some traces of the art are said to remain. Many pictures on canvas were hung against the walls; but there was no merit in any of them, nor any well-marked peculiarities, such as lend an interest to Byzantine frescoes and other works of art. The *iconostasis* also, or altar screen to separate the sanctuary from the rest of the church, was absent; in fact, this does not seem to be found in Armenian churches. In the wall of the south aisle there is a curious pulpit, which is reached from behind by a dark staircase through a side chapel. In front of the pulpit is a cushion, on which rests a volume of the Gospels, but it is so low that it is necessary to kneel in order to read it. On the opposite side of the church is a chapel of St. John the Baptist, the entrance doors of which are inlaid with tortoiseshell and mother-of-pearl.

Before leaving, we went out to sketch the monastery, from a point on the road by which we had arrived. On the way, we stopped to examine the grottoes in the rocks which we had noticed the evening before, and found them to consist of regular chambers, opening out into one another, and arranged with numerous niches at the sides. The view of Argaeus, from this point, in the opposite direction to the monastery, was remarkably fine, for owing to our having retired to a distance from it, the summit towered up, sharply cut, in solitary grandeur above the lower peaks. The hills on the opposite side of the plain below us, which may have been five miles distant, belong to the same range as that which we had crossed in coming from the Halys to Kaiserieh, and consequently they intervene between Surp Garabed and that river. It was no easy matter to escape from the crowd of people who tried to follow us wherever we went; indeed here, as previously at Tchakmak, we were much struck with the rudeness and extreme inquisitiveness both of the visitors who were staying in the place and of the domestics; nor was our opinion of these last improved when we discovered that several articles of wearing apparel belonging to our dragoman had been stolen. When we required that a search should be made, one of these was ultimately found, concealed in a cupboard, but the others we could not recover.

After paying a farewell visit to the old superior, we started in the company of one of the monks, who paid us the compliment of escorting us. He was a Vartabed, or monk of a higher grade—a name which is peculiar to the Armenian Church, as is also the office to which it is attached. It properly means a preaching monk, or Doctor, but those who bear it form a special class in the ministry, intermediate between bishops and priests. As we had been struck with the ignorance of this person the evening before on questions relating to the history of his society, we were now all the more impressed with his readiness and intelligence on all matters of business in talking to the farmers and peasants whom we met. The track lay along ledges of rock, like that by which we had approached Surp Garabed, formed by the breaking away of the cliffs as they descend to the plain, and here also the ground was everywhere bare above, but varied below with numerous trees, where the water breaks out in copious springs. At intervals there were villages, and in one of these was a house belonging to the monastery. When we had passed the last of them, the Vartabed took leave of us, and after this striking in among the hills we entered an uninteresting tract of country, five hours' riding over which brought us to the point where our path joined the regular road between Kaiserieh and Sivas. Shortly afterwards, a salt lake, covered with a white incrustation, came in sight on our left, and in it we recognised the same which we had seen forming a conspicuous object from the summit of Argaeus. Close as we were to it, when the sunlight fell on its surface, it looked quite like water. The soil throughout this region, and indeed for the greater part of the way to Sivas, is volcanic, and these salt formations are connected, I suppose, with the same set of phenomena. It has often been thought that the Halys obtains its name from this cause, but this derivation is probably erroneous.[1] Not far from this lake we halted by a small spring, where there was a single tree, the first we had seen for many hours; but though the sun at this time was hot, it was so tempered by the coolness of the wind as almost to render shade unnecessary.

When we had resumed our journey, we noticed about an hour further on that we were approaching

---

[1] The name is also written Ἅλυς, and is therefore probably unconnected with ἅλς.

a remarkable building having a lofty outer wall in which were numerous towers. When we reached it, we found that it was entered through a porch, elaborately ornamented with honeycomb-work, and within was a court about forty yards square, at the sides of which were arched recesses supporting an upper storey, with a similar arrangement to that which we had seen in the Timour-khané at Amasia, while the arches underneath formed a passage or aisle. In the middle of this court stood a detached tower of two storeys, the lower of which was open and composed of piers and arches, so as to give the effect of a second portal. Here again there was honeycomb-work, and the face of the stone was traced with ornamental patterns like those on the tomb of Houen. A gateway at the further end leads into a splendid edifice, of great size and fine proportions, being perhaps sixty yards long, which in its arrangement more resembles a church than any other building, for it has a lofty nave and two side aisles formed in the same way as the recesses of the outer court. A certain space at the inner end is separated off by a low breast-wall, and over the centre rises a cupola, now ruined, though the roof in other parts is perfect. The building generally is dark, and I did not notice that there were any windows in it. Hard by, in contrast to these remains of former magnificence, was a small, poverty-stricken village, and we learnt from some of the inhabitants that the structure was called Sultan-khané, and was believed to have been built by Sultan Murad (probably Murad IV.), though whether as a khan, or a palace, or a mosque, they did not know. We regretted that we could not devote more time to investigating this interesting place, but the afternoon was far advanced, and we had still three hours before us ere we could reach our resting-place, the village of Sariola. This appeared in view when we were still a long way off, and it was difficult to believe that our arrival could be so long delayed; but owing to the clearness of the air, distances are very deceptive in this country to an unpractised eye. To this result the elevation contributes, for throughout this stage from Kaiserieh to Sivas we were between 4,000 and 5,000 feet above the sea, and the atmosphere is as pure and invigorating as that of the Engadine. We also found that the estimate of hours along this road was unusually long. The element of uncertainty that is thus introduced into the computation of distances is very unfavourable to accuracy of measurement, and consequently renders precise numbers extremely vague for scientific purposes. In fact, so much depends on the rate of going and other accidental causes, that it may almost be questioned whether, within certain limits, round numbers are not the safest guide to truth. On arriving, we found that our zaptieh had procured comfortable quarters for us at the house of a Turkish landowner, who was, however, absent himself at the time.

Let us now hurry onward on our way to Sivas, for the intervening country presents but few objects of interest. In nearly six hours the following morning we reached the village of Karagheul or Black Lake, which is so called from a muddy pool in the midst of the houses, in which at this time numerous buffaloes were lying. Though the name of the place is Turkish, the inhabitants are all Armenians, and as we rested in a shady spot by the side of the pool, their chief men came round us to tell us their grievances. Foremost amongst these were the depredations of the Circassians, who, they said, used to carry off their cattle, so that the lands at some distance from the village had to be left untilled. They complained also of the heavy taxes they had to pay, but these appeared to be the kharatch or poll-tax, together with the tithes and other imposts, which undoubtedly are very heavy, but are not irregular, so that they were not worse off than the rest of the Christian population. When we asked to whom they were paid, they answered that they were sometimes collected by the kaimakam in person, sometimes by yuzbashis (captains), or zaptiehs. At the time of the famine they said they had suffered greatly, but were better off now. As we crossed a low ridge some distance further on, we turned to take our last view of Argaeus, the beautiful outline of which was distinctly visible, though it is here nearly seventy miles off. We passed the night at the village of Kayapournar, which stands on a rocky hillside overlooking a well-cultivated plain. Throughout the whole of this district the harvest was still going on, showing how much colder the climate is than in the neighbourhood of Kaiserieh. Our dinner was cooked here on cakes of tezek piled on the hearth, and the evening was chilly enough for us to find a fire not unwelcome.

The next day we crossed the plain in the midst of the harvesters, and passing the large Turkish village of Sheher Kishla, which was distinguished by a minaret, pursued our way over higher ground to a place called Hamma, where also the population was Mahometan. Here we wished to stop, but as the rays of the sun were scorching, and there were no trees in the neighbourhood, we were forced to look out for a house to rest in, and this was not altogether easy to obtain, for the male population were all at work in the fields, and the women were naturally shy of entertaining strangers. However, as none of them were veiled, we did not suppose they were very conventional in their ideas, and so it proved, for before long two elderly females agreed to give us shelter, and when once we were lodged in their house they became exceedingly communicative. They had several of their grandchildren with them, and with tears in their eyes they complained that the Government had taken away their sons to the war, and asked how these poor children were to be supported. Sixty men had gone from this village, and not one had returned, notwithstanding which the taxes were demanded of them. The two daughters-in-law came in afterwards, and all of them were large and powerful women, worthy mothers of Turkish soldiers, though we had noticed that the Turks in Asia Minor, though strongly made, are not usually large men. The zaptiehs, no doubt, are often of great stature, but then they are a picked body. They were much interested in all that belonged to us, and privately expressed their conviction that our spurs must be of silver and our holsters full of money. During the winter, they said, the house was covered with snow; and when I asked them what occupation they had then, they pointed to their dresses and the carpets, and said they made them.

At this time they were engaged in spinning. I may here remark how great a mistake was committed at the time of the Russo-Turkish war, when it was said that the Turkish soldiers were at a disadvantage for a winter campaign in Bulgaria or the Balkan, from being unaccustomed to endure excessive cold. In reality Asia Minor, which is the great recruiting ground for the Turkish army, has, as we have often noticed, a remarkably severe climate in winter; and those who are inured to its extremes of temperature must possess very hardy constitutions.

Three hours more brought us to the village of Kurd-keui, situated on the side of a gentle hill, where we determined to pass the night. Its name implies that it was once occupied by a Kurdish colony, but its present inhabitants are entirely Turks. The room in which we were lodged was so characteristic a specimen of the accommodation that is found in the best houses in these villages that it may be worth while to describe it. The door of entrance leads into a large stable, and from this again another door opens on one side into a good-sized room, with an arcade of wooden pillars running round two sides of it, and thus separating off from the rest of the apartment a certain space which is slightly elevated. Sometimes the floor is of clay or stamped earth throughout, but usually the elevated part is boarded over. In one part of this there is a fireplace, the front of which, above the hearth, is formed of cement ornamented in patterns; and at the opposite end stands a small wooden platform, raised about four feet from the ground, and intended for sleeping on. The windows, which are unprotected even by shutters, are very small, to prevent the wind and cold from entering. One house of this kind may be found in almost every village in these parts, even though most of the others may be mere hovels, and consequently we were able to dispense with our tent entirely for the present. The chief difficulty which the traveller encounters in such places arises from the movable furniture which the natives think it right to import into your abode; for they do as they would be done by, and show their hospitality immediately after your arrival by introducing rugs, carpets, pillows, and mattresses, which are essential to the Oriental notion of comfort, but usually swarm with vermin, and must be kept out at all hazards if you are to enjoy any rest. We had often to rack our brains for excuses to get rid of them, but usually succeeded in doing so without giving offence, the remoteness of our country and the strangeness of our dress serving in some measure to explain the outlandishness of our habits.

We were now but six hours' distance from Sivas, and this last stage of our journey we accomplished without a halt. As we had diverged from the road in order to reach Kurd-keui, we were forced to explore our way at first, and thus lost some time, as our zaptieh had rather vague ideas about the direction. However after four hours, during the latter part of which we had been steadily and sometimes rapidly ascending, we reached the summit of a high ridge from which Sivas was visible. The view from this point was extensive and very striking. In the valley, which descended a thousand feet below us, the silver stream of the Halys was flowing, and all around were steep clayey mountain-sides, above which to the north rose a lofty flat-topped height, probably the Chamlu Bel Dagh in the direction of Tokat, while the eastern horizon was bounded by the distant peaks of Anti-Taurus, the outline of which is far finer when seen from here than it appeared from Argaeus. Between these in front, and somewhat withdrawn from the course of the river, lay the extensive city of Sivas, forming a long line of trees and clustered houses on a space of level ground. We descended to the river by a steep winding road on the face of the mountain, and crossed it by a newly-built bridge of numerous arches, paved with flat slippery stones. On some meadows in the neighbourhood of the bridge numerous Circassian families were encamped with their flocks and herds. The Halys at this point looks at first sight as large as it did at Tchok Gheuz Kiupri, where we first saw it in approaching Kaiserieh. This of course is impossible, and as a matter of fact at this time of year it can be forded anywhere; but when it comes down in flood, it was described to us as having a great volume of water and prodigious force. From thence we rode to the city, and passing through its tortuous streets, made our way to the residence of the pasha, who at this time was occupying a country house in the suburbs, pleasantly situated in the midst of trees and runlets of water. He was himself indisposed, but we were received by his son, an agreeable young man, who was dressed, like so many of the younger Turkish gentlemen of Constantinople, in Frank costume except for the fez cap; he spoke French fluently and well, though he had not been in France, but had learnt it at Constantinople. At our request he undertook to provide us a lodging which we might occupy during our stay.

The house to which we were conducted was in the centre of the town, and proved to be the handsomest dwelling that we had seen in Asiatic Turkey. It was very large, according to the average size of houses in these parts, and the rooms were lofty, spacious, and tastefully decorated, the ceilings and alcoves being enriched with plaster ornaments. These were so finely executed that we hardly supposed they could be native work, but we found that they had been made by Armenians residing on the spot. But if the house was interesting, its proprietor was still more so. He was a Turkish gentleman called Kangal Aga, or the lord of Kangal, and though he was now in a private position, he had not always been so. At Yeuzgatt, when we stayed in the house of Tchapan Oglou, we had been entertained by a descendant of the Dere-beys, but we had not hoped to see a live Dere-bey, still less to be entertained by one. Yet such was, or rather had been, our present host. His patrimony of Kangal is situated in the Anti-Taurus, about a day and a half's journey from Sivas, and there he resided in his earlier days, and ruled the neighbouring country as an independent feudal chieftain, though recognising, in name at all events, the suzerainty of the Porte. There also he grew rich by receiving bribes and making extortions; in fact, if what we heard of him was true, he must have been a miscreant of the first water. But gradually the Government, following out the policy which Sultan Mahmoud had practised so successfully both in Europe and Asia, got hold of him, and forced him to leave his stronghold and live in the town, where he is treated with the greatest honour, and allowed to enjoy an ample income, but is practically a prisoner. His appearance is not striking in any respect, and certainly has nothing to indicate either force of character or brutality. We found him a courteous and agreeable entertainer, though he did not visit us very often.

The position of Sivas is one of great importance, because it commands the approach to the one main pass which crosses the Anti-Taurus from Anatolia into Armenia, and forms the line of communication between the Black Sea by way of Samsoun and the interior of Asia Minor on the one hand, and the valley of the Tigris and the Persian Gulf on the other. Under these circumstances it is not surprising to find that the site has been occupied from ancient times. It is probably the same place which we hear of as receiving the name of Megalopolis from Pompey, but it was not called Sebasteia until the imperial times, for Pliny is the first writer who mentions it by that name. At a later period it was made the capital of Armenia Minor, a province the boundaries of which varied at different times, but which may be described in general terms as the district comprised between the Halys and the Euphrates. Under the Byzantine emperors it was one of the most flourishing cities of Asia Minor. In the eleventh century, in consequence of the inroads of the Turks into Armenia, a large number of Armenians migrated into the valley of the Halys, and from that time onward a considerable part of the population of this city and of the neighbouring districts has been composed of that race. At last the place fell into the hands of the Seljouks, from whom it subsequently passed to the Ottomans. The most important event in its history was the siege by Timour the Tartar, at the time of his campaign against Sultan Bajazet in the year 1400 A.D. On that occasion it was vigorously defended for eighteen days, but at the end of that time a breach was made in the walls, which are described as having been very massive, and the place was taken by storm. Timour massacred the whole of the Christian population, who formed the most industrious portion of the inhabitants, and the city seems never to have recovered from this great calamity. At the present day it is estimated to contain from 35,000 to 40,000 souls, and it is said to be increasing. The modern pronunciation of the name gives evidence of its classical origin, for it is strongly accented on the last syllable, thus retaining the accent of Sebasteia (Σεβάστεια). The Armenians here, and everywhere eastward of this, speak Armenian as their native tongue, and the lower classes know Turkish but imperfectly. This is an evidence that we are approaching their proper home, for further to the west we had found the opposite of this to be the case.

As seen from within, Sivas appears to be surrounded on three sides by low hills, while in the middle of the town rises a rocky prominence of no great height and level at the top, on which stands the castle. Persons approaching it from the north are struck with the flat roofs of the houses, but to these we were already accustomed, as this is the regular mode of building in Kaiserieh. The dwellings seem to be constructed more in blocks than is usual in these towns; but the feature which more, perhaps, than any other attracts the eye in a general view, is the numerous chimneys, rising to a high-pitched covering, like a gable, which probably serves to cast off the snow in winter. There are but few objects of interest in the place, the principal being the fronts of two mosques of the Seljouk period, in different parts of the town, which are handsomely ornamented in the same style as similar buildings which I have noticed elsewhere. Sivas has a bad reputation for evil odours; so much so, that Dr. Van Lennep remarks that 'uninitiated travellers generally enter the town involuntarily holding their hands to their noses.' When we first rode through that part of the town which leads to the pasha's residence, we thought it had been harshly judged, but we found good reason to change our opinion afterwards, for some of the streets are not paved at all, and in many of those which are so, the pavement is broken away in places, so as to form large hollows, where half-liquid filth collects, emitting most noxious exhalations. The consequence of this is that typhus is prevalent in the early spring—a circumstance which the pasha's son attributed to the people living closed up in dirty houses during the winter, but which the American missionaries accounted for with much greater probability by referring it to the thawing of this objectionable matter, after it had been frozen during the cold season. The elevation of Sivas above the sea, according to our consul-general, Colonel Wilson, who, as I have already said, is an authority in these matters, is 4,614 feet. This estimate is higher than what previous travellers have computed is to be, and what our own aneroid gave; but it is probably correct, as it is the result of careful measurement under very favourable atmospheric conditions. Dr. Van Lennep makes it 4,481 feet. In consequence of the great height of this region (for the city stands but little above the level of the river-bed) very few vegetables can be grown here; and at dinner time Kangal Aga informed us that those which we were eating had come from Tokat, between this place and Amasia, which is lower and has a warmer climate.

We remained here during the afternoon of our arrival and the following day, in order to make preparations for our journey into Armenia. Just as we had settled ourselves in Kangal Aga's house, we received a visit from Mr. Block, a young Englishman acting as Colonel Wilson's dragoman, who had heard of our coming, and brought me some welcome letters. This gentleman is the firstfruits of the admirable system of student-interpreters, first set on foot when Lord Derby was at the Foreign Office, according to which young men, selected by competition, are sent out to Constantinople, with salaries from the English Government, with a view to learning the languages of the native races in Turkey on the spot. The object aimed at by this measure is one of primary importance, for our consular service in Turkey is lamentably deficient in this respect, and in England the facilities for learning even Turkish are few or none. We found that Mr. Block spoke Turkish fluently. Later on we visited Colonel Wilson, and the next evening he kindly entertained us at dinner. He was located in an agreeable, airy house at no great distance from our quarters, which was entered through a courtyard, and formed an excellent summer residence, though it would be difficult to keep warm in winter. He had reached Sivas about the same time that we first visited Kaiserieh, and spoke of the heat at that time as having been very great, the thermometer on the day of his arrival marking over 100° in the shade. In the course of his journey overland from Smyrna, which he had made in the company of Mr. Block and, as far as Kaiserieh, of Captain Cooper, he was struck by the absence of any military force, and in fact of any power that could keep order in case of a rising. In this place there was a body of 100 cavalry, but otherwise they had met with no soldiers at all. We afterwards found the same thing to be true of almost every part of Armenia. Fo doubt, from one point of view the absence of the Turkish soldiery is favourable to tranquillity, as they are apt themselves to be a disturbing element. Thus the worst of the outbreaks which had taken place in the previous spring consisted in attacks by these on the Christian population in the district of Malatia and Marasch in the southern part of the Anti-Taurus; this was a very bad affair, and was being now investigated by the Turkish authorities. But at the present moment the general exhaustion more than anything else seemed to be the cause of temporary quiet. At the same time there were ugly signs of a spirit of lawlessness in the towns. At Kaiserieh there had been attacks by Mahometans on Christians, and disputes accompanied by violence between various Christian sects. And at Sivas the state of things was even worse, for a man who until lately was in no position at all, had assumed to himself all the power in the place, was employing

Circassians to do his bidding and using violence as he liked, and had thus overawed the population and the authorities. Colonel Wilson had been much impressed by the results of the famine, as seen in the districts he had passed through, and did not think the country had more than half recovered the effects of that calamity.

During our stay we also visited the American missionaries, Messrs. Perry and Hubbard, partly with the view of obtaining money, for, as I said at starting, the missionaries had become our bankers through the kind influence of their secretary at Constantinople. We spent some time pleasantly in conversation with them and their ladies, and were glad to have the opportunity of obtaining information from persons so well acquainted with the people. With regard to the relations of the Mahometans and Christians in these parts, I described how in the villages where we had stayed they seemed to be much on an equality, and when they met they appeared to be on friendly terms; and then I inquired whether this really represented the true state of the case. Mr. Perry replied, that I should be much mistaken if I thought so. In their dealings with one another there was much outward show of politeness, but notwithstanding this there was a deep-seated alienation between them. The Mahometans asserted themselves as the dominant class and made the Christians feel it, and the Christians in turn repaid this by hatred; and this statement applied to the country as well as to the towns, for there the Mahometans were equally oppressive to their Christian neighbours. Everywhere it was understood by both sides that a request made by one of the ruling race was equivalent to a demand. I asked whether in those parts of the country where the Christians bear arms they had not a sufficient security. He answered, No; for they do not usually dare to use their arms against a Mahometan, because if one of that creed is killed, it is sure to go against the Christian in the law courts, whereas in the opposite case the Mahometan would have every advantage. This was afterwards confirmed to me at Erzeroum, where I was told that, in consequence of a Mahometan having been found dead in a Christian village, the fourteen chief men of that village had been arrested on suspicion, a thing which would never have happened if a Christian had been killed. Mr. Perry mentioned a case of a member of his own congregation at the time of the war, which was a period of great hardship for the Christians, because the soldiers who were then recruited or levied used to make raids on the Christian villages, and demanded presents of money, and that the girls should be given up to them for their lust. On one of these occasions, an Armenian Protestant, driven to desperation by the insults offered to a woman of his family, used his knife and killed a soldier. In consequence of this he was condemned to fifteen years' imprisonment, and was now dying in prison, all the attempts of the missionaries to obtain his release having been met by excuses and delays. When I asked whether a Christian's evidence was received in the law courts, the reply was in the negative. At the same time Mr. Perry disclaimed all personal preference for the Christians, for in the ordinary affairs of life the Mahometans, he said, were more agreeable to deal with.

As we are now on the eve of quitting Asia Minor, it may be well for me here briefly to state my impressions with regard to the condition and prospects of that country. That it is a land with a great capacity for development there can be no doubt at all. Even now it produces a large quantity of corn, and if all the arable land were brought under cultivation, this might be increased at least fourfold. For this reason, as the present population is small in comparison of the area, their ordinary wants are supplied with comparative ease. The sheep also, both the Angora and the broad-tailed breed, are very valuable, and might be made a large source of revenue. In like manner, the mineral wealth of the country is undoubtedly great, though for the most part it is undeveloped, and where mining operations have taken place, they have for the present ceased. Nor is any hindrance to progress offered by the populations which inhabit it, for both Christians and Mahometans belong to vigorous races, and the Armenians at all events have no lack of ability. But however this may be, certain it is that the present condition of Asia Minor is deplorable. The immediate cause of this, no doubt, was the famine to which I have so often alluded; but as an interval of five years has elapsed since that occurred, the country ought to have recovered from its effects under any other than the most unfavourable conditions. But, as I have already remarked, if there had been any reserve of supply, the population could not have been reduced to a state of destitution by a single blow; and the same cause which brought about the severity of the calamity, destroyed all power of rebound. Under these circumstances the weight of taxation, burdensome at all times, was felt to press doubly heavily, especially the tithe of corn, which was paid in kind, and the sheep and goat tax, which amounted to $2\frac{1}{2}$ piastres (about 5*d.*) for every animal. These were paid by all the people alike, and in the case of the Christians there was the capitation tax besides; but there can be no doubt that at the present time, owing to the great destruction of the male population during the war, the Mahometans are in a worse plight than the Christians. The case is altogether different in Armenia, as we shall see hereafter; but that this is so here, even the Greek Bishop of Kaiserieh, a good and able man, remarked to Colonel Wilson and Captain Cooper. The consequence is universal disaffection against the Government at Constantinople. The people feel that the only object of their rulers is to obtain their money in the form of taxes, and their men for soldiers; that nothing is done to promote any local objects; that marauders are allowed to prowl about the country; and that trade is paralysed by national bankruptcy. Such a measure as the abolition of the copper currency—which, though the coins were admirable, yet in one day, and without any notice given, ceased throughout the provinces to be a legal tender—was an act of bad faith towards the whole population sufficient to account for any amount of mistrust and indignation. But, from what we could gather, none of these grievances were as deeply felt as the venality of justice. This complaint was on everybody's lips, and the feeling that no case, however slight, could be decided without the payment of bribes, and that the Government officials grew rich by this means, rankled in their minds. Accordingly, the opinion prevailed that the present *régime* was intolerable. On this subject there was no difference; Mahometans and Christians, natives and foreign residents, all thought alike. The one thing that every person was inquiring for was some power which might replace it. And what power could that be?

It suffices to ask this question, to show how nearly hopeless the situation is. Hardly any point, in fact, connected with the future of Turkey is so difficult of solution. No one supposes that the presence of a few consuls, however vigorous and able they may be, if armed only with the power of protest and representation at head-quarters, can do more than slightly modify the evil. A native Government is an impossibility, for the antagonism of creeds is too strong to allow of the people spontaneously acting together. The jealousy of other nations must prevent any European State from undertaking the task; and even the idea that by the combined action of the Great Powers an independent State might be formed under the guidance of some vigorous ruler seems to be outside the sphere of practical politics. Besides, the great numerical preponderance of the Mahometan element in the population renders it probable that, as long as an Ottoman Government exists, Asia Minor will continue to be directly subject to it. Yet, unless the narrowing of the area of its dominion forces the Porte to a complete revolution in its mode of administration, the condition of the country is likely to grow worse and worse. There is no period in the life of a people so full of misery—as the later centuries of Byzantine history amply show—as that of the protracted death-sickness of a decaying empire.

The best thing that can be hoped for is some partial development of local self-government, which may secure that a portion of the money demanded in the form of taxes may be expended on the country itself. Of reform on a more extended scale there can hardly be said to be any hope.

CHAPTER VIII.

ANTI-TAURUS AND EUPHRATES.

Armenia—Its geographical features—Sketch of its history—The Armenian Church—Influence of the Armenians—Guide-book for Armenia—Departure from Sivas—Pass of Delik Tasch—Visit of Count von Moltke—Village of Allaja Khan—Hekim Khan—Character of the Anti-Taurus—First view of the Euphrates—Ferry at Keban Maden—Two streams of the Euphrates—Its lower course—The Euphrates in history—Village and mine of Keban Maden—Arrival at Mezireh.

THE land of Armenia, which we are now about to enter, is in some respects one of the most remarkable countries in the world. It occupies a great part of the triangle which lies between three seas—the Mediterranean, the Euxine, and the Caspian. Its elevation above the sea is very great, reaching 6,000 feet in the plains which intervene between Erzeroum and Ararat in the northern part of the district. These form, as it were, the roof of Western Asia, from which the chief rivers of this part of the world flow in different directions, the Euphrates towards the Persian Gulf, and the Araxes to the Caspian. It is bounded and intersected by vast ranges of mountains, the most important of which are the Taurus towards the south, dividing it from Mesopotamia, and containing the sources of the Tigris, and the Anti-Taurus towards the west; besides these, it attains a great altitude in the volcanic summits of Bingheul Dagh in the centre of the country, of Sipan above the lake of Van, and of Ararat in the east, which rises to a height of more than 17,000 feet. The lake of Van itself forms a remarkable geographical feature, being a large expanse of brackish water, deeply sunk amongst the mountains, and without an outlet, while at the same time it is between 5,000 and 6,000 feet above the sea. The whole country forms a link to join the great central plateaux of Asia, which were the seats of the famous Oriental monarchies, with the lower, but still elevated, regions of Anatolia. In consequence of its thus standing between Greece and Rome on the one side, and Persia and Parthia on the other, it was the scene of continual struggles, either for its own independence, or in the contests between those empires. Its climate, as might be expected, is even more rigorous than that of Asia Minor, and the ground is deeply covered with snow during many months of the year—a circumstance on which Xenophon dwells in recounting the sufferings and privations which he and his soldiers experienced in passing through Armenia in the course of their famous retreat.

The Armenian race, by whom this country has been inhabited from an early period, belong to the Indo-European branch of the human family, as is proved by the evidence of their language. The same evidence goes to show that they are more closely related to the Persians and their kindred tribes than to any other races of the same stock. The native name of this people was Haikh, while that of Armina was given to them by the Medes and Persians. Their early homes, when they migrated from Media, seem to have been in the eastern part of the country, about the lake of Van, and both on the northern and southern sides of Ararat. The former of these two districts, the neighbourhood of Van, is the Togarmah of the Bible, where the name occurs, both in the genealogy of the sons of Noah in the book of Genesis,[1] and in Ezekiel, where there is mention of commerce in horses and mules as existing between Togarmah and the people of Tyre.[2] Here they were attacked by the Assyrians, but that great kingdom never thoroughly subdued them, though its civilisation exercised great influence on them, as is shown by the employment of the cuneiform character in this part of Armenia, where numerous inscriptions in this mode of writing still remain. Afterwards Armenia formed part of the empires of Persia, of Alexander the Great and his successors, and of Rome, but yet retained sufficient independence to be governed at frequent intervals by native sovereigns. In the time of Augustus it was a bone of contention between the Romans and the Parthians, who were the most dreaded enemies of the masters of the world. Again, in the third century of the Christian era, when the Sassanid or later Persian kingdom was founded, Armenia was frequently conquered by the princes of that dynasty, but it was enabled as often to reassert its freedom by the help of the Roman arms. When its prince Tiridates embraced Christianity in 276 A.D., the struggle became embittered by the introduction of a religious element, for the Persian monarchs were bigoted followers of the doctrines of Zoroaster, and each subsequent invasion of Armenia was accompanied by violent persecutions of the Christians. This state

[1] Gen. x. 3.   [2] Ezek. xxvii. 14.

of things reached a height when the country was partitioned between the Romans and Persians, first under Theodosius the Great, in 390 A.D., and more completely afterwards, in the time of the younger Theodosius, about 429 A.D. After the fall of the Sassanidae in the seventh century, it was disputed for by the Greek empire and the Saracens, but from 859 to 1045 A.D. it was again ruled by a native dynasty of vigorous princes, the Bagratidae. This was brought to an end by the suspicious and short-sighted policy of the Byzantine emperors, who conquered and annexed this province, thereby laying open their whole eastern frontier to the invasion of the Seljouk Turks, who shortly before this had commenced their attacks, and might have been successfully resisted by these hardy mountaineers in their powerful strongholds. The result was fatal to both parties, for Armenia was overrun and desolated, and by the battle of Manzikert, in 1071 A.D., in which the Emperor Romanus IV. was defeated and made prisoner by Alp Arslan, the whole of Asia Minor was left at the mercy of the Seljouks. A relative of the last native sovereign, called Rupen, escaped into Cilicia, and there established a principality, which attained to some importance and lasted for several centuries, being ruled by a dynasty called from him the Rupenian. But the mother country passed into the hands of various Mahometan powers, until at length the greater part of it was incorporated in the Ottoman Empire. The last great calamity which fell upon it happened in 1605, when Shah Abbas of Persia removed 12,000 families from their homes, and settled them near Ispahan. The districts which lie to the north of Ararat have gradually passed into the hands of Russia.

The Armenian Church is the oldest of all national Churches. The people were converted by St. Gregory, called 'The Illuminator,' who was a relative of Dertad or Tiridates, and had been forced to leave the country at the same time with him, and settled at Caesareia, where he was initiated into the Christian faith. These youths returned to their own land, as Dr. Neale says, 'the one to reassert her independence, the other to enlighten her.'[1] Both prince and people embraced the Gospel, and thus presented the first instance of an entire nation becoming Christian. The persecutions they subsequently suffered endeared the Church to the people, and it has been identified with them and bound up with their national existence throughout their long history. At first it was subject to the See of Caesareia, but when a written character was invented for the Armenian language, and the Scriptures were translated into that tongue, by St. Mezrop, one of their most famous saints, at the beginning of the fifth century, it obtained an independent standing-ground. After the Council of Chalcedon, in which they took no part, the Armenians adopted the views of the Monophysites, and since that time have been separated from the rest of the Christian world ; but the cause of antagonism between them and the orthodox Eastern Church was as much political as doctrinal, since it arose in great measure from the attempt of the Greeks to assert their ecclesiastical supremacy over other races. Their descendants at

---

[1] Neale, *History of the Eastern Church*, i. 66.

the present day would no doubt maintain that they hold the views of their forefathers, but whether these, if stated in other than technical language, would prove to be different from the doctrine of the Church at large, is more than doubtful. In other respects, such as organisation and ceremonial, they do not very greatly differ from the Greek Church. As I have already said, their spiritual head is the Patriarch of Etchmiadzin, which place is now within the borders of Russian Armenia, not far from the northern foot of Ararat; but those who reside in the Turkish dominions are directly subject to the Armenian Patriarch of Constantinople, according to an arrangement entered into with the Porte. At one time two rival patriarchates existed, the one at Sis in Cilicia, which was in connection with the Rupenian kingdom, the other on the small island of Akhtamar in the lake of Van; but both these schisms have now been reconciled. A certain number, not inconsiderable, have joined the Roman Church, and are known as United Armenians; but the great bulk of the nation has adhered to the national communion. It is generally agreed that in numbers, in intelligence, and in wealth, they constitute by far the most important Christian communion of the East excepting the Russian.[1]

Though the majority of the Armenians in Asiatic Turkey—especially the agricultural population—have been too much ground down by centuries of oppression to show many signs of spirit or energy, yet there can be no doubt that their national character

---

[1] Neale, *History of the Eastern Church*, i. 65. Stanley, *Lectures on the Eastern Church*, p. 7.

is a powerful one, and will exercise a marked influence in determining the future of the East. The American missionaries in the country itself describe those of their pupils who are of this race as being highly intelligent, and I heard the same thing many years previously from one of the teachers in the school at Bebek, near Constantinople, who described the Armenian mind as having great depth and sobriety. Those of the upper class are known throughout Turkey as leading bankers and merchants, especially at Constantinople, where sultans and grand viziers have been fain to borrow money of them, and their shrewdness and aptitude for business are proverbial. They are also to be found engaged in trade in most of the capitals of Europe, and throughout the length and breadth of Asia, including India. In this manner the calamities of the nation have become in one sense the cause of its greatness, for this wide dispersion and consequently extended influence have resulted from the enforced emigration brought about by invasion and persecution—at first, during the early inroads of the Seljouks, who carried off innumerable prisoners and sold them as slaves, and afterwards on various other occasions down to the time of Shah Abbas. At the present day many from the lower classes also emigrate for a time in search of employment, and are to be found at Constantinople engaged in various trades and occupations, especially as porters, for the *hamals* of that city are to a great extent Armenians. They may be regarded as types of their race, which is characterised in its political and social life by industry, perseverance, and long-suffering endurance. The total number of this nationality in Asiatic Turkey is variously estimated at from three-quarters of a million to more than two million souls.[1] The other race which forms a considerable element in the population of Armenia is that of the Kurds; of them we shall have to speak further on.

The guide-book which we used for our journey in Armenia was an original one, but proved admirable, and is in reality the only book at present existing which is of service in the country. It was the tenth and part of the ninth volumes of Ritter's 'Erdkunde.' In this comprehensive work, which with the exception of the first volume is devoted to Asia, the great geographer has brought together all the accessible information about the different parts of that continent, so that the successive volumes form an epitome of what was known of each country up to the time of their publication. Vol. X., which is especially devoted to Armenia, was published in a second and revised edition in 1843, and comparatively little has been added to the stock of our knowledge of the country since that time. It contains, besides historical and other summaries, a notice of the various routes through Armenia, with abstracts of the accounts given by the travellers who have followed them. Great care is taken in estimating the distances, and in noticing the objects of interest

---

[1] Mr. Ravenstein in his very careful paper in the *Journal of the Statistical Society* for Sept. 1877 (p. 455) reckons them at 760,000. Mr. McCoan (*Our New Protectorate*, i. 135, and *note*) says more than two millions. 'An Eastern Statesman' in the *Contemporary Review* for April 1880 (p. 535) puts the number for the whole of Turkey at two millions, and from this more than one hundred thousand must be deducted for the European dominions.

on the way. Thus it is quite possible, by means of careful study beforehand, to make it serve as a guidebook; and if it is less methodically arranged than such handbooks usually are, it contains a far larger amount of valuable information. The bulky volume, however, printed on the very worst of old German paper, is highly unsuitable for use in travelling, and accordingly I had it bound in four separate parts before leaving England. In addition to these I took the latter part of Vol. IX., which describes a portion of the country near the Persian frontier. I can recommend this arrangement to future travellers.

At six o'clock in the morning on August 12 we left Sivas, issuing from the town on its southern side. The stage for which we had engaged our horses was as far as Kharput, a journey of six days, and included the passage of the Anti-Taurus and the crossing of the Euphrates. The road that we were to follow was the regular post-road to Bagdad, but all accounts agreed in describing this part of it as traversing a most desolate region. The zaptieh whom we took with us was to accompany us the whole distance—an arrangement which we had insisted on with some urgency, for at first the authorities tried to persuade us to change our escort from day to day at the villages where we passed the night; we knew, however, that in this way we should get inferior men, and when they found that we insisted on what was our undoubted right, they provided us with an excellent attendant, quick and intelligent, and well acquainted with what proved to be in places a somewhat intricate road. He was an old man, but so smart and military in his bearing that we at once surnamed him the 'Old Colonel.' We had not gone far before we reached the Halys, which is here crossed by a bridge considerably further up the stream than that by which we had passed it before. This bridge has the peculiarity of not being straight, but constructed at an obtuse angle, the apex of which stands in the middle of the current so as to break the force of the water. All about here the corn was piled in large cocks in the fields, waiting for the tax-gatherer; for as the taxes are taken in kind, the collector has to inspect it and determine the tithe before it is stored. The proprietor, however, is allowed to thresh it, but not to winnow, for the latter process is supposed to offer opportunities for cheating. Anyhow, whether in the fields or the threshing-floor, the corn has to remain exposed, sometimes for a long period, and if bad weather comes it is liable to be spoilt. This proceeding is customary throughout Turkey, and the people are accustomed to it, but still it is everywhere felt to be a hardship.

When we reached the further end of the plain in which Sivas lies, we took leave of our friends Mr. Block and Mr. Hubbard, who had accompanied us for a certain distance. As we began to mount the hills beyond, we obtained a fine view of the city behind us, lying outspread in the midst of environing mountains. Our road continued over the clayey spurs of Anti-Taurus, until after five hours we reached a spring, in the neighbourhood of which were the ruined arches of a building that may perhaps in former days have been a khan; here we were glad to shelter ourselves from the sun and rest awhile. When we resumed our journey, we passed some way further on one of those salt lakes, covered with a white incrustation, which I have already spoken of as existing in the east of Asia Minor. Our course thus far had been almost due south, but at this point we turned towards the south-east up a lateral valley, at the bottom of which were green meadows intersected by a clear mountain stream. Above us to the left rose lofty limestone peaks, but below these, and also on the opposite side of the valley, were igneous rocks, the broken faces of which exhibited patches of deep colour, red, yellow, and green. A gradual ascent led us up a mountain-side interspersed with dwarf juniper trees, the thick stems of which showed their ancient growth, until we reached a rock that rises 150 feet above the road, called Delik Tasch, or the Hollowed Rock, from a shallow cavern at its base. From this both the pass at its back and the neighbouring village have taken their name. The pass, to say the truth, has but little about it that is characteristic, for it crosses open ground, where there is a slight depression in the mountains; but still it is the highest point in the road across the Anti-Taurus, and as it is 1,600 feet above Sivas, reaches the height of more than 6,000 feet above the sea. It is owing to the great elevation of the neighbouring plains that it appears insignificant. The watershed thus formed is one of great importance, for whereas all the streams that we have left behind us drain into the Halys, and so into the Black Sea, those that we shall henceforth meet flow into the Euphrates, and are carried by it into the Persian Gulf. On the further side we obtained extensive views over a succession of level ranges, reaching for a great distance in the direction of Armenia, which were now tinged with pink by the evening light. The village, which lies immediately below the summit of the pass, presented a peculiar appearance from the flat tops of the houses being surmounted with large hayricks. The hay is probably obtained from the meadows over which we had passed in the valley, and was in itself an unwonted object, for we had seen nothing of the kind since leaving Ladik between Samsoun and Amasia.

The house to which we were conducted belonged to a relation of Kangal Aga, our host at Sivas, for here we are in the neighbourhood of his ancient patrimony, and Kangal, the place from which he took his name, is situated at some little distance to the left of the road which we followed the next day. We occupied a spacious room, not unlike those which we had met with in the villages of Asia Minor; but it was not long before we recognised in this a place of almost historical interest, for it was evidently the same which was occupied by Count von Moltke in 1838, and of which he has given a description in one of his published letters. At that time he held an independent commission from the Sultan in connection with the Turkish army, and was on his way to the frontiers of Armenia and Syria, which were threatened by the forces of Ibrahim Pasha, who commanded for Mehemet Ali. It was the middle of March, and the whole country in this neighbourhood was deeply covered with snow, and it was snowing heavily as the Prussian officer and his Turkish attendants crossed the pass of Delik Tasch. Curiously enough, he speaks of this as the watershed between the Black

Sea and the Mediterranean. It appears from his account that the Porte was already circumscribing the power of the Dere-beys in these parts; so far, at all events, as to have full command of this important road. He writes as follows:

'We noticed the foundations of a strong fort, built by some Dere-bey or Lord of the Valleys with the view of holding the pass in his power. Reschid Pasha, however, established there an Ayan, whose duty it is to maintain the security of the road, as a sort of margrave. After our fatiguing ride we received a most agreeable welcome at his house; a grand fire crackled on the hearth; the ceiling of the large apartment was covered in with closely-fitting pine trunks, which with earth trodden in upon them serve for the roof; while the floor was strewn with clean carpets, and slender wooden pillars separated the central space destined for the more distinguished guests from the daïs occupied by the servants. With a strong sense of comfort we stretched ourselves out on the cushions, and shortly afterwards the large tin tray appeared, on which the numerous dishes of a Turkish meal are served; for pewter dishes with covers of the same metal, wooden spoons, and a very long napkin of half silken texture, form the dinner service of the upper as well as of the poorer classes. My Turkish attendants greatly enjoyed a good cup of Russian tea, or possibly the rum that was in it.'[1]

Our route the following day continued in a southeasterly direction, and for six hours we were traversing bare undulating plains, where for the greater part

[1] Von Moltke, *Briefe über Zustände und Begebenheiten in der Türkei aus den Jahren* 1835 *bis* 1839; 2nd ed. Berlin, 1876, p. 207.

of the way there was sparse cultivation, so that it cannot quite rightly be described as uncultivated, as it is in Kiepert's map. In this part of Turkey the ground usually lies fallow alternate years, but in the remoter districts it often appeared to us as if it must be tilled at much longer intervals. Von Moltke naturally speaks of this region as a desert, for when he saw it there was a waste of snow as far as the eye could reach, and the traveller was almost blinded by the reflection of the sunlight from the white surface. The snow lay four feet deep, and the difficulty of the journey was increased by its having so far lost its consistency as not to allow of walking over it; the only passage was along a path two feet wide, where the snow had been beaten hard by the feet of beasts of burden during the winter. As ill luck would have it, in the middle of this he met a heavily laden train of camels and asses, and before the two lines could pass one another the whole of the baggage had to be unpacked, and an entire hour was lost in this process.

At last we descended into a stony valley, where a khan had been newly built on the site of what had been a notorious resort of robbers. Strange to say, this was the first khan which we had seen, except in the great towns, since leaving Amasia; so little communication is there along the roads in the east of Asia Minor. While we were resting there, a long drove of camels went by, but not laden, for they were on their way from Arabia to Kaiserich to be sold; the people at the khan informed us that they fetch somewhat more than 10*l.* Turkish each, which seems a small price.[1] From this place the ground again

---

[1] The Turkish pound is intermediate in value between the napoleon and the sovereign.

rises, until it attains a considerable elevation, though still 200 feet lower than Delik Tasch, and now the eastern horizon began to be varied with the outlines of higher mountains. We passed the night at the village of Allaja Khan, the zinc-tipped minaret of which had attracted our notice as we descended to it from above. This place, if one may compare small things with great, reminded me of Spalato on the coast of Dalmatia, where the greater part of the modern town is comprehended within the magnificent walls of Diocletian's palace; for here half the village lies within the inclosure of an old khan or caravanserai, which must have covered a vast space of ground. At present the building is a mass of ruin, but an entrance gateway remains in one part, the round arch of which is formed of stones alternately blue and white, and the minaret also is diversified by bands of black stone. This feature accounts for the name of the place, for *allaja* in Turkish signifies 'streaked' or 'variegated.' Owing to the way in which the dwellings are massed together, it is possible to wander for a considerable distance over their flat or slightly sloping roofs. Like most of the villages of the Anti-Taurus, Allaja Khan has a mixed Turkish and Armenian population.

The next day was mostly spent in following downwards the course of a valley, which wound among finer mountains than we had hitherto seen in this part of our route. The stream that flows through it finds its way into the Euphrates somewhat above the junction of that river with the Tokma Su, the ancient Melas, which waters the district that was called Melitene (now represented by the town of Malatia), and is one of the most important of the early tributaries of the Euphrates. The natives here call their river Kirk Gheuz, or the Forty Eyes, a common Turkish name for sources and streams. All about its bed great patches of feathery tamarisk were growing. Ten hours brought us to the large village of Hekim Khan, or 'the Physician's Inn,' which is reputed, whether rightly or wrongly, to have taken its name from a caravanserai built by a person of that profession. The word *khan*, which is attached both to this name and to that of our last night's abode, clearly shows the origin of these villages—that is to say, that they were at first resting-places on the line of traffic, round which other houses were subsequently congregated. So thinly populated is this district, that though we had now journeyed 100 miles since leaving Sivas, the only villages which we had passed on the way were those in which we slept. The position of Hekim Khan is striking, for it lies high above the river, in a hollow on the mountain side surrounded by fine cliffs, while a curious conical hill, capped with rock, rises on one side of it. A stone-built mosque and minaret form conspicuous objects among the other buildings. Some travellers speak of a castle as existing here, but the only building, as it appeared to me, which at all resembled such an edifice, is the ruined wall of a large khan—probably the original one—in the neighbourhood of the mosque.

At this point the two roads from Sivas to Kharput diverge, the one following the river-valley and passing by Malatia, the other leading over the mountains and crossing the Euphrates at Keban Maden. The former of these is the easier, and the line of telegraph runs along it; but the latter, though it traverses rougher ground, is the shorter by several days, and for this reason we preferred it. We now ascended over the mountain sides towards the east, in the midst of more interesting country, for the ground was covered with much oak-scrub, and the surrounding scenery was really fine. By this time we had discovered the true character of the Anti-Taurus. The view of it which we obtained from Argaeus had prepared us to find that it was not a very grand or very lofty chain relatively to the neighbouring country, but now we had learnt that it is not so much a range of mountains as a great mass of elevated land, about 100 miles in breadth, which is more broken into peaks and deep valleys on its eastern than its western side. To us, who crossed it diagonally, the distance of course was greater. Our road now became a mere horse-track. Hitherto it had been fairly wide where the country was level, though in gorges or rocky places there was no attempt at engineering, and it would be impossible for a carriage to come from Sivas to Hekim Khan. The fact is that in this part of Turkey the best roads are only scratched on the surface, and that mainly by bullock-carts or passing caravans, and in difficult ground they are left to take care of themselves. As some one epigrammatically expressed it, 'Turkish roads are constructed by mules.' In the course of this day we saw somewhat more cultivation, and passed one or two villages, but the inhabitants appeared to be wretchedly poor. Here, indeed, as in the more poverty-stricken parts of Asia Minor, there was no sign of starvation, for the people generally looked well-fed, but their clothing was miserable. In one hamlet we saw a child stark naked, and another boy in a small threshing-floor close by had nothing on his body but a rag hanging from one shoulder. At one point in our route we again reached a considerable elevation, though much lower than Delik Tasch, and here on our left hand there rose a line of fine basaltic rocks with vertical stratification. The streams that we crossed were flowing southwards towards the Euphrates. In the evening, after riding between eight and nine hours, we arrived at Tahir-kéui, a village which stands high up on a hillside, overlooking a wide extent of country.

The fourth day of our journey brought us to the Euphrates. The early part of it was spent in traversing the dreariest uplands that we had seen in the Anti-Taurus, so that we were reminded of the country between Yeuzgatt and Kaiserieh; but after about seven hours we began to descend through a rocky valley by a steep and rugged Alpine path. Here at a turn of the road our eyes were suddenly greeted by the sight of the first green reach of the river lying far below us. It was a wild, but most impressive scene. The mountains on either side of the stream, but especially those opposite to us, though perfectly bare, rose to a great height and presented a striking multiplicity of form, so that Von Moltke compares their general aspect to the waves of a stormy sea;[1] and in addition to this they were richly coloured in places with red and yellow. As we descended further, the whole was softened and deepened by the light of the westering sun, which cast numerous shadows over the folds of the hills, and a wider curve of the winding

[1] *Briefe*, p. 210.

THE EUPHRATES AT KEBAN MADEN.

river displayed itself, closely hemmed in between its rocky barriers. The level of the stream proved to be fifteen hundred feet below the entrance of the gorge. When we were still two hundred feet above it, we stopped to sketch at a point where a sharp bend of the stream, and a conspicuous church crowning a rocky knoll, with a ruined village on the ridge above it, composed a striking view; after which we descended to the water and bathed, while the first of our party were being ferried across. The mud on its banks was worse even than that of the Halys, for the water, notwithstanding its clear green tint as seen from above, is very turbid; it was difficult to get in without sinking half-way up to one's knees, and the leg when pulled out again was clothed with a brown stocking. In order to plunge, it was necessary to clamber for some distance over projecting stones. We found the stream cold, partly no doubt from its being full and deep, but also probably from its flowing in shade owing to the narrowness of the gorge above.

We next proceeded to cross the river. Its breadth at this place is about 300 feet, though it becomes wider lower down, and the current is strong. The bank from which we started was covered with a shingly beach, but on the opposite side frowning rocks rose from the water, and only admitted of landing at a point where they slightly recede somewhat further down. Von Moltke compares it, not unreasonably, to the Moselle, though there is nothing in its surroundings to recall the bright vegetation that lends a charm to that beautiful river.[1] The ferry-

[1] *Briefe*, p. 221.

boat was an extremely rude and primitive construction, which almost defies description. It was some 30 feet long by 15 feet wide, flat-bottomed, with sides formed by upright beams about 10 feet high. Had it been roofed over, it would not have made a bad Noah's Ark. The sides sloped upwards from front to back —I hardly like to say from the bows to the stern, so little resemblance was there to either—and the forepart descended nearly to the level of the water, so as to allow of horses and merchandise being embarked and disembarked; and here also were the oars by which the vessel was propelled, one on either side, and each worked by two men—if oars indeed they may be called, for they were nothing more than planks with a handle. At the back or upper end stood a rough kind of poop, from which projected a long pole with a rudder attached, the whole thing being nearly as long as the boat itself. Four of our horses with the man who accompanied them and 'the Old Colonel' had already crossed, and we now followed with our dragoman and the two remaining horses, together with two bullocks, the property of another passenger. When all were on board, the vessel was pushed off from the shore, and for a minute or two moved quietly onward, but when it got fairly out it was caught by the current, and would have been whirled down with great rapidity had it not happened that the wind was blowing up stream, and so moderated its force. We thus slid gently down, and brought to under the steep cliffs where there is just room to land. In order to return to its original starting point, the boat has to be taken across, and then paddled up stream in the lee water.

The point at which we have thus passed the Euphrates is an important one in its course from being close to the place where it becomes a single river, for higher up it flows in two separate streams, which join their waters only a few miles above the ferry. What is the exact distance of the confluence it is hard to say. Von Moltke says one hour; the boatmen told us half an hour, which perhaps it may be for a boat descending the rapid current; but in the neighbouring village of Keban Maden it was estimated at three hours, and this is probably the truest computation. The two streams, with which we are to become intimately acquainted in the course of our journey, are called respectively the Frat and the Murad—the former rising near Erzeroum, and flowing through the west of Armenia, while the latter has its sources in the mountains southward of Ararat, and waters the eastern and southern districts of that country. The deposit that the river contains below the junction is derived from the Frat, which is a turbid stream almost from the first, while the water of the Murad is clear. The Murad is the larger of the two, and is probably the Euphrates which Xenophon speak of in his 'Anabasis,' but it was the Frat which regularly bore that name among the Romans.[1] At the present day, the combined river at this ferry and in the earlier part of its course is called the Murad, but lower down it is known as the Frat, which name is of course, wherever it is found, a corruption of the ancient name. Below Keban Maden it continues to be hemmed in by a mountain

---

[1] Armenian writers apply the name of Euphrates to both arms. See Bunbury, *History of Ancient Geography*, i. 353 *note*.

gorge for a distance of ten hours,[1] and escaping from this into the plains near Malatia, bends round towards the east, and forms together with the upper course of the Murad a remarkable loop, within which in ancient times lay the province of Sophene, and which now contains the town of Kharput and the principal source of the Tigris. Again it resumes its southerly course, and here, as it descends towards the lower ground, occur a series of extraordinary rapids, where the stream is inclosed by precipitous rocks, and the water rushes through in a succession of cataracts. One traveller has made the passage on a raft, and from the account which he has given of the dangers of the transit, it is hardly likely that it will be attempted again. The hero of this daring exploit was the man who was afterwards to be the great strategist of the German army, Von Moltke.[2] When these are passed, the Euphrates flows to the south-west, towards the innermost angle of the Mediterranean, and into that sea it would discharge itself, were it not for the intervening range of Taurus; but being diverted at that point, it makes a sharp bend, and flows towards the south-east with many windings, between the fertile districts which once were Mesopotamia and Babylonia, and the Arabian deserts, until it reaches the Persian Gulf. Its whole course extends to 1,780 miles.

It is impossible not to feel that it is an event in any man's life when he reaches for the first time this mighty stream, which has played so prominent a part in the history of the world, and around which so many memories are gathered. Especially is this

[1] Von Moltke, *Briefe*, p. 221.   [2] *Ibid.* pp. 290 foll.

the case when we meet with it, as here, in the land of its birth, and when it has just become an united stream. As early in the Bible as the second chapter of Genesis its name occurs as one of the rivers of the Garden of Eden.[1] The patriarch Abraham passed it on his way to the Promised Land, and in the covenant which God made with him the dominions of his posterity are to extend from this river to the river of Egypt.[2] The impression which it made upon the minds of the Jews is shown by the titles of '*the* river,' 'the great river,' which they apply to it. In the Psalms, the vine—by which the chosen people is symbolised—is described as stretching out 'her boughs unto the sea, and her branches unto the river.'[3] At a later time it was associated in their minds with the captivity in Babylon. It is introduced into the allegorical imagery of the book of Revelation, where 'the sixth angel poured out his vial upon the great river Euphrates; and the water thereof was dried up, that the way of the kings of the east might be prepared.'[4] Nor is the position that it holds in profane history less prominent. Its fertilising waters, and the consequent productiveness of the neighbouring lands, were the cause of the early civilisation which showed itself in the great kingdoms that arose on its banks. It became the recognised boundary of the Roman Empire, which overstepped it only for a brief period in the time of Trajan. It saw the defeat of Pharaoh Necho by Nebuchadnezzar at Carchemish; that of the younger Cyrus by his brother Artaxerxes at

[1] Gen. ii. 14.
[2] Gen. xv. 18.
[3] Ps. lxxx. 11.
[4] Rev. xvi. 12.

Cunaxa—from which event commenced the retreat of the Ten Thousand; and the death of Alexander the Great at Babylon: Crassus under the Roman Republic, and Julian under the Empire, passed it on the way to meet their fate. It witnessed the brilliant campaigns of Heraclius, and the successes of the Caliphs. In modern times it has often been thought of as a possible highway from England to India, and this idea has been revived in our own day.

When the whole of our company had disembarked, we again mounted our horses, and ascended by a steep path over the rocks. We were now in the true land of Armenia—for in ancient times the province to the west of the Euphrates was called Lesser Armenia, and at the present day, though numerous Armenian families are found in the country that we have traversed, yet, from this time onward, we shall meet with them in much greater numbers. A little way above the landing-place stands a row of cottages, which look as if they were half constructed in the cliff; leaving these below us, we passed between the ruined houses which we had noticed from the opposite side, and the Greek church, which proved to be a large building with an apse standing in an inclosure. From this point fine views were obtained of the great bend of the river, and of part of its course lower down. Crossing the ridge, we shortly afterwards reached the village of Keban Maden, which is situated in a lateral valley descending transversely on to the stream, and is separated from the ferry by a rock-encrusted hill, on the steep side of which it is built.

The surroundings are charming notwithstanding the barrenness of the wild lofty mountains that look down upon it, for beautiful runlets of water are conducted through it for purposes of irrigation, variegating the place with a mixed vegetation of poplars, willows, and mulberry trees, which grow among the houses, and run in a green line, refreshing to the eye, far up the valley. The house at which we were entertained for the night was the property of an Armenian gentleman, who resided there with his aged father; from the number of the servants, and the size and style of the rooms, which were those of a town house, and quite unlike anything that we had seen since leaving Sivas, it seemed to be a prosperous establishment. It was one of the highest in the village, and its windows commanded a reach of the Euphrates. The height of the river above the sea at the ferry is 2,425 feet, so that we have descended considerably since we quitted Asia Minor. At supper-time we had further evidence that we were in the neighbourhood of warmer climes, for amongst other dishes that were provided for us was the most delicious melon I ever tasted, exquisite in flavour and melting with ripeness. As we had hitherto met with hardly any fruit except the commonest pears and apples, this was a treat indeed. We were informed that it came from Kharput, but it had probably been brought thither from Diarbekir in the valley of the Tigris, for that place supplies most of the finer fruit that is found in these parts.

Like the house which we occupied, many of the dwellings here had a well-to-do appearance, and the large number of handsome headstones with inscriptions in a cemetery in the outskirts of the village also bore witness to its former importance. But its prosperity is a thing of the past, for the mine which was the source of it, and from which the place derives its name (*maden* signifies 'mine' in Turkish), is worked no longer. This was a silver mine, or rather one of lead and silver, and though it seems never to have been a successful speculation, owing to the feebleness with which the operations were carried on, yet it gave employment to a large number of people. A traveller's account of it in the middle of the last century represents it as being worked at a great disadvantage, and according to Von Moltke's computation, in his time it was carried on at a ruinous loss.[1] The Turks were the managers, and the smelting operations were performed by the Armenians, but the miners were Greeks, who came from the mountains at the back of Trebizond. We were told that in former days there were as many as a thousand Greek houses here; this is probably an exaggeration, for one visitor's notice, written at the time, computes the whole number of families of all nationalities employed as from 400 to 500, but the size of the neighbouring Greek church shows that the workmen of that race must have been very numerous. The work was discontinued eight years ago, and now there are only eight Greek families here, the rest of the inhabitants being either Turks or Armenians. The effect of this is shown in the numerous ruined houses in the village itself, and those which we had passed as we approached it; the

[1] See the accounts in Ritter's *Erdkunde*, x 801.

old smelting-houses, also, on the further side of the place, are falling into decay.

On leaving Keban Maden the next morning we followed the valley upwards, down which runs the Maden river, as it is called, on its way to join the Euphrates. A considerable part of its stream is drawn off higher up to feed the watercourses by which the village is supplied. The views here were very grand, owing to the contrast between the steep rocks above and the rich vegetation below. When the trees came to an end, we continued to wind along the numerous folds of the hillsides, and on our way passed a gang of twelve prisoners in manacles, who were guarded by two mounted zaptiehs. They proved to be robbers, who had been captured near Arabgir, a town situated some distance from here towards the north, and were now being conducted to Kharput. When we reached the head of the valley, we found that we had risen 2,000 feet above the level of the river; in this part the entire mountain that we were crossing was composed of fine granite. Here very extensive views over open, though not level, country were displayed before us, and towards this we descended gradually in an easterly direction, until after six hours we reached the Armenian village of Arpaüt, where we rested for awhile. We now perceived that we had entered a well-cultivated district, for the ground for a great distance on both sides of the road was carefully tilled, and as we advanced the villages became numerous. A range of hills still intervened between us and Kharput, and we had to ride for four hours more, until the evening began to close in. At last we approached a broad belt of vegetation, which extended before us in a plain, though half hidden owing to its level being lower than that of the undulating ground which we were crossing ; the northern end of this was bounded by a long line of steep flat-topped heights. We were told that we were near our destination, and wondered that we saw nothing of the town, but supposed that, as in some other Oriental cities which we had seen, the houses were concealed by the foliage.

On the edge of the first plantations we reached a group of official residences, and as we were requested by our zaptieh to dismount, no further doubt remained on our minds about our having arrived at Kharput ; and we were soon occupied with the question of getting a night's lodging, for the buildings were closed and their occupants had departed. While we were debating what it was best to do, a number of Armenian gentlemen came up, wearing fez caps, but otherwise in Frank costume ; and one of them, who, as we afterwards learned, was a man of great influence in these parts, offered us hospitality. This we willingly accepted, and as his house was hard by, we soon found ourselves installed in a delightful resting-place. This was a large stone-built *kiosk* or summer-house, open on one side, which was divided into three compartments, the middle one of which contained a fountain, while those on either side were devoted to our use, and with the help of a little furniture, which was soon brought, formed most comfortable living and sleeping rooms. In front was a broad tank of cool water, beyond which extended a pleasant garden, while the view was bounded by the fine range of Taurus, stretching along the southern horizon. When we were fairly installed, we inquired about the position of the town, and were amused to find that we were not at Kharput at all—for that place was situated on the heights above, about half an hour's ride off—but at the village of Mezireh, which is the official station for that place, and the residence of the pasha. We did not quarrel with our fate, for we were exceedingly well off, and the entertainment we received was most considerate. Some of the wine made on the spot was brought to us, and we found it strong and pleasant to the taste; this was one of the very few occasions on which we met with wine in Armenia. When night came on, the stars, as seen from our airy abode, presented a magnificent spectacle in the cloudless sky from the transparency of the air.

We had hardly finished breakfast the next morning, when one of the American missionaries at Kharput, Dr. Barnum, came to claim us as his guests. We found that our coming had been telegraphed from Sivas, but we had arrived a day earlier than we were expected, otherwise he would have met us the previous evening. Dr. Barnum was a middle-aged man of striking appearance, with an intellectual forehead, and handsome but careworn features; he had now been a resident in Kharput for many years. When he proposed that we should accompany him to the town, our kind entertainer at first demurred, but ultimately admitted that he had the previous claim. The relations existing between the Protestant missionary and these Armenian churchmen—for by this time several of them had come to visit us—seemed to be exceedingly friendly, and I discovered that our host had two members of his family at the American college. When I questioned Dr. Barnum on this point, he returned the same answer which I had often received before from both sides, that at one time an opposition existed to them on the part of the native clergy, but that these now recognised the Americans as their benefactors, because they had elevated their nation by means of education and friendly assistance, and that they respected them accordingly.

CHAPTER IX.

KHARPUT AND THE WESTERN TIGRIS.

Town and castle of Kharput—Crusaders confined in the castle—Position and history of Kharput—The Jacobites—Origin and fortunes of the sect—Armenia College—Its students—Course of study pursued—Relations with the Mahometans—A summer retreat—Armenian grievances—The girls' school—Estimate of the American missions—Plain of Mezireh—Lake Gheuljik—Construction of a dike—Head waters of the Tigris—No connection between the Euphrates and Tigris.

In order that we might approach the town from the side where it presents the most striking appearance, it was proposed that we should ride round to the southern foot of the heights on which it stands, sending our baggage by the direct road, for Mezireh lies south-westward from it. These heights, which, as I have said, bound the plain towards the north, rise very steeply, and towards the summit are precipitous; and so entirely are the buildings on this side confined to the upper level, that but little of them is seen from below. This circumstance accounted for our having failed to discover the position of Kharput on the previous day, for though we had noticed what seemed a village or group of houses on the ridge, there was nothing to suggest that it was a place of any extent. Following Dr. Barnum as our guide, we now skirted the hills which here project in a kind of spur, until we reached a village called Husseinik, which stands at the mouth of a deep gorge that penetrates to the foot of the castle-rock. At this point we turned northwards, and ascended by a steep winding path along the left side of the ravine, with a most striking view in front of us, for the precipitous cliffs which close it at the further end are crowned by the picturesque ruined walls of the mediæval castle, while at their base nestle the buildings of a part of the Armenian quarter, backed by the rock, and rising in terraces one above the other, interspersed with trees. We stopped to sketch this scene, notwithstanding that the rays of the sun beat down fiercely upon us; and then proceeding onwards until we reached the first houses, threaded our way along the steep streets, and turned round the east side of the cliffs, where the Jacobite quarter is built in an equally steep position. Up the irregular, slippery pavement of this it was no easy matter for the horses to scramble, but at length we found ourselves on the summit, where the town and castle stand.

We were first conducted to the castle, which occupies the most prominent projection of the cliffs. The entrance to it is on the north side facing the town, and here there are lofty towers of solid masonry. Near the massive portal several figures of animals are inscribed on the stones, one of them being a tiger. After entering, we passed through a succession of ruined walls, and then emerged on to a small platform of ground, at the edge of which is the precipice. From this dizzy height, a thousand feet above the lower ground, there is a superb prospect over the rich plain, studded with numerous villages, and bounded on the southern side by the Taurus range, which contains the sources of the Tigris, and separates this country from the lowlands of Mesopotamia. To east and west lay an expanse of undulating ground, stretching on the one hand towards the Murad into which this district drains, on the other in the direction of the Euphrates. The length of the plain to the foot of Taurus is said to be fifteen miles, while the Murad is sixteen miles distant. It was described to us as being a most beautiful sight in the spring-time, when the whole is one vast carpet of green. According to the natives, the number of villages it contains is 365, and they also maintain that here was the Garden of Eden—' in fact,' said Dr. Barnum, pointing to a spot far in the distance, 'just where that village stands you may believe that Adam first saw the light.' While we stood gazing at this glorious view, four magnificent vultures were wheeling about in front of us. After the dreary scenery of the greater part of the Anti-Taurus, I hailed with delight the change to bold, sharply-cut mountain outlines, and brighter colouring, for as evening approached the distance was overspread by a deep tint of violet. We seemed to have reached a new and more romantic land.

An especial interest attaches to this castle, because it was the scene of strange incidents with a tragic ending during the period that followed the first crusade. The circumstances are related by several authorities, both Christian and Mahometan. In the year 1122, at the end of a campaign between the crusaders and the Mussulmans on the confines of Syria and Mesopotamia, the Emir Balak, who ruled an extensive district from Aleppo to Mosul, was secretly retreating, when the Franks discovered his line of march, and their leaders, Jocelyn of Courtnay, Count of Edessa, and Waleran, set off in pursuit with a body of horse. They found him posted in a strong position, and making a reckless charge on his forces, were defeated and taken prisoners. The two counts were loaded with chains and taken to Kharput (William of Tyre calls it Quartapiert), where they were thrown into prison, while twenty-five of their companions were conducted to the neighbouring fortress of Palu on the eastern Euphrates, which we shall presently visit in the course of our journey. Of Jocelyn we are told that he was sewed up in a raw camel's hide, which, when it dried upon him, contracted to such an extent as to leave him helpless, and prevent him from making any use of his limbs.[1]

The following year Baldwin II., King of Jerusalem, made an expedition to avenge his comrades, but himself fell into an ambuscade laid for him by Balak, and was taken prisoner together with his nephew, and thrown into the same dungeon at Kharput with Jocelyn and Waleran. A few months later, however, a plan was set on foot for delivering them. A small band of Armenians from the neighbourhood of Edessa—Matthew of Edessa says they were fifteen, William of Tyre fifty—made their way to Kharput, and after watching the fortress for some time found that it was carelessly guarded, and that the garrison was small. Accordingly, they disguised themselves as monks, and pretending that they had come about the affairs of their

[1] This incident is mentioned in *Ibn Athir*, vol. x. p. 419, quoted by Mr. Taylor in the *Geographical Society's Journal* for 1865, vol. xxxv. p. 34. Mr. Taylor was the first person to notice these events in connection with Kharput.

monasteries, approached the gate, and managed to put themselves in communication with some persons within. After a time they forced an entrance, and having slain the guards whom they met, and closed the gates, reached the prison where the king and his companions were confined, and freed them from their fetters with transports of joy. They then liberated the rest of the captives, among whom were a number of ladies, and the Franks became masters of the castle. After this, Jocelyn hastened to Antioch to obtain succours; but meanwhile Balak, who was at Aleppo, having heard of what had occurred, left that place 'with the speed of an eagle,' and in fifteen days appeared before Kharput. This place he besieged with such vigour —undermining the cliffs, and thereby causing the fall of one of the towers—that its defenders were panic-stricken and surrendered; whereupon he flung all the prisoners, except Baldwin, his nephew, and Waleran, amounting to sixty-five men and eighty 'beautiful ladies,' over the walls down the precipice. By Jocelyn's negotiations Baldwin was subsequently ransomed, but his nephew and Waleran were put to death.[1]

When we left the castle, we passed through the Turkish and the chief Armenian quarters, which occupy the space behind it, until we reached the house occupied by Dr. Barnum and his family. This stands not far from the edge of the precipice, and commands a view but little inferior to that from the castle. It was a delightfully clean and comfort-

---

[1] *William of Tyre*, bk. xii. chapters 17-19; *Matthew of Edessa*, (Dulaurier's translation), chapters 234-236; Abulfeda, *Annales Muslemici*, ed. Reiske, vol. iii. pp. 413, 421.

able abode, and the books and furniture that were about the rooms gave it a look of home, which was all the more welcome because we were so little accustomed to it. In its neighbourhood were the houses of the three other missionaries, and also the buildings of the college, of which I shall have more to say presently. The air here is fine, but as the town is exposed to the sun, and there is no drainage, and refuse of all kinds is thrown into the streets, it is unhealthy during the summer months, and the Americans are glad to escape, for the night at least, to a purer atmosphere in the neighbouring country. We estimated the height above the sea at this point as 4,470 feet.

From a strategic point of view the position of Kharput is very commanding—more so even than that of Sivas, since it stands not only at the exit of the pass over the Anti-Taurus, but also at the head of the Tigris valley. Consequently this site has been continuously occupied by a city from very early times. That it was so in Nero's reign is proved by a Roman inscription of that date which has recently been discovered there.[1] By some it has been identified with Carcathiocerta, the capital of the province of Sophene, and of this the modern name is possibly a corruption, strange though it may appear. The termination *certa*, which is also found in Tigranocerta, once the capital of Armenia, is the same as *gerd*, which signifies 'town,' in Armenian. The former part, or the native name which it is intended to represent, appears in Armenian writers as Kharpert

---

[1] See Mordtmann's paper in the *Hermes* for 1880, vol. xv. pp. 289 foll.

or Garperd, but by the Syrians it was known as Korthert. But the modern form is at least as early as the eleventh century, for Cedrenus, the Byzantine historian of that time, writes the name in almost identically the same manner (Χάρποτε).[1] During the Middle Ages, as might be expected, it frequently changed hands. At the beginning of the twelfth century we find it in the possession of a prince of the Turcomans, from whom it was captured by the crusaders. At the end of the fourteenth century it belonged to a Mongolian chieftain, who in turn had to cede it to Sultan Bajazet.[2] It is now the headquarters of this part of Armenia. The total number of houses is 5,000, of which 70 are Jacobite, 500 Armenian, and the rest Turkish;[3] the villages in the plain are almost entirely inhabited by Armenians.

The Jacobites, whom we meet with here for the first time, deserve some notice, as they are a peculiar body of Eastern Christians. Their head-quarters are at Diarbekir, where their patriarch resides; but when I inquired about their race I could obtain no answer, for, as my informant remarked, 'creed and race are sometimes so curiously intermingled in these parts, that it is impossible to distinguish the one from the other.' Their proper ecclesiastical language is Syriac, but Arabic is often used in its place, and here the church service is performed in Turkish. Their

[1] Cedrenus, *Compendium Historiarum*, ii. 419, ed. Bonn.
[2] See Ritter's *Erdkunde*, x. 811.
[3] The mode of computation by houses, though it often gives the nearest approximation that can be obtained, is of necessity a vague way of counting, because the numbers it represents depend on the number of inhabitants allowed to a house. In Asia Minor, Texier reckons this as five persons (*Asie Mineure*, p. 544), and this is the usual allowance, but other writers give more.

Church is a lineal descendant of the ancient Church of Syria, which was the oldest of all the Gentile Churches. 'In its capital, Antioch,' says Dean Stanley, 'the name of "Christians" first arose: in the age of persecution, it produced Ignatius, and, in the age of the Empire, Chrysostom and John of Damascus. In the claim of Antioch to be founded by St. Peter, the Eastern Church has often regarded itself as possessing whatever privileges can be claimed by the See of Rome on the ground of descent from the first Apostle. To the chief pastor of Antioch alone in the world by right belongs the title of "Patriarch."'[1] After the condemnation of Eutyches, at the Council of Chalcedon in 451, the Monophysite doctrines with regard to the divine and human natures of our Saviour were widely adopted, though in a modified form, by the Syrian Church; but the movement that gave rise to the distinctive name of the communion of which we are now speaking, belongs to a later period. Of this Neander has given the following account:—

'The credit of having done most to preserve, establish, and extend the Monophysite party in Syria and the adjoining countries, belongs to a man distinguished for indefatigable zeal in the cause to which he had devoted himself, for enterprising activity and a courage that despised all dangers. In those regions, owing to the deficiency of clergy, of which the Emperor Justinian had found means to

---

[1] Stanley, *Eastern Church*, p. 9. The authority for the last statement is Theodore Balsamon, quoted by Neale, *History of the Eastern Church*, i. 126, who says: 'The Patriarch of Antioch is the only Prelate who has a claim to that title: the proper appellation of the Bishops of Rome and Alexandria being *Pope*, of Constantinople and Jerusalem, *Archbishop*.'

deprive them, the Monophysite party was threatened with becoming gradually extinct, when certain imprisoned bishops of this sect united together and ordained, as the general metropolitan of their Church, the monk and presbyter Jacob, from the cloister of Phasitla, in the district of Nisibis, a man inured to deprivations and hardships, and of unshaken firmness and constancy. With great rapidity, and not without many dangers, he traversed, under the disguise of a beggar, the Syrian provinces and those adjacent; he confirmed, by his exhortations, the oppressed party, and ordained clergy for them; he gave them a superior in the Patriarch of Antioch; and laboured for them himself during a period of thirty-three years, until A.D. 578, as a bishop, probably at Edessa. From him proceeded the name of Jacobites, which was applied sometimes to the whole sect, sometimes to a part of it only.'[1] He is usually known as Jacobus Baradaeus—Al Baradai, 'the man in rags'—from the circumstance, it is said, of his going about as a beggar.

The Jacobite Patriarchs of Antioch, however, were unable to reside in that city while it remained in the power of the emperors, and consequently settled themselves at Amida on the Tigris, now Diarbekir, at which place, as I have said, they still have their head-quarters. Unlike the Maronites, who have descended from the same Syrian Church, they have never given their allegiance to the Church of Rome, but remain as an independent communion. Though in their Monophysite doctrines they are at one

[1] Neander, *Church History*, iv. 272 (Bohn's edit.).

with the Armenians, they hold no communion with them, being separated from them by differences relating to various opinions and rites. But the alienation between these two bodies dates from a very early period, as it arose from the jealousy of the Armenians towards the Syrian clergy on account of their overweening influence in the south-west part of Armenia. In fact, before St. Mezrop invented the Armenian alphabet, at the beginning of the fifth century, only Syrian Bibles were in use in Armenia, and in the part just mentioned, the bishops, who were Syrians, wrote and officiated in their own tongue, and at last they aspired to the Armenian patriarchate itself.[1] One peculiar custom exists among them, that the same name is transmitted from prelate to prelate, the patriarch being always called Ignatius; and though this custom arose at the end of the sixteenth century, there can be little doubt that the name is derived from that of the saint who was the first bishop of Antioch.[2]

In the afternoon we visited the college—or Armenia College, as it is called, since it is intended for the whole country. This institution had been established three years before—principally owing to the exertions of Mr. Wheeler, its president, an intelligent and vigorous man, who collected 12,000*l*. in America for this purpose—with the view of diffusing Christian civilisation throughout the country, by preparing intelligent Christian leaders in all departments. It thus holds a higher position than the

---

[1] Ritter's *Erdkunde*, x. 572.
[2] Stanley, *Eastern Church*, p. 9; Neale, *History of the Eastern Church*, i. 152.

primary schools which are found in the other American mission stations; here these are maintained by the native Protestant community, but they admit all who are willing to pay the usual fees. The college, which has an independent status, is divided into two parts, the normal school, and the higher school or college proper. The former of these, which we visited first, occupied a large airy room, and consisted of eighty scholars; but this was not their full complement, for, as it happened, our visit fell on the first day of their term, and some who came from Diarbekir and other distant places had not yet arrived. For the same reason they had no lessons prepared, but the rapidity with which they did addition and subtraction sums from a board with movable figures astonished even my companion, who as bursar of a college in Oxford was accustomed to tolerably quick computation. The subjects which they are taught are: elementary English and Turkish, arithmetic, algebra, history, &c., together with the study of the Bible. They come from all parts of the country, from Egin on the Frat towards the north, to Diarbekir and Bitlis on the south and east, being selected from the local schools that are connected with the missions.

The higher school, or college proper, which was assembled in another room, was composed of thirty-three students. The payment for board and lodging for each of these—and also for those in the normal school—is 5*l*. per annum, while the sum paid for instruction is somewhat less. Of this amount those who are able pay all, while some assistance is given to those who cannot. We undertook to pay for one

—a process which is dignified with the name of 'founding a scholarship'—and the next day we learnt that one scholar, who was without means, and was expecting to have to discontinue his education, had been retained by means of a donation out of what we had given, to which a number of his associates had agreed to add a piastre (2*d*.) each per week. Some of those in this department were from the Jacobite community, though they had now become Protestants, but the great majority were Armenians. In order that we might have an idea of the different languages represented amongst them, different pupils were desired to stand up and recite the Lord's Prayer in Turkish, Kurdish, and Old and New Armenian. The great difference that there was between the two last showed us how little the ordinary Armenians can understand of their Church service, which is in the old tongue. When I remarked that none of these languages was represented in my University, Mr. Wheeler asked one of his students whether he would like to go to Oxford, if requested, as professor of Armenian; and to this he at once replied in the affirmative. The youth who knew Kurdish was a particularly interesting fellow, for though he had held a good position in a school connected with the missions somewhere in Kurdistan between Diarbekir and Bitlis, he was so anxious to learn, that he could not be kept from coming to the college. His sharp features formed a strong contrast to the large noses, dark eyes, and generally ponderous faces of the Armenians, and I subsequently recognised in them the Kurdish physiognomy. The dialect of Kurdish which is spoken in that part of the country, between the two main branches of the Tigris, differs so much, I was told, from the ordinary language that it is unintelligible to the other Kurds; and this was afterwards confirmed to me by Major Trotter, our consul at Erzeroum, who was acquainted with that speech. The course of studies pursued is very wide, including, in addition to the higher branches of the subjects studied in the normal school, the Greek, French, and Persian languages, law, natural, mental, and moral philosophy, geometry, astronomy, and physiology, theology, music and drawing. We found that the pupils could read English well, and, at the request of their teacher, we both of us made them a short address in our own language. Afterwards we visited the library, and inspected the lecturing apparatus, which seemed fairly complete. In carrying on this work Mr. Wheeler is assisted by native teachers.

The only objection that I had to bring against this admirable system of instruction was that it was too elaborate for its purpose. Mr. Wheeler, however, was not of this opinion. Those who are educated in this way, he said, get an enthusiasm for civilisation, and, when they return to their homes, exercise an elevating influence on their communities. In common life this is seen in greater cleanliness in the cottages, in prints hung about the walls, and in other evidences of an interest in something beyond everyday concerns. Besides this, they obtain positions of usefulness as teachers in local schools, pastors of Protestant congregations, &c. When I asked about the position which the college holds relatively to the Mahometans, he answered that they were quite willing to receive persons of that creed as pupils, and that not a few Turks would be willing to send their sons if they dared, but they are discouraged by fear of the ridicule, perhaps of something worse, to which they would be exposed at the hands of their co-religionists. In the earlier days of the mission, the Mahometans showed strong signs of opposition, but now they have come to be friendly except in times of excitement, when there is a tendency to lawlessness or outbreak; then threatening language was often heard. At all times, however, they look upon it with suspicion, because they are aware that education is likely to undermine their supremacy. 'Besides this,' he added, 'they fear our pens'—meaning by this that flagrant abuses cannot be perpetrated with the same impunity as formerly, because they are apt to be reported to head-quarters. Thus the missionaries, though they abstain on principle from taking any part in politics, exercise indirectly something of the influence of an European consul. Mr. Wheeler told me that he was frequently in communication with Sir Henry Layard, who requested him to supply him with information about what was passing. In consequence of this some time ago a pasha, who openly manifested his ill-will towards them, received a sharp reprimand from Constantinople.

In the evening we rode out with Dr. Barnum to a garden, about a mile distant from the town, containing two cottages, where the missionaries pass the night during the summer to avoid the unhealthiness of the place. The path lay along steep slopes, where the ground begins to fall towards the precipitous cliffs, but at one point we diverged from this, so as to reach the top of the ridge, which here is somewhat more elevated than the town itself. The view which it commands is a splendid mountain panorama, embracing the long line of Taurus to the south, and that of Anti-Taurus to the west and north, the latter reaching to the neighbourhood of Arabgir and Egin, and beyond them to the upper valley of the Frat, while an intermediate depression, where the ground sloped away from our feet, marked the course of the Murad. When we reached our destination, we found that it occupied a pleasant position on the hillside, and here were assembled the other members of the mission, Messrs. Wheeler, Allen, and Browne, together with five ladies and several children. We dined in the open air, in the court in front of the cottages, and afterwards sat and talked with the assembled party. Naturally our conversation turned much on the condition and prospects of the country. Mr. Wheeler strongly advocated the English sooner or later assuming the government of Armenia, and thought that the consuls who were now being sent out might in the course of time assume the position of 'residents' or authoritative advisers, and that this might pass into a more definite control. When I shook my head, and referred to the natural jealousy of other European Powers at such a course of action, he suggested that if the change was insensible this would probably disappear. Beyond this he thought there was no hope, for they all agreed that the Armenians were unable of themselves to govern the country.

The principal grievance of the Armenian population in these parts, and the main cause of their sufferings, is their treatment by the Kurds, who occupy the mountains on either side of the plain of Kharput, and throughout the country generally, while the lowlands are cultivated by the Christians. These tribes have long exercised a sort of suzerainty over the neighbouring Armenians, the chiefs requiring tribute from them, each from a certain number of villages; and this burden is in addition to the kharatch or tribute, and the other taxes that are paid to the Turkish Government. But lately this state of things has become worse, for whereas formerly only the chiefs used to make these demands, since the confusion that has arisen in consequence of the war, their sons and relatives have begun to do the same; and this at times takes the form of pillage, for in one village all the male inhabitants were bound by the Kurds, and their carpets and other possessions carried off. When I inquired how the women fared on such occasions, the answer was that they are not usually maltreated, it being significantly added that the Kurds in this respect are better than the Turks. 'But the truth is,' one of the missionaries remarked, 'that the Mahometans here have no sense of justice in dealing with the Christian rayahs. I can illustrate this by what happened to myself. In the course of last spring a servant of mine, an Armenian, had bought for me three horse-loads of straw in the bazaar. As he was going away a Turk seized one of these loads, and carried it off, and on seeing this another seized the second. Fearing that he might lose the whole of his purchase, the man begged that they would, at all events, leave him the third, on which they laid hold of him and proceeded to beat him. The next day, when it was found that the straw belonged to an American, it was restored and an apology was made ; but had it been the property of a native, you may be sure he would have regained nothing. It would be no use bringing the matter before a court of law, for in the courts there is always a bias in favour of a Mahometan.' I asked, referring to what I had heard on the subject at Amasia, whether, if the Christian was rich and offered a bribe, he might not gain his suit. 'Perhaps so,' was the reply, 'but then the bribe would have to be much larger on his side, in order to counterbalance this bias.' After hearing of this state of things, we understood the reason of the suspicious behaviour of the people of Arpaüt the day before, who answered, when we asked them to sell us cheese, eggs, and other things, for our midday meal—'We have nothing; how can you expect anything from us ? we are Christians.'

Another, though much slighter, grievance which the Armenians were feeling at this time, was the impressment of their beasts of burden for Government use, on which occasions they receive very little in payment. This we discovered from the difficulty we experienced in obtaining horses for our onward journey, which forced us to make application to the person appointed by the authorities to search for them, as the peasants conceal them. Ultimately Dr. Barnum succeeded in getting them for us from a man who lived several hours' distance off in the plain, but who undertook to have them in readiness for us the following morning. Just then the scarcity was increased owing to the number employed for the campaign of Dervish Pasha against the Kurds of the Dersim mountains to the north and north-east of Kharput. These wild tribes had been the principal offenders in the attacks on the Christians both during and since the war, and this commander had been sent with a force of 20,000 men to endeavour to reduce them, to a great extent in consequence of the representations on the subject that had been made to the Porte from Western Europe. On the spot, however, it was not expected that this would have much result, since in former campaigns with the same object the Kurds had always professed perfect submission, and after doing so had bribed the military leaders, who thereupon sent word to Constantinople that tranquillity had been re-established. Before leaving Armenia in the autumn, we were informed that much the same thing had happened on this occasion.

It was already dark when we took leave of our pleasant American friends. Mounting our horses, we rode back to the town under Dr. Barnum's guidance, and passed the night at his house.

The next morning we visited the girls' school, which is intended to hold somewhat the same position for women as the college does for men: here also the pupils are boarders, and come from various parts of the country. Of these there are about thirty-five, but their numbers have greatly fallen off of late, partly owing to the prevailing poverty, and partly to want of sufficient appreciation of the benefit of female education. It is much to be hoped that this will revive, for almost the first thing to be desired for the regeneration of a people is the education of the future mothers of families, as has been shown by the great work accomplished by Dr. Hill's school for girls at Athens, which, founded at a time when the Greeks had but just escaped from slavery, has exercised a most important and beneficial influence on Greek society. The subjects taught here are: arithmetic, English, Turkish, the Bible, and other more advanced subjects. Several of the girls were good-looking, and the bright colours of their dresses, and the gold earrings that they wore, which in many cases were coins, had a picturesque effect. They sang some hymns, both in English and Armenian, to American tunes, and the singing was nice, though with a little roughness, which was not out of place. Then followed calisthenics, which consisted of gesticulations with the arms, up and down, and backwards and forwards, together with clapping of the hands, and moving in and out, and from side to side. The effect of the whole was not unlike that of a ballet, and this was increased by the dresses, and the Verdi airs to which they moved. This school is conducted by two unmarried American ladies.

It remains now to speak of the mission to which these schools belong, and the representatives of which we have already met with at Kaiserieh and Sivas, and shall meet with at Van and Erzeroum. Kharput is its most important centre, and its influence here extends over numerous villages, reaching for six or seven days' journey towards the south, and for three or four towards the north. It will be seen from this how great is the civilising power which is exercised over the country; but the missionaries themselves would be the first to say that religion and not education is their primary object. Now their aim as religious teachers is not so much to reform the existing Armenian Church, as to establish separate Protestant communities composed of members of that Church.[1] This part of their work—let it be said once for all—I cannot wholly approve. Quite apart from questions of Church government, I hold it to be an important principle, not to be deviated from unless under very exceptional circumstances, that one communion of Christians should not interfere in the affairs of another communion, nor make proselytes from among its members. Besides this, I am myself a strong believer in National Churches, especially in the East, where the spirit of nationality is the strongest of all forces. Notwithstanding that the pure evangelical doctrines which these missionaries preach contain far more spiritual teaching, and have a far better effect on practical morality, than what is to be derived from the native priests; notwithstanding also that the Armenian Church is in many respects a corrupt communion; yet I believe that ultimately more would be gained for Christianity by 'gathering up the fragments that remain,' because, come what

[1] It is a difficult matter in a few words to express an opinion on a complex subject without appearing to be unfair to one side or the other. The original object of the missions was to reform the Armenian Church, but as the method of doing this was to teach Protestant Evangelical doctrines to individuals, and to expose the superstitions of that Church, it might have been foreseen from the first that a rupture would be the consequence. The immediate cause of the separation, however, was the persecution of the converts by the Armenian Patriarch. The Evangelical Armenian Church in Turkey was first constituted and recognised by the State in 1846; since that time the various communities have had native pastors under the supervision of the missionaries.

will, the great majority of the people will adhere to their Church, which has given them what Christianity they possess, and has been associated with their national history both in good and bad fortune. I therefore unhesitatingly prefer the system which Dr. Hill pursued at Athens in the schools already mentioned, of promoting religious education without interfering with the Church of the country, and leaving it to enlightenment to promote reformation. Still, I cannot expect everyone to agree in this view, least of all persons who belong, as these missionaries do, to the Congregationalist (Independent) body. From their own point of view their success has been very great, since they have established their communities so widely throughout the land ; and it may be that the rivalry thus caused, and the example shown, may tend to promote reform in the Armenian Church itself, as has certainly been the case with the schools, which are now being rapidly established by the Armenians themselves. Of the American schools I can speak in terms of unqualified praise. The benefit of these is recognised by the people, and this in great measure reconciles them to the religious work, which would naturally call out their antagonism. And the missionaries themselves, fourteen of whom we met in the course of our journey, are above commendation. When we consider the self-denial of their life—the absence from home and civilisation on the part of cultivated men, the solitariness of the position, the severity of the climate, and the hardships of the journeys they undertake, especially in the winter-time, in visiting their flocks—we feel that they are men of a truly evangelical spirit, and that the example thus set cannot be wholly lost. We found them shrewd, practical men, and cautious in judgment, for without this they could never have succeeded as they have done in the midst of so many difficulties. 'Hence to anyone who wishes to understand the true state of the country the information they can impart is invaluable, because they are intimately acquainted with the people from their long residence amongst them, and speak their languages, both Armenian and Turkish, and judge what they see without prejudice.' I will add one remark more— I should strongly deprecate any interference with them. Though their mode of proceeding may not wholly approve itself to us, yet intermeddling would only introduce an element of confusion. Their system has taken root deeply, and another agency might impede them, but could hardly flourish by their side.

In the course of the morning (August 19), at an earlier hour than we had ventured to hope, our horses and mules appeared; the latter being especially recommended to us on account of the ruggedness of the tracks which we should have to follow during the next stage of our journey. Our proposed course lay eastwards, in the direction of the lake of Van; but first we intended to make a slight détour towards the south, in order to visit a lake called Gheuljik, which lies at no great distance off in that direction, and in the neighbourhood of which the sources of the western branch of the Tigris were said to be. At 10 o'clock we left Kharput, and descended the mountain side by a steep, winding path, until we reached the plain of Mezireh below. So far one of the missionaries, Mr.

Browne, had accompanied us on horseback to speed us on our way, but here he bade us farewell, and returned to the city. The plain in this part slopes away very gradually towards the south, and as we followed it downwards, we passed numerous vegetable gardens, which were still green owing to the careful irrigation; the soil was light and rich, and the thickly planted villages testified to its productiveness. At the further end of this we rounded a spur which projects from the foot of the cliffs below Kharput, and crossing a stream which carries the combined waters of the plain towards the Murad, made for the foot of the Taurus range, which we reached after about four hours. Here we rested awhile on the lower slopes, in a pleasant spot, where the scanty foliage of some fruit trees offered a somewhat imperfect shade, and then followed a path upwards towards the southeast, ascending sometimes steeply, sometimes more gradually, along the mountain sides, with ochre-coloured rocks above us, and deeply-rifted clefts and gorges below. In proportion as we mounted, the views became more extensive over the plain, which was still half covered with vegetation, until at last the summits of Anti-Taurus began to reveal themselves behind and above the mountains of Kharput.

When we had passed the crest, and descended a little distance on the further side, the bright-blue waters of the lake came in sight; and as we proceeded, reach after reach opened out, so that when we saw it in its whole extent, it appeared to be some fifteen miles in length, but narrow in proportion, stretching from north-west to south-east. As its name, Gheuljik, signifies 'the little lake,' we were not prepared to find it so large; it is deeply embedded among fine mountain summits, the highest being those on the further side. The point at which we reached it was about the middle of its length, and thence we made for its eastern end, sometimes following the water's edge, at others climbing along the rocky paths above. As evening drew in, the peaks became tinged with beautiful colours—dull red, lilac, and violet—and our previous impression was confirmed, that we had reached a land of brighter tints and sharper forms. At the head of the lake stood an old khan, but this was now ruined and afforded no shelter, so we were forced to ride half an hour further in the dusk to a similar building some way up the hillside, which bore the name of Khan Chezi. This stands on the high road from Kharput to Diarbekir, and was consequently crowded with muleteers, who had taken up their quarters for the night in various parts of the inner court. One room there was, but this was so stifling owing to the smallness of the windows, that we preferred to pitch our tent in the road outside, and there we passed a cool and agreeable night.

My anxiety to explore this lake was increased by some facts connected with it of which I had heard at Kharput. Under ordinary circumstances its waters have no outlet, being closely locked in by the mountains which surround it; but towards its south-eastern angle there is a dip in the hills, the lowest level of which can never be very much above the surface of the lake. Now for some time past the waters have been steadily rising, and at last, a few years ago, they overflowed their banks at this point, and flooded the valley which descends from here towards the upper waters of the Tigris. The damage caused by this was so severely felt, that the Government undertook to cut a dike in this direction, in order to carry off the surplus water, and in this way the lake has become at certain seasons one of the principal feeders of that river, and may for the time be regarded as perhaps its main source. We now started to examine this point under the guidance of a man from the khan. That building is separated from the lake by a range of hills, and in order to round these we had to follow downwards for a short distance the valley at the head of which it stands, and then ascend that through which the cut is made. In half an hour we reached the lake, and as the highest part of the dike has not yet been connected with that piece of water, we found at this point a marsh formed by the inundation waters, which was thickly covered by gulls, storks, herons, ducks, and other water birds; while snipes and wild geese were to be seen flying above. In the winter time, our guide told us, a great body of water flows down here; as we saw it, however, a narrow strip of dry ground separated the lake and the marsh, cutting off all connection between them, though it is possible that the water filters through underneath. We next rode down to a point where six labourers were at work, either clearing or continuing the dike, under the superintendence of a Turkish inspector. From this man, who seemed an intelligent person, I learnt that the work had been begun about two years ago. I then questioned him about a plan, of which I had heard at

R

Kharput as having been once contemplated, for drawing off the water on the opposite side of the lake, so as to make it flow into the Murad. He told me in reply, that towards the north-west end of the lake there was a place where the hills were only about 600 feet (*iki yuz meter*) above the surface, and that this had been examined with a view to that object. The idea had been abandoned, however; and there is no need to say that, owing to the much lower depression at this end, it was a wholly unnecessary proceeding. The height of the lake above the sea is about 4,000 feet.

We then followed the dike downwards, and found it in some places 15 or 20 feet deep, with a stream running in it, which if it did not arise from infiltration from the lake, must have been the drainage of the surrounding soil. Unfortunately the cut was very badly made, for instead of having a good outward slope, the banks were quite steep, so that they would fall in with the first rush of water. We were not so much surprised, however, at the work being done imperfectly, as at its being done at all, for a Government which lacks money for the most ordinary purposes could certainly not be expected to undertake a local improvement of this sort. But when we inquired about this afterwards, we were told that by the Government in a case like this, is meant not the central Government at Constantinople, but the individual agency of a local pasha; and thus it sometimes happens that in remote provinces, when a pasha is called upon for his contribution to the revenue, he declares that none is forthcoming, and then employs what money he can get on some local object which has taken his fancy. It is sincerely to be wished that more of what is taken from the pockets of the people might be used in a similar way. At the distance of a mile and a half from the lake towards the south we came to a stream into which the dike opens, flowing from the north-east from the direction of the khan; and about the same distance further down again this is joined at right angles by a larger stream from the west, which is separated from the lake by the mountains on its southern side. Just at this point a peasant mounted on a donkey came riding across the fields towards us, so I asked him, 'Where does this stream flow?' 'To Bagdad,' he replied. He could not have given a more comprehensive answer, for these are the head waters of the Tigris. He gave the name of Houshousi to the stream that was flowing here; lower down the river is known as the Shatt. From what I could learn at Kharput from persons acquainted with this neighbourhood, this branch of the Tigris has no well-marked source, but is formed by the confluence of a number of small streams like those which meet at this point. After viewing this we returned to the khan, following for some part of the way the Diarbekir road, which is here a well-constructed causeway. We found that one of the chief tributaries of the stream that receives the water from the dike, is that which wells up in the middle of the courtyard of the khan, and which no doubt determined the selection of that spot for the building.

The examination which we had now made of the eastern end of the lake, and the answers I had obtained to my questions, had satisfactorily settled a point of considerable interest in geography. This is the question of a possible communication in this neighbourhood between the waters of the Euphrates and Tigris. The idea was first suggested by a passage in Pliny's 'Natural History,' where that writer states, on the authority of Claudius Caesar, that in the upper part of its course, in the region of Arrene, the Tigris flows so close to the Arsanias, that when their streams are swollen, they flow together, yet without mingling, for the water of the Arsanias being lighter, floats on the surface for the distance of about four miles, after which it separates again and falls into the Euphrates.[1] The river here called Arsanias is the Murad or eastern branch of the Euphrates, and though some of the details here given may at once be pronounced fabulous, yet it seems probable that there were some peculiar phenomena which served as a foundation for the story. Now the relative position of the Tigris and Euphrates in this part is so peculiar that it is not surprising that the idea should have been suggested that what Pliny speaks of might be found to occur here. I have already mentioned the loop formed by the Murad and the lower Euphrates. The interval left by this at its neck or narrowest part is about 20 miles wide, and it is just here that the Gheuljik and the principal independent source of the Tigris lie. The latter, in fact, according to Kiepert's map, at the nearest point is only five miles distant from the Euphrates; and though there can be no idea of their meeting there, as a steep mountain range intervenes, yet it is a remarkable fact that the two great rivers, which join at last not far from their

---

[1] Pliny, *Hist. Nat.* vi. 27, § 31.

entrance into the sea, after flowing separate for so great a distance, all but touch one another in the land of their birth. Between the Gheuljik and the Murad the distance is greater, but still only about twelve miles; and as the position of the lake is intermediate between that river and the Tigris, and its neighbourhood was only partially explored, it was thought that it might be possible for its waters to communicate at times with both of them. One explorer, Von Mühlbach, even speaks of the Gheuljik as having a slight, though only a slight, outflow towards the Murad.[1] But this is certainly not the case, and never could have been so, unless we suppose some extensive alteration of the ground to have taken place, and of this there is no evidence. All along the northern and eastern sides of the lake the ground rises for several hundred feet, the lowest point, apparently, being that which the overseer of the works had mentioned; and the valley towards the east, in particular, which we subsequently followed, runs up to an elevated watershed. In fact the only depression in the rim of the basin is at the point where we found the dike being made, so that ordinarily, as I have said, the lake has no outlet; but as in former days its waters may have risen periodically in the same way as they have lately done, a connection may have existed in ancient times also between it and the Tigris: with the Euphrates, however, whether in its upper or lower course, nothing of the kind could have happened. No doubt it is possible that, notwithstanding this, the story in Pliny may have originated from the nearness of the waters of the two

[1] In Ritter's *Erdkunde*, x. 105.

rivers without any further foundation in fact; but when we come to the eastern sources of the Tigris near Bitlis, we shall find, I think, that the features of the ground in that part correspond more closely to the phenomena which he describes.

CHAPTER X.

THE KURD COUNTRY.

Valley of the Murad or Eastern Euphrates—Town and castle of Palu— Cuneiform inscription—St. Mezrop's dwelling-place—Effects of the Ramazan—The Dersim Kurds—Kurdish village of Grolla—The Kurdish race—Their religion—Kizilbashes—Wild mountain road— Chevli — Birds in Armenia — Terbassan — Kurd physiognomy — Manna—Changeli, or Surp Garabed of Mush—The church—Manuscript of King Hatoum—Ziaret—A Hindoo colony—Zenobius's account of it—St. Gregory the Illuminator—Conversion of the Hindoos.

As Diarbekir was only two days' journey distant from our present halting-place, we should have been strongly tempted at another season to visit that interesting city. But this excursion, even if we had had time for it, would have involved descending the Tigris valley and entering a region of great heat, whereas our object was all along to keep on the upper level, on the northern side of the mountains that separate Armenia from Mesopotamia, and thus to insure cool nights, and no unreasonable exposure during the day. The path that we now followed led eastward, at right angles to the road from Kharput to Diarbekir, gradually ascending a long valley in the midst of the mountains; and after we had proceeded in this way for several miles, we turned to look back on the lake as it lay embedded among the mountain summits. Its appearance, as seen from this point, would quite justify its title of 'the little lake,' since it is foreshortened and the effect of its length is lost; but the view was very beautiful, owing to the gem-like effect of its bright surface in contrast with the deep blue of the range on its southern side. Near this spot we met some camels descending the valley, accompanied by several Arabs, one of whom carried a long lance according to the custom of his country; this sight reminded us that the Arabian desert was at no great distance off. After the head of the pass was reached, we first made our way through a succession of gorges splendidly coloured at the sides by red porphyry and green basalt, and then descended into a more open fertile valley leading down to the Murad, in which lies the village of Sarikamis, surrounded by a considerable amount of cultivated land, and itself in the midst of trees and other vegetation, which it owes in part to its copious source of water. Here after four hours' march we rested awhile, and then in another hour and a half arrived at the river, the level of which is somewhat more than a thousand feet below the lake Gheuljik.

We were now on the left bank of this eastern branch of the Euphrates, and at most times of the year, when the stream cannot be forded, we should have been obliged to keep on this side until reaching the town of Palu, as there is no bridge below that place; as it was, the water was said to be low enough to admit of our crossing it, and this we determined to do, as an hour's journey is saved in this way. None of our party, however, was acquainted with the ford, so a peasant boy was summoned from the neighbouring fields to show us the passage. The valley in which the river flows is at this point about three miles wide, and it is sad to see how that which otherwise might be a source of fertility, has become by long neglect a cause of ruin and desolation, for the stream wanders over the whole of this area, being divided into eight or nine branches, only one of which has a considerable body of water. This was the second that we reached, and at the place where we forded it, which was just above the head of a rapid, it was about 180 feet wide, and the stream was clear and strong, though not deep, for it nowhere reached to our stirrups. The greater part of the intervening ground is a bare mass of stones and shingle, but here and there it evidently had not been overflowed for a long period, for it was overgrown with tamarisks and other plants. When we arrived at the further side of the valley, we continued our course over the heights which bound it in that direction, sometimes overlooking the bright serpentine courses in which the river wanders hither and thither at will. At last the castle-rock of Palu appeared in sight, but as it was still an hour's distance off, and the evening with its short twilight was fast closing in, we determined to stop at the village of Seidili, which lies not far from the stream, in the midst of irrigated lands and watercourses, along which we had to thread our way in order to effect an entrance into the place. The tax-gatherer had evidently already paid his visit here, for the corn was being winnowed, and that process is not permitted until it has undergone his inspection. While we were looking about for a night's lodging, we spied a good-looking house, with one peculiarly tempting newly-built chamber on the first floor, with windows on all four sides, and when we asked permission to take up our abode there, the owner, who proved to be a well-to-do Turkish farmer, called Achmet Aga, readily agreed. We remained in the courtyard below for some time while it was being prepared for our reception; at the end of this he welcomed us kindly, and we spent the night in great comfort.

Early the following day we reached Palu. It is a large town of 1,500 houses, and presents an imposing appearance as you approach it, for the peaked rock on which its castle stands rises steeply to the height of 900 feet above the river, and the river itself here flows in a single bed with a fine green stream, while from the opposite bank a hillside rises in a mass of verdure, being thickly clothed with plantations of poplar and mulberry trees. On the southern side of the castle-cliff a level platform of rock projects, on which the main part of the town is built, and from this again there is a steep descent to the river, which flows round it on three sides. At the back of the castle, and separated by it from the rest of the buildings, is a suburb or upper town, which is mainly occupied by the wealthier classes. In the direction of this we first ascended, until we were nearly half-way up the castle-rock, where a road runs round it, forming the communication between the two parts of the city; here we obtained a guide from among the Turks who were lounging about in the neighbourhood, and having ridden up the steep slopes under his guidance until riding was no longer possible, dismounted, and clambered by rough ways to the summit. The view it commands is fine, for the town on both sides is outspread beneath you, and the river may be seen as it makes the circuit of the southern portion, and also both its upper and lower course for several miles to the east and west of the place. The bridge by which it is crossed from the left bank is on the eastern side, and must once have been a solid construction, but now appears to be patched with woodwork. All along towards the south the Taurus runs at no great distance off, forming a fine line of peaks, while towards the north the ground is more level, and bears a large quantity of corn. On the summit itself there is no castle or other fortification, but a little way below walls of rough construction run round the steep rock. It was here, no doubt, that the Crusaders were confined, who, as I mentioned before, were taken prisoners and brought hither by the Mussulmans.[1]

Within these walls, a short distance below the summit on the northern side, there is a cuneiform inscription on the face of the rock—the first that I had ever seen *in situ*. The plate or smoothed tablet on which it is engraved is about twelve feet in height, and six in breadth; and as the material is a rough limestone, the inscription is somewhat worn by exposure to the weather. The upper half of this surface is quite covered with writing; below this a space occurs, and further down again there is a shorter inscription. The series of inscriptions to which this belongs is more fully represented at Van, and I will speak more at length about them when we reach that place; we must now turn to another kind of monument, which seems to be connected with it. Just below this tablet

[1] See above, p. 220.

a rough path leads down the face of the otherwise precipitous cliffs, until a narrow portal in the rock is reached, with a rude attempt at an arch above, and pilasters with capitals at the sides, hewn in the stone. This serves as the entrance to a rectangular chamber, about twenty-five feet by twelve in dimensions, and from this again three other square chambers open out, all with flat roofs, all excavated in the rock, without ornament, and lighted only from the door. They are consequently, of course, very dark. Following the same path, a little further down we came to a second portal, larger than the former one and square-headed, which leads into another set of chambers, of the same size as those we had just seen, and arranged in the same manner. These, our Turkish guide informed us, were the dwelling-place of St. Mezrop, the Armenian saint, who invented the Armenian alphabet about 406 A.D., and translated the Scriptures into that language. His name, though little known in Europe, is still in great repute in his native country, and with good reason; for if any holy men deserve to be held in pious remembrance, those have an especial claim who, like Ulfilas, the apostle of the Goths, and Cyril and Methodius, the apostles of the Slavonians, and Mezrop, have invented alphabets for those among whom they preached the Gospel. In their time, and for the nations they evangelised, they did a hardly less important work than the inventors of printing subsequently did for the world at large. From a political point of view, also, St. Mezrop was a great benefactor to his countrymen, for whereas, up to that time, from the absence of a native version of the Scriptures and liturgy, they had been ecclesiastically, and so to some extent politically, subject either to the Greeks or the Syrians, they were thenceforward able to assert their independence. Our guide said that numerous pilgrims come here on account of the associations of the place, and that they always leave a piece of money behind them, which however is usually the prey of the next comer. He himself, being a Mahometan, and consequently free from scruples on the subject, had sometimes visited the place in quest of such windfalls. Anyhow, the story that the Armenian alphabet was invented at Palu by St. Mezrop is no modern fable, but an ancient tradition both of the place itself and of the Armenians generally.[1] A third set of chambers, in most respects similar to the other two, is reached by a flight of steps, which starts from a point a little lower down than the path which has been mentioned. All these excavations closely resemble those of the castle-rock of Van, and the presence in both cases of a cuneiform inscription close at hand suggests that the chambers were the burial-places of kings, while the writing was the commemoration of their exploits.

We now rejoined our attendants, who had waited for us below, and wound round the castle-rock by a terrace-path, until we reached the town which lies on its southern side. Our first object was to obtain a fresh zaptieh to accompany us, for the one we had brought with us from Kharput was a mere boy, and unacquainted with the country : we therefore rode straight to the police station, and as the kaimakam was absent for the moment, we asked permission to occupy one

[1] See the authorities on this point in Ritter's *Erdkunde*, x. 715.

of the chambers, to eat our breakfast in, pending his arrival. While we were waiting there, we were greatly struck by the rudeness of the officials to one another, which formed a strong contrast to the ordinary Turkish politeness. They were in fact thoroughly quarrelsome and out of temper, and for some time we were at a loss to account for this, when suddenly the reason flashed across us. The month of Ramazan, the great Turkish fast of the year, had just commenced, and this being the third day, they had not yet become accustomed to its privations and were irritable in consequence. This fast occurs in various months according to a cycle, and its severity greatly depends on the season of the year in which it falls, owing to the relative length of night and day. As the nights during the Ramazan are devoted to eating and drinking, not to say feasting, the enforced abstinence of the daytime is not greatly felt during the winter, when the days are short; but in the summer, when the interval between sunrise and sunset is long, and the heat of the sun exhausting, the rigour of the fast is very oppressive, since neither food nor drink nor smoke is allowed to pass the lips during all those hours. The upper classes manage in some degree to adapt their life to it by sleeping the greater part of the day, and transacting business between their meals during the night; but those who work in the fields suffer dreadfully, especially from being unable to quench their thirst. At last the kaimakam appeared—he had no doubt been asleep at the time of our arrival—and a zaptieh was provided to accompany us, though there was some difficulty in arranging this, for the police here were merely armed peasants. Real zaptiehs, we were told, had been promised to be sent from Constantinople, but they had not come. The person on whom the office now devolved—a ponderously built man—betrayed extreme unwillingness, and made so many objections, that at last one of the officials lost his temper, and taking him by the shoulders pushed him bodily out of the room. He accompanied us, however, and at the same time observed the fast throughout very strictly. This is not absolutely necessary when on a journey, and on other occasions when we had travelled in Turkey during Ramazan, we had found our guards much more lax in their observance; but it is to some extent a question of preference, for those who break the fast in this way, are expected to observe so many more days after the expiration of the month, as an equivalent.

The part of our journey which commenced at this point lay through one of the least frequented districts, and one which has a bad name for insecurity. This arises from its nearness to the country of the Dersim Kurds, who are the terror of this whole region, and against whom, as I have already said, the Turks had now sent an armed force. One of the American missionaries, whom we afterwards met at Bitlis, had been stopped and robbed by the Kurds at one point in the road. The natives only pass this way in large companies; and an Armenian gentleman, whose acquaintance we also made at Bitlis, was waiting at that time to make the journey in the opposite direction until a caravan of from seventy to a hundred people should have been formed. And now, when we arrived at Palu, we found another Armenian waiting, in hopes of being allowed to join us, for the sake of the protection which our company was supposed to afford. He was on his way to Van, on account of some money transactions with the pasha of that place, and had heard at Kharput that we were intending to make the journey. His appearance was rather an exaggeration of the usual Armenian type, for he had a large head and heavy frame, and was slow-moving, subservient and taciturn. We made no objection to his coming with us, but on more than one occasion we experienced the disadvantage of having such companions, for they endeavour to attach themselves to you, and obtain hospitality gratis at the houses where you pass the night.

We left Palu about midday, issuing from the eastern side of the town, and skirting the steep slopes of the castle-rock in that direction. After an hour and a half, we passed through the Armenian village of Hoshmat, which contains some considerable houses. For the rest of the day our course lay towards the north-east, gradually mounting over dry hot hillsides and through open valleys, until an hour before sunset we reached the Kurd village of Grolla, which lies round a small open common between a range of hills and a stream that flows in the bottom. Near this we pitched our tent in a pretty position by the side of a watercourse, which is shaded by a long line of poplars. The houses here were half underground, more deeply buried than any that we had yet seen in Armenia, and this feature now became more strongly marked the further east we advanced into the country. On the flat roofs of some of them ricks of corn were standing, while on others plates of tezek were piled, like a breastwork, to the height of two feet. Many conical stacks of dry branches and leaves for winter use were to be seen on the hillsides close by. The dress of the inhabitants had no very peculiar feature; but the men, as is usually the case among the Kurds, could be distinguished from Turks and Armenians by their white drawers coming down just below the knee, and leaving the rest of the leg bare. They hardly spoke a word of Turkish, so that we had difficulty in communicating with them; and we found them very suspicious, demanding a high price for the articles, such as milk and cheese, which we bought of them, and requiring that the money should be paid on the spot. The women, to judge from their loud shrill voices, ought to be viragos, and their looks did not belie this character. Some of them were engaged in making butter in skins suspended from poles in front of the houses, by working them backwards and forwards with their hands. As these people have the reputation of being arrant thieves, and are especially clever in horse stealing, we collected our saddles, bridles, and other property close round the tent, and picketed the horses just beyond, our attendants sleeping in the middle.

As this is the first occasion on which we find ourselves among the Kurds, it may be well here to notice the most important facts relating to them. The evidence of their language shows that their race is of Median origin, and therefore belongs to the Indo-European family, for notwithstanding that a considerable number of Arabic and Turkish words have found their way into the speech of the people,

s

yet both in grammar and vocabulary it is closely allied with the Persian. Consequently, notwithstanding their national antagonism, the Kurds are also akin to the Armenians. They are the same people who were called Carduchi in ancient times, and their name also appears in that of Cordyene or Gordyene, which was applied to the district they inhabited. This corresponds approximately to the modern Kurdistan, being, roughly speaking, the country intersected by the upper waters of the Tigris and its eastern tributaries on the frontiers of Turkey and Persia. Here we find them at the time of the retreat of the Ten Thousand, between the dominions of the Great King and the plateaux of Armenia; but at a later period they spread into the last-named country, for we now find them there in great numbers, and naturally, as the Armenians emigrate, they take their place. Throughout their history they have been known for their wildness and independent character, and they were the most formidable of all the foes whom Xenophon had to encounter. From that time to the present day they have maintained themselves in their original seats notwithstanding all the changes that have passed over Western Asia, and have been included within the various empires that have successively held sway there—Greek, Roman, Parthian, Byzantine, Saracen, Persian and Turkish—though owing but a temporary and partial allegiance to any of them, and maintaining a semi-independence under their local chieftains. The most eminent historical character that has arisen from amongst them is the great Saladin, who is said by Abulfeda to have been a Kurd. Their number in Asiatic Turkey has been estimated by a careful authority at about 1,600,000 souls,[1] but others think that they do not exceed a million.[2] Of these a considerable number are nomads. Their chief men always speak Turkish or Persian in addition to their native tongue, and the common people in Turkey usually understand something of Turkish, though, as we found in this village, this is not always the case. They cannot be said to possess any literature, but some of their stories have been collected, and published in Kurdish and German.[3]

In respect of religion they are mostly Mahometans, though the Nestorian Christians, who are found on the borders of Turkey and Persia in this neighbourhood, also belong to this race. The Mahometan Kurds, however, with the exception of those who dwell in the larger towns, are usually Kizilbashes. This name, which signifies in Turkish, 'Redheads,' is a term of reproach applied by the Turks to a certain class of sectaries, who are widely spread through Asia Minor and Armenia. In both those countries we were told that their distinguishing characteristic was their being Shiites; that is, they hold like the Persians, that Ali, the companion of Mahomet, and fourth in succession of the caliphs after him, was the vicar of God, and regard the three intervening caliphs as usurpers. They are said to hate the Turks, who are orthodox Sunnites, more than they do the Christians: and this is perhaps true, if the principle be admitted, that in religious controversy

---

[1] Mr. Ravenstein, in the *Journal of the Statistical Society* for 1877, vol. xl. p. 455.
[2] Ritter's *Erdkunde*, ix. 621.
[3] In Lerch's *Forschungen über die Kurden*. St. Petersburg, 1857.

the acrimony 'varies inversely as the distance.' But underneath this tenet, which is common to the Kizilbashes at large, there seems, according to the accounts of various authorities, to lie a great variety of opinions. Of those in Asia Minor, Dr. Van Lennep remarks—' They hold the transmigration of souls, have mysterious and obscene rites, in which the initiated alone take part, heartily hate the Turks while they outwardly profess their religion, and do not believe in a Supreme Being, but have particular objects of veneration.' These religious tenets he would refer to a heathen origin, and adds : ' They are said to carry on their worship in great secrecy, guards being placed in the neighbourhood with orders to keep away intruders under pain of death. Their worship consists of dances, in which men and women take part, each sex standing in a group by itself. The Turkish authorities have succeeded in falling upon them and dispersing them in the midst of their saturnalian nightly orgies.'[1] Mr. Taylor, formerly consul in Kurdistan, mentions one set of Kurds, who are ' neither Moslems, Christians, nor real Kizilbash. They swear by a church, and never by a mosque, or the Deity, or any of the prophets. After a good deal of intercourse with them in different places, I could not make more of their belief than what is expressed in the formula of faith which their headman repeated to me in Turkish. . . . . "A thousand ways he showed himself, but many remained in doubt: if he should show himself in one way, a great many would come to the faith." And they explained it by saying that all the prophets mentioned in the Torat, Enjeel,

---

[1] Van Lennep, *Travels in Asia Minor*, i. 293, 295.

and Koran, were nothing more than one and the same person, who had appeared at different epochs in different forms. They thus ascribe divinity to all, though they forbear to mention one name more reverently than the other. But, as they consider that the last shape he assumed was that of Ali, they attach more sanctity to his name than to Moses or Christ, while Mahomet they ignore entirely. In this respect they are not unlike the Ali Illahees of Persia, and Kizilbashes of other parts of Kurdistan, who seem to regard Ali as the personified Deity, and holding, therefore, a much higher position than the Prophet of Islam.'[1]

Elsewhere the same writer speaks of the Kizilbashes of the Dersim as not practising circumcision, but observing a mixture of pagan and Christian rites, as they worship, or rather reverence, the sun and stars, and also employ the Christian sacraments of Baptism and the Lord's Supper. They respect our Saviour and the Apostles, but believe that God visited earth in different forms, and will again visit it. 'From one of their religious books called the "Booywick," that fell into my hands,' he says, 'I find their respect for Mehemed is simply a blind to deceive the Moslems, for they have nothing in common with them; no really obligatory fasts, stated prayers, ablutions, or belief in the Koran. They teach the ubiquity and omnipotence of Aly, the creator of everything in heaven and earth, and in contemplation of his magnitude and primeval existence, worship venerable natural objects, as huge oaks and large

[1] Taylor's *Travels in Kurdistan*, in the *Geographical Society's Journal* for 1865, vol. xxxv., pp. 28, 29.

isolated masses of rock. They adore the sun at rising and setting, reverence fire, and pray and sacrifice at the sources of rivers.' The pagan observances Mr. Taylor regards as remains of their old heathenism, while the idea of the several incarnations of the Deity he considers to be a part of the Hindoo worship introduced into the neighbouring province of Daron, of which we shall have hereafter to speak.[1]

Shortly after leaving Grolla the next morning, we were met by a number of men driving asses, who stopped to inform us that a band of Kurdish robbers, from ten to fifteen in number, were lying in wait for us on the road some distance further on. This intelligence had anything but a cheering influence on the minds of our party, for this was just the part of the road where the greatest risk was to be apprehended. 'Ils peurent tous,' our travelling servant observed to us in his remarkable French, and certainly he was himself not to be excluded from the number of those affected in this manner. Whether our zaptieh was white-livered, or whether his languor proceeded from the exhaustion of fasting, we could hardly say, but he certainly always left it to one of us to lead the way where there was any suspicion of danger. As practical jokes are not in vogue in Armenia, there was some probability that the story was true; but be this as it might, the only thing to be done was to go forward. One of the company suggested that we should hire some Kurds from a

---

[1] Taylor's *Journal of a Tour in Armenia*, &c. in the *Geographical Society's Journal* for 1868, vol. xxxviii., pp. 319, 320, and the authorities there quoted. Mr. Taylor considers these Dersim Kizilbashes to be originally of Armenian, and not Kurdish, extraction.

village on the mountain side, to act as interpreters between us and the brigands, but this proposal did not find much favour, for the probabilities were that the one would speak as much, or as little, Turkish as the others. Our course now lay over very fine mountains wholly uncultivated and uninhabited, and commanding extensive views towards the north. The solitude of these uplands was most impressive, and the elevation throughout some part of the route was between six and seven thousand feet above the sea. Among the masses of fallen rock large blocks of black obsidian were visible, and all about grew tall-stemmed flowering plants, which a month before must have been a beautiful sight; as it was, no blossoms were to be seen anywhere except a few campanulas.

Descending at last by a steep and rugged track, we reached the first village, called Kalender, having heard nothing more of the reputed robbers, who, if they had ever been there, had thought better of their attack upon us. The valley in which this village is situated contains a large number of fruit trees, and close to the village itself, notwithstanding the great elevation (5,000 feet), several luxuriant walnuts grow, under one of which we rested. The mountain sides also in this neighbourhood are covered with much more dwarf vegetation than usual, and this gives the country a refreshing look of green. The Kurdish inhabitants here spoke Turkish, and provided us with a plentiful supply of excellent milk. One of their employments is collecting manna, which they call *ghezenghi*; it is found throughout a considerable part of the south of Armenia, and is exported. Here it is gathered from the oak-scrub, the leaves of which were covered with a shiny substance which looks as if it exuded from them; and as we descended the valley, we found the tree-tops lopped off to facilitate the collecting of it. Gradually the oaks became more numerous, until at last they formed a small low forest, and through this we continued, partly along the bed of a stream, partly over a succession of ridges, until a large plain, inclosed by grey mountains, came in sight below. Before reaching this, we crossed into a parallel valley—it might almost be called a trench from the regular embankment it forms on either side of a wide river bed—near the mouth of which lies the village of Chevli. This is inhabited by a mixed population of Turks, Kurds, and Armenians, and contains about 400 houses; but it is a poor place, and we were fain to pass the night in a dusty corner of a court sheltered from the wind, on the roof of an Armenian peasant's dwelling.

The stream of Chevli joins that which descends from Kalender shortly after they enter the plain, and their united waters flow towards the Murad, which at this point is only a few hours distant. We crossed the combined stream, and for two hours kept along the northern edge of the plain, partly on the level itself and partly on the neighbouring slopes, in order to avoid the watercourses by which the ground is intersected. At the further end of this was the village of Chibsur, where the Mudir of Chevli was now residing, owing to whose absence from that place we had been unable to obtain better quarters the night before. We now gradually ascended the hills towards the east, following a track but slightly marked, and thus showing how little this route is traversed; fortunately the men who accompanied our horses were acquainted with it, for the zaptieh betrayed complete ignorance. The scenery resembled that of the previous day, except that the ground was more open, and the stunted oaks less thick; but throughout this region, notwithstanding the small size of the trees, there was more woodland than we had seen since leaving Amasia, or were to see again in the rest of Armenia. The birds here were very numerous, and among them I noticed partridges, pigeons, and ringdoves, hoopoes, magpies, and various kinds of finches. The partridge, according to my observation, is a much commoner bird in Asiatic, than in European, Turkey. Here and there we met a few wild-looking Kurdish peasants, but we passed no villages in the course of the day; it was altogether a most solitary country, and the thickets were excellently suited for lurking-places for ill-disposed persons, if such there were. When midday came, we halted under a tree by the side of a beautiful mountain stream, which was especially welcome, as we had met with no good water since leaving Sarikamis on the left bank of the Murad. Above this the hills contract so as to form a graceful dell, in which, besides the oak and ilex, even ash trees appeared. Owing to the abundance of acorns this whole district would be a perfect paradise for pigs, but, strange to say, throughout our whole journey we did not see a single specimen of that animal, which in Europe is almost characteristic of a Bulgarian village. We thus reached the summit of a pass which crosses a range called by our muleteers Soulahan-daghlar, and descended again through pretty glades, which only wanted turf to make them perfect, with fine views of distant mountains. The outline of these was generally level, but their clearness gave them beauty, for the transparency of the atmosphere in this country surpasses everything that I have seen elsewhere. At sunset we crossed a considerable river, the Tachtali-chai, which runs transversely in a deep depression; and now, as no human habitation appeared, we were beginning to wonder where we should pass the night, when, after mounting on the further side, we entered a long open upland valley, completely different in appearance from what we had left behind—well watered, but bare of trees, and inclosed by sloping hills. In the middle of this we halted at the small Kurdish village of Terbassan, after a journey of eleven hours.

This place was quite the most miserable that we had yet met with. It was composed of four human habitations, and about three times that number of stables to contain the cattle at night and during the winter. These dwellings were formed of low walls, the stones of which were piled together and roughly covered in; they were sufficiently tenanted by their usual occupants, and the only sleeping-place they had to offer us was two small platforms, not much more than wide ledges, attached to the outside of one of them, but these were so little inviting that we determined to pitch our tent, notwithstanding the gale that was blowing and the lateness of the hour. The village is built on a mound overlooking a stream; but this is too complimentary a description of its position, for the mound is in reality a dustheap, and the dust seemed to be everywhere; while the tent was being set up it blew in our faces, and when we were inside we heard it pattering on the canvas. Nor was this simple dust, but a mixture of clay, chaff, feathers, rags, manure, and other kinds of filth, which was inexpressibly offensive. We were all the more provoked the next morning when we found that this discomfort might easily have been avoided. We had inquired of our muleteers, who, as I have said, were well acquainted with the route, about the position of Khareba and Boglan, two places in this neighbourhood which we had heard of at Kharput. It was quite evident that a valley containing so much arable land must have a larger population than the inhabitants of this miserable hamlet; but notwithstanding this, they declared that they knew nothing of Khareba, and that Boglan was far away beyond the hills. When daylight came, we found that the former was less than half an hour distant, and the latter in a conspicuous position at the head of the valley. The fact was that they wanted to stop, and had no scruples about deceiving us.

The Kurd physiognomy, as seen in these parts, is striking, and strongly marked. The shape of the face is a long oval, and the eyes are dark brown, those of the children being sometimes very beautiful; but the most characteristic feature is the nose, which is aquiline, and hooked downwards at the end, with large and strongly lined nostrils, like those which we are accustomed to see on old Greek coins. The expression is seldom good. The men sometimes shave the hair in front, and leave it long behind, like the Albanians; the women generally have black elf-locks hanging down, which give them a Megaera-like appearance. They also have a partiality for full red trousers. There seemed to be much sickness among the people of Terbassan, which I can only attribute to the filthiness of their persons and dwellings; for it is difficult to think the situation can be unhealthy in so fresh an upland valley, unless perhaps the neighbouring irrigation may cause it to be so. One woman was ill in bed, and they applied to me for some medicine for her, since no medical aid is attainable in these remote parts, and the cure has ordinarily to be left to nature. Under these circumstances anything administered by a stranger, especially if it has a strong taste, is apt to be of service, owing to the effect on the imagination; so I left some quinine for her, which is usually the most successful remedy, and this was thankfully received.

Another long day's journey from this place might have brought us to the town of Mush, which was our next halting-point on the way to Bitlis. We determined, however, to make a slight détour in order to see a famous Armenian monastery situated in these parts—that of Surp Garabed, or St. John the Baptist, which is only second in importance to the convent with the same appellation near Kaiserieh, which we had already visited. To the Kurds it was unknown by that name, and it was not till we called it Changeli, or 'the place of bells'—its Turkish name, for *chang* means 'bell' in that language—that they recognised what place we meant. As none of our company knew the road, we hired one of the inhabitants of the village to act as our guide thither, and it proved to be six hours distant, on the further side of a steep mountain range. The Kurd, we found, had an excellent notion of making a bargain, and, poor though he seemed, would rather have refused to come than obtain any but a high price for his services. While we were on the road, I had ridden on a little distance in front of my party, when three Kurds met me, and one of them offered to show me something curious which he was carrying in a strong bag. He then produced what looked like a large mass of stone, a heavy lump with broken edges, greenish-grey in colour, with small bright particles, which shone somewhat like the mica in granite. Before I had finished looking at it my companion came up, and thought it must be some kind of petrifaction. I then asked the man what his object was in carrying a stone, to which he answered by proposing that we should taste it—a suggestion which looked at first rather like banter. However, a piece was broken off, and when we put it into our mouths it proved to be manna, and was very sweet to the taste, though not so much so as the white and sickly stuff which is sold by chemists in England. When gathered from the leaves it is compressed into a solid mass of this kind, and is thus in a convenient form for exportation. In the country it is used for making sweetmeats.

After five hours of almost constant ascent the ridge of the mountains was reached, and from this a magnificent view presented itself. From our feet the ground descended in steep oak-clad slopes to the great plain of Mush, which stretches away in one unbroken level for forty miles towards the east, environed by fine mountains; through the nearer part of it the winding course of the Murad may be traced like a silver thread, which ultimately disappears into a gorge at its western extremity. From this point, as far as Palu, the river forces its way through a succession of rocky valleys, which have never yet been explored. The ride from the ridge to the monastery is one of the most beautiful in all Armenia, for it follows a terrace-path along the mountain side through low forests, and commands a succession of such views as I have described. Scenes like these, the appearance of a great expanse from a high terrace-walk—whether from the Malvern Hills overlooking the valley of the Severn, or from the steep face of the Monte Generoso above the Lake of Lugano, or from the heights behind San Remo over the Mediterranean—have always appeared to me the most exquisite things that nature has to show. We were in no hurry to reach our journey's end, when on crossing a shoulder of the mountain we came in sight of the towers of the monastery, which occupies a small table of ground, with steep slopes both above and below it, at a height of 6,000 feet above the sea, and 2,000 above the plain. We then descended by grassy lawns, passing a group of blue-gowned youths, scholars apparently, who were seated under the shade of some spreading willows, and shortly afterwards reached the outer gate of the building.

The square inclosure within which the monastery stands is surrounded by a wall, and the numerous trees, chiefly poplars, which grow around this, give a refreshing appearance to its otherwise dreary structures. After passing through this outer space we dismounted, and entered the building by a passage which leads into the inner quadrangle. This strongly resembles a large caravanserai or khan with a church in the middle, for it is composed of two storeys, the lower one of which supports a large gallery running all round, and giving access to the rooms of the upper storey. In both of these the chambers are mainly intended for the accommodation of pilgrims. The day of our arrival (August 24) coincided with the festival of the Assumption—or rather, to use the name applied to it by the Easterns, the Repose—of the Virgin, which is observed by the Armenians on August 10 (Old Style) and the two following days; this day, being the Sunday following the festival, was the highest day. In consequence of this the court was full of men, women, and children, more gaily dressed than any that we had yet seen in this land of sadness, picnicking in groups on the ground. Earlier in the day, we were told, there had been as many as four thousand of them, and one thousand still remained. Some of the women had one nostril pierced for a silver ornament (or rather disfigurement), consisting of a ring with filigree work projecting on one side, decorated with small blue beads in imitation of turquoises. This is one of the great Armenian places of pilgrimage, ranking next in importance after Etchmiadzin, Jerusalem, and Surp Garabed of Kaiserieh; the last named of these, though a smaller foundation, ranks in every respect before it, but the Superiors of both are archbishops. Owing to the insecurity of the country, the number of pilgrims who come hither from a distance has greatly diminished, and most of those present at this time came no doubt from Armenia itself; but the regular order of pilgrimage for those from abroad is first to visit

Kaiserieh, then to come hither, and finally to proceed to Etchmiadzin in Russian Armenia. The Armenian who had accompanied us from Palu informed us that he had been brought hither on pilgrimage when a boy. The great object of veneration at Surp Garabed of Mush, as this place is called for the sake of distinction, is the body of St. John the Baptist, whose head is at Surp Garabed of Kaiserieh. The fame of this saint is widely spread through all this neighbourhood, and even far into Kurdistan, and curious legends are told concerning him. Thus Mr. Rich, in his 'Narrative of a Residence in Koordistan,' speaks of being informed in that country that—'the saint there' (i.e. at Tchengedeh, which is a corruption of the name Changeli) 'is celebrated for teaching arts and trades—all except music—and he will allow of no women to come near him for the sake of Herodias.'[1] The monastery was founded by St. Gregory the Illuminator, the Apostle of the Armenians, whose fountain is still shown on the hillside above, where he is said to have baptized a thousand heathens; and in the narrative of his contemporary Zenobius, who was the first bishop of this see, the translation of the relics of John the Baptist from Caesareia hither in St. Gregory's time is mentioned, by which means even at that early period this monastery became a great place of resort.[2]

As soon as our arrival was announced the monks came out to receive us, and conducted us to the further part of the building beyond the east end of the church, overlooking the plain, in which the principal rooms

[1] Vol. i. p. 376. Women are excluded from the chapel of St. John the Baptist in the cathedral of Genoa, except on one day of the year, for the same reason. See Murray's *Handbook of Northern Italy*, p. 119.
[2] Ritter, *Erdkunde*, x. 704.

are situated. The one in which we were entertained was, like all the rest, a small chamber with a barrel roof of stone, and reminded me of those in which travellers pass the night at the Great St. Bernard. In the space between these and the church were a number of white marble tombs of former Superiors of the convent. The Superior at this time was absent at Constantinople; besides him there are 20 monks, and about 180 lay brethren. In the company of our entertainers we found a priest, who was one of the chief men about the Armenian Patriarch at Constantinople; he proved a well-educated man, and spoke French fluently, so that he was of service to us in obtaining information. After the monks had regaled us with what they had at hand, we were conducted to see the church. This building has three towers, one over the western porch, with a broad octagonal structure below, and a smaller one above, both constructed with pointed arches, and open at the sides; and two at the eastern end, of smaller dimensions and not open. These two in many respects resemble the towers at Ani, the old Armenian capital, now in Russian Armenia;[1] but the larger one is much more like that of the porch of the cathedral of Etchmiadzin.[2] On the façade are ornamental carvings in interlaced patterns, closely resembling what may be found in Ireland, and over the central door is an imitation of honeycomb work roughly coloured. Inside, the area of the church forms nearly a square, and is divided into a nave and four aisles, separated from one another by

---

[1] See the plates in Fergusson's *Handbook of Architecture*, pp. 974, 976 (1st ed.).

[2] Figured in Neale's *Eastern Church*, i. 260.

pointed arches, heavy in style and rude in execution. As usual in Armenian churches, there is no altar-screen or *iconostasis* between the body of the building and the sanctuary, as there regularly is in the Greek places of worship. Altogether the effect its architecture produced upon us was that of a curious mixture of the East and the West. The most valuable object which it contained was a large manuscript of the Gospels in Armenian, written on vellum in gold letters, with numerous full-page illuminations. The execution is beautiful, and it has the interest of being a royal work, having been written by a King Hatoum[1] with his own hand. This is the only book of interest preserved here, for the library was pillaged during the last century. Beneath the floor of the church a King Sempad (one of many of that name) and other Armenian princes are buried, but they have no tombs, and the places where they lie are only marked by slabs. Evidently the monastery was once a resort of great personages.

After leaving the church we were conducted to the schoolroom, a large gloomy stone-built chamber, where about thirty pupils were assembled; but the whole number was not present, for some had gone home to spend the festival. They mostly come from Mush, and are preparing for the ministry. To give us an idea of their music, they sang in chorus an Armenian national song. The voices were extremely harsh, but their singing was vigorous and the air forcible. New school buildings have lately been in course of erection along the outer wall of the inclosure facing the monastery, for the accommodation of more

[1] There were several kings called Hatoum from A.D. 1227 onwards.

students, but the work has had to be discontinued for the time from want of funds. Having thus exhausted the objects of interest within the monastery, I climbed up the steep ground at its back in order to find a point of view for a sketch, in company with the Constantinopolitan priest, who pointed out to me St. Gregory's fountain. The appearance of the place from above was curiously Oriental from the wide extent of flat roofs, but its stiff outlines formed a good contrast to the mountain spurs immediately below and the expanse of plain beyond. On leaving, we were presented with an introductory letter, addressed to various dignitaries at Van and elsewhere in this part of the country. Its contents were a sealed book to us, as they were in the Armenian language and character; but it was inclosed within a tasteful border of flowers, and headed by a medallion representing the baptism of our Lord, with angels on either side, and below, a highly idealised likeness of the three towers of the church, together with the head of the Baptist and other emblems. The chief monks begged us to let our countrymen know, that the hopes of the Armenians are now fixed on England. This was a remark that we had often heard elsewhere.

We now descended from the monastery by a steep path to the plain of Mush, and riding along it, after two hours reached the village of Ziaret, or 'pilgrimage,' so called, apparently, as being the resting-place of pilgrims who visit Surp Garabed. Here we established ourselves in an untenanted house in the outskirts of the village. Towards nightfall, while I was enjoying the stillness of the evening, I seemed to hear at intervals as it were a fairy chime coming from above, far away. At the time I thought it must be an illusion. However, on comparing notes with my companion the next morning, I found that he had heard the same sound; and this no doubt was the vesper peal of Changeli, rightly called 'the place of bells.' We must remember that, except in a few favoured spots in Turkey, the use of this accessory of divine worship is forbidden to the Christians, while they are not employed by the Moslems.

An unusual interest attaches to this monastery, both on account of the very early date of its foundation, and because it appears to occupy the site of a heathen place of worship, which, strange to say, was the head-quarters of a colony of Hindoos. The story of the first occupation of the site by the Christians forms a remarkable episode in the history of the conversion of Armenia, and shows that in some parts the new religion was propagated by the help of the sword. The account we have received of it is given by a contemporary, Zenobius, who was a Syrian bishop, and primate of the convent called Innaknian (the nine fountains), and flourished in Armenia in the beginning of the third century. This convent was none other than that of which we are speaking, for the Armenian geographer Vartan, who wrote in the thirteenth century, says that Surp Garabed was still called Innagnea-vank, from its nine sources of fresh water, and Klaga-vank, from the name of its first Superior, Klag, who was succeeded by Bishop Zenobius.[1] He wrote a work called the 'History of Daron,' which was published in Armenian in Venice in 1832. Daron or Taron, which is here mentioned, was the district

---

[1] Vartan's *Geography*, in Saint-Martin, *Mémoires sur l'Arménie*, ii. 431.

that comprised the plain of Mush and the neighbourhood of the upper course of the Murad.¹ 'The narrative,' its translator, Mr. Avdall, remarks, 'was evidently written in Syriac, and intended for the Syrian nation, though the writer seems to have subsequently rewritten it in the Armenian language, but with Syriac characters; the letters of our [the Armenian] alphabet having been invented a century posterior to that period.'

The following is Zenobius' account of the Hindoo colony and its history. 'This people had a most extraordinary appearance. They were black, long-haired, ugly and unpleasant to the sight. They claimed their origin from the Hindoos. The story of the idols worshipped by them in this place, is simply this: Demetr and Keisaney were brothers, and both Indian princes. They were found guilty of a plot formed against their king, Dinaṣkey, who sent troops after them, with instructions either to put them to death or to banish them from the country. The felons, having narrowly escaped the pursuit, took shelter in the dominions of the King Valarsaces, who bestowed on them the principality of the country of Taron. Here a city was founded by the emigrants, who called it Vishap or Dragon. Having come to Ashtishat, they raised idols there in the name of those they worshipped in India.² Fifteen years after this settlement in the country, both of the brothers were put to death by the king, for what fault I do not know. He conferred the principality on their

¹ Ritter, *Erdkunde*, x. 552.
² Ashtishat means 'the place of offerings,' and Avdall compares it as a centre of sacrifices with Juggernaut. Ritter, *Erdkunde*, x. 553, 554.

three sons, named Kuar, Meghti, and Horain. The first built a village, and called it after his own name Kuars. The second founded a village on the plain, and called it after his own name Meghti. The third also built a village in the province of Palunies,[1] and gave it the appellation of Horains.

'After a certain space of time, Kuar, Meghti, and Horain, of one accord, resolved on changing their abode. They sojourned on the mountain called Karki, which to a delightful temperature added a fine and picturesque appearance. It abounded in game, herbs, wood, and all that is adapted for the comfort and convenience of man. Here they raised edifices, where they set up two idols, respectively dedicated to Keisaney and Demetr, in honour of whom attendants were appointed out of their own race. Keisaney had long flowing hair, in imitation of which his priests allowed the hair of their head to grow, which custom was afterwards prohibited by authority. This class of people, on being converted to Christianity, were not deeply rooted in their faith. They durst not, however, openly profess the religion of their pagan ancestors. They continued therefore dissemblingly to allow their children to wear plaited hair on the crown of their heads, in resemblance of their idolatrous abominations.'

Mr. Avdall remarks that it is difficult to determine at what period they emigrated from India, but the Valarsaces here mentioned was grandson of Arsaces the Parthian, and brother of Arsaces the Great, by whom he was appointed king over Armenia a century and a

---

[1] Ritter suggests that Palunies is to be identified with Palu, but the position of that place seems hardly to agree with this.

half before Christ. They must therefore have been in the country 450 years before they were converted.

The story of their conversion is as follows. After St. Gregory had destroyed the heathen temples in the rest of Armenia, he was informed that two remained in the province of Taron. The narrator, who was present on the occasion, thus continues:

'Hereupon our course was changed to the place where these temples stood, with a view to effect their demolition. Having arrived in the country of Palunies, in the extensive village called Keisaney, near the town of Kuars, we met there some of the heathen priests. Having ascertained from the prince of Hashtens that on the following day the great images of Keisaney and Demetr were to be levelled to the ground, they repaired to the temples in the dead of the night, and removed from thence all the treasure into subterraneous places. Intimation of the impending danger was forthwith sent to the heathen priests in Ashtishat, who were earnestly urged to collect warriors, and quietly join them on the morrow in order to take an active part in the battle which was to be fought by the great Keisaney with the apostate princes. In like manner the inhabitants of Kuars were also instigated to lie in ambush in the hedges of gardens, and ruffians were sent to waylay the Christians in the forests. The head-priest, called Arzan, and his son Demetr, took the command of the troops stationed at Kuarstan, and halted there, awaiting the arrival of reinforcements from other quarters. On the following day they made a descent to the skirts of the mountain, in order to indulge in marauding and pillage.'

Then follows the account of the conflict, which was protracted, and consisted of a number of engagements, varied by single combats. One of these may be mentioned, as the scene of it was this very spot.

'The rebel attacked our army with the greatest fury, and was flushed with the success of his arms. Hereupon the prince of the Seunies cried to him in a contemptuous voice, " Thou whelp of a wolf! thou beganst to display the disposition of thy father, and feel a delight in feasting upon carrion." The rebel replied in a bold and reproachful manner, " Thou vain-glorious eagle! thou only piquest thyself on the power of thy wings; but if thou ever fallest in one of my traps, thou shalt soon feel the weight of my arms." The prince of the Seunies could not brook this taunt, but furiously rushing upon him, directed the axe which he held in his hand to his helmet, and having driven him to some distance from his troops, pursued him to the eastward of the mountain. Here, opposite to the convent of Innaknian, he brought him to the ground by a violent shove from his horse; and having himself alighted, instantly severed his head from his body, which he precipitated headlong from the mountain. " Now," said he, " let vultures behold you, and know that the eagle has killed the hare." Immediately after this, the prince of the Seunies returned to the army; and the place where the prince of Hashtens fell, is to this day called by the appellation of the Eagles.'

Finally both Arzan and Demetr are slain, and the heathen sue for peace. ' The heathen temples were razed to the ground, and the images of Keisaney and Demetr were broken to pieces. They were both made of brass. The length of the former was fifteen feet, and that of the latter twelve feet. The priests of the idols, with tears in their eyes, entreated the victors to put them to death, rather than destroy their mighty Keisaney. Six of the priests were killed on the spot, for the resistance they offered to the Armenians.' Most of the neighbouring people were induced to embrace Christianity, and 'being duly prepared for baptism' were baptized by St. Gregory. But four hundred refused to abjure the religion of their forefathers, and 'were imprisoned and their heads shaved.'[1]

As the name Keisaney seems to be Armenian, and Demetr Greek, it is doubtful whether they were the original ones; and Lassen, the famous Indian scholar, while he does not doubt the truth of the story, thinks it more likely that the worship and the idols came from India, than that they were called after the princes.[2] Attempts have been made to identify these Hindoos with some of the modern tribes who are found in Armenia. But the subsequent migration of the gipsies from India into Western Asia must render it very difficult to arrive at any certainty on the point.

[1] Avdall, *Memoir of a Hindu Colony in Ancient Armenia*, in the *Journal of the Asiatic Society of Bengal*; ed. Prinsep, vol. v. p. 331.
[2] Lassen in *Erdkunde*, x. 557. Ritter with his usual erudition has collected all the information there is to be found on this point.

CHAPTER XI.

BITLIS AND THE EASTERN TIGRIS.

Town of Mush—State of the neighbouring population—Quartering of Kurds on Armenians—Plain of Mush—Armenian villages—The Kara-su—French-speaking natives—Trials of a loyal Turk—Pass into Kurdistan—The watershed—Eastern source of the Tigris—Accounts of Strabo and Pliny—Communication with the Euphrates—Xenophon's route—Bitlis—A retreat in Kurdistan—Mode of collecting manna—Castle of Bitlis—First view of the lake of Van.

IN one hour from Ziaret we once more reached the eastern Euphrates, which flows hither through the mountains from the neighbourhood of Ararat, where we shall meet it near its source at a later stage of our journey. Here it forms a single stream one hundred and fifty feet in width, and about the same depth as where we last forded it below Palu: being fairly confined within its banks, it does no damage to the adjoining country. Our course now continued by the foot of the hills which bound the southern side of the plain, and along these we passed numerous villages. The land, which though productive was rudely cultivated, seemed for the most part to be devoted to the growth of corn, but melon and vegetable gardens were not infrequent, and many bullocks and buffaloes might be seen pasturing. At last we rounded a spur, and entered a recess of the plain, which gradually contracts into a confined valley; at the head of this lies the town of Mush, which we reached after five hours' journey. All that you see of the place as you approach is a portion of the upper part which occupies a steep mound, and the most conspicuous object is a picturesque minaret, variegated with black and white stone. The rest of the town is so plunged in a deep ravine that it is hidden from view. In the plots of ground on the outskirts cabbages of extraordinary size were growing, and high up the neighbouring slopes, both here and elsewhere along the mountain sides, were bright green vineyards, a surprising sight, as the plain itself is 4,000 feet above the sea. On entering the place we found it to be quite the filthiest town that we had met with in Turkey; in fact, on this point every traveller that has visited it appears to be agreed. The pavements were broken and ragged; every street was an open drain, and the stenches were fearful. It is, however, a considerable place, containing 3,000 houses, of which 800 are Armenian. We rode at once to the Serai, or official residence of the governor, a building which corresponded to the general aspect of the place, being dirty and ruinous, half barrack and half offices. The governor was absent, and his deputy was attending the Ramazan service at a mosque at some distance off; so thither we bent our steps and met him as he was returning. When we requested a lodging, he ordered us to be conducted to what proved to be a khan—a dwelling the only good feature in which were two ancient stone lions, carved in bas-relief on the capitals that support the arch at its entrance; these appeared to be Saracenic work. This treatment showed scant courtesy towards the bearers of a firman, so my companion, leaving me to superintend the baggage, returned to the Serai to expostulate. He found the deputy in the usual Ramazan condition, sleepy and peevish; but an Armenian gentleman in the employ of the Government, who happened to be with him at the time, kindly offered to entertain us, and conducted us to his house, which occupied an airy position in the highest part of the town.

The interior of this dwelling presented curious contrasts. The lower part might have been mistaken for the abode of a common artisan, for the floors were of clay and irregular in their level, and the stairs, which were little more than a ladder, led through a large trap-door into the upper floor; but when this was reached, we entered a well-furnished room, provided with three sofas, two easy-chairs, and a cushioned divan in the window, which commanded a fine view over the town and the wide plain beyond. Our host was a polished gentlemanly man, and from him we obtained much information as to the state of the country. From what we had heard elsewhere, we had gathered that the district of Mush was a sort of centre or culminating point of misgovernment and oppression in Armenia, and certainly what we now learnt confirmed this view. For some time past, he said, the Kurds from the neighbouring mountains —not those of the Dersim—had been accustomed to descend on to the plain, and burn the crops, and rob and murder the inhabitants. To some extent this was going on still, and quite lately in one village the newly-gathered harvest had been fired. I asked what the Government did under these circumstances.

'Now and then,' he replied, 'a man is caught, and is imprisoned for a year at Erzeroum, but that is all.' 'But are there no Turkish soldiers,' I inquired, 'to restrain the Kurds?' for we had passed a squadron of regular cavalry, who were encamped outside the town. 'Yes,' he said, 'but their behaviour in the villages is still worse, for they take the opportunity of violating the women.' This confirmed what I had heard on this subject from Dr. Barnum at Kharput. These grievances, however, hard as they are to bear, are temporary; the evil which is now to be mentioned is more deep-seated, because it is a long-standing system, and is recognised by the Government. This is the quartering of the nomad Kurds on the Armenian villages in the plain in the winter-time. During that season these mountaineers and their cattle are distributed among the Christian population, who provide them with everything and receive no payment in return. I was aware that this state of things prevailed in former times, but was not prepared to find it still existing; yet all that I heard on the subject at this place was afterwards confirmed to me at Van. The knowledge of this at once explained what seemed to us an anomaly as we journeyed through the plain—that while the villages were stored with abundance of hay, corn, and tezek, the inhabitants seemed poverty-stricken, and the children were half-naked. Neither the richness of the soil nor the industry of the people can keep off want, when parasites of this description live upon them during half the year.

I inquired about a fine manuscript of the Gospels, which the American Bishop Southgate saw in one of the churches here.[1] Our host replied that it was no longer in Mush itself, having been removed to a place two hours and a half distant. From this I should conclude that it is the same which Mr. Taylor mentions as existing at Arakolets Vank, a monastery in this neighbourhood—'a fine old manuscript copy of the New Testament in Armenian, written on vellum.'[2] I was much struck by the apparent absence of valuable MSS. in Armenia. In fact, that at Surp Garabed was the only one of any importance which I saw or heard of in the course of our journey. This was all the more disappointing because during the previous spring the Armenian Patriarch at Constantinople had told my friend Canon Curtis of that city, that MSS. had lately been discovered in tombs in this country. I confess this seemed to me an unlikely thing, and certainly such places were unfavourable for their preservation, but anyhow I could find out nothing about them. The district of Mush is famous for having produced two persons of importance to Armenian literature—St. Mezrop, the inventor of the alphabet, and Moses of Chorene, the national historian; both these celebrated men were born near this place.

At Mush we obtained fresh horses, and a new zaptieh, who was in all respects a contrast to the one who had accompanied us from Palu, being a bright active young fellow, and one of the most attentive and intelligent that we met with anywhere, so that he was of real service to us in identifying places. We started at an early hour, and descended through the steep

---

[1] *Erdkunde*, x. 677.
[2] *Geog. Soc. Journal*, vol. xxxv. p. 43.

streets of the town to the plain, along which we rode as before, keeping nearer to the southern than the northern range of hills that bound it. On the way we passed numerous villages, which resembled collections of large ant-hills, for when the walls of the cottages have been built up to a certain height, and trunks of trees laid across to form a roof, earth is piled up over the top and sides, and from this the chimneys protrude like small mud volcanoes, though here and there large pots are used for this purpose; sometimes an aperture is made on one side to serve for a window, and usually some kind of air-hole is constructed in the roof. The largest of these groups of houses, called Has-keui, is a considerable place, where an extensive manufacture of clay jars is carried on, but it is built in a similar manner to the others. It is interesting to remember that it was here that Xenophon first made acquaintance with the Armenian houses, which from his description must have closely resembled those of the present day, though he speaks of them as subterranean, an epithet which has often been repeated in narratives, and is so still, but, to say the truth, is rather an exaggeration. But as he and his soldiers had in this part of their march to wade through snow, and some of them had lost their eyesight and their toes in consequence, we can well believe that these warm dwellings seemed a delightful shelter, especially as they contained plenty of provisions, and beer (οἶνος κρίθινος), which they evidently enjoyed.[1] It is worthy of notice that Xenophon makes no mention of dung-fuel, but speaks of there being plenty of wood for firing, from which

[1] Xen. *Anab.* iv. 5.

we may gather that the country was well provided with trees at that time, and that its present denuded aspect arises from long devastation, and does not represent its primitive condition. Now, however, tezek is felt to be the first constituent of human comfort. In one village we saw the cakes of it constructed into an ornamental fortification with buttresses. It was evidently regarded as a material worthy of artistic treatment.

The tributary of the Murad by which the south-eastern portion of the plain of Mush is watered, is the Kara-su, or Blackwater, an important stream, which deserves its name from its turbid current. It winds considerably, and we had to ford it several times in the course of the day. Its bed is deeply cut, and has high banks; in one part, where the harvest was going on, we saw a huge wain, drawn by four oxen, struggling down the bank and through the heavy bottom. After five hours we rested at Ahkevank, a village with a cemetery in its neighbourhood, within the inclosure of which is a chapel. It has been spoken of as a monastery, but this is a mistake, though the termination of the name, *vank*, has that meaning, and possibly such a building may have existed here at some former time. The inhabitants were all Armenians, and were not less inquisitive than that race usually are. Poor things! it made us sad to think what they must suffer in the winter with their scanty clothing: one little boy wore simply a cap and an old waistcoat. We were surprised twice during this day by meeting persons who spoke French. The first of these was a gentleman who visited us before we left Mush, having been sent by the archbishop of that place with letters of introduction for us to persons at Bitlis and Van. He was himself a native of Van, and spoke cordially of the American missionaries in that city. The other was a peasant, whom we passed on foot as we rode along the plain. He saluted us in that language, and we found that he spoke it admirably. When we inquired how he had learnt it, he told us that for twenty years he had been employed in the shop of a Frenchman at Constantinople, where his brother was still, and added that he wished he was there too. 'What!' exclaimed my companion, 'when you have this rich plain to cultivate, and those fine mountains all round you!' He replied, 'The corn of the Turks does not flourish! When the Turks deprive us of our possessions and our earnings, how can you expect us to prosper?' These words might serve as a brief summary of the reasons for the emigration of the Armenians.

After again fording the Kara-su, we passed Marnik, the last village in the level country, and entered an angle of the plain, behind which at some distance off rises the grand mass of the Nimrud Dagh, which separates the district of Mush from the lake of Van. Ascending a little from this point we reached a small round marsh with a clear stream running from it; this was spoken of by our zaptieh as the source of the Kara-su, but a considerable body of water joins it from above, and on the following day we found its highest springs to lie at some distance off. A little way higher up lay the village of Nurshin, which is now Turkish, though formerly inhabited by Kurds. Here we were received by a kindly, simple old Turk, called Hamed Aga, who inhabited a small stone-built house, commanding a fine view over the length of the plain. Dinner was served immediately after our arrival, and when we expressed our surprise at its being ready at once, for he had had no notice of our coming, the old gentleman replied that as he lived at the foot of the pass that led from Kurdistan into Armenia, he was accustomed to receive visitors, and liked to have a meal ready to welcome them. It was a graceful explanation, though hardly probable, and we fancied it was invented in order to overcome any scruples that we might have felt in interfering with his Ramazan dinner. He was a specimen of a loyal subject, who respects the central Government which he only knows from a distance, while he is scandalised by the abuses he sees going on around him. Two of his sons had been killed in the war, and two had not yet returned, but he did not complain of this, nor yet of the burdensome taxation in itself, apart from the peculation of the local agents. 'I grudge nothing of what I pay,' he said, 'if it really reaches Constantinople; what I cannot bear is that it should go into the pockets of the kaimakams and the other officials.' He was deeply indignant at the maladministration of justice. Not long before this he had procured the imprisonment of a number of robbers; but by paying a medjidié (about 3s. 6d.) apiece to the Mudir, these miscreants had regained their liberty. On discovering this, he had appealed to the pasha at Mush, but no notice had been taken of his communication. Another grievance was the management of the Government monopoly of tobacco. We had observed a few fields of that plant about this place, and a good deal more growing near Mush, but the cultivation of it in this neighbourhood, we were told, had greatly decreased of late years owing to increased taxes and the use of cigarettes instead of the old-fashioned pipe; by these means the consumption had been reduced, and it was found not to be worth while to produce it so far from head-quarters, since it was not allowed to prepare or sell it on the spot. In reality, however, the consumer has suffered more than the producer from this cause; for as the prepared article is only allowed to be issued from certain centres, and is sent out in packets of limited size, it is usually dry and powdery, and a very different thing from what the people used formerly to enjoy. The annoyance arising from this is very generally felt throughout the Asiatic provinces.

At Nurshin we took leave for a time of the Armenian houses, for the same mode of construction is not in use in Kurdistan. In this place, however, close below our abode, were several of the usual earth-covered ant-hill structures, and these had a round hole at the top for the smoke to escape through, with a large flat stone lying close by, with which it was covered in during the winter. We now continued the ascent (August 27) over a gently inclined plain behind the village, and after an hour reached an upland expanse, which formed a sort of pass between graceful oak-clad mountains, those on our left being an offset from the Nimrud Dagh. This is pronounced Nemrut Tagh in this part of the country, both words affording instances of the use of *t* for *d* in the pronunciation of Turkish in Eastern Armenia; another peculiarity which we noticed is the corruption of *k* into *tch*, as *itchi* for *iki*, 'two.' Though the ground here is almost level, it took us another hour to reach the summit of the pass between Armenia and Kurdistan (5,650 feet above the sea), but the watershed itself is indistinguishable, and I saw green spots where there were marshes in winter, from which the water might flow in either direction; so at this point it appears that the head waters of the Tigris, which rises here, join those of the Kara-su, which is a confluent of the Euphrates. We were strongly impressed by the remarkable position of the plain of Mush, situated as it is at so great an elevation among the mountains, with so gradual a rise from its level to this point. Towards the east a dip in the mountains forms an opening towards the lake of Van, which our zaptieh spoke of as 'the sea' (*deniz*), and truly it deserves that name from its vast expanse; from here, however, its waters are not visible, though the summit of the lofty Sipan Dagh, which rises from its northern shore, is seen far away. The road which we followed towards Bitlis now turned at right angles, and thus we had before us the meeting-place of three valleys—three great cross-roads, so to speak, of nature's making—which lead respectively to the plain of Mush, the lake of Van, and the valley of the Tigris.

The point which we have thus reached is one of considerable importance for ancient geography, because the eastern source of the Tigris was the one recognised in antiquity as its real source, and about it there grew up a number of curious legends. The first detailed account of it that has come down to us occurs in Strabo. When enumerating the lakes that are found in Armenia, that writer says : 'There is too the lake Arsene, which is also called Thopitis, and this contains potash, and serves for cleansing and fulling clothes ; and for this reason also its water is not drinkable. The Tigris also flows through it, after rising in the mountain district over against Niphates, and preserves its stream unmixed owing to its swiftness, from which it gets its name, for among the Medes *tigris* means "an arrow ;" and whereas there are many kinds of fish in the river, in the lake there is one kind only. But at the extremity of the lake the river falls into a chasm, and after running underground for a long distance rises again in the district called Chalonitis.'[1] The lake here called Thopitis, which Pliny more accurately calls Thospites, is undoubtedly the lake of Van, for this is called by Armenian writers, Lake of Dosp, from its being situated in the province of Dosp, of which the city of Van was the capital.[2] What Strabo relates as to its cleansing properties is true at the present day, for the natives use the incrustations that are formed on the surface for washing clothes.[3] The water of the

---

[1] Strabo, xi. p. 529. The last statement is impossible, as Chalonitis is far away in the eastern part of Assyria. Mr. Bunbury (*History of Ancient Geography*, ii. 289) suggests that there is a mistake in the name.

[2] Saint-Martin, *Mémoires sur l'Arménie*, i. 55, 131.

[3] Bp. Southgate says (*Narrative of a Tour through Armenia, Kurdistan, Persia, and Mesopotamia*, ii. 306) : 'I found in the bazaars at Van a singular substance, which the people informed me rose and formed on the surface of the lake, and was collected and used by them in washing clothes. It was in flat cakes, none of which were more than an inch thick. It was white, imperfectly crystallised, and extremely fragile. An analysis of a specimen which I brought to the United States, and submitted to Professor Cleaveland, of Bowdoin College, shows it to be "alkaline salts, composed chiefly of carbonate of soda and chloride of sodium."'

lake of Van is too salt for drinking. The idea that the stream passes through the lake without mixing with it is found in many other places, and is naturally suggested by the difference in colour of the water of the two for some distance below the point where the river enters—a feature which many of my readers will have noticed at the head of the lake of Geneva, where the current of the Rhône is traceable for more than a mile. What is stated about the fish may have been suggested by the same thing which occurs at the present day, viz. that the fish are found to congregate about the mouths of the streams, where they are caught in great quantities. And finally, as the lake has no visible outlet, and the real sources of the eastern branch of the Tigris are at this point but a few miles distant from its western extremity, and with only a low watershed between, the universal fondness of the human mind for tracing a subterranean connection between waters, would easily suggest that the river which was here formed, was in reality the reappearance of the former one after having escaped the contamination of the lake and the dangers of an underground journey.

Having thus examined Strabo's account, let us turn to that given by Pliny. 'The Tigris,' he says, 'rises in the district of Greater Armenia, from a conspicuous source in a level spot. The name of the place is Elegosine; that of the river, where its course is slower, Diglito; from the point where its speed increases, it begins to be called Tigris from its rapidity, for this is the word for an arrow among the Medes. It flows into the lake of Arethusa, which supports whatever heavy substances are brought down into it, and exhales natron in clouds; it contains but one kind of fish, and these avoid the current of the river as it passes, and in like manner the fish from the Tigris do not pass into the lake. The river is distinguished from it as it flows along both by its current and its colour, and after passing through it disappears into a chasm where Mount Taurus meets it, and after flowing underground, bursts out on the further side at a place called Zoroande. The identity of the stream is shown by objects dropped into it being carried through. Subsequently it passes through a second lake called Thospites, and again descends into an underground passage; after a course of 22 (Roman) miles it reappears near Nymphaeum.'[1]

It is not difficult to see that the story here given is an adaptation of the former one, with such amplifications as are usually found in a later version. Thus the idea of its waters supporting ponderous objects was suggested, no doubt, by its saltness and its incrustations, which correspond to the phenomena of bituminous pieces of water like the Dead Sea, which have that power; though, as a matter of fact, when we swam in it, we did not discover that it possessed greater buoyancy than the sea. Similarly, the notion of proving the continuity of streams which pass underground by the reappearance of objects cast in

[1] Pliny, *Hist. Nat.* vi. 27, § 31: The story of the disappearance of the Tigris is found in other Latin authors of the post-Augustan age; thus Lucan writes (*Pharsal.* iii. 201):

> At Tigrim subito tellus absorbet hiatu,
> Occultosque tegit cursus, rursusque renatum
> Fonte novo flumen pelagi non abnegat undis.

And Seneca says (*Natural. Quaest.* iii. 26): 'Idem et in Oriente Tigris facit, absorbetur et desideratur diu, tandem longe remoto loco, non tamen dubius an idem sit, emergit.' See Ritter's *Erdkunde*, x. 80.

higher up—a test, we may be sure, which has been more often imagined than applied—was familiar to the Greeks in connection with the lakes devoid of outlet, and the subterranean passages of their limestone mountains. Of some of the names which occur in this passage, such as Elegosine, Diglito, and Zoroande, it is impossible to give any account, though Diglito is not very unlike what Tigris or Tigreta might be in the mouth of a race averse to the use of hard consonants.[1] As to the course of the stream before it reaches the lake, we can only say that the river which flows into the head of Lake Van is the Bende-Mahi-su, and that it is a torrent of no great size, which rises in the mountain range to the south of Ararat. The lake here called Arethusa—a purely Greek name—is probably, to judge from the similarity of form, the same as the Arsissa of Ptolemy,[2] and that again seems to be a more accurate form of the Arsene of Strabo;[3] and the original of Arsissa, it is thought, is to be recognised in the town of Ardjish,[4] on the northern shore of the lake of Van, on its eastern arm, which is still called Lake Ardjish after that place. The only question is as to the antiquity of the town, but we find it at all events as early as the tenth century, when it is mentioned by Constantine Porphyrogenitus,[5]

---

[1] Since writing this, I have discovered that Kiepert also identifies the name Diglito with Tigris, but he considers Diglito to have been the earlier form. *Lehrbuch der alten Geographie*, p. 79.

[2] Ptol. v. 13, § 8.

[3] Kramer's Strabo, vol. ii. p. 495 *note*.

[4] Saint-Martin, *Mémoires sur l'Arménie*, i. 56.

[5] *De Administr. Imp.* c. 44, vol. iii. pp. 191, 192 ed. Bonn. It is there called Ἀρσες and Ἀρζες. Assyriologists find a name corresponding to Arsissa in the accounts of the Assyrian invasions of Armenia; see Duncker, *History of Antiquity* (Abbott's translation), i. 520, 521.

in whose time it was in the hands of Mussulman princes. Now as this eastern arm of the lake of Van is in so many respects a separate piece of water, so that it might easily be distinguished from the rest of the lake; and as Pliny ascribes to the lake Arethusa the same characteristics as Strabo does to the lake Thospites; the natural conclusion is that, being an uncritical writer, he has adopted a less accurate version of the story, and has made two lakes out of Strabo's one. But it hardly requires to be pointed out that both these writers, and in fact the ancients generally, whatever elements of truth there were in their notions about the sources of the Tigris, had very vague ideas on the subject.[1]

The passage that immediately follows Pliny's account of which we have been speaking, has been already quoted in reference to the Gheuljik lake, as it mentions the connection in times of inundation between the waters of the Tigris and the Arsanias, which latter is the name by which Pliny knew the Murad.[2] We there saw that the two streams do not communicate, and never could have communicated with one another near the western source of the Tigris, and therefore this phenomenon, if it is to be found at all, must be looked for elsewhere. Now at this watershed such a feature is actually to be seen, not indeed corresponding to the details given by Pliny, for those would be impossible anywhere, but still sufficiently well marked to form the foundation of the story, and certainly of a nature to attract

[1] See, on several points connected with this, Bunbury, *History of Ancient Geography*, ii. 409.
[2] See above, p. 244.

attention. The idea of one river flowing on the surface of another, which is there introduced, is as old as Homer, who relates it concerning the Peneius and Titaresius in Thessaly.[1] We know, however, from having traced the waters of the Kara-su up to this point, and having seen the ground slope away to the valley of the Tigris on the other side—and to this point I purposely devoted especial attention—that a confluent of the Murad (Arsanias) actually has a common origin with that river, and this no doubt must be more evident in the wet season. It is true, therefore, that the Tigris and Euphrates, which—though, as Pliny rightly remarks, they originally had separate mouths [2]—now enter the Persian Gulf as one river, had communication with one another also in the upper part of their courses; and this curious fact probably gave rise to the more elaborate story of their flowing for some distance in a common channel.

But we have not yet done with classical antiquity, for another point of great historical interest remains to be noticed. This place is the position of which we can speak with the greatest confidence in the retreat of the Ten Thousand, and which we can therefore use as a starting-point in determining more disputed questions as to their route. It will be remembered that that devoted band, according to the account left us by their intrepid commander, after the ruin of their cause at the battle of Cunaxa near the banks of the Euphrates, crossed the Tigris, and followed the left bank of that river upwards until they reached its tributary the Zabatus, now called

---

[1] *Il.* ii. 753, 754.   [2] *Hist. Nat.* vi. 27, § 130.

the Greater Zab, which flows from the north-east through Assyria. It was here that their generals were treacherously seized and murdered by the Persian commander Tissaphernes, and as they were henceforth in the midst of declared enemies, it was impossible for them to follow the high road westward to the Euphrates, which would have been their direct route towards Ionia; and consequently they were forced to penetrate into the mountains towards the north, in order to reach the highlands of Armenia, where they might pass the Tigris and Euphrates near their sources, and so descend towards the Euxine. This mountain region was the territory of the Carduchi, the modern Kurdistan; and in forcing their way through its intricate valleys, while continually harassed by its warlike inhabitants, they experienced their greatest losses. At last, after seven days, they came to the valley of the Centrites, now called the river of Sert, a confluent of the Tigris, rising due south of the lake of Van, from which it is separated by a lofty mountain chain. In two days more they passed the sources of the Tigris, which must have been these above Bitlis, for the only practicable route from Kurdistan into Armenia in this part is by way of that place. The principal difficulty that here presents itself in interpreting Xenophon's account is the omission of all notice of the lake of Van, for it is hard to think that he did not hear of it, when it was only a few miles distant. It is clear, however, from their not having seen it, that they must have proceeded onwards by the same route by which we have ascended; and from this it follows unavoidably that the next river which they reached, the Teleboas, was the Kara-su, and that when, after struggling through the snows of the Armenian uplands, they came to the Euphrates, this must be the Murad, the Arsanias of later writers, at the further end of the plain of Mush.[1] Their subsequent course, after fording that stream, we shall have an opportunity of speaking of when we again cross their track at a later period of our journey.

Our visit to Bitlis was an excursion, for it led us away from our direct course towards the lake of Van; but we were anxious to make acquaintance with that interesting town, and also to explore the head waters of the eastern branch of the Tigris, as we had done those of the western. At various points along this route there are massively built stone khans, which are intended as refuges for travellers at unfavourable seasons of the year, like those we are accustomed to see on Alpine passes; these, however, had more pretensions to architecture than can be found in the Alps, and seemed to date from a considerable antiquity. One which I entered on the side towards Nurshin had arched recesses at its sides, and one of those towards Bitlis possessed an ornamented portal. As we descended, we passed at intervals a number of limpid brooks, which contributed their waters to swell the stream of the infant Tigris, and after three hours' riding down the bare stony valley we found ourselves at the entrance to the town.

---

[1] Bunbury, *History of Ancient Geography*, i. 349-353. It is true that Xenophon makes it three days' march from the sources of the Tigris to the Teleboas, but here as elsewhere in the narrative Mr. Bunbury's remark is just, that it is 'utterly impossible to explain the distances given' (p. 356).

When approached from this side, Bitlis comes upon you as a surprise, for until you are within it there is nothing but a few trees to suggest that an inhabited place is near. It lies completely below the level of the upper valley, which here suddenly makes an abrupt descent, so that the river, which has now been swelled into a fair-sized torrent, breaks into rapids and cataracts in its passage through the town. In the middle of the place it is joined by another stream from the mountains toward the north-west, and the buildings climb up the hillsides at the meeting of these valleys, rising one above the other with a striking effect; while the Bitlis-chai (Tigris), thus reinforced, breaks its way through the deep chasms below, and for several days' journey descends with great rapidity towards the lower country. As we entered, we were struck with the massiveness of the stone-built houses, with large courts and gardens surrounded by strong walls, the coping-stones of which were constructed so as to rise to a sharp angle at the top. Another marked feature was the abundance of trees, which formed a strong contrast to the bare flanks of the mountains that towered above. In the middle of the town between the two streams rises the castle, occupying a platform of rock, the sides of which fall away precipitously, and like all the cliffs around have vertical cleavings; the space which it covers is large, and it forms a very conspicuous object with its square and circular towers, following the sinuosities of the ground. The only thing wanting in the appearance of the place is colour, for there is a certain monotony in the brown sandstone of the buildings exactly corresponding to the hue of the mountains. Owing to the neighbourhood of Arabia, towards which country it faces, the climate here is milder than on the table-land of Armenia, and the barometer rarely falls below zero in the winter, though this is often the case further north. The elevation is still great, being 4,700 feet above the sea.

On inquiring for the Armenian gentleman to whom we had brought an introduction from Mush, we found that he lived in the upper part of the town not far from where we entered it; but as our desire was to be near the American mission, and that proved to be a long distance off, on the heights occupied by an outlying quarter towards the southeast, we determined not to request hospitality from him. Dropping down through the steep streets, and passing under the castle-rock with the Tigris on our left hand, we threaded our way through the cool bazaars, and then crossing the stream mounted again in the direction of the mission station. The view from this side is remarkably fine, as it commands nearly the whole of the town, lying in its rocky basin with the castle in the centre. In order that we might not take Mr. Knapp, the missionary, unawares, we left our horses and baggage at the corner of a street, and proceeded on foot to his house, to inquire if he could give us information about a lodging. As it happened, we arrived at a fortunate moment, for he was on the point of starting for the country, where he was encamped for the summer months, and he invited us to spend the day with him. He was delighted to see us, for here, as elsewhere in this remote country, we found the average number of European visitors to be one in two years; but as he was wholly unprepared for our coming, we seemed to him—to use his expression—to have dropped from the clouds. The girls of his native school being now absent, he offered us for our accommodation their schoolroom, the largest chamber in a building close by his house, which had been the palace of some former Bey, and stood within an inclosure of garden ground. We gladly accepted the offer, for though the room with its closely barred windows, stone floor, and massive walls, bare of everything except maps, had very much the aspect of a prison, to us it was an ideal residence, being clean, cool, airy, and free from objectionable furniture.

Leaving our servant here to make arrangements for us, we again mounted our horses, and accompanied our new entertainer on his country ride. Our road lay along the side of a valley towards the southeast, through which a stream descends transversely towards the Tigris; and when we had crossed this brook and mounted the steep slopes beyond by a winding path, after three-quarters of an hour we reached an encampment of two large tents, which were occupied by Mrs. Knapp and her two little girls, together with thirty Armenian boarders from the girls' school. The position was superb and wonderfully solitary, for the town, which was 600 feet below, was completely shut out by an intervening spur, and the grand mountains of Kurdistan rose above us all around. Here we spent the afternoon, and subsequently dined, under the shade of a spreading walnut tree, one of several in this neighbourhood, for the whorls or knots in the trunks of these trees are collected by merchants for use in veneering, in consequence of which it is worth while to cultivate them. They are mostly exported to France, where they are called *loupes*; the excrescences of those in this place had already been cut off. We had heard of this trade at Amasia; in fact it goes on throughout Asia Minor and Armenia, wherever these trees are found. In the neighbourhood was a small village, which, like almost all the villages near Bitlis, had been pillaged by the Kurds during the Russo-Turkish war; that period was one of great suffering to the Christians, for the Mahometan population were wholly unrestrained by any fear of punishment. Mr. Knapp himself had been obliged to remain in Bitlis during that time; now, however, quiet had been restored. In many ways the mission here seems to have had a hard struggle, and the solitude of the life for a single family must be very great. Close to the tents was a source of clear water, which finds its way down into the brook below. This whole district is a land of springs, and several of these have mineral waters. One is chalybeate, while another, a sample of which was sent to America to be analysed, seems to contain somewhat the same components as Vichy water. Some of this, which I tasted from out of a bottle, had a mild flavour of ink.

Mr. Knapp gave us some information about the manna, and the mode of collecting it. It is obtained from the leaves of a variety of trees, and not from the oak only, though from that it is procured most easily. Dry years are especially good for it, and this year in consequence there had been a great harvest. It is collected in two different ways. Sometimes the leaves on which it lies, when gathered, are steeped in water, which is then strained, and the sugary matter collected; in this case the leaves communicate to it that greenish hue which we had noticed in the lumps we had met with in the country. Sometimes, on the other hand, the leaves are left to dry, and the white deposit scales off. As to its origin, the people are not agreed. It is generally regarded as exuding from the leaves, and its appearance when seen on their surface would lead you to suppose that such is the case. But this the people of Bitlis deny, for they say it lies on any plant without reference to its nature, and even on men's garments. Hence they conclude that it is deposited by the air, a view in which Mr. Knapp agreed with them; and he thinks that it arises from the aromatic exhalations carried by the wind from Arabia in this direction. Another substance which is largely collected here is the gum Tragacanth, which we have already spoken of as growing about Mount Argaeus.

At dinner we were provided with a dish of potatoes of home produce, which were a great treat, for vegetables were the article of food the want of which we had most felt in the course of our journey. The growth of vegetables, I have often observed—especially of those which require some care and thought—is one of the best tests of the state of civilisation in a country. Here potatoes are hardly ever found, except where they have been introduced by the missionaries, though they flourish well where they are grown. At last, when the shadows began to lengthen on the Kurdish mountains, we bade farewell to our kind entertainers, and led our horses down the zigzag path to the valley. Mounting at the brook, we guided ourselves towards the town by following the line of a watercourse. The more distant mountains towards the west rapidly deepened into blue in the brief twilight of this climate, and the moon was already shining before we entered Bitlis. The lofty summits of this district, which form the conclusion of the Taurus chain, are the Niphates of antiquity, the range which Virgil and Horace regard as embodying the enemies of Rome in Asia, and on the highest peak of which Milton makes his Satan to alight.[1]

We remained the next day at Bitlis, and found the rest welcome after our rough experiences of the previous week. Several visitors came to see us, and among them an Armenian, who was about to become a professor in the college at Kharput, but was waiting to make the journey thither by the same route by which we had come, until a sufficiently large caravan should have been collected to insure a safe transit. He had been educated at first at Kharput, and afterwards at Basle, and spoke both English and German well. In the afternoon we explored the castle, in the company of a zaptieh, whom we had requested the pasha to furnish us with for that purpose, but we found neither inscriptions nor any object of interest within it. On the outer face of the walls, however, there are some inscriptions in the Arabic character. Its date is unknown; the inhabitants ascribe it to Alexander the Great, but it probably belongs to

---

[1] Virg. *Georg.* iii. 30: 'Addam urbes Asiae domitas, pulsumque Niphaten.' Hor. *Od.* ii. 9, 20: 'Cantemus Augusti tropaea Caesaris, et rigidum Niphaten.' Milton, *Par. Lost,* iii. 741: 'Nor stayed, till on Niphates' top he lights.'

the time of the Saracens, when the emirs of Bitlis were important personages. At the same time it is likely enough that the same site was previously fortified, since an ancient Armenian city, called Paghesh, existed here,[1] and so commanding a position as this rock could hardly be neglected. The town of Bitlis itself during the Middle Ages was surrounded by a wall, as we learn from Abulfeda, whose description of the place is on the whole accurate; he adds that in his time half this wall was in ruins.[2] Until comparatively lately the place was governed by semi-independent Kurdish Beys. The last of these, called Sherif Bey, was still in possession when Colonel Shiel visited Bitlis in 1836, and that traveller says in his narrative: 'We were lodged in the Governor's house, a large stone square building inclosing a wide court, and placed on the top of a high hill, where it stood alone, overhanging a part of the city.'[3] This palace, Mr. Knapp told us, was situated some way above where we were living, but has now been entirely pulled down. The Bey, who is reputed to have been a great tyrant, was seized by the Turks and carried to Constantinople, where he was kept in confinement till his death.

Bitlis is said to contain about 3,000 houses, of which 2,000 belong to the Kurds, 1,000 to the Armenians, 20 to the Turks, and 50 to the Syrians (Jacobites). Our host estimated these as representing 30,000 souls, a computation which allows a greater

[1] Saint-Martin, *Mémoires sur l'Arménie*, i. 103.
[2] Abulfedae *Geographia*, in Büsching, *Magazin für die neue Historie und Geographie*, vol. v. p. 311.
[3] Shiel, *Journey from Tabriz through Kurdistan*, in the *Geog. Soc. Journal* for 1838, vol. viii. p. 71.

number of inhabitants than usual to each house; but this would seem to be justified by the number of large isolated buildings which it contains. The Kurdish girls here frequently wear the same nose-ring as I had seen worn by Armenian women at the convent of Changeli. The younger men of that race whom we saw in the bazaars were often very handsome, with black eyes and hair, regular features, and a determined look. These also were well dressed, wearing over their bright-coloured waistcoats short dark sheepskin jackets with the wool on, open in front and without sleeves. Unlike the Kurds of the mountain districts, and those that inhabit the plain of Mush, they are not Kizilbashes or Shiites by religion, but Sunnites like the Turks. They were quite the wildest population that we had seen in any town, and we were not sorry to be accompanied by a zaptieh whilst sketching the castle; in fact the people crowded round us so, that, had he not been present, it would have been impossible even to see the objects which we wished to draw.

The Ramazan is certainly not a favourable time for travellers in Turkey. When you are wanting to make an early start, your attendants arrive late, and numerous things are found to have been neglected. This was what we experienced on the morning of our departure from Bitlis (August 29); our newly hired horses had not been shod, a blacksmith had to be sent for, and after the night's revel everyone was half asleep. In consequence of this we did not start before eight o'clock. The impression we had formed of the inhabitants of Bitlis was fully confirmed by the behaviour of our new zaptieh and katirjis. All of these were Kurds, and the former, in particular, was a very rough specimen. It was not his fault, no doubt, that nature had made him very ugly, and had provided him with a shock head of carroty hair, a very unusual feature in this land ; nor could we blame him for his tattered and patched uniform, which seemed rather to hang upon him than to be worn by him, for he probably received neither pay nor clothing, like most of his corps, who consequently have to maintain themselves by exactions from the *rayahs* ; but for his surliness and disobliging ways he certainly was responsible, and these made him a very unamiable companion. Our way lay up the valley by which we had approached Bitlis two days before, but as we now kept above the left bank of the stream, on the opposite side to our previous track, we did not descend into the town, but only skirted its outlying buildings. Following the foot of the mountain slopes on the southern side, we passed the watershed in which the Tigris rises, and as we overlooked it our previous impressions with regard to the formation of the ground were confirmed. To the eastward of this, at a somewhat higher elevation, a level plain extends, hemmed in on either side by lofty mountains ; those towards the north were green with undergrowth of dark oak, and behind them the higher summits of the Nimrud Dagh were visible. Here the cornfields were carried up the slopes to a surprising height, showing how much more of the land might be brought under cultivation, if necessary. We were all anxiety to catch a glimpse of the lake of Van, and it seemed to be long in appearing. The cap of Mount Sipan, which dominates its northern shore, had been for some time in sight, and now we were admiring other fine ranges which showed themselves at a distance on the right, when suddenly the ground sloped away in front of us, and the glittering expanse was seen. It was a beautiful view, owing to the numerous bays, the succession of headlands, and the finely cut outlines of the ridges ; but as yet it gave no idea of the magnitude of this inland sea. The part here visible was only the narrow western arm, a pretty inclosed piece of water, with intimations of a wider surface beyond, and a suspicion of shadowy mountains in the far distance. Immediately below us, on the edge of the innermost bay, lay the village of Tadvan, and at the side of this a mass of rocky ground, broken into two crests, rose from the shore. Towards this village we now descended after five hours' journey from Bitlis.

CHAPTER XII.

THE LAKE OF VAN.

Remarkable character of the lake—Village of Tadvan—Shores of Lake Van—Powdery volcanic soil—Akhlat—The Kharaba-sheher, or 'ruined city'—The castle of Akhlat—Dust storm—The upper valley—History of Akhlat—Tunuz—Adeljivas—Ascent of Mount Sipan—Village of Norshunjuk—The crater—View from the ridge—Summits of Sipan—Height of the mountain—Legends relating to it—Walls of Adeljivas—Circassian colonies—Boats on Lake Van—Crossing the lake—Armenian sailors—Landing-place of Avanz.

WE felt a natural excitement at reaching this famous lake, which had been in my thoughts for many years, and which appeared in some ways to be the goal of our journey. Independently of the grandeur of its scenery, it is a very remarkable natural phenomenon, for its water is salt, owing apparently to the volcanic nature of much of the ground by which it is surrounded, and though it receives the contributions of numerous streams, it has no visible outlet. Its extreme length is ninety miles; its breadth, where it is widest, about thirty; its area is, perhaps, twice as large as that of the lake of Geneva, and it is more than 5,000 feet above the level of the sea.[1] Its striking elevation is brought home to you with great force as you approach from this side; for after having wondered at the neighbouring plain of Mush, with its expanse of forty

[1] Our aneroid made it 5,200 feet; it has been estimated as high as 5,467 feet (*Erdkunde*, x. 287).

miles in length, lying at so great an altitude, you learn with astonishment that this vast piece of water is a thousand feet higher still, and only about five hundred feet below the uppermost source of the Tigris. To all this must be added the objects of interest in its neighbourhood—Mount Sipan, an extinct volcano of imposing form and the highest summit between Argaeus and Ararat; the ancient city of Akhlat with its remarkable remains of antiquity on the northern shore; and on the southern, the castle-rock of Van, which may without exaggeration be spoken of as one of the wonders of the world, from its extraordinary formation, its rock-hewn chambers, and its cuneiform inscriptions.

The village of Tadvan is composed of a small number of scattered houses, situated in the midst of gardens and fruit trees, which are irrigated by the waters of a neighbouring fountain. As our object was to visit Akhlat and ascend Mount Sipan before reaching the town of Van, our course from this point lay in the neighbourhood of the northern shore. After resting for an hour we continued our journey over hills sloping to the water, and enjoyed such views as are obtained in skirting a lake, when its surface assumes different hues as seen from above and from below, with a succession of bays on both sides, and ever-shifting promontories. One of these headlands, at the back of which we passed, stood up conspicuous with a strongly marked outline. As we advanced, the expanse of bright blue water became gradually wider, but there was no point at which we were unable to see both shores. On our left, away from the lake, lay the Nimrud Dagh, which since leaving

Mush we had seen on three sides; from here it has the appearance of being a considerable range, but in reality it is one great volcano, and at Van we were afterwards informed, though it is difficult to believe it, that the crater of this is from five to seven miles across. Our Kurdish katirjis now began to show signs of insubordination. As it was owing to their fault that we started late from Bitlis, we determined that they should make up for lost time by an evening march, and this they resented. For some time they had lagged far behind, and at last when we reached a point where a road diverged from the main track towards a distant village, they took themselves off in that direction, and our servant, whom we had left to watch them, rode up to say that they threatened if we went any further, to throw down our baggage in the road. This they were quite capable of doing; so I sent back the zaptieh with injunctions to force them to follow us at all hazards—an order which he dared not disobey. This brought them to their senses, and they now returned to the main road and came after us, though with an increasing interval.

The ground throughout this district was everywhere volcanic, and the soil, which was simply dust, was being scratched by the rudest kind of plough I have ever seen, for it had no tailpiece at all; so powdery was the earth, that it seemed as if a violent wind might destroy all the furrows. Towards sunset we obtained a view over the north-westernmost bay of the lake, at the head of which Akhlat lies, while the massive form of Sipan rose in its full proportions behind. Flashes of lightning now appeared on the horizon at several points, betokening a change of weather. As the evening was drawing in, we found it necessary to wait for our company, who arrived at length, silent and subdued, in a very different frame of mind from that in which we left them, when they were wildly shouting at one another and gesticulating. The zaptieh undertook to conduct us to a village, but if he was not extemporising a way, he must have missed his track, for our course through the fields was very vague and circuitous. At last by the light of the moon we reached a place called Karmunsh, situated on a hillside overlooking the lake, and this on inquiry proved to be less than an hour distant from Akhlat. Here our tent was pitched, not without difficulty, on the hard surface of a threshing-floor.

On waking the next morning we heard a rushing sound, as of the sea, and this proved to proceed from the water of the lake being dashed on the beach below. During the night a strong east wind had arisen, and now the shore was fringed with foam. The country between Karmunsh and Akhlat was composed of dusty hills, and valleys full of copious clear springs, which welled out of the rocks, and were surrounded by poplars and willows, and an abundance of green turf, forming a refreshing sight. As we approached the latter place, we threaded our way along watercourses by intricate paths, until we reached the official house of the Mudir, which is situated in an orchard filled with walnut, plum, and apricot-trees; the fruit on the last-named of these was very small, but so abundant as to bend the branches, and of excellent flavour. The Mudir himself was absent, but his place was supplied by a Bimbashi (colonel), and before him our attendants from Bitlis were at once brought up to answer for their misconduct. The katirjis received a severe reprimand, and the uncivil zaptieh was sent home without the usual *bakshish*. His place was taken by an intelligent local zaptieh, also a Kurd, but in features and complexion more like a peasant from Central Italy. He was cheery and communicative, and we found him an excellent guide to the neighbourhood.

In order to make the following description clearer, I may notice at starting, that Akhlat at present consists of three parts—the Gardens, the Kharabasheher or 'ruined city,' and Akhlat Kalessi, or the 'castle of Akhlat.' The first of these, in which the Mudir's house and a few other scattered buildings stand, is on the upper level, the second in the valley below, the last on the shore of the lake, which is about half a mile distant. The surrounding district forms a gently-sloping table-land, seamed by narrow gorges with steep sides which have been carved out by the mountain torrents. In the middle of the deepest of these there rises a long flat-topped hill or table of rock, which divides the valley into two parts, while on its western side runs a full clear stream, which covers the neighbouring ground with vegetation. On and about this hill is the Kharabasheher. Descending by a steep track from the gardens to the stream, we rode along underneath this, and noticed numerous caves in the steep sandstone cliffs of which its sides were composed; these were for the most part artificial chambers, and fifteen of them were now inhabited, like those which we had first met with on the banks of the Halys. Above, the foundations of the castle walls which surrounded the summit were to be seen at intervals, some of them being well built, others of ruder construction. Passing under the southern end of this rocky table, we crossed the stream, and ascended on the opposite side of the valley towards the east, just where a large detached mass of wall, which belonged to some ancient edifice, stood up in a picturesque position on the edge of the slope. This is one of a number of pieces of masonry which we found extending over a very large area, though we could discover no trace of city walls. Arrived at the level ground beyond, we came in a few minutes to a small old mosque, by the side of which stood a fine tomb in perfect preservation. The plan of this was circular, and on the ground-floor was a closed chamber intended for the sepulchre, while another above this was open to the air halfway round, with a colonnade of low pillars supporting round arches; the whole was covered by a roof which sloped upwards to a point. This building, which was composed of the sandstone of the neighbourhood, was covered on the outside with rich ornament in the Saracenic style, especially with the angular interlaced work, and round the cornice there ran a long inscription in Arabic characters. We saw some seven other tombs in the course of our exploration of the city, and they all resembled this in their general shape; but though equally high they were smaller in their ground plan, and consequently were more taper. In the upper chamber there was always a recess in the direction of Mecca. They bore a strong likeness to those we had seen at Kaiserieh, and those which we subsequently saw at Erzeroum. The one I have described stands on the outskirts of a large cemetery,

MOUNT SIPAN AND LAKE VAN.

in which were a number of tall headstones, some of them as much as ten or twelve feet high, carved with arabesque designs and Arabic inscriptions. These were of the same material and probably of the same date as the tombs.

At no great distance from this point towards the south-east by the seashore, is the inclosure now called Akhlat Kalessi, or the castle of Akhlat. This is a large rectangular fortress, measuring about 600 yards from the sea to the crest of the hill, and about 300 yards across. The walls which inclose it are massive, with towers at intervals, some round and some square; and it is entered by two gates, which stand opposite one another in the middle of the eastern and western walls. The shore-line seems to have been undefended; at least at the south-east angle where I examined it, there was no trace of anything more than a rude breastwork, which had evidently been thrown up at a later time. The principal buildings within it are two mosques of some antiquity, massively built, with little ornament. The rest of the area is occupied by fruit trees, in the midst of which stand ten inhabited cottages. In respect of their construction the walls much resemble those of the castle of Bitlis. While we were sketching these, the clouds began to gather on the summit of Sipan, and before long a heavy storm of thunder and lightning was raging round it, and threatened to descend upon us. Before it arrived we had taken shelter within the inclosure, and then it appeared in a different form from what we had expected, as a dry dust storm of the most obnoxious description, filling the whole air as it swept violently by. This continued for nearly half an hour, during which we regaled ourselves with the luscious little apricots that had fallen from the trees.

Returning now to the cemetery, we kept along the heights on the eastern side of the valley, overlooking the 'ruined city,' and when we had pursued these upwards for some distance, we scrambled steeply down and crossed to the cliffs opposite. At this point the effect of the sheer rocks, and the clear stream breaking into cascades, was extremely picturesque. On both sides there were numerous rock habitations, one of which on the eastern cliff was called Kara Keliseh, 'the black church,' while another opposite bore the name of Takht-i-Soliman, or 'Solomon's throne'—a widely spread appellation, which may be found at intervals from this place to the heart of Afghanistan. Thus the two great historical characters, whose fame has made the greatest impression on Western Asia, are found to be commemorated within a limited space in this remote region; Solomon, the embodiment of wisdom, being represented at Akhlat, and Alexander, the great conqueror, at Bitlis. The rock chambers resemble in most respects those of Cappadocia, and here too there are niches cut both in the walls of the habitations themselves, and on the face of the neighbouring cliffs, but these are much ruder, and the chambers do not open into one another. From this point we returned by a sloping path to the Gardens.

The history of Akhlat shows its great importance in former days, and at the same time illustrates in a remarkable way the vicissitudes to which all this country has been exposed. Its origin is unknown, but at an early period we find it existing as a leading

Armenian town, under the name of Khelat. During the ninth century of our era it was conquered by the Saracens, but the Imperial author, Constantine Porphyrogenitus, who wrote in the first half of the tenth century, states that in the reign of his predecessor, Leo VI. (the Philosopher), this and the neighbouring towns, or the emirs who held them, had been tributary to the Byzantine empire; adding that as they had since been lost, it was the duty of the emperor to regain them.[1] This was accomplished before the end of the same century, when after the eastern frontier had been gradually advanced by the great warriors, Nicephorus Phocas and John Zimisces, Basil the Second, who is more famous as the conqueror of the Bulgarians, made himself master of this country in 993 A.D. Afterwards Khelat fell into the hands of independent Kurdish chieftains, though at the time of Alp Arslan's invasion we find it occupied for the moment by a Turkish garrison; and here one of those curious contrasts of West and East presents itself, which are so characteristic of the Middle Ages, for the force which was detached by the Emperor Romanus IV. to besiege Akhlat, shortly before the fatal battle of Manzikert, was commanded by a Frank adventurer whose name is given by the Byzantine historians as Oursel, but was in reality Russel Baliol.[2] The Kurdish rule, however, became so oppressive, that after a time the inhabitants invited a Turkish adventurer to assist them and be their prince. He drove out the Kurds, and founded a

---

[1] *De Administr. Imp.* c. 44, vol. iii. p. 196, ed. Bonn. He writes the name Χλιάτ or Χαλιάτ.
[2] Finlay, *History of Greece* (new edit.), iii. 31.

Seljouk dynasty (A.D. 1099), taking the title of Shah Arman, 'king of Armenia.' The century that followed was the flourishing period of the greatness of the city, which henceforward bore the name of Akhlat; at the present day, as I found by inquiry, the Armenian name of Khelat is quite unknown. The castle of the upper town was the palace of these princes, and we may conjecture that the tombs and other monuments belong to this time. This coincides with the era of the three first Crusades, with the rule of the Comneni at Constantinople, and with the reigns of our two first Henrys.

In 1207 Akhlat was again seized by a Kurdish prince of the family of Saladin, who held it until 1245, when it was captured by the Mongol bands of Genghis Khan. During this interval it was three times besieged by Gelaleddin, khan of the Khoarasmians, which nation had founded a powerful empire on the shores of the Caspian. These sieges are an evidence both of the strength of the place and the severity of the climate. Gelaleddin's first attack was made in 1226, when he remained a long time before it, but was forced to withdraw for a while by a heavy fall of snow. Returning after a few days, he made several fruitless assaults, and ultimately raised the siege on account of the great cold. But at the end of 1229 he came and besieged it for the third time with greater success. On this occasion he attacked it from the side towards the lake with twenty military engines, and passed all the winter there. The siege was long and severe, and the inhabitants were reduced to great extremities, so that a pound of bread was sold for a gold piece. At last the city was carried at the point of the sword;[1] but Gelaleddin was forced to evacuate it not long after by Alaeddin, the Seljouk sultan of Iconium, after a bloody battle which is known as the battle of Akhlat.[2] The Mongols afterwards ceded it to a Georgian princess, called Thamtha, who had married a Kurdish chieftain, also of Saladin's family. At the end of the thirteenth century Abulfeda speaks of it as being regarded by some as the most famous town in Armenia; and in his description, which was derived from a native, compares it to Damascus in respect of its streams, and praises its gardens, though the climate, he says, was extremely cold. As to its size his authorities differ, one saying that it was a small city, another that it was as large as Damascus.[3] A hundred years later another geographer, Bakoui, describes it in the following terms: 'It is one of the principal towns of Armenia, and abounds in fruits, streams, and trees. Its inhabitants are partly Mussulman, partly Christian; they speak Persian, Armenian, and Turkish, and are clever locksmiths and workers in iron. The fish called *thamrikh* also comes from there, and is exported in great quantities.'[4] The place continued to be in the possession of Kurdish princes, who were sometimes independent, and sometimes acknowledged the suzerainty of the Turks, until at last it was incorporated in the pashalik of Van.[5]

[1] Deguignes, *Histoire générale des Huns, &c.* vol. ii. Pt. 2, p. 284.
[2] Finlay, *History of Greece* (new ed.), iv. 336.
[3] Abulfedae *Geographia*, in Büsching, *Magazin für die neue Historie und Geographie*, vol. v. p. 311.
[4] Bakoui's *Geography* in *Notices des Manuscrits de la Bibliothèque du Roi*, vol. ii. p. 513.
[5] Ritter, *Erdkunde*, x. 326–328; Saint-Martin, *Mémoires sur l'Arménie*, i. 103.

It is a difficult point to determine the relative date of the town and castle inland, and the walled inclosure or castle (Akhlat Kalessi) on the shore of the lake, and to decide which of them is spoken of at the period above mentioned. Ritter thinks that the upper town belongs to quite the earliest period, and that it was the latter of the two that was besieged by Gelaleddin; but this is hardly possible, for as the walls of this fortress reach to the water's edge, it would have required a flotilla to attack it from 'the side toward the lake.' Abulfeda, again, can hardly refer to it, as he speaks of the city walls as having been thrown down, whereas those of the lower castle are still almost perfect. If we regard him as meaning the upper town, the destruction of the walls may have been the result of Gelaleddin's siege, and this would partly explain the absence of any traces of a wall there at the present day. We may add that the narrow area of the lower castle forbids us to suppose that it can be the important city which was so famous in the Middle Ages, though at the same time the massiveness of the walls seems to imply that it is a place of some antiquity. In default of all direct evidence, I should be disposed to conjecture that this fortified enclosure was made in the convenient position it occupies by the lake after the original walls of the town fell into ruin—perhaps during the fourteenth century—and that this and the old town existed side by side; though it is not improbable that at a later period, when the population decreased, the inhabitants may have retired for safety within the fortification.

Leaving Akhlat, we now proceeded eastwards in

the direction of Adeljivas, which place lies immediately at the foot of Mount Sipan, on the edge of the lake. Our road lay behind the Kaleh, and when we had passed this, we reached a long grove of trees extending down to the shore, within which is concealed the village of Erkedan. A dense black storm once more shrouded all view of the mountain in front, and this the strong east wind, which had all the relaxing effect of a scirocco, was constantly threatening to bring down upon us. We proceeded notwithstanding, being emboldened by remembering how the bad weather had kept off during the morning; when all at once it burst upon us in a tempest of hail and violent rain, which continued for twenty minutes with unabated violence. At the end of that time we reached the Mahometan village of Tunuz, and though the storm had now cleared off, we were glad to remain there for the night. The rain was a new sensation to us, for with the exception of a few drops at Ladik, when we were on our way to Amasia, we had seen nothing of the kind since leaving Paris. Tunuz is prettily situated not far from the shore in the midst of a forest of fruit trees. We would gladly have pitched the tent in one of the orchards, but of this the violence of the wind did not allow; so we had to be content with a room, which formed in reality part of a large dark stable, though elevated a few steps above the ground. We carried our point that the cattle should not be quartered here alongside of us, though this had been the owner's original intention; and thus we passed a tolerable night, notwithstanding a rather overpowering effluvium.

The next morning opened bright and clear, but

the strong east wind still continued. The lake, along the northern shore of which we pursued our way, had now all the appearance of a sea, for its expanse was crested with white waves, and these, as they rolled in and broke on the rocks, dashing the spray into our faces, emitted a briny smell. In fact, the views throughout this part strongly resembled marine scenery from the massiveness of the cliffs and the absence of trees and shrubs, so that there was nothing of the softness which is usually associated with a lake. The gulls too, that floated on the surface or soared above it, contributed to the illusion; and our travelling servant, whose ideas on general geography were not very definite, shook his head doubtfully when we tried to persuade him that it was not an arm of the sea; indeed, I am not certain that he ever quite cleared up his views on this subject. From time to time, when we ascended the heights, we looked down the steep cliffs into graceful bays far below, where the blue water shoaled into clear green. In places the path was worn in the rocks, and was so slippery to the horses' feet that prudence suggested dismounting in order to avoid the risk of a broken leg, an accident not pleasant to contemplate in such remote regions. At last after four hours, as we were crossing a ridge which overhangs the water at a great elevation, we caught sight of the ruined castle of Adeljivaz below us on the edge of an open bay, where a steep rock rises to a height of 400 feet above the lake, crowned by a large keep. Between the foot of this and the water's edge run strong mediaeval walls, and wherever the edges of the cliffs are not absolutely precipitous, corresponding lines of fortification have been built, joining these to the upper castle. When we had descended to it, we found it to be in a very ruinous state, and the masonry appeared rough after that of the castle of Akhlat. Like that inclosure, it has two gates opposite one another in the two walls, and the space between them was so narrow, that we had passed in at one and out at the other within a few minutes. On the further side stood two rows of rough shanties, which may be dignified by the name of the street of the village; but the principal houses, as at Akhlat, are situated in the midst of gardens in the valley beyond, which, like all the other inhabited valleys in this part, is a mass of verdure.

In one of these gardens, about half a mile from the lake, stood the house of the kaimakam, and at a little distance off, separated from it by a clear rushing stream, was his place of business, a sort of police station, such as is usually found where these officials reside. To this we were conducted, and were soon comfortably lodged in its one apartment, which had a clay floor, a rough divan, four unglazed windows without shutters but protected by bars, and, as its sole furniture, a chest, which, we presumed, contained the archives, but anyhow it served us for a dining table. It was a most pleasant abode, being shaded by walnut trees, and refreshed by mountain breezes, with a sound of falling water close at hand. Here we deposited all but the lightest part of our luggage, and immediately proceeded to make inquiries about Sipan. We knew that it had been ascended from this point in 1838 by Mr. Brant, in company with Captain Glascott and Dr. Dickson, and we found that we could not do better than follow their route, proceeding at once to Norshunjuk, the highest inhabited village, in order to secure an early start the next morning. The kaimakam, a young Turk of European appearance, provided us with a zaptieh to conduct us thither. He also arranged to our satisfaction a new dispute that had arisen with our refractory katirjis, who wished to break their engagement with us and leave us in the lurch.

In the afternoon we started, lightly equipped, and rode up the valley behind the village. The first part of the way led through gardens and orchards, in the midst of turf and innumerable runlets of water; and the views which we obtained looking back might recall many of the peeps of the Mediterranean from the valleys of the Riviera, if you take poplars to stand for cypresses, for now the mountains on the opposite shore of the lake were obscured by mist, and there seemed hardly any limit to its expanse. The upper castle of Adeljivaz on its massive rock formed a striking object on the right hand of the picture. But as soon as we emerged from the cultivated ground all was changed. Nothing was now seen but the barest hillsides, except where a small Armenian monastery stood high up in a side valley, surrounded by a square wall, with a whitewashed church and pointed belfry. Thus far Sipan had not been visible, for Adeljivas lies too close at its foot to allow of its being seen from thence; but when at last we reached the summit of a steep ridge, it burst upon us close at hand in full detail, being separated from us only by a wide upland valley, deeply sunk in the heart of the mountain, at the further end of which lay the village of Norshunjuk. Though in its upper parts it has too much of the uniform shape of a volcano to be strikingly beautiful, yet there is much grandeur in its steep slopes and the massiveness of its form. The dip into which we now descended was mostly covered with pasture land, but in the neighbourhood of the village a large quantity of corn was grown, and yellow heaps of grain were conspicuous among the mud hovels. This was a remarkable sight, for the elevation of the place is not much less than 7,000 feet above the sea.

Our resting-place proved to be a mass of dust, and its Armenian inhabitants were a set of rude mountaineers, and excessively inquisitive; this, however, was hardly surprising, when so unwonted guests made their appearance on the scene. Among them we were not gratified at seeing a Circassian; he was the first of that race whom we had met with in Armenia, and his presence struck us as being an ill-omened sight. The pitching of the tent became an embarrassing operation owing to the number that crowded round to look on. Several of them said they had ascended the mountain, as did also our zaptieh, but his replies to questions were so evasive that we were unwilling to entrust ourselves to his guidance, and the statements of the others also we discounted liberally, knowing how very vague the views of persons on this subject are apt to be. Ultimately we agreed to take the head man of the village, whose name was Chaspar, for our guide, and he proved a genial companion and a good walker, but afterwards confessed that he had never reached the summit. The next question was about the course to be followed. The general opinion was in favour of the southern face of the mountain, and this appeared to correspond to the route which Mr. Brant had taken; but the east wind was still violent, and if it should continue, it threatened to rake this line of approach with tremendous effect. Accordingly we traced out a promising route along the western side towards what appeared to be the highest point, and persuaded our guide both of its intrinsic merit, and of the importance of following it on the morrow—wrongly, in all probability, for no one is aware of the difficulties of any particular line of ascent until he has tried it; and certainly ineffectually, for in the night time our native was fully at liberty to indulge his natural propensity *stare super antiquas vias*. Fortunately for us the wind moderated, and caused us hardly any inconvenience.

Our mountain expedition was once more favoured by a brilliant full moon, for a month had elapsed since we ascended Argaeus, and again the sky was perfectly cloudless. We started at three o'clock in the morning. At first the lake behind us was dimly seen in the moonlight, but the view of it enlarged as we mounted upwards. Our way lay over rough slopes, covered with stones and low-growing plants, and the ascent was gradual at its commencement, but became more steep as we proceeded. At half-past four the daylight began to appear, and half an hour later the sun was gilding the ridges above us. In one place we found the footprints and other recent traces of a bear—we had heard of these animals as frequenting the mountain before leaving the village—and we also put up some flocks of quails, and several partridges, which were unconscious of the import of the day to their brethren in England, for it was the first of September. Higher up the ground was strewn with large blocks of black obsidian, the surface of which resembles polished coal. The flowers were almost entirely over, but some pretty pink Alpine asters were still in blossom. It was a rugged climb, though nowhere difficult, and thus far I had mounted to the best of my ability, but at last I was forced to confess to myself that my walking powers had forsaken me. This was the result of numerous nights of sleeplessness or broken rest throughout the journey, by which I had been seriously weakened. My wind was still good, and my legs strong, but I simply had not the force to carry me on. Under these circumstances I begged my companion, who was in good condition, to press on with the guide towards the summit, leaving me to follow at my leisure. In this way I ultimately reached the ridge which we had seen from below.

Great was my satisfaction at doing so, for here the whole character of the mountain was revealed to me. Below me towards the north lay a large and perfect crater with no break in its wall of circuit, about three-quarters of a mile wide and 500 feet deep, the bottom of which was partly occupied by a green pear-shaped lake. This was fed by a stream flowing from vast masses of snow, which sloped at a very steep angle from beneath my feet to the base of the depression; in the upper part of one of these there was a large crevasse full of water, which gave the snow-field the appearance of a glacier. The lake has no visible outlet; and though Chaspar maintained that its waters reappear and find their way down the south-western side of the mountain, yet, as we have seen in examining the ancient legends about the Tigris, the human mind is sure to discover an escape for waters, even where none exists. On the opposite side of the crater there rose on the left front a number of small peaks, forming the summits of a long ridge, that sloped in parts towards the basin; and on the right front a broad tower-like mass of rock, also crowned by a number of conical points. These two were joined by a line of cliffs covered with much talus, on the further side of which lies another snow-basin, bounded by peaks still more distant. Thus the upper region of Sipan is much more truly volcanic in its appearance than that of Argaeus, which has no marked crater remaining; but this is not the case with its lower part. There are indeed several fairly well defined craters about the foot of this mountain, and one round lake called Aghir Gheul, on which you look down from above in the direction of the lake of Van, evidently occupies a basin of this character, but there is no such belt of volcanic cones as encircles the Cappadocian mountain. The view from the ridge over the lake commands all the western inlet towards Tadvan, and all the broad bay that extends southwards to the city of Van, together with the mountains of Kurdistan behind, and even beyond these some still more distant, probably in the direction of the country of the Nestorian Christians; but all this as I saw it was much obscured by mist, which detracted from the beauty of the scene. The appearance of the lower slopes of Sipan was exceedingly bare, not a tree being visible anywhere.

It was not easy to decide from the point where I stood which is the real summit of the mountain.

It was evidently to be found in one of the two groups of peaks I have described, but here they appeared to be of about equal elevation. We had hitherto supposed it to be the north-westernmost point, for that had been constantly in view as we approached from the side towards Akhlat; and for this accordingly Mr. Crowder made. Descending along the inner face of the crater towards the left to a depth of about 200 feet, he then ascended again at the foot of these peaks, and finally reached the highest after an hour's good walking. As seen from thence, the opposite peaks towards the east appeared to him somewhat higher, and the view of the mountain which we obtained when afterwards crossing the lake, left but little doubt upon the subject. The latter group was the one which Mr. Brant and his companions ascended, and they seem not to have questioned that they arrived at the highest point.[1] On the northern flanks of the mountain, Mr. Crowder reported great masses of snow to be lying. The view in that direction was even more obscured by mist than that towards the lake, but one object *was* visible. This was Ararat, which stood up above everything else to the north-east, in shape like a truncated cone, deeply covered with snow; the lesser Ararat was hidden. The north-western peak of Sipan proved to be 400 feet higher than the rim of the crater which I reached, but the absolute height of the mountain is more difficult to determine. Mr. Brant estimated it approximately at from 9,500 to 10,000 feet, but Sir Henry Layard observed, when he was in this neighbourhood, that this calculation seemed to

---

[1] Brant in *Geog. Soc. Journal*, x. p. 409.

be under the mark.[1] My aneroid marked 12,600 on the north-western summit, but this was probably too high, for the aneroid, however good the instrument may be, when once it has been subjected to low pressure, as this one was for the first time on Argaeus, is apt not to recover itself, and consequently its subsequent readings of heights are in excess.[2] But to one who looks at Sipan from the lake, which is itself more than 5,000 feet above the sea, it seems almost impossible that it should be only 5,000 feet higher;[3] in fact, from Norshunjuk the summit appears to rise fully that height above, and that village, as I have said, is not much under 7,000 feet. To this I may add, that the time occupied by Mr. Crowder in his steady ascent—four and a half hours to the ridge, and five and a half to the summit—implies at least that elevation. From all this I conclude that we shall not be far wrong in estimating it as 12,000 feet.

I was quietly descending, when my companion

[1] Brant, as above, p. 411; Layard, *Nineveh and Babylon*, p. 15. Mr. Brant was unable to use his barometer, as it was out of order.

[2] My friend Mr. Tuckett, who has had excellent opportunities of testing this instrument, writes to me: 'So far as my experience goes, the heights determined by aneroid readings are almost invariably in excess of the true ones—at any rate after some ascents have been made with the instrument, which being slow in recovering its elasticity after being subjected to low pressure, and in fact never doing so altogether, develops by successive increments a very considerable minus error. Its readings being thus too low, the resultant height comes out too high.' At the same time I should remark that our estimates of lower elevations throughout this journey, as high as the level of the lake of Van, were usually less than those of former travellers, where we had the opportunity of comparison.

[3] Most travellers who have judged by the eye have attributed to Sipan a height of 11,000 or 12,000 feet: see Shiel in *Geog. Soc. Journal*, viii. 60; Wilbraham's *Travels in the Trans-Caucasian Provinces of Russia, &c.* p. 341.

and the guide overtook me. We intended to have returned by the same route which we had followed during our ascent, but unfortunately Chaspar lost his way, and conducted us over rugged mountain sides and rocky slopes, such as no mountaineer loves at the end of an expedition. At last we reached Norshunjuk at noon, where we were soon refreshed by a bath and copious draughts of milk, for there was hardly a trace of water on the stony parched declivities. In the afternoon, as we rode down to Adeljivas, the heavy thunderstorms that gathered over the lake reminded us that we had done well in devoting the early part of the day to our excursion. In conclusion, I may mention the legends which former travellers report as having grown up round this mountain. One of these, which is found among the Kurds, turns on the name. According to this, the ark touched this mountain before resting on Ararat, upon which Noah exclaimed, ' Subhanu-llah ! ' (Praise be to God !), which expression has been converted into Sipan.[1] This story, however, apart from what refers to the name, is not confined to this mountain, for it is told also of Argaeus by those who live in its neighbourhood. Another tradition relates, ' that a large city existed on the very spot where the mountain now stands ; that the inhabitants were so buried in sin that the Almighty caused three mountains to move from the east, the north, and the south, and suspended them above the devoted city. The inhabitants, however, were so blind to their impending ruin, that they mistook the dark mass which hung

---

[1] Shiel in *Geog. Soc. Journal*, viii. 61; cp. Wilbraham, *Travels in the Trans-Caucasian Provinces of Russia, &c.* p. 340.

above their heads for a thunder-cloud, and their destruction came upon them unawares. Subterranean passages are said still to exist beneath the mountain, by which some daring adventurers have succeeded in penetrating into the heart of the buried city.'[1] Perhaps, as Ritter suggests, this latter legend may have been suggested by some outburst of volcanic agency, and by hollows in the earth.[2]

We had now reached a critical point in our journey. As the objects of interest about the lake of Van lie partly on its northern, partly on its southern shore, we perceived, when we were planning our journey before leaving England, that much time would be saved if we could manage to cross the lake; the only other alternative being to make the circuit of it, and this would occupy four or five days. I discovered that one traveller had crossed it many years ago in a boat, but it appeared that the natives only made such voyages in the finest weather. When inquiring about this point at Constantinople from Mr. Baldwin, the secretary of the American Missions, we learnt from him that the missionaries at Van had lately had a small steamer sent out to them in pieces for use on the lake, and that they hoped to put it together and launch it this summer; but whether they had accomplished this he was not aware. While we were at Bitlis, Mr. Knapp telegraphed for us to his associates at Van, to request—not the use of the steamer, that seemed to us too daring—but that a boat might be sent across to meet us at Adeljivas by a certain day. That day had now arrived, but no boat had appeared. By great good luck, however, there

---

[1] Wilbraham, as above.   [2] *Erdkunde*, ix. 977.

happened now to be a native boat at the little port—a rare occurrence, for there is no traffic from here, and passing vessels rarely find it worth their while to touch—and its owners agreed to take us across to Van for a tolerably high remuneration, if we required it. But the question was not yet wholly solved, for the wind was still strong, and until it abated the sailors altogether refused to attempt the voyage. In consequence of this we were forced to remain at Adeljivas the day after our descent from Sipan—a delay which we should have had little cause to regret owing to the pleasantness of the place, had there not been a possibility of our being detained as prisoners for an indefinite time.

During the day we descended from our umbrageous residence to the lake, in order to bathe and to visit the ruins of the old town. The two lines of walls which I have already described, run down at their extremity for some distance into the water, thus forming substantial piers; from the extremity of one of these we were able to plunge, and the water proved to be not merely brackish, but decidedly salt.[1] It is clear that there could have been no navy on the lake in ancient times, for here, as at Akhlat, there was no sea-wall. The width of the inclosure at the shore, when paced, proved to be 250 yards. Within it one ancient mosque with a minaret remains, and also part of another considerable building. The mosque, which is now used as a storehouse for corn, appears to be of the same date as those in the castle of Akhlat; it is massively built

[1] Captain (Sir R.) Wilbraham speaks of the water as being far bitterer to the taste than that of the Caspian. *Travels*, p. 342.

of stone, with but little ornament, and its arches are pointed and slightly ogived. This lower inclosure between the foot of the rock and the lake must have been the town as distinguished from the castle above; at the present day it contains a few poor dwellings. Of the history of the place little is known, in fact its ancient name is not certainly determined. But as Constantine Porphyrogenitus, when enumerating the fortresses in this part of the country, mentions Khelat, Aljike, Arzes, and Perkri,[1] and the first of these is now Akhlat, and the third Ardjish on the north-eastern arm of the lake, while the last, at the head of that arm, retains its old name almost unchanged, it is difficult to avoid identifying the second, Aljike, with Adeljivas, especially when we consider the partial similarity of the names. I may notice in passing, that in Bitlis and some other places, we regularly heard the place called Aljiwas. Now Aljike ('Αλτζίκε) seems to be the same as the Armenian town of Ardzge,[2] which is a different place from Ardjish; and this again corresponds to the Ardje ("Αρτζε) of Cedrenus.[3] As this historian mentions that Ardje was besieged and taken by the Turks during the early period of the Seljouk invasions, we must suppose that Adeljivas was the scene of that occurrence.

We also obtained further information about the Circassians in this neighbourhood, for we noticed some of them here as we had already done at Norshunjuk. It appears that several colonies of that race are settled about on the mountain side, and the

[1] Constant. Porphyr. *De Administr. Imp.* cap. xliv. vol. iii. pp. 194 *seq.* ed. Bonn.
[2] Saint-Martin, *Mémoires sur l'Arménie*, i. 105.
[3] *Hist. Compend.* vol. ii. p. 577, ed. Bonn.

Armenian peasants complain that both they and the Kurds are constantly stealing from them. While we were at Norshunjuk the place was full of a story of a girl from the village, who had been carried off by a Circassian on the morning of the day on which we arrived (August 31) during the absence of her relations. These latter immediately on hearing of it went in search of her to a neighbouring Circassian village, and on the following morning the heads of that village came over to make inquiries, but up to the time of our departure no clue had been discovered. Deeds like this are the natural effect of a number of men fully armed being planted in the midst of an unarmed population; in fact, the first condition of an improvement in the position of the people in Turkey is that all should be disarmed; or, if that cannot be in this wild region, that all should be allowed to carry arms, without distinction of race or creed.

On the morning of the 3rd the wind had dropped, and our boatmen sent word that they were ready to start, so we prepared at once for our departure. Having placed our baggage on two asses, which we hired for the purpose, we made our way to the lake, where we found the boat attached to the pier from which we had bathed. It was about 30 feet long, and of very rough construction, but better than I had anticipated, for at all events it was not flat-bottomed like the one that Colonel Shiel saw in process of building on the shore of the lake.[1] The sides were very high, and in the forepart stood a mast with a long yard for a lateen sail, while the stern was occupied by a small

[1] Shiel, as above, p. 64.

poop on which two persons could sit, one of them steering. The boatmen, however, had not yet arrived, and it was not until the zaptieh who accompanied us to Norshunjuk had gone in quest of them, that they at last presented themselves. Even then much remained to be done before we could start. One of them had to swarm up the mast, to put the sail-rope through a hole in the top of it. Then one of the oars proved to be out of order, and the blade, which was formed of a flat piece separate from the rest, had to be fastened on with pegs, after which it was secured by a cord passed through a number of holes by the help of a large packing-needle. However, at last we were off. Our company consisted, besides our two selves and our servant, of the two sailors, and two stalwart young Turks of the lower class, who were allowed to make the voyage gratis. One of these was a handsome fellow, and something of a dandy withal, for his eyelids were unpleasantly stained with henna. We were not far from land, when a Turkish captain appeared on the beach with his wife, servant, and baggage, and demanded to be taken on board also; but this was too much, and we were obliged to leave him behind, violently gesticulating.

At first there was but little breeze, and that little was not in our favour, so we were forced to make our way along the shore by rowing; but after we had reached a slight headland a gentle wind sprang up and carried us out towards the middle of the lake. The view of Sipan now became remarkably fine, and as we proceeded we could see more clearly than from the western side that the summit is truncated, and has thoroughly the form of a crater. Undoubtedly from here the eastern summit appears to be the highest, and the boatmen said it was so. When we asked them about the little round lake near its foot, on which we had looked down from above, they told us that its name is not Agri Gheul (Painful Pool)—as Kiepert, following the authority of Brant,[1] gives it in his map—but Aghir Gheul, i.e. 'slow' or 'motionless' lake. They added, quite gravely, that from time to time there emerge from it wonderful horses with six legs, though in other respects resembling ordinary horses, except that they live under the water. They had often been seen, but none had ever been caught, for they at once retired when watched by any number of persons. These sailors were Armenians, and one of them, we discovered to our surprise, could speak a little Greek; this he had learnt at Constantinople, where he had been employed in a barber's shop at different intervals, once for five, and afterwards for four years. The boat belonged to Van, and it was only by accident they had come to Adeljivas—a lucky accident for us. They declared—and this is very generally believed—that there are no fish in the lake, but only at the mouths of the streams which flow into it, where the fishery takes place in the spring. Dr. Reynolds, however, one of the Americans at Van, assured me that when riding on high ground above the lake, he had seen numbers in the clear water, and, as Mr. Brant has well remarked, their existence is proved by the presence of cormorants and other water-birds which live only on fish. Whether the lake fish are the same as those in the rivers, Dr. Reynolds did not know. The latter, which

---

[1] Brant, as above, p. 410.

are caught in basket-traps, are about the size of a herring. They are salted for exportation.

Between sailing and rowing we made gradual progress during the day. There was very little motion, and yet our Turkish fellow-passengers were sea-sick. The gnats or small flies that gathered about us were so numerous as to be quite a phenomenon; they settled so thickly on the sail as to look like soot, and the rudder appeared to have a covering of felt. A tack was always followed by an unpleasant disturbance of insect life. Towards evening the wind fell, and the views of the grand mountains encircling the calm expanse of the lake were most beautiful, as the sun set in the midst of gold-fringed clouds over its western end. In that direction the great Nimrud Dagh stood up conspicuous, appearing no longer as a ridge, but as a single mountain. We were now approaching the southern shore of the lake at the entrance of the bay which leads up to Van, just where a little rocky island called Anabad lies off the coast, with a monastery of St. George at the foot of its cliffs—a picturesque place, for the buildings were prettily grouped together round a white cupola. Here our boatmen proposed that we should stop for the night, and the spot was a tempting one, but we still had hopes of reaching Van, and accordingly determined to proceed. Between the island and the mainland ran a reef, where the water was so shallow that they found it necessary to wade in order to get us over; this was accomplished with some skill, and altogether throughout the voyage they showed more seamanship than we had expected of them. However, when we had gone some distance further, they said they were tired and could row no longer; so, as the breeze did not seem likely to rise again, we put to shore, and having fastened our boat by a rope to a big stone in true Homeric style, pitched our tent upon the shingly beach. A romantic solitude it was, as we sat there in the moonlight, not a little satisfied at having solved the problem of crossing the lake.

The next morning after a bathe and breakfast we continued our voyage. In our wake followed five sailing-boats, heavily laden, which proved that the amount of communication by water is not as small as has been supposed. They came from Ardjish, on the north-eastern arm of the lake, which is the greatest corn-growing neighbourhood in these parts, and like ourselves were making for Van. Gradually the lofty mountains of Kurdistan which back the southern side of the lake revealed themselves in fuller detail, and at last our eager eyes caught sight of the rock on which the famous castle is built. After four hours' sailing before a gentle breeze we reached the landing-place of Avanz, a mean little harbour with a small jetty, which is distant about a mile from the city; within it several boats resembling our own were lying. A curious mass of rock rises immediately above it, and commands a most striking view. In front stretches a level plain, which from its appearance must be marshy in parts during the winter, and beyond this rises the solitary castle-rock, the slopes of which on this side are defended by a succession of irregular walls, while its long outline is diversified by towers and other fortifications, and a minaret. Both to left and right of it runs a dark green line, marking the course of a stream through the plain, the waters of which are shaded by poplars and other trees; and in the background stands up the steep mass of the Varak Dagh, a serrated mountain of splendid form, which dominates the view. We found that we were expected, for an Armenian boatman in the service of the American missionaries was on the look-out for us; so we hired two donkeys that were waiting there to carry our baggage, and proceeded on foot under his guidance to the city.

CHAPTER XIII.

VAN.

Situation of Van—Its appearance and population—The great inscription—Telegrams in Turkey—A Christian assistant-governor—Castle of Van—Naphtha well—View from the summit—Excavated chambers—The caves of Khorkhor—The cuneiform inscriptions—Object of the rock chambers—Unhealthiness of Van—History of the city—Moses of Chorene's account of its foundation—Legends of Semiramis—Assyrian influence—Later history—Timour's siege—Difficulty in obtaining horses—Armenian ponies—Lake of Artschag—Karakenduz—First view of Ararat—Head of Lake Van—Pergri.

THE castle-rock of Van is about two-thirds of a mile in length, and 300 feet in height, running nearly due east and west, and standing quite alone in the plain. At either end it rises by a gradual ascent, with a slight depression in the ridge on both sides of the long and nearly level summit; in this way its outline seems to be divided into three parts, of which the two lateral heights are crowned by forts, and the central one by a castle, the walls of which are dressed with unbaked bricks and 'cob.' Colonel Shiel appropriately likens it to a camel's hump. On the northern side, which faces the lake, the slopes though steep are not abrupt, but in the opposite direction the cliffs fall in sheer precipices from top to bottom throughout its whole length, forming, as seen from that side, a most imposing wall, the like of which it would not be easy to find elsewhere. The city, which is in shape an irregular oblong, lies entirely beneath this, towards the south, and consequently is not seen from the opposite side; it is not of great extent, and is inclosed by two lines of Turkish walls with tall battlements. The famous inscriptions are found for the most part on this side of the cliff, and the most important of all occupies an inaccessible position half-way down the precipice; but there are some too on the rocks which face the lake. The rock-hewn chambers, also, are entered through openings which overlook the city.

When we had crossed the plain, we reached the gate which stands at the western foot of the rock— Iskele-kapousi, or Gate of the Port, it is called—and entering the city, passed round to the southern side. The houses are for the most part built of sun-dried bricks, which give the streets rather a poor aspect; through these we were conducted nearly the whole length of the place, gazing as we went along at the marvellous line of precipitous cliffs which rose on our left, in some parts surmounted by fortifications. The inhabitants whom we met—Turks in large turbans and flowing robes, wild-looking Kurds in sheepskin jackets, and Persians in tall felt hats—appeared the most old-world people we had seen anywhere in Turkey. At length we stopped at the shop of a chemist connected with the mission—the missionaries themselves were not in town—and after some delay he obtained for us a clean room in the house of an Armenian gentleman not far off. From a wooden balcony which ran partly round a small court in the interior of this house, we could see high above us on the cliff the great inscription of which I have spoken. This vast tablet with its numerous lines of cuneiform letters, as it lies outspread on the face of the rock, has been compared to a sheet of the 'Times' newspaper, and no description could give a better idea of it. Strange indeed it is to behold such a work in such a position, completely inaccessible both from above and from below. The inscription is trilingual, being written in three parallel columns, and is much later in date than the other inscriptions which are found here. It commemorates the exploits of Xerxes the son of Darius, and is very nearly word for word the same as those of that king at Hamadan and Persepolis.[1] When it was copied, a telescope was required to read it.

During the afternoon we received a welcome visit from Dr. Reynolds, the medical man of the mission, and Captain Clayton, our newly-appointed vice-consul, who had heard of our arrival, and had ridden in from the suburbs to welcome us. The non-appearance of the boat at Adeljivas was now explained. The telegram from Bitlis had arrived in a half-unintelligible form, and was interpreted as a request for the use of the missionaries' steamer. Now that steamer had been launched, and had made a trip on the lake—we had heard of her as being seen by the natives on the opposite side—but her engine soon required repair, and at present she was unserviceable. They had not thought of sending any other boat, as that did not seem to form part of our request. This was not the first instance we had met with of incorrectness and irregularity in the Turkish telegrams. A gentleman at Bitlis informed me that on one occasion when he had sent one, a fortnight elapsed before

[1] Layard, *Nineveh and Babylon*, p. 394.

the reply came. Captain Clayton said that he had lately received one from Erzeroum, but he doubted whether he more than half understood it. When Major Kamsaragan, the Russian vice-consul, who had arrived here subsequently to Captain Clayton, left Erzeroum on his way hither, he telegraphed his coming the day before he started from that place, but his telegram did not arrive until the day after he reached Van. In passing through the country I had often admired the completeness of the Turkish telegraph system, as I saw the wires stretching along through remote and almost uninhabited regions, and had attributed much credit to the Government for the way in which it had been carried out; but the results are a satire on its management. Like most other schemes in Turkey, it has been elaborate in conception, expensive in execution, and almost barren of practical utility. Before our visitors departed, it was arranged that they should accompany us to inspect the castle on the morrow; and thus we had the satisfaction of feeling that we should see without let or hindrance a place to which many had been denied admittance. Most of the earlier travellers, as Shiel, Monteith, and Wilbraham, had been unable to see the interior; and even comparatively lately (in 1864, I believe) Mr. Ussher was not permitted to enter.

At the appointed hour the next morning our friends appeared, accompanied by a goodly company, including Major Kamsaragan, and a number of natives of some position, headed by the Mouaveen, or Christian assistant-governor. Strange to say, though some of these gentlemen had resided several years in Van, none of them had ever visited the castle, so it was altogether a great occasion. The Major was a small wiry man, with a bright eye and very dark complexion, and a lively cheery manner, who spoke Armenian and Turkish fluently—Russian also, I suppose, though of this we heard nothing—but no language of Western Europe. This seemed surprising in a Russian officer, but was accounted for by his being an Armenian by birth. Whether he could put in a claim to royal blood I do not know, but his name is a famous one in early Armenian history, for the Gamsaragans were a branch of the Arsacidae. The Mouaveen, who had already paid us a complimentary visit before breakfast, was a pleasant gentlemanly man, who had resided some years in Western Europe, and spoke both French and Italian well. He was an Armenian, and acted as assistant to the pasha, for here and in some other places an officer of this kind has been appointed as a means of communication—'buffer' was the uncomplimentary expression we heard applied to him—between the Christians and the Turkish authorities. He is supposed to have much power, but in reality, we were assured, has very little, so that he is not much more than a convenient agent of the governor. However, his position has this advantage, that he is only removable by the central Government at Constantinople, and not at the will of the pasha for the time being.

We now started for the castle under the guidance of a common soldier, who was said to have lived there ten years, and to be well acquainted with its antiquities; about these, however, we found remarkable ignorance to prevail. On the way I obtained what information I could on general topics from the Mouaveen. He said the city contains 30,000 inhabitants, of whom three-fourths are Armenians. On account of the nearness of the Persian frontier, which is only sixteen hours (about fifty miles) off, there is a garrison of 400 soldiers—an unusually large number, for we found Armenia, as well as Asia Minor, at this time almost denuded of troops. As to the population of Armenia at large, he said the Kurds and Armenians were about equal in number, if the nomad Kurds were included, but that in estimates made in the country itself they were not usually calculated. The entire number of Protestant Armenians was about 30,000. He expressed a warm regard for the American residents, adding that though at first there were differences between the Protestants and the members of the Armenian Church, yet now all, including the higher clergy, liked the missionaries, because they felt they did so much good to the cause of the Armenians. This corresponded to what I had heard elsewhere; in fact, the only person from whom I received a contrary opinion was the priest at Surp Garabed of Mush (Changeli), who was one of the following of the Armenian Patriarch at Constantinople. When I questioned him on the subject, it was not without a feeling of humour, as I was sure from his position what his reply must be. 'Do you think the Protestants do harm or good?' I said. 'They certainly do not do good,' he answered; 'their influence is owing to the destitution of the country.' The Mouaveen confirmed what I had heard on the spot about the quartering of the Kurds on the Christian peasants during the winter in the plain of Mush; and generally, as may be supposed, he gave a distressing account of the sufferings of the Armenians.

We entered the outer fortifications of the castle at the western end, close to the Iskele-Kapousi, through which we had passed on the previous day. The wall in this part is composed of immense blocks of stone, evidently of ancient construction, and other courses of masonry at the base of the fortifications on the ridge of the cliff are also massive, and apparently of the same date. These blocks are attributed by the people to Semiramis, for in old Armenian books, the Mouaveen said—referring no doubt to Moses of Chorene—Van was called Shemiramagerd, or the City of Semiramis. Ascending the hill by a sloping road along its northern side, we came to the inner line of fortifications, and just inside this were conducted to a curious narrow hole running down vertically into the rock. A pole somewhat resembling a huge ladle was now brought, and thrust deep into it, and when this reappeared, it was covered with a brown half-liquid mixture, which looked like treacle, but was in reality naphtha; the hole was the entrance to a naphtha well. After this we reached the ridge, and mounted along it to a point close to the summit, where was the commandant's house; here we were forced to wait, while the inevitable coffee was handed to the whole company. The panorama from the highest point was enchanting, for on the one side lay the expanse of the blue sparkling lake, with its circuit of mountains, among which Sipan and the Nimrud Dagh were conspicuous, while in the opposite direction the broken Varak Dagh formed a noble object on the further side of the plain. In one of the upper valleys of the last-named mountain lies an important monastery, which is the residence of the archbishop, and has a good school. Towards the west, close to the shore of the lake, an island with a peaked rock was pointed out to us as Akhtamar, once the seat of a rival patriarchate in opposition to that of Etchmiadzin; here during the war two years previously Dr. Reynolds and his family took refuge, as fears were entertained that the city might be sacked by the Kurds. The town at our feet, as we looked down the wonderful precipices on to it, was itself a remarkable sight from the roofs being universally flat, except here and there, where round-domed mosques and a few minarets appeared. The beauty of the views which thus met us at every turn greatly enhanced the pleasure of visiting the castle and its antiquities. Near the summit we saw a number of old bronze cannons, some of which were curiously ornamented; and most of them were marked on the muzzle with a broad arrow, which is said to signify that they are no longer fit for use. Several were lying on the ground, and only a few were mounted on carriages. Among those still in use there was one that we regarded with feelings the reverse of friendly, for during this Ramazan season it was fired off at intervals during the night just over our heads, to the detriment of our slumbers. The last report was especially obnoxious, as it came just two hours before sunrise, being intended to warn the faithful to prepare their last meal before the fast commences.

We now descended for a little distance, and rounding the eastern face of the cliff, reached a recess on its southern side, where the surface of the rock was smoothed, and a sort of terrace had been made in front of it. Here was a square-headed portal opening into an excavated chamber with a round barrel vault, the dimensions of which may be roughly estimated as 25 feet in height, 30 feet in length, and 20 in width; from this again four dark chambers open inwards, two from the long side opposite the entrance, and one from either end. In order to explore these, tapers had to be lighted, for the daylight only enters through the single outer doorway. In one of the chambers two niches had been cut in the stone, but there was nowhere any sign of ornament; still, the amount of labour expended on the work must have been very great, owing to the extreme hardness of the calcareous rock. Returning to the outer air, we were conducted to the entrance of another large chamber close by, where the *subterranea* were still more elaborate in their arrangement; for not only do three other chambers open from the first one, two at the sides and one in front, but from the one in front, the entrance of which faces the outer portal, three others open into the heart of the rock with a similar arrangement. The work throughout these is very careful, but there are no inscriptions, either within, or on the neighbouring cliff. The floors of some of them were covered with large stone cannon balls, over which we had to pick our way in order to penetrate further in; when I asked how these came there, the soldiers who accompanied us answered, with a power of anachronism which was almost grand, that they were of the time of Semiramis. As I stood, three chambers deep, within the innermost of these recesses, which was faintly lighted by the taper of a zaptieh, and looked out towards the first hall, where the rest of the company were standing near the door by which the sunlight entered, the scene was worthy of the pencil of Rembrandt.

Returning next along the northern slopes, we noticed at one point a cuneiform inscription built into the wall, and then descending on the outer side of the Itch Kaleh or inner castle, reached a point in the ridge about half-way between the Iskele-kapousi and the summit, at a considerably lower elevation than the terrace which we had just left. Here numerous steps are cut in the side of the rock, and the rock itself has been levelled so as to make a small platform. From this a polished staircase descends the southern face of the cliff, for some twenty feet, and so steep it was that some of the party declined to come, and the hand of a soldier was welcome while clambering in slippery boots along the edge of the precipice. Here the vertical rocks, which are brownish in colour with red stains, had been smoothed into a glassy surface, and on this were engraved several cuneiform inscriptions of the most elaborate finish, still retaining their original sharpness, though parts had been defaced, apparently by some projectile which had struck them in the course of one of the many sieges which this castle has sustained. At the foot of the stairs is the entrance to another group of chambers, which former travellers have called Khorkhor Mugaralari, or the caves of Khorkhor; but this title had been forgotten, though the Mouaveen said that a garden immediately below bore the name of Khorkhor. The main hall, which is first entered, is about equal in dimensions to the former of the two that I have described, but the roof instead of being arched is flat. In different parts of the side walls are ten large niches, and opposite the entrance towards the left there are steps in the upper part of the wall leading to the roof; what object these could have served is not clear, but it looks as if they must have supported some wooden platform or other temporary erection. In the face of the wall there are holes at intervals, and these may possibly have been intended for the same purpose, but it is more likely that they received the fastenings of metal plates like those which we have noticed at Amasia. From the hall lead four inner chambers of exquisitely polished stone on the same plan as the former ones, only in all of these there are niches; the one on the left leads again into a further recess, which is smaller and descends to a lower level. By throwing down a stone I discovered that it was not very deep, but otherwise it was impossible to estimate it, for the darkness was so great that a taper did not suffice to illuminate it, and this the numerous bats that were flying about threatened to extinguish. On the wall of the main chamber opposite the entrance was inscribed the name of M. Texier, the famous French traveller.

Leaving this extraordinary place we once more passed through the outer fortifications, and descending to the plain followed the foot of the hill on its northern side. Here about half-way along, at a point where the rock fell inwards, were three tablets bearing cuneiform inscriptions; and beyond these some way up the hillside, were two arched recesses in the rock, in the easternmost of which stands another inscription. Continuing our walk, we at last re-entered the city by its eastern gate, having thus made a complete circuit of the castle height.

Let me now add a few remarks on the cuneiform inscriptions. Besides those that remain on the rock itself, others have been found in the neighbourhood of the city, and also at various points on the shores of the lake, and elsewhere in the south of Armenia, as for instance at Palu. With the exception, however, of the Xerxes inscription, and one or two others, they remain a riddle to philologists. They were first copied by Schulz in 1827; in fact, our knowledge of them may be said to be due to that intelligent explorer.[1] From the time that they became known through him, various attempts have been made to discover their meaning, but hitherto these have been unsuccessful. Though the Assyrian character has been employed, the language is certainly not Assyrian, and consequently we are driven to the conclusion that this mode of writing was borrowed by another people who used it to represent the sounds of their own tongue. A further difficulty arises in determining who this people were. The attempt has been made to prove that they were the ancestors of the present Armenian population, but the latest authorities discountenance this view, and are inclined to think that the language is more closely connected with the modern Georgian than with any other, and that though it is mixed with Aryan elements, yet these do not predominate. Those who spoke it, therefore,

---

[1] Schulz's paper on the subject, which was published together with his transcriptions after his lamented death, is in the *Journal Asiatique* for April, May, and June 1840, pp. 260–323. He was murdered by the Kurds in 1830.

were distinct from the Armenians proper. What has been deciphered amounts for the most part to certain names of kings, and such portions of words as serve to give evidence with regard to the inflectional structure of the language. M. Lenormant, who has discussed the subject at length in his 'Lettres Assyriologiques,' decides that all but four of them are of the seventh century B.C.[1]

The chambers also deserve a few words, especially as we have now reached the last of that remarkable series of excavations which we have met with in the course of our journey at Amasia, on the banks of the Halys, on the summit of Mount Argaeus, in the neighbourhood of Urgub, at Palu, at Akhlat, and finally at Van. In the first place, I should at once divide these into two separate classes, according as they appear to have been rudely fashioned for human habitation, or wrought by art for a special purpose. Nothing is more natural than that a primitive population, who had not developed the art of building, especially in a country like Asia Minor where wood was scarce, finding a soft material like tufa rock, which admitted of being easily hollowed out, should have excavated dwellings for themselves in these; and the habitations thus made would naturally be improved and adapted as time went on, as we find them to have been in the valley of Gueremeh. This would account for those which we have noticed in Cappadocia, and those of Akhlat. But the same

[1] *Sur l'ethnographie et l'histoire de l'Arménie avant les Achéménides*, in *Lettres Assyriologiques*, i. pp. 121, 124, 129. Compare also Prof. Sayce's paper 'On the Cuneiform Inscriptions of Van' in Kuhn's *Zeitschrift* for 1877, vol. xxiii., pp. 407-9, and his *Introduction to the Science of Language*, ii. 184.

explanation will not apply to elaborate chambers like those of this castle, or those of Palu or Amasia. These, notwithstanding the absence of ornament, imply a considerable advance in cultivation, as being the production of skilled workmen. Of those at Amasia I have already spoken as being sepulchres; but those also at Van, and those of Palu, which though ruder are closely similar in plan, seem most probably to have served the same purpose, and at all events could not have been intended for habitations of the living, for which use their darkness totally unfitted them. It is highly probable, as Sir Henry Layard remarks of the caves of Khorkhor,[1] that the neighbouring inscriptions record the victories and deeds of certain monarchs, while the chambers themselves were their places of burial; and this would apply to Palu, where also the two are in juxtaposition. Where this is not the case, they may have been treasuries; but from the analogy of similar constructions, it is much more likely that they also were intended to contain the dead.

Our morning's work being thus concluded, we now mounted our horses to ride out to luncheon with Dr. Reynolds, who lives in a village or suburb about three miles to the east of the town. Our road thither followed the line of the trees which we had noticed as forming so conspicuous an object in the plain when we first approached the place; these are the gardens of Van, watered by copious runlets, along which, on either side of the dusty track, numerous dwellings of the wealthier classes are built, including the private residence of the pasha. Dr. Reynolds's house occu-

[1] *Nineveh and Babylon*, p. 395.

pies a slight rise in the ground, and its level roof commands a lovely view, including the castle, with the green line of trees in front, and the blue lake behind, and in the other direction the Varak Dagh close at hand. The castle-rock as seen in profile from this point strikingly resembles Windsor Castle. The other missionaries, Messrs. Barnum and Scott, live hard by, and the English and Russian vice-consuls about a quarter of a mile nearer to the city. The reason why they have chosen this neighbourhood, which in some ways is inconveniently remote, is the unhealthiness of Van. This might easily be accounted for by the marshiness of the ground that surrounds it, though this is dry during the summer; but our host, who as a medical man spoke with authority, referred it rather to the accumulation of filth in the place, and also to the large amount of irrigated ground shaded with trees in the neighbourhood, which he regarded as an especially dangerous element.

We passed two pleasant hours here in the society of Dr. and Mrs. Reynolds and their friends, and in the midst of European cleanliness and comfort, but the time soon came when it was necessary for us to return to Van, in order to secure horses for our onward journey. We had anticipated some difficulty with regard to this on account of the bad repute for insecurity attaching to the route that we proposed to pursue in the direction of Bayazid and Ararat; and already on the day of our arrival, my vigilant companion had been making inquiries on this subject, and found that the means of transit were not readily forthcoming. We succeeded in interesting the Mouaveen on our behalf, and when negotiations had been set on foot with a katirji, he put a gentle pressure upon him—'though of course,' he remarked to us, 'if he refuses to go, I cannot force him.' As yet, however, neither the man nor his horses had appeared, and since in this land of slippery bargains it is necessary to see both at an early stage of the proceedings, we were anxious to be on the spot that we might not miss our chance. When we arrived, Mr. Crowder set off at once on this quest, and also to ransack the bazaars for *souvenirs*, which were not easy to find, the principal works of art being rather commonplace ear-rings, and nose-rings—filigree-work in silver or silver gilt—more curious than beautiful. I stayed at home to write letters, and while thus occupied received a visit from the Archbishop of Van, who came accompanied by other Armenian dignitaries. He was a rather fine-looking man, with a dark complexion, and wore a purple garment and a cap of the same colour. When sunset came, we were once more taking the now familiar road through the gardens, but this time to dine with Captain Clayton. That gentleman was engaged in reconstructing a native house, which had the makings of an agreeable abode; but it appeared likely to require considerable pains to render it a fitting residence for the winter, for that season, as may be supposed in so elevated a region, is very severe. Here we were hospitably entertained, and among the guests was Major Kamsaragan, who, notwithstanding his deficiency in languages, was evidently a favourite. I am glad to be able to report that at that period the diplomatic relations of England and Russia at Van were not 'strained.' We rode back by the light of the moon, and our horses, fortunately for us, were sure-footed and accustomed to the journey, for the broken road was full of pitfalls, which might easily have been dangerous owing to the deep shadows cast by the trees. The serai of the pasha, as we passed, was brilliantly lighted, for the nightly festivities of the Ramazan were proceeding. At last the city appeared, and we rode in under the rocks and towers of the citadel, now illuminated by the moonlight. Just outside the entrance two camels squatted on the ground presented a weird appearance, the moving of their long necks being the only sign that they were living creatures.

It remains to give a brief sketch of the history of the city, the antiquity of which is proved by the cuneiform inscriptions, independently of any further evidence which we have respecting it. As we have seen, its foundation is attributed by the Armenian historians to Semiramis, and the account of this, as given by Moses of Chorene, who wrote in the fifth century of our era, is as follows. He describes how that queen, whose name has become a byword for profligacy, for—

> A vizio di lussuria fu sì rotta,
> Che libito fe' licito in sua legge—

became enamoured of Ara, king of Armenia, from hearing of his beauty, and made war upon him in order to become master of his person. He was killed, however, in the course of the campaign, and his troops also were defeated. After this the historian proceeds:

'Semiramis, having rested a few days in the plain called Ararat after the name of Ara, passed to the southern side of the mountain, wishing—as it was then the summer time—to enjoy herself in the valleys and the flowery plains. When she saw the beauty of the country, the purity of the air, the limpid fountains that burst out on all sides, and the rivers flowing grandly with pleasant murmurs, she cried, "In a land where the atmosphere is so salubrious, and the waters so pure, we ought to build a city, a royal residence, that we may pass a fourth part of the year, that is, the summer season, in Armenia, in the midst of all these delights, while the three other cooler seasons we will pass at Nineveh."

'After having visited a number of sites, Semiramis reached the eastern districts, where, on the shores of a salt lake, she saw a hill oblong in form, stretching lengthways from east to west, and sloping slightly towards the north; on the southern side a cavern rose perpendicularly upwards towards the sky, and at some distance off in that direction was a level valley which extends to the east of the mountain, while as it descends to the edge of the lake, it becomes wide, grand, and deep. All this neighbourhood was traversed by sweet waters, which descended from the mountains through rifts and valleys, and joining at the wide base of the hills formed actual rivers. On either side of the streams rose numerous villages in this deep valley. Eastwards from the smiling hill stood a slight mountain.'

We are then told how Semiramis sent for numerous bands of workmen from Assyria, and built the city, which is elaborately described as it existed at the later period. The writer, however, does not seem to have visited the place, for he speaks of having received the account from others. The embankment of the stream which passed through the town is remarked on as especially worthy of notice.

'Semiramis first caused the embankment of the stream to be constructed of squared blocks, vast masses of stone fastened together by cement, forming a work of considerable size and height, which is said to remain to the present day. In the cavities of this passage (so report tells us) the robbers and vagabonds of the country now take refuge, feeling themselves as secure there as in the remote caves in the mountains. Let a man but try to pull out from this mass of masonry a single sling-stone, and he would fail to do so for all his efforts; so exactly do the stones fit, that a person examining them would fancy that their joinings are formed by wax run into them. This embankment, which is several stadia in length, reaches to the city.'

The following is the description of the castle:

'As to the extremity of the town and the wonderful edifices that exist there, the real state of the case is so little known that it is impossible to give an account of them. Semiramis furnished the summit with walls, contrived puzzling entrances, hard of access, and raised a royal palace with dreadful dungeons. No one has given us an exact description of the plan or arrangement of these buildings, so that we cannot present this in our history. All that can be said is that from the accounts given us, of all royal edifices this is the first and the most splendid.

'On the eastern side of the cavern, where at the present day owing to the hardness of the flintstone it is impossible to trace a single line with an iron instrument, chapels, chambers, treasuries, and long recesses have been formed. How such extraordinary constructions could be erected no one can tell. All over the face of the stone, pages on pages have been inscribed, as it were with a writing instrument on wax, so that the sight of this marvel by itself is sufficient to amaze everyone; but this is not all. In several other places in Armenia, Semiramis caused columns to be erected, and further had the remembrance of some event inscribed on these; and at various points set up boundary stones with inscriptions traced in a similar manner.'[1]

The account here given is interesting, both as embodying the traditional legends of the place, and as acquainting us with the ideas entertained concerning it at that early period. The name of Semiramis has perpetuated itself in these parts, not only in connection with the city, but also by being attached to a stream to the southward of Van, which is still called Shemiram-rud, or Semiramis' stream,[2] and another Assyrian name, that of Nimrod, is found in the Nimrud Dagh, which has often been mentioned as closing the western end of the lake. But while the presence of these names is not accidental, modern criticism has proved that the elaborate story of the Armenian chronicler is really the growth of a later time, and was suggested by the inscriptions themselves, and by other evidences of Assyrian influence. That the two peoples came into contact, we have ample proof from the Assyrian monuments. As early as the reign of

---

[1] Moses of Chorene (Vaillant de Florival's French translation), bk. i. chapters xv. xvi.
[2] Ritter's *Erdkunde*, ix. 987.

Tiglath Pileser I. (1130-1110 B.C.) the kings of Assyria seem to have invaded the eastern part of Armenia; and from this time onwards their annals frequently contain notices of wars with that country, which from time to time became tributary to them. In the Assyrian inscriptions the land of Van is mentioned by name (*mat vannai*) beside that of Urarti or Ararat, and each of these is ruled by its own prince. The power that was exercised over the people of this land by the civilisation of the Assyrians is shown by their having adopted from them the cuneiform mode of writing; and in the representation in the palace at Khorsabad of the capture of an Armenian town, the style of architecture and the plan of the Armenian temples, together with the altars and ornaments, if these at all faithfully represent the originals, would seem from their similarity to have been borrowed from the same quarter.[1]

To come down now to a later period—shortly before Alexander the Great's expedition into Asia, according to the Armenian historians, the city was further decorated by one of its native princes;[2] but the statement with which this is coupled, that he was called Van, and gave his name to the place, is disproved by what we have just seen of the existence of that name at an earlier period. It must, however, have been subsequently destroyed, for two

[1] Duncker's *History of Antiquity* (Abbott's translation), i. pp. 517, 519, 521, and the authorities there quoted. Any statement on this subject, however, requires to be made with reserve, for if M. Lenormant's view is correct that the language of these inscriptions is altogether distinct from Armenian, then we must admit his conclusion that they are the work of an earlier population.
[2] Chamich, *History of Armenia* (Avdall's translation), i. 44.

centuries after this (149 B.C.) Vagharshag or Valarsaces, the first Armenian king of the line of the Arsacidae, found it in ruins and rebuilt it; and one of his successors, Tigranes, established there a large colony of Jewish prisoners, whom he had brought away after an invasion of Palestine.[1] In the middle of the fourth century of our era it was again destroyed by Sapor II., king of Persia; but its ruin could not have been complete, for its ancient monuments are described, as we have seen, by Moses of Chorene, who wrote somewhat more than a hundred years later. To the Greeks the place was almost unknown, though it is probably to be identified with the Armenian city of Bouana mentioned by Ptolemy.[2] Before the eleventh century the Armenian princes of the Ardzruni family had made it their capital; but during that century it was surrendered to the Byzantines, for at the time of the early Seljouk invasions under Togrul-beg, in the reign of Constantine IX., we hear of the troops of the Eastern Empire retiring thither on one occasion, when Cedrenus, the Byzantine historian, calls it Ivan, and describes it as the capital of Vaspourakan, the frontier province of Armenia.[3] Otherwise it is hardly noticed in the annals of the Empire, probably owing to its remote position on the southern side of the lake of Van, while the tide of invasion passed to the north of that lake. The same explanation must be given of the greater importance attributed to Akhlat at this period.

---

[1] Moses of Chorene, bk. ii. chapters xiv., xix..
[2] Ptol., v. 13. See Saint-Martin, *Mémoires sur l'Arménie*, i. p. 138.
[3] Cedrenus, *Hist. Compend.* vol. ii. p. 580, ed. Bonn.

Van soon passed into the hands of the Seljouks, and while in their possession was besieged by Timour and his hosts. The Mahometan chronicler who has given an account of this siege, calls the place Avenik—a form not unlike that found in Cedrenus—and says that the city was captured at the first assault, and its walls destroyed; but that the Turkish commander withdrew into the citadel, and for some time withstood the furious attacks of the besiegers and their engines of war. But first the outworks of this were carried and the buildings within destroyed by catapults, and afterwards the foremost of the enemy forced their way into the rocky galleries and over vaulted passages, until they approached the highest battlements and threatened to render the place untenable. Thereupon the garrison, who had already begun to suffer from want of water, deserted to the besiegers, and forced their commander to surrender himself and the citadel to Timour, who sent him prisoner to Samarcand. The conqueror, we are told, desired to destroy the monuments which he found there, but was unable to do so owing to the solidity of their construction.[1] In 1533 it became the possession of the Ottomans, and has been held by them since that time, except for a short period in the seventeenth century, when it was taken from them after many years' siege by Shah Abbas of Persia in 1636.[2]

On the morning of September 6 we prepared to leave Van, and to our great satisfaction the promised horses, which notwithstanding my companion's exer-

[1] Cherefeddin, *Histoire de Timur Bec* (De la Croix's translation), quoted by Ritter, *Erdkunde*, ix. 981, 982.
[2] See generally Ritter, as above; Saint-Martin, *Mémoires*, i. pp. 138, 139.

tions we had not yet seen, made their appearance. Their owner still professed himself the victim of compulsion, and refused at first either to accompany them himself or to allow any of his men to come with us —a mad threat, which we knew to be unmeaning. He was not afraid, he said, of making the journey in our company, but of losing his beasts during their return. However, a bargain, highly advantageous to him as regards hire, was struck, and he on his side provided us with an excellent attendant. Ultimately we took these horses with us the whole way to Erzeroum, so that he had reason to be more than satisfied, as the communication between that place and Van was comparatively safe, and this was also a line of traffic by which he might have the opportunity of transporting some merchandise. His reluctance was not surprising, for the nomad Kurds of the Haideranli tribe, through whose country our projected route lay, have long been the terror of this neighbourhood, and M. Texier and Mr. Ussher, both of whom travelled from Bayazid to Van, speak of the risks of the journey, and their expectation of being attacked at certain points. We subsequently learnt that a few months after our visit a party was pillaged in this very district. This insecurity in part arises from the neighbourhood of the Persian frontier, which at Van, as I have said, is only fifty miles off, and at Bayazid is much nearer; in consequence of which it is easy for marauders to escape pursuit by passing from one country into the other. The horses proved to be good, as might be expected from the land of Togarmah—the Scriptural name of the region of Van—which was famed for its beasts of burden.[1]

[1] See above, p. 180.

Xenophon also—no mean judge, for he was both a sportsman and a writer on horses—speaks in terms of praise of the spirited ponies of Eastern Armenia.[1] Ponies they are universally in these uplands, and small ones, but we can testify to their sure-footedness, for we had no mishaps from first to last. Shortly after we had filed out of the city, one of our new team signalised himself—from no fault of his own, but to our great dismay—by scattering to the winds the few metal pans, plates, and cups, which constituted our service for the kitchen and table. The bag which carried these had been carelessly fastened on his back, together with the other baggage, and slipping round between his hind legs, caused him to gallop round a neighbouring inclosure, kicking and plunging, until the unhappy contents were dispersed far and wide over the land. This accomplished, his excitement ceased, and all the articles were recovered, much out of shape, but still serviceable.

Our course lay towards the north-east, and the views were interesting, as long as the castle and the lake remained in sight behind us. But this was not for long, for we soon entered a succession of stony valleys, bare, waterless, and shapeless. At one point on our left hand we passed a low hill, on which stood the foundations of an ancient town, square in plan, and composed of two or three courses of massive blocks; it was in excavating this, I believe, that a number of objects covered with Assyrian inscriptions were lately found, some of which are now in the British Museum. For nearly six hours we rode through this monotonous country, until about the middle of

[1] *Anab.* iv. 5, § 36.

the afternoon a lake of some size, called Artschag, came in sight, which was bright blue in colour, and edged with a white incrustation of salt, and emitted a strong, offensive odour. The scenery here was striking, for in contrast with these hues, the surrounding hills were deeply tinged with iron and sulphur. Towards the head of this piece of water we halted near a village, where the only spring was in the level plain, welling out of the ground in numerous small sources, which formed muddy pools a short distance below. Here it was interesting to watch the care with which the buffaloes were being groomed. They were brought to the pool, splashed with water, persuaded to lie down in it, and finally well rubbed with the hand, during all which process they looked as if they were in perfect bliss. From the trouble that was thus expended upon them one would suppose them to be very valuable animals, and, as a matter of fact, they are of great service for draught owing to their strength; but they were not the only creatures that were treated in this way, for we saw even a donkey coming in for his share of the refreshment. Such consideration for the brute creation, from whatever cause arising, was pleasant to witness in a land where it is rarely found; at the same time I do not think the people in Armenia are often cruel to animals.

Our resting-place for the night proved to be only an hour further on, near the eastern shore of the lake Artschag. It was the large village of Karakenduz, a regular Armenian dustheap with anthill structures, such as we had seen before. We went through it, to discover if there was any tolerable accommodation, but even the best houses were so absolutely repulsive, that we determined to pitch our tent at the further end of the extensive village green, where we were sheltered by a wall and an inclosure of trees. At Van we had heard reports of a stone with a cuneiform inscription being built into one of the interior walls of the church of this place, so thither we repaired, under the escort of one of the numerous natives who had crowded round our little encampment. When we arrived there service was going on, and after we had been present at this for a short time, the heat and the foulness of the atmosphere so overpowered us, that we were glad to beat a hasty retreat without seeing the object of our search. We soon found, however, that we had only exchanged one evil for another, for the cattle were now returning for the night, and the air all about our road was full of the dust they made by literally turning up the substratum of the village. From this we escaped by the expedient—an easy one in Armenia—of walking over the house roofs.

The following day brought us to the head of the lake of Van. Owing to the irregularity of the outline of the lake in this part our course since leaving the city had been far removed from it, nor had we at any point caught sight of its waters. Nearly the whole day was occupied in traversing very lofty mountains—the highest point in the road was 6,725 feet—notwithstanding which the views were not fine, owing to their barrenness and commonplace outlines; but to me it was signalised by my obtaining my first view of Ararat, the summit of which, as we were crossing a pass, appeared above the nearer ranges. It was here about sixty miles distant in a direct line, a mass of white snow, which in shape resembled a beehive, varied only by a few protuberances. To see Ararat at all is something, and a mountain with so many associations cannot fail to be impressive; besides which, so extensive a snowy surface standing out against a clear sky, especially in a southern country, is suggestive of great elevation: but in itself the shape of the summit could not be described as imposing. A long and steep descent at last brought us to the level ground about the innermost angle of the lake, which here appears as a narrow inlet of blue water, for eastward of Adeljivas its surface contracts, and throws out a long arm—the lake of Ardjish —towards the north-east. In this neighbourhood we saw it for the last time. In the background the fine form of Mount Sipan rose very conspicuous. We skirted the hills at the upper end of the plain, and were not sorry to avoid the shore of the lake, which had a marshy and unhealthy appearance. At the further extremity lies Pergri, the chief place of the district and residence of the kaimakam; here we had intended to pass the night, but being informed that at present it was occupied by soldiers, and that in consequence there would be small chance of obtaining the necessaries of life, we halted at the neighbouring village of Kutchuk-keui, and encamped by the side of a large grove of poplars. These we did not fail to remember, for they were the last trees, whether wild or cultivated, that we saw until reaching the upper waters of the eastern Euphrates.

The valley which here opens out from the mountains towards the north-east is a point of some strategical importance, because through it runs the line of communication between Persia and southern Armenia. The hosts that invaded the country during the Middle

Ages constantly passed by this way. Consequently Pergri, which commands its outlet, though now neglected, was once a carefully guarded position. The name of this place is given by some travellers as Berghiri, probably owing to the pronunciation of the Turks, who always prefer to insert a vowel between two consonants, but it appears in mediaeval writers as Perkri (Περκρί), and this has been but slightly changed in the course of ages. Constantine Porphyrogenitus speaks of this and the fortresses on the northern shore of the lake as especially important to the Byzantine Empire, because they formed a strong barrier on the frontier.[1] In the eleventh century we find it in the hands of a Saracen emir, called Aleim, who delivered it up to the Emperor Romanus III.; and a body of six thousand Byzantine troops, under a Bulgarian patrician, was stationed to defend it. Aleim was, however, dissatisfied with the reward he received, and opened communications with the Persians, whom he contrived to introduce into Perkri. The Byzantine garrison was surprised and put to the sword; but a powerful body of native troops and Russian mercenaries soon regained possession of the place, which was taken by assault, and Aleim was put to death.[2] It is curious to find some of these names, which have been rendered so familiar to us by recent events, occurring in connection with this remote locality at so early a period. The ruined towers of the old fortress, which we passed the following morning, occupy a detached height overlooking the course of the Bende-Mahi-su, which issues from the valley.

[1] *De Administr. Imp.* cap. xliv. vol. iii. p. 197, ed. Bonn.
[2] Finlay, *History of Greece*, ii. 403 (new edit.).

CHAPTER XIV.

THE HIGHEST UPLANDS.

The Bende-Mahi-su— A friendly warning—The nomad Kurds—Kurdish encampment— Description of the tents—Lofty ridge—Grand view of Ararat—Noticeable points respecting it—Village of Diyadin—The roof of Western Asia—Head waters of the Murad—Geography of the district—Sketch of the Russo-Turkish campaign—Monastery of Utch Keliseh: its church—Persian villages—Description of native dwellings—The Turkish currency—Plain of Alashgerd—Pass of Delibaba —Meeting with Englishmen—Battles in the pass—The Persian traffic—The Araxes—Plain of Pasin—Deveh Boyoun—Arrival at Erzeroum.

THE modern village of Pergri proved to be a very mean place. We halted there a few minutes to visit the kaimakam, and when he appeared he was as drowsy as his co-religionists usually are on the days of Ramazan. Our object was to ask for two more zaptiehs, for though we had brought two with us from Van, it seemed more prudent to increase our escort now that we were about to enter the country of the Haideranlis. However, he informed us that all the zaptiehs were absent, but that the body of troops who had been quartered there the previous night would be ahead of us, and their presence might act as a protection. We now followed the valley upwards into the heart of the mountains, along the banks of the Bende-Mahi-su, which is a clear and rapid torrent with a considerable body of water, though for some distance its stream was diminished by being partly carried off by a large watercourse for purposes of irrigation. It was an extremely desolate region; all around extended rough and unproductive moorland, inclosed by rocky hills; not a village, not a habitation, was to be seen; and the only human beings we met were a few wild-looking peasants driving oxen, which bore bags of hay or grain, for throughout this district these animals are used as beasts of burden for carrying purposes. The day was showery, and heavy rain-storms were sweeping over the sky. We several times crossed the stream, which usually flows in a deep trench, but elsewhere is fringed with beds of rushes, and when we finally took to its right bank, we passed a recess in the hills, where the Turkish soldiers we had heard of were encamped. The river-valley now trends more towards the east, and would have led us out of our way, as its waters rise in the mountains to the southward of Bayazid. Accordingly after four hours we left it, intending henceforth to pursue a more northerly course; but before proceeding further, we halted a while for our midday meal by the side of a tributary spring.

While we were resting at this point, three Kurdish horsemen suddenly appeared on the scene. The chief man among them, whose name, we afterwards discovered, was Ali Bey, was gaily attired in a turban and a long blue robe, with a light white shawl thrown over his shoulders and clasped at the throat in front; in his hand he carried a long bamboo lance, which he rested on the ground when he stopped. In other respects he was fully armed, and even carried a revolver. The two other Kurds were his attendants. He conferred for some time with our zaptiehs, and then rode away with his two subordinates down the valley by which we had approached. After his departure, the blank consternation that fell upon our party was really comical. In our dragoman we were not surprised at this, for he suffered from Circassians and Kurds on the brain, and he had cried 'wolf' so often that we had ceased to pay any attention to him. But the zaptiehs also were evidently much alarmed, and probably they estimated the situation better than we did ourselves. It seemed that Ali Bey, who professed himself a friend, had turned aside from his road on seeing us, and brought word that it would be most dangerous for us to pursue the straight road to Bayazid, as we were intending to do, because fighting was going on in that direction between the Turks and part of the Haideranli tribe, who had been plundering and burning villages both in that district and towards the Persian frontier. He was himself a Haideranli, but the part of the tribe to which he belonged was still on good terms with the Ottoman Government. We did not know what to make of this communication. We were aware that the Kurds of the Julamerk district, south of Van, were in open insurrection, and there were rumours of a general rising of the Kurdish tribes, who were supposed to have made a secret league against the Porte; but, on the other hand, the Mouaveen had led us to suppose that we should make our way through without difficulty, if accompanied by two zaptiehs. Only Captain Clayton had suspicions that all was not right in this quarter, and we gathered vaguely that the soldiers whom we had passed were destined to take part in some such service. Still it was annoying to have to quit our intended route, and we had no guarantee that the author of this information was either friendly or trustworthy. Our difficulty in arriving at a decision was greatly increased by the obscure and confused way in which the communication had been retailed to us.

Meanwhile Ali Aga had sent back one of his attendants with the offer, backed by his urgent recommendations, that he should conduct us to the head-quarters of that part of the tribe to which he himself belonged; so under this man's guidance we started again, following for the time the same direction which we had previously taken. Ararat was now once more in sight, directly to the north of us, still retaining the beehive form, but much nearer and grander than before. Presently our guide began to bear away towards the west, whereupon we grumbled and remonstrated, and for the moment felt disposed to push our way through at all hazards. Ultimately, however, our zaptiehs became so urgent in the matter, that we felt compelled to yield. We had now entered a land of upland pastures, and the Kurdish encampments began to be very numerous, so that in one view as many as fifty-seven black tents could be counted in separate groups. Here and elsewhere in this neighbourhood, the plains in the midst of the mountains presented a strange aspect from their being covered in parts with masses of igneous rock, which were so thickly clothed with a green lichen as to wear at first sight the appearance of a dwarf forest. The Kurd conducted us to a camp, where on his recommendation another guide was provided to accompany us in his stead. After we had waited half an hour he appeared in the shape of an old man, bearing a lance, and riding a mare which was accompanied by its foal. My companion, who had been among the Arabs, remarked that the Kurds whom we met, like that people, always rode mares, and that these were unshod; and also, among other points of resemblance, that their lances were of bamboo which would bend almost double. Following him, we pursued our way over the grassy mountains in a direction generally bearing north-west, and towards this point of the compass our route continued until we reached the valley the next day.

At last we arrived at a small village, the only one that we saw in the whole district, and our wanderings seemed so interminable, that we half made up our minds to spend the night there, but our zaptiehs and dragoman, who were now wrought up to a high pitch, entreated us not to do so, as it was a very unsafe place; so before long we were off again, with a new guide, and a foal in company as before. Late in the afternoon we descended into a dip among the uplands, and here found the large encampment of which we were in search, not far from the course of a clear mountain stream, with numerous tents forming a long line, some large and black, some smaller, round and white. The men who were hanging about them were a wild and surly-looking set, with hair streaming down in long locks. The dress of most of them was composed of white trousers and a sort of frock-coat of a light material, resembling cretonne, usually red in colour, with a belt and turban. All of course were armed. Their possessions might be seen about the encampment—sheep, goats, oxen and cows, herds of horses, big mastiff dogs, and greyhounds clothed with small coats. The whole formed a highly picturesque scene.

We had entered the encampment about the middle of the line, and while our tent was being pitched in the midst of the Kurdish tents—a process which greatly roused the curiosity of our new acquaintances—I was anxious to find some place in which to rest, for I had been suffering from face-ache during the day, and was very tired; so seeing a nice-looking white tent close by, I asked whether I could betake myself thither. '*Yok, yok, yok,*' was the reply; 'oh no! not on any account; that's the chief's, that's Mirza Aga's tent!' Well, I don't know whether leave was obtained, but in the course of our journey we had learned to be no great respecters of persons; anyhow in less than a minute my spurs were off, and I was reclining on Mirza Aga's carpet, with my head on his cushions, and was soon asleep. How long I remained there I do not know, but I was awaked at last by a light tap on my shoulder, and found a Kurd kneeling by my side with a small cup of Turkish coffee in his hand, of which I partook with much refreshment. It was, besides, a token of friendship. Coming as we did amongst this wild people, whom it is usually the traveller's object to avoid, we might have seemed to be running into the lion's jaws, but somehow things had gone so smoothly for us hitherto, and we had got so much into the habit of regarding ourselves as strange animals whom the natives did not like to molest, that it never came into my mind to feel any apprehension; but if it had, the offer of this cup of coffee would have dispelled it, for one might feel certain that here, as amongst the Arabs, the bond of hospitality was a sacred one. The result proved that both our persons and our property were in perfect security.

At sunset the Muezzin uttered the usual call to prayers, in front of the chief's tent door, and thereupon many of the community engaged in worship in an independent style, each Kurd kneeling on his carpet near his own abode. They were Kizilbashes, I suppose, like the rest of these nomads, but in their mode of devotion there was nothing to distinguish them from ordinary Mahometans. During the evening, Mr. Crowder paid a visit to the chief, and was courteously received in the tent which I had so unceremoniously occupied. Mirza Aga, who was a large man and wore a high turban, consoled him for our deviation from our intended route, by saying that we should certainly have had our throats cut if we had continued as we proposed. He also informed him that in a fortnight's time he was intending to descend to the villages in the neighbourhood of Bayazid and Diyadin—a resolution which we fully approved when the night came, for it was very cold, especially towards morning, and no wonder, for the height of the encampment was 7,275 feet above the sea. A first look at the Kurd tents gives a person the idea that they must be chilly habitations, but this disappears on a nearer inspection. There are indeed great spaces between the covering of the tent and the sides, and these latter are not pinned closely to the ground; but as they are occupied by day as well as by night this arrangement is necessary, for otherwise when the sun is on them the heat would be unbearable. But within the inclosure of the larger tents are separate rooms parted off, and both these and the sides of the tent itself are formed, not of any thin material, like canvas, but of a stout wickerwork of canes, each bar or cane of which is cased in worsted work or embroidery of gay colours, and in this way the whole is firmly compacted together. Within there is always a plentiful store of carpets, rugs, and pillows. In the larger encampments there are separate tents for the women.

The next morning Mirza provided us with an old white-bearded Kurd, armed as usual with a lance, and riding an unshod mare, to act as our guide, and we started in the expectation of taking the route to Bayazid, for at first our direction lay rather to the east of north, and by our long détour we had avoided the dangerous region. That place was said to be twelve hours distant. The dip up which we rode was partly a stony bottom, partly pasture land intersected by small streams, the smell from which, or from the ground in their neighbourhood, was highly bituminous. After crossing a ridge nearly 9,000 feet in height, we were surprised at so great an elevation to find just below the crest another, though smaller encampment. When we halted here for breakfast, our old guide suddenly disappeared; he seemed to have vanished like a spirit, and we never saw him again. We were allowed to occupy a compartment of a large picturesque tent, which was open towards the north; this room was appropriated to a Mollah, a handsome man, who had many books about him. The floor was covered with a thick dark felt carpet, at the edge of which a number of posts were driven into the ground from which to hang arms. At this point we found that no further guide was forth-coming, the probable reason being that the nomad Kurds do not like to venture singly into the lower country; and as Bayazid was said to be seven hours distant, with no halting-place between, while Diyadin was only two, and the path thither was easy to find, we were obliged to yield to our zaptiehs, who were strongly in favour of the latter destination.

We reconciled ourselves to this as best we could, and were descending towards the north-west over a very wild and solitary region, when an object came in view which made ample amends for our disappointment. This was Ararat—not now the dome only, as in former views, but the whole mass revealed from base to summit, a splendid sight. The highest point is here about thirty miles distant towards the north-east. Below us the ground descended rapidly some two thousand feet to the valley, and the interval between this and the foot of the mountain was occupied by a succession of rolling hills. Owing to the high elevation from which we looked, this is probably as fine a view as any that can be obtained from this side, for it need hardly be remarked that from the lower ground at the foot of a mountain, when you look up at it, a great part of its height is lost. It was a stormy day, and rain-clouds at intervals were sweeping over the summit, but not so as to prevent us from seeing it thoroughly. For a mountain of so great elevation—for it reaches somewhat more than 17,000 feet, and is consequently 1,200 feet higher than Mont Blanc—the amount of snow was not large, though towards the west, where the slope is easier, wide snow-fields were seen; on the southern side, which is exposed to the sun, its extent is naturally less than on the northern, and the season at which we saw it, the beginning of autumn, is just that when there has been time for the last winter's store to disappear, and no fresh snow has begun to fall. This year also had been one of great heat and drought throughout all these provinces. It is mainly on its great mass that the mountain has to depend for its impressiveness, for it has none of the sharp outlines, or well-cut peaks, or steep precipices, which render the Alps so beautiful. It is a volcano, and has the rounded summit and gradual slopes of such a mountain. In fact, its shape reminded us forcibly of that of Vesuvius, and like Vesuvius it has graceful outlines, far more so than the straight unvaried sides of Etna. As seen from here, it has lost the beehive form, for the western slope is continued in a long and massive ridge. At the eastern foot appeared the pyramid of the Little Ararat, which looked almost like a model of its greater brother, and in the dip between them rose a ridge which seemed to connect their bases. Low as the lesser mountain looked by comparison, its height is still nearly 13,000 feet. On the other side, towards the north-west, the upper valley of the Murad had also come in sight far below us, for we now once more meet the stream of the Euphrates, which takes its rise in this neighbourhood, almost within sight of Ararat. So surrounded are we here by objects of immemorial associations!

My friend Professor Bryce in his 'Transcaucasia and Ararat,' which contains the account of his adventurous solitary ascent of the mountain, has treated so exhaustively almost everything connected with it, that

I feel myself absolved from the necessity of enlarging on the subject; but there are a few points which it may be worth while to notice. Its Turkish name is Aghri Dagh, or the Painful Mountain, while by the Armenians it is known as Massis. The name which is most familiar to us, Ararat or rather Airarat, originally signified 'the fruitful plain,' and was applied to the ground about the middle course of the river Araxes, that is, the district on the northern side of the mountain. In the primitive legends of the Armenian nation the same thing has happened that so often occurs in the later Greek mythology; that is to say, the geographical features have been worked into the genealogy of the race. According to these, Haikh was the father of Armenak, the Armenian nation, and Armenak's grandson and great-grandson were Amasiaj and Arast, which names represent respectively the mountain Massis and the river Araxes.[1] At the present day Ararat forms the grandest boundary stone in the world; for it, or rather the two Ararats, are the meeting-point of three great empires, the northern slopes of Great Ararat being in the possession of Russia, and the southern forming part of Turkey, while a portion of Little Ararat belongs to Persia. The first ascent, that of the German traveller Parrot, was made from the western side, but those who have subsequently attempted it have done so almost entirely from the opposite quarter, starting from the dip between the two mountains, and ascending along the eastern ridge. In the spring of 1879, however, Mr. Cole, one of the American missionaries at Erzeroum, again attacked it from the

---

[1] Duncker, *History of Antiquity*, i. 516.

west; and though he failed to reach the summit, in consequence of his companion being exhausted, his opinion was that, as the slopes on that side were more gradual, that approach would prove the easier. The same is the opinion of Professor Bryce, though for one who ascends alone, as he did, he considers the eastern side to be preferable. In reality the ascent presents no great difficulties to a practised walker in good training, except such as arise from the absence of guides, and the want of the ordinary appliances of mountain climbing. In our case, however, it was out of the question, for even if I had been in a condition to undertake it, our limited time and the unfavourable state of the weather would have rendered it impossible.

The two hours which had been allowed for our journey to Diyadin from the last Kurdish encampment had become four before we reached that place, in accordance with the usual inaccuracy in computing distances which prevails in these mountainous regions. Notwithstanding the length and steepness of our descent, we found the elevation of the village to be still 6,000 feet above the sea. I had read so much about Diyadin that I had expected to find it a town of some size, but it is in reality a miserable place, with the usual dust-heap appearance. But the remains of a large fortress close by, with several strong towers still standing, testify to its former greatness. Beneath its walls a tributary of the Murad, which joins that river just below, has cut for itself a deep bed through vertical walls of basalt. Near this we established ourselves, by the side of an outlying house of greater pretensions than the rest, and here the kaimakam and two of his associates paid us a visit in the course of the evening. They seemed much pleased to see us, and it may easily be believed that a visitor is a godsend in so remote a locality. When we spoke of the state of the Kurdish district through which we had passed, he said that the ravages we had heard of as having taken place in the country south of Bayazid were to be attributed to Persian Kurds who had crossed the frontier; but at Erzeroum we afterwards learnt that it is usual with the authorities, in case of any atrocities happening on these borders, to lay the blame on those for whom the Turkish Government cannot be held responsible. What was the official view taken of our friend Mirza Aga we discovered from the remark of a zaptieh here, who said that if he ever was caught he ought certainly to be put to death.

We remained at this place the following day, I to rest, and my companion to make a short excursion in the direction of Bayazid, in order to obtain a nearer view of the sides of Ararat. The town of Bayazid, we were told, had been ruined during the late war, and had not yet recovered the damage it then sustained, so that whereas it formerly contained a thousand houses, it is now composed of only a hundred, which are almost entirely inhabited by Armenians. It is difficult to suppose, however, that it can long remain in this depressed state, in consequence of the importance of its position. It is the frontier town of this part of Turkey towards Persia, and commands the great caravan route that leads from the Black Sea to that country, passing between Ararat and the mountains which we have lately been crossing. How important this is we shall have frequent cause to remark in the course of our subsequent journey. It was therefore a just stipulation of the Berlin Treaty that this place and its neighbourhood, which had been conquered by the Russians, should be restored to Turkey. It would have been wholly unreasonable that the main line of communication and traffic between two great countries should be at one, and that the most important, point in the hands of a third Power.

We now began to turn our faces homewards, for it was not part of our programme to enter either Russian or Persian territory. The country through which we were passing for the next six days on our way to Erzeroum, is that which I have already termed the roof of Western Asia, being formed by a succession of very elevated plains for the most part not much less than 6,000 feet above the sea, from which the waters drain off, on the one side to the Persian Gulf, on the other to the Caspian. It is a district more attractive to the geographer than to the lover of scenery, for its monotony of bareness is wearisome to the eye, and but few of the mountains in its neighbourhood are striking in form. Yet this great watershed, which divides this vast continent in two parts and mainly determines its configuration, sending forth its streams to fertilise lands so far removed from one another, can hardly fail to excite the imagination. In order, therefore, to make the general character of the country more clear, and at the same time to enable us to pass over it with less delay, I will at once describe its principal features.

I have said that we are again in the immediate

vicinity of the Murad. That river, the eastern branch of the Euphrates, rises in the lofty Ala Dagh to the south-west of Diyadin, about fifteen miles from that place, its head waters being formed by the contributions of a number of brooks which trickle from the mountain side.[1] At that village its stream turns at right angles, and flows in a direction somewhat north of west through level uplands confined by parallel mountain ranges, until it reaches the great plain of Alashgerd, where it trends away to the south-west, after receiving the numerous tributaries that flow from that plain. Thence it makes its way through the mountains which lie to the north of Mount Sipan and the lake of Van, and passing near the town of Melazgerd—famous in the Middle Ages as Manzikert, the scene of the great victory of Alp Arslan over the Byzantine emperor—reaches at last the plain of Mush, where we last saw it. Its modern name, I may here remark, is derived from that of the Sultan Murad (Amurath) IV., being so called, according to Von Moltke, because of the numerous bridges, roads; and khans which are said to have been constructed by him in this land.[2] Whether Bayazid also, which is not an ancient town, was called from the sultan of that name (Bajazet) 1 do not know, but it would seem probable.

From the point where the Murad begins to bend towards the south, the plain of Alashgerd extends for some twenty miles, watered by the numerous western tributaries of that river. The most conspicuous

---

[1] See Mr. Brant's account in vol. x. of the *Geographical Society's Journal*, p. 418.

[2] Von Moltke, *Briefe aus der Türkei*, p. 221.

mountain in its neighbourhood is the lofty Keuseh Dagh, at the north-western angle, at the foot of which in a recess of the plain stands Toprak-kaleh (Earth-castle), the most important place and strongest position in the district. On the northern side of the Keuseh Dagh in the direction of Kars stretches the Soghanli Dagh, the scene of Mukhtar Pasha's retreat after the capture of that city, while towards the south it is continued in another broken range, which forms the watershed between the eastern Euphrates and the Araxes. Over this there are several passes, the most direct being that called the pass of Delibaba from the village of that name at its western exit. As soon as the summit of the ridge is reached, the waters, which have hitherto descended towards Mesopotamia, begin to run towards Central Asia, for the plain on the further side is that in which the Araxes flows. That river in the upper part of its course comes from the south-west, through the district called Pasin, rising in the Bingheul Dagh ('mountain of a thousand lakes, or sources'), which lies half-way between Erzeroum and Mush; and then passing at the back of the Keuseh Dagh and the chain which joins that mountain to Ararat, runs for a while almost parallel to the Murad, only in an opposite direction, and ultimately finds its way into the Caspian. The road to Erzeroum crosses it about the middle of the undulating plain, which is even more extensive than that of Alashgerd, and from this point follows its western confluents upwards, passing the fortress of Hassan-kaleh, until the way is again barred by the transverse ridge of the now famous Deveh Boyoun, or Camel's Neck. At the foot of those heights on the further side the city of Erzeroum lies, and here once more the streams begin to find their way towards the Persian Gulf, for about twenty miles to the north of that place are the sources of the Frat or western Euphrates; this flows through a third plain, which stretches away from the city at an elevation equal to that of those already mentioned, and then winding through the mountains towards the south-west, joins the Murad above Keban Maden.

The district which I have now described was the scene of important movements during the late war between Russia and Turkey, and a great part of it was traversed more than once by the armies of both those nations. The first evidence that we were on the war-track came to us in rather an amusing form, for when we inquired for fowls and eggs on our arrival at Diyadin, we were told that the Russians had eaten them all two years before, and there had been none there ever since; but it was not long before we found much sadder proof of the devastation those marches had produced. At the risk therefore of lengthening out these preliminaries, I will introduce a very brief account of the operations that took place there at that time, in order that we may understand what happened at the different points we reach in our journey.

It will be remembered that at the beginning of the campaign the Grand Duke Michael, who commanded the Russian army in Asia, crossed the frontier in three columns, the right of which advanced on Ardahan, the centre on Kars, and the left on Bayazid. The Turkish commander-in-chief, Mukhtar Pasha, had disposed his forces in a corresponding manner, though moving on a more concentrated base of operations; thus the Turkish line of defence ranged along these upland plains from Bayazid to Erzeroum, while their centre was advanced in front of it as far as Kars. The Delibaba pass was in reality the key of their position, because it lay midway between the two extremities, and at the back of the approaches to Kars. The Russian left, which was commanded by Tergukassoff, struck the first blow by marching rapidly on Bayazid and capturing that place without a shot having been exchanged. Ardahan also was taken by the Russian right wing, and in consequence Mukhtar, who was at Kars, found himself obliged to retire to a strong position on the Soghanli Dagh, and at the same time drew in his right, which was now threatened by Tergukassoff, who had advanced from Bayazid, to Mollah Suleiman near the western end of the plain of Alashgerd, and afterwards within the Delibaba pass itself. Subsequently, when he found the Russians to be weaker than he expected, he ordered Mehemet Ali, who commanded the right wing, to attack them, and the result was the battle of Tahir-keui in the pass on June 16, where, owing partly to the strength of the Russian artillery, and partly to the bad tactics of the Ottoman commander, the Turks were disastrously beaten, and driven right through the defile. This was a critical juncture for the Turkish cause, since for the moment Mukhtar's army had Loris Melikoff with the Russian centre in front of him, and Tergukassoff in his rear. From this position he extricated himself with great promptitude. The Russians had established themselves in a strong position at the village of Eshek

Elias towards the western end of the pass, and here the Turkish commander-in-chief attacked them in person on the 21st, and at the price of a tremendous sacrifice of life to his soldiers, forced them to retire to the head of the Alashgerd plain. Then returning to the Soghanli Dagh he awaited the advance of the Russian centre, and having repulsed them with great slaughter on the 25th, drove them back almost to the frontier. Up to this time Tergukassoff held on in the neighbourhood to see whether Melikoff would succeed; but after hearing of this battle he retired with all speed, knowing that his communications were threatened by a Turkish force under Faik Pasha, which was advancing from Van to Bayazid. Kurd Ismail Pasha was ordered to pursue him; but the Russian retreat was carried out with so great skill and boldness, that they not only kept at bay a foe that was three times their strength, but also conveyed with them their sick, wounded, and prisoners. When they reached Diyadin, they found that Bayazid was already invested, and consequently were forced to retire over the mountains to Igdir in Russian territory to the north-west of Ararat. Shortly afterwards Tergukassoff, profiting by the supineness of the Ottoman general, moved rapidly from Igdir, and on July 8 threw himself on Faik's forces, and defeated them with heavy loss, and before Ismail's troops could arrive in support, had relieved the besieged garrison and retired safely across the frontier.

During the rest of the summer the war seemed to languish, but it was only the lull that precedes a more formidable struggle. Mukhtar Pasha, whose strength lay in concentrating his forces, had now extended his line of defence, and the result was the great battle of Alaja Dagh, which ruined the Turkish cause. Upon this he retired, closely followed by the Russians, over the Soghanli Dagh into the Araxes valley, intending to make a stand at Kiuprikeui, where is the bridge over that river in the plain of Pasin. The day after the battle Ismail also received orders to retreat from the neighbourhood of Bayazid, and the question now was whether he would succeed in getting through the Delibaba pass, before the Russians who were advancing from the north should intercept him. It was a race against time ; and so near a thing was it, that one who then accompanied his force described to me how, just as their rear emerged from the pass, the head of the Russian column appeared on the road which here converges from the north. In this way he was able to join Mukhtar with 8,000 men. Mukhtar was now gradually driven back through the Araxes plain, from Kiupri-keui to Hassan-kaleh, and thence to the heights of Deveh Boyoun, which had been entrenched with a view to defence. Here a final stand was made, but the Turkish troops, being now thoroughly demoralised, gave way, notwithstanding their commander's gallant endeavours to rally them, and retired into Erzeroum. That place held out successfully, and the winter season, which had now fully set in, was in favour of the defenders. It was not captured, though in February of the following year the Russians were allowed to occupy it during the negotiations for peace.

We left Diyadin on September 11. Shortly after starting we reached the infant Euphrates, which is here a small clear mountain stream, and like its tributary which we had seen as we approached, has cut for itself a deep bed through steep walls of rock. During the day and a half that we followed its mazy course through the plain, we watched it gradually increasing in volume from the numerous tributaries which it received from both sides. The scenery was interesting as long as the Great Ararat and its attendant satellite were in view behind us, but when they were hidden there was nothing to relieve the bareness of the narrow plain and the ranges by which it was bounded. We had not proceeded far before a large building appeared in sight just above the left bank of the river at the foot of the hills, which proved to be the monastery of Utch Kelisch. In order to reach it from the road we had to force our way through tangled masses of prickly shrubs, which have overgrown the neighbourhood of the stream. The area occupied by the monastery is small, and square in shape, and is surrounded by a high wall flanked by towers; the dwellings are attached to the inner side of this, and anywhere but in Armenia would appear to be of a humble character. But the church, which occupies the centre of the quadrangle, is a magnificent structure, and quite out of proportion to the rest of the edifices; it was in fact the finest ecclesiastical building which we saw in all this country. Alas! though not in ruins, it was in a sad state of disrepair, having been sacked by the Kurds together with the rest of the monastery two years ago at the time of the Russian invasion. In consequence of that attack, also, the only occupants of the place were one monk, who had belonged to the body before that time, and a few lay brethren or peasants. Previously there had been four monks and a school for fifty children. I gather from the accounts of former travellers that this convent, once a place of great importance and the resort of numerous pilgrims, had greatly declined in prosperity during the present century;[1] but its present condition represents the lowest depth of misery. Its Turkish name of Utch Keliseh signifies 'Three Churches,' but what is the origin of this appellation I am unable to discover, for there is no sign at present that more than one church ever existed here. Dr. Neale thinks that it means the Holy Trinity,[2] but this as a Turkish title is improbable, and Etchmiadzin, to which the Turks have given the same name, has received it for a different reason.[3]

Both in arrangement and architectural features this church greatly resembles some of the Lombard churches. It is built of large blocks of black and grey stone, and the construction throughout is very massive. None of the windows are of considerable size, but in various parts there are numerous small ones. The arches are usually round, but those of some of the entrance-doors are pointed; the arch of the western door has a rude cable-moulding over it, and about it much interlaced ornament, such as we

---

[1] Ritter's *Erdkunde*, x. 650.
[2] Neale, *Eastern Church*, i. p. 106. Mr. Brant was informed that the name was derived from its being the largest of three churches, one of which was in the plain, and one on the neighbouring mountain side; both were destroyed, though the monks said the traces of one were visible. This explanation may very well be the true one, though the name itself would easily suggest these statements. *Geog. Soc. Journal*, x. 423.
[3] *Erdkunde*, x. p. 516.

have already noticed both in Saracenic and Christian buildings. The church faces east. Over the centre rises a large cupola supported on strong piers, and to the west of this is one large bay, which forms a lofty nave with a barrel roof; at the sides are small low round-arched aisles which run the whole length of the building; the crossing is open from side to side. Directly east of the crossing runs a low wall a few feet high, which marks off the choir from the rest of the building, and one bay east of that again the sanctuary commences, which is raised five steps, and ends in a large apse. The dimensions, when paced, proved to be about 114 feet in length to the commencement of the apsidal recess, and 84 feet in width; the height from the pavement to the top of the interior of the cupola we estimated at 70 or 80 feet. Over the altar is a double row of round arches, supporting a massive octagonal stone baldacchino, which reaches nearly to the roof; the arches of this rest on triple engaged pillars. Frescoes remain in places about the choir and sanctuary, but they are sadly defaced. Outside the building the monk showed me three tombs that contained the bodies of patriarchs of Etchmiadzin who died here.

At no great distance from Utch Keliseh the stream of the Murad is spanned by a bridge, the existence of which proves that the river, though small, is not easily forded at every season. From this point we were conducted along the southern side of the valley, and as this road seemed to lead us away from the direct track, we inquired the reason of it. We then found that the monk at the monastery had related numerous stories of plundering and murders on the part of the Kurds in this neighbourhood, which had happened within the last few days, and in consequence of this our dragoman, katirji, and zaptichs had arranged among themselves to take us by a longer route on the left bank of the Murad. From what we afterwards heard from Major Trotter, our consul at Erzeroum, these stories were probably true, but just then we were sick of tales of robbers, and we reflected that if the Kurds wanted to attack us, the difference of so slight a distance could hardly affect the question, so we immediately ordered a return to the main road. In the evening we reached the village of Gerger, and were at once struck by the appearance of its inhabitants, whose long faces and peaked features, as well as the thick mushroom caps of black or brown wool that they wore, showed that they belonged to a distinct nationality from the other races of the country. They were Persians, and we found that several other villages in this part are occupied by this people. They seem to have been settled here since about 1835, when they migrated from near Erivan in Russian territory. Perhaps this movement may have been connected with a counter-migration of the Armenians of the plain of Alashgerd, who before that time quitted their country in great numbers to settle in Russia.

The village of Gerger occupies a knoll of ground overlooking the Murad, near where the more inclosed levels open out into the wide plain of Alashgerd. A mound of this kind or a sloping hill-side is chosen by preference for the site of a village, because it offers greater facilities for burrowing into the earth. As the house which we occupied here was a favourable specimen of the native dwellings, and I have not yet given a full account of their interior and mode of construction, it may be worth while for me to describe it. After you have entered by a low door, you find a considerable area, divided up into a number of compartments, which ramify in all directions from and through one another; these compartments are formed, partly by low cross-walls plastered with clay, partly by poles which reach to the roof. These pens are almost entirely stables for cattle, but one inner compartment, which, fortunately for the occupants, has a small window in the roof, is devoted to human beings. The floor of this is composed of clay, while the stables are roughly paved. The low side-walls are formed of large stones piled together, and these support trunks of poplars laid at intervals, with numerous branches across and between them, while the whole is covered by a thick layer of clay which forms the roof. When you are resting within, small fragments either of the branches or the clay frequently detach themselves and fall upon you, or make strange sounds in the stillness of the night. When the house is built on level ground, earth is piled all over it so as to form a heap, but if it is partly excavated in a mountain side, it is only necessary to cover the roof. The weight of all this clay and earth requires very strong supports to sustain it, and it is in consequence of the value of its stems for this purpose that the poplar is so extensively grown throughout Armenia. I must repeat what I have before remarked, that the term 'underground' as applied to these dwellings is deceptive; in the strict sense of the word they neither are nor ever were so, and the ideas about them which

I myself brought with me to the country proved quite erroneous. When we arranged to sleep in one of these places, our first stipulation was that the beasts should not be allowed to enter, and this, though it excited surprise, was always agreed to, and the animals were housed elsewhere; but it would sometimes happen that before we retired to rest a belated buffalo would come lumbering in, and express reluctance and indignation at his subsequent ejection. During the summer the animals are only kept in at night, but this is necessary owing to the danger of thefts if they are left abroad; throughout the winter season, however, when both ground and houses are covered with snow, they never leave the stables; and if we found the smell of these noisome when they are vacant, what must it be when they are tenanted for months together? Yet Mr. Knapp, the missionary at Bitlis, assured us that he often passed the night in these places, together with all this company, when visiting his country congregations at that time of year; but he added that it was great suffering.

This village was the first place where we met with any difficulty with respect to the money of the country. Once or twice before we had found the people a little suspicious of the existing coinage, but here at first they flatly refused to take it, and it was only after long remonstrance and explanation that they were persuaded to do so. The reluctance which they showed is connected with one of the standing grievances of the population in Turkey, the insecurity of the currency. I have already noticed how a few years ago a proclamation was suddenly made throughout Asiatic Turkey, that no payments for taxes would be received in copper money, though that was the regular exchange for the lower classes; and this was equivalent to its withdrawal from circulation. At the present day, though it passes to some extent in Constantinople, it is never seen in the provinces. How great the loss was to the peasants, and how great for the time the injury to trade, it is not difficult to imagine. However, its place was taken by a coinage of alloyed metal, which was known as *metallique*; this was the only exchange besides gold and silver, and came to be universally recognised. It was this to which the Persian villagers objected, for their confidence was shaken by the previous act of bad faith on the part of the Government, and they feared lest they should once more lose their money. This seemed unreasonable enough at the time, but their apprehensions, though founded on no good reason, have been justified by the sequel. Six months later than this, in the middle of March 1880, we were astounded to hear through the newspapers, that a decree had been issued, lessening by one-half the value of the metallic currency. It was not surprising to learn by the same telegram that symptoms of revolution had shown themselves in consequence in various parts of the empire. Who can save a Government that treats its subjects thus?

We now entered the plain of Alashgerd, and halted in the middle of the day at Kara Keliseh, not far from the point where the Murad begins to bend away towards the south. This village contains a mixed population of Persians, Turks, and Armenians, and was once a place of some importance, but many of the houses were now in ruins, for it was sacked by the Turks during the war. Its dilapidated condition rendered it even more dirty than the ordinary villages of the country, and the dust raised by an approaching thunderstorm nearly blinded us. Beyond this the plain is intersected by many streams, tributaries of the Murad, in the neighbourhood of which numerous herons and plovers were to be seen. We passed a large Persian caravan on its way from the Black Sea to Persia, encamped near one of these ; only two or three tents were visible, but large quantities of merchandise were heaped on the ground all round them, and on the other side of the stream more than a hundred beasts of burden were feeding in the stubble. At one point we obtained a very distant view of the summit of Sipan, far away to the south, through a depression in the nearer hills. Before us towards the west the Keuseh Dagh was a conspicuous object, for it rises some 5,000 feet above the plain in a lofty pyramid with a steep face on this side ; as we approached nearer it assumed more and more the appearance of a broken-down crater, and the hills round its base looked as if they had once formed the remainder of the rim of this. The effect of the whole group was very grand owing to the thunderclouds that hung about them during the afternoon. We had hoped to reach Mollah Suleiman, a place of some size towards the end of the plain, before nightfall, but being belated, we remained at an Armenian village called Koshlian.

The whole of the following day was occupied in crossing the Delibaba pass. As Mollah Suleiman lay at the foot of the heights towards the north, it was altogether out of our course, but it was necessary to obtain a fresh zaptieh from thence, for the one whom we had brought from Diyadin was only authorised to accompany us thus far. Accordingly we sent our dragoman thither with the firman under this man's escort, with orders to meet us at the angle of the plain. It was not long before we reached the mountains, near where Tergukassoff for some time occupied a strong position in the early part of the campaign. On the way we were met by a long train of 170 laden camels, and these were followed some hours later by another, though smaller, caravan. The pass for some distance is composed of a succession of hills and valleys which have to be crossed one after the other; but towards the middle a fine glen is formed, with ridges crowned by basaltic pinnacles, and as this is deep and winds much it ought to be easy of defence. The eagles, of which bird we had seen great numbers in Eastern Armenia, were here sufficiently tame to remain perched on the telegraph posts within easy pistol-shot as we passed. Beyond this a long ascent through grassy uplands leads to the summit, which is a sort of double *col* with a low valley between; on the first of the two heights is a small redoubt with rifle-pits. Looking down from this point towards the south we saw below us another road leading from Bayazid to Erzeroum; this on the maps is called Kara Derbend, and is the lowest and easiest pass through these mountains between the valley of the Murad and that of the Araxes, but far the most circuitous. It is the usual caravan route, and is free from snow much longer than the other tracks; by it the Turks retreated from Bayazid to join Mukhtar Pasha after the battle of

Alaja Dagh. It will thus be seen that this watershed is a point not easy to defend, because any one of the passages through it can readily be turned. On the further side of the *col* numerous pyramidal mountains now appeared in the foreground towards the west, and behind them portions of the distant plain of Pasin opened out at intervals.

As we were commencing the descent, in one of the most solitary spots in the pass, some baggage-horses were seen approaching, the luggage on which had an unmistakably English look. On inquiry we learnt that this belonged to an Inghiliz pasha, and a few minutes afterwards, at a turn of the road, the Inghiliz pasha himself appeared in the shape of Captain Everett, our newly-appointed vice-consul at Erzeroum, who was accompanied by another young Englishman, probably a student-interpreter. It was a mutual surprise, and after many greetings and questions, in the course of which Captain Everett recognised our dragoman as having been his travelling servant in the Balkans earlier in the year, we discovered that they were on their way to investigate the disturbances which had been reported from the country further east. 'So far,' he said, 'we have found nothing amiss, but we expect we are now entering the disturbed districts.' We laughed, for this was the part we had just traversed, but it appeared certain that even caravans had been lately pillaged there by the Kurds, and during this day our zaptieh was continually riding to commanding points in order to reconnoitre, and expressed his anxiety that our party should keep together. There was no time for a long parley, but we agreed to exchange our zaptiehs as they had come from different sides of the pass, that they might return at once to their homes, and then parted with warm shaking of hands. To us this meeting with two countrymen, and the few fragments of news they imparted to us, seemed like a ray of light let in upon us from Europe.

At the foot of the first descent is the Armenian village of Tahir, which was destroyed by the Turks at the time of the war. The valley in which it lies was the scene of the great defeat of their right wing, by which their cause was almost ruined in the early part of the campaign. The fighting on that occasion continued, I believe, for eight hours, and the result gave the Russians the command of the pass, and a position in Mukhtar Pasha's rear. Again the intricate path mounts to another *col*, and from thence there is a long descent, until you traverse a narrow gorge of crumbling red and grey limestone, and emerge into an upland level deeply sunk amidst steep heights, where stands the village of Eshek Elias, inhabited by Kurds. The position is very fine, though the surroundings are bare. This place, where we encamped for the night, witnessed another great engagement, five days after that at Tahir, in which the Turks, now commanded by Mukhtar himself, turned the tables on their adversaries, and drove them from their entrenched positions, though with great loss of life, mainly owing to their not availing themselves of the cover afforded by the ground, and exposing themselves unnecessarily to the Russian fire. This victory rendered it possible for the Turkish commander-in-chief to fight the great battle of Zewin on the Soghanli Dagh four days later.[1] The name of

---

[1] The battle of Tahir is described by an eye-witness in the *Times* of

the place is a puzzle, for Elias seems to be that of the Jewish prophet, who is venerated as a saint by the Eastern Christians, while Eshek, which is the Turkish for 'ass,' sounds like an uncomplimentary prefix. The idea suggests itself that it may have been originally an Armenian village, called Surp (Saint) Elias, and that a Kurdish population which succeeded them may in contempt have changed the title into Eshek; but this is guess-work. It will have been remarked, however, how varied are the nationalities that are found along this line of country—Persians, Turks, Armenians, and Kurds; and we know that many of the Armenians have emigrated.

From Eshek Elias we followed a stream downwards for several hours in the midst of grand mountains, the road from time to time being hemmed in between lofty rocks of fine colours, until we reached the wide valley of Delibaba from which the pass gets its name. Before arriving at this, we passed on our right the entrance to a valley, by which there is another route to Mollah Suleiman by the foot of the Keuseh Dagh; this, we were told, is two hours shorter than the road which we followed, but it is a fatiguing journey. The village of Delibaba—that is, Crazy Father, so called probably in commemoration of some dervish—now came in sight, but as it was some distance from our route, we entrusted our firman to our zaptieh, with orders to send on his successor from thence. At this point the scenery changes, and instead of fine broken heights we have wide dreary

July 9, 1877; that of Eshek Elias in the same paper of July 20. See also Mr. Norman's (the *Times* correspondent) *Armenia and the Campaign of* 1877, pp. 107-120, and 151-155.

undulations, extending far away towards the west, and marking the line of our subsequent journey. On the horizon towards the north-east the lofty Soghanli Dagh is visible, which intervenes between this neighbourhood and Kars. The Araxes is here about six miles distant to the north, but it is not within view, and the mountains on the other side of the valley in which it flows have a level and commonplace outline. Again we met two Persian caravans, whose approach was notified some time beforehand by the clanging of large bells, for these are usually attached to the camels, being sometimes hung round their necks, sometimes suspended from the sides of their loads, so that one beast will even carry as many as five of these appendages. Many of the packages had French titles outside; but however this may be, I was assured at Erzeroum that most of the goods transported are of English manufacture. I have seen it stated that the Russian railway from Poti on the Black Sea to Tiflis in Georgia has diverted a great part of the Persian traffic, but this does not seem to be the case. On the contrary, the captain of one of the French steamers that ply between Trebizond and Constantinople told me that, instead of declining, the Erzeroum trade has increased of late years.

The small village of Jaliak, where we rested in the middle of the day, was inhabited by Turks, and had been ruined by the Russians during the war. Along the whole of this route we were told that the Christian villages were destroyed by the Turks, and the Mahometan villages by the Russians; but the 'Times' correspondent, who was on the spot at the time, attributes the destruction to the Kurds; so much so, that he says that in the district we have hitherto passed through, out of 126 villages all but nine were abandoned in the latter part of the campaign owing to their depredations. It seems improbable that the commanders on either side, knowing that they might have to retreat along this line, which in fact they had to do, should willingly have allowed the sources of their supplies to be ruined. Our afternoon's ride was one of the dullest in our whole journey, for the levels over which it lay were brown and bare; the one object that relieved the view was a rocky summit among the mountains far away towards Erzeroum, which stood out against the sky, in form closely resembling a cathedral, with a square central tower, and nave and choir. In the evening we were indemnified by a magnificent sunset, the sun going down clear in front of us, and leaving the cloud racks illuminated with gold, and the mountains below of the deepest blue. We stopped at a place called Amrakom, inhabited by Turks and Persians, which possessed shops, and a greater appearance of prosperity than the rest of these villages.

At about an hour's distance to the west of Amrakom, the road to Erzeroum crosses the Araxes, or Bingheul-chai, as it is here called, in consequence of its rising in the mountain of that name. It is a clear stream of some width, but not deep, so that we forded it easily. At this point it turns at right angles, and from having flowed towards the north, now takes an easterly course, and runs at the foot of the mountains in a deep bed which it has cut for itself. The position is an important one, because here the road from Kars to Erzeroum joins that from Bayazid, and consequently the neighbouring village of Kiupri-keui has been fortified, and Mukhtar Pasha attempted to make a stand there in his hurried retreat. The bridge (*kiupri*) which is thrown across it is the finest, I think, of all the bridges that I have seen in Turkey. It is composed of six arches massively built of stone, and rises from the right bank, which is on the level of the stream, to the left, where it abuts on steeper ground. Both on the upper and the lower side the piers are supported by large buttresses, and some of these have ornamental string-courses. The plain that extends to the west is watered, like the corresponding part of the plain of Alashgerd, by the tributaries of the main river, and these we now follow upward towards its head. Half-way along on the northern side stands the fortress of Hassan-kaleh, the position of which closely corresponds to those which the Greeks chose by preference for the sites of their cities, being a spur that runs out into the lower ground at the foot of the higher mountains. It has several lines of fortifications, and commands this part of the plain. A small town lies on its western side. As we advanced further to the west, we learnt that all the villages beyond in the direction of Erzeroum were in ruins, and consequently we were forced to stop at Arjalash, a Mussulman village situated on the slope of the hills towards the south.

From the retreat of Mukhtar we must turn for a moment to that of Xenophon, for we are now once more on the track of the Ten Thousand, whom we left in the plain of Mush, after they had passed the watershed between Kurdistan and Armenia. In that plain they crossed the Euphrates (Murad), and then after some days reached a river called the Phasis, in the neighbourhood of which was a people called the Phasiani.[1] Now as the plain through which the Araxes here flows is at the present day called Pasin, it seems probable that they crossed the intervening mountains, and thus reached this district, which in fact would be the most natural course for them to pursue in endeavouring to find their way towards the west.[2] Their course henceforward is extremely obscure, but fortunately the configuration of the ground is such that the general direction of their journey was almost necessarily determined for them. Finding at this point a mountain chain facing them towards the north, a river flowing east, and its tributaries coming from the west, they would naturally follow the latter upwards, since that route would lead them towards their home. They would thus find their way into the plain of Erzeroum, and thence, though every outlet was difficult, they could hardly help taking—what must have been at all times a line of communication—the course which we are about to take to reach Trebizond.

Throughout this day, as we advanced along the plain, we had observed a long flat-topped ridge at the end, closing it up on its western side. These are the heights of the Deveh Boyoun, where the Turks made their last stand. The following morning (September 16) we reached the foot of the ridge, and crossed a low pass between it and two detached hills with slight fortifications on their summits, which rise towards the south. Then comes a deep depression, succeeded by a further ridge of some elevation, from which is the immediate descent into Erzeroum. The whole of the

---

[1] Xen. *Anab.* iv. 6, § 4, 5.
[2] See Bunbury, *History of Ancient Geography*, i. 355, 378.

mountain barrier along this line is included in the common name of Deveh Boyoun, but the part which the Turks defended is the first ascent, where the ground slopes upward at a considerable angle, thus forming a strong position. The heights directly above the city are crowned with forts, which are of the utmost importance to hold, because if they are captured the place itself becomes untenable. As we descended, the extensive plain of Erzeroum came in view, inclosed on the further side by finely shaped mountains; and at last the city appeared, which, however, does not lie in the plain itself, but on the lowest slopes at the edge of it, half encircled at the back by a lofty chain, of which the Deveh Boyoun forms a part. As seen from without, it seemed the most imposing city, with the exception of Amasia, that we had reached in our journey, owing to the numerous minarets and other striking buildings that rise up from its midst. Before entering the walls we passed a large tomb, resembling in its shape those which we had seen at Akhlat and in the neighbourhood of Kaiserieh—tall, with a stone roof rising to a central point, and containing an upper chamber with small windows. The walls themselves have been engineered on scientific principles, but now there are gaps and breaches in them. The interior of the city is fairly clean, and the houses gave us the idea of great sumptuousness in contrast to the hovels to which we had for some time been accustomed, for most of them were built of two, and some even of three, storeys. A few of them were partly excavated in the hill-sides, but these had very slight claim to being called subterranean. We were received with great kindness by our consul-general, Major Trotter, who entertained us during our stay. If our meeting with two Englishmen on the Delibaba pass seemed like a ray of light from Europe, at Erzeroum we felt ourselves on the outskirts of that continent: we appeared to have come from so much further east, and to be now so much nearer to a port, which would be a starting-point for reaching civilised countries.

CHAPTER XV.

ERZEROUM AND BAIBURT.

Erzeroum: its history—The Persian quarter—Principal buildings of the city—The castle—Prospects of famine—Consular reports on the country—Possible remedies for its disorders—Warm springs of Ilidja—The Frat, or Western Euphrates—Pass of the Kop Dagh—River Tchoruk—Baiburt: its castle—Ancient buildings at Varzahan—Armenian architecture—Intricate passes—'Thalatta! Thalatta!'—Route of the Ten Thousand.

ERZEROUM is the most important place in Armenia. The ground on which it stands has been occupied by a city from ancient times, as might be expected from its position on the edge of an extensive and fertile plain, and at the entrance of a pass on the main line of communication between the Black Sea and Persia. The earliest name that it bore was Karin, but in the year 415 of our era this was changed to Theodosiopolis in honour of the Emperor Theodosius the Younger, when the place was fortified by Anatolius, the general of the armies of that prince in the East. From that time it became the principal stronghold of the Roman Empire in this country. Its modern name is a corruption of Arzen-er-Rum, or Arzen of the Romans, the title which it received from the Saracens. Being a frontier fortress, it several times changed hands between the Greeks and the Moslems during the early period of the Middle Ages. In the thirteenth century it was stormed and pillaged by the Mongols, and when their power came to an end it fell into the hands of the Turks, to whom it has since belonged. During the campaign of 1829 it was captured by the Russians, but in the late war they failed to take it, and it was only ceded to them as a material guarantee while the terms of peace were being negotiated. The population, which once was very large, has greatly declined of late years, and at present is estimated at only 20,000. Owing to the great elevation of the place—about 6,000 feet above the sea—the cold is extreme in winter, and continues far into the year, so that snow has been known to fall even as late as the commencement of June ; but in the height of summer, as is often the case in high plateaux, the heat is excessive.

The quarter of the city which we passed through on our way from the gate of entrance to Major Trotter's house was inhabited by Persians. These people form an important element in the population, for they number about two thousand, and most of the carrying trade with Persia is in their hands. In consequence of this they enjoy greater freedom and consideration here than they do elsewhere in Turkey. Thus the spectacle of the Muharram—a yearly celebration in honour of Hussein and Hassan, the sons of Ali, and in lamentation for them—which in Constantinople and elsewhere has to be enacted in private, here is carried on in the open streets. Mr. Cole, an American missionary who resides here, described to me the scene, when the devotees, clothed in white robes, go in procession through the city at nightfall, carrying swords. With these they gash their heads, and the wounds thus inflicted are slight at first ; but when the actors become excited, they are so dangerously severe, that the relations of those who take part in the ceremony are wont to accompany them in order to parry the blows. The ghastliness of the sight is naturally increased by the contrast between the red bloodstains and the white dresses. In Constantinople this takes place within a large caravanserai, and there, owing to the more confined space, it is more disgusting and less imposing.

On the day after our arrival we visited the principal buildings of Erzeroum, accompanied by Major Trotter, who had obtained for us special permission to inspect the castle and some ancient edifices, which, being used by the Government as depositories for stores and for similar purposes, are not otherwise allowed to be seen. The shops which we passed as we walked through the streets appeared to be good, and those for provisions were well supplied, for the festival of Bairam, with which the Ramazan concludes, was to commence that evening. A great abundance of fruit was exposed for sale, including even grapes, but these last were not grown in the neighbourhood, the climate of which is too severe for them, but had been brought from a place about eighteen hours distant towards the Russian frontier. Erzeroum is supposed to be celebrated for its brass work, but we could neither see nor hear of anything in that line but what was quite common.

The first building that we visited was that called Tchifteh Minareh, or the 'Pair of Minarets,' from two of those erections, which rise to a considerable height above the façade, and are constructed of brick, with small engaged pillars of the same material all round them. They differ in style from the rest of the edifice, and were evidently added at a later period. The portal in front is surmounted by fine honeycomb work, and the stone at the sides is also elaborately decorated. Within is a broad nave, the span of which must have been fine when the roof was in its place and the arches that supported it were standing; there is also a crossing, and instead of aisles on the two sides are rows of arches forming two storeys, one above the other. The ornament was mostly incised, and contained much interlaced work. Hamilton believes that this was originally a Christian church,[1] but I could see no signs of this in the building itself, and as it points exactly towards Mecca, it is more likely that it was a mosque. Attached to the further end of it, though forming apparently a separate building, was a large polygonal edifice, corresponding in its general features to the tomb which we had seen outside the walls, but much larger and loftier. It had numerous small windows pierced high up, and niches with honeycomb work round the lower part inside. Some of the details of these buildings were not easy to investigate, in consequence of portions of them being built up as store-chambers, and the people who were in charge of them knew nothing of the purpose for which they were originally designed. Not far off, but on the opposite side of the castle, was another brick column, called Bir Minareh, or the 'Single Minaret;' this corresponded in style to the former ones, but was much more elaborately ornamented, and numerous pieces of blue encaustic tiles were introduced in patterns on its surface.

[1] *Researches in Asia Minor*, i. 179.

The castle occupies a height of no great area in the middle of the city. It contains no object of interest except a small Saracenic chapel, but the view from the walls all round is very fine, comprising the mountains at the back, the plain, the circuit of the modern walls, the numerous minarets, and the busy streets. The extent of the fortifications is very great, and a considerable space intervenes between the walls and the city; to defend them properly not less than 20,000 men would probably be required. Major Trotter, who was within Erzeroum during the late siege, pointed out to us the fort on the heights in the direction of the Devch Boyoun which the Russians momentarily entered. They were almost immediately driven out again, but had they held it they would have commanded the city. The attack was part of a combined movement, for another Russian detachment had been sent round during the night to descend on the place by a pass through the steep mountains towards the south, and thus to distract the attention of the besieged. In the darkness, however, they lost their way, so that they did not reach the heights till daybreak, and as the descent was long they were easily kept in check by the Turkish artillery. This accident probably saved the city, for the Turks required all their men to resist the masses that the Russians brought up to retake the fort on the heights.

During the evening Mr. Cole dined with Major Trotter to meet us. From him we first heard of the alarming prospect of famine in Armenia during the coming winter, which has since been so lamentably realised. It seemed that the harvest in this country, instead of having been abundant, as we had found it in Asia Minor, had been almost a total failure, owing to the want of rain. The peasants had stored far less grain than they had sown, and flour in consequence was six times as dear as it had been a year before, the measure that then cost $2\frac{1}{2}$ piastres being purchased at this time for 15 piastres. Yet tithes, taxes, and Government exactions remained the same as in more favourable seasons. It was clear that, when the small remaining supply of corn was exhausted, starvation would be the inevitable result. From all that we could learn the normal condition of the Christians in this neighbourhood was very bad; nor did there seem to be much loyalty among the Turks, though there is no openly declared disaffection, as there is in Asia Minor. The troops in Erzeroum had received no pay for four years, and nothing but loyalty to the Sultan and devotion to their religion kept them from mutinying; even so, it was a question how long their allegiance would continue. The pasha was anxious to give them a month's pay at this festive season, but in order to do this he was forced to borrow 1,200*l.* on his own responsibility, for nothing was forthcoming from Stamboul. Owing to the proximity of the Russian frontier we had expected to find that amongst the Armenians of this part Russian influence was predominant. But this was not the case, for that nation was not in good odour in Erzeroum owing to the intemperance and incontinence of their soldiers at the time of the occupation. On the other hand, the Ottoman authorities and leading Mussulmans, both here and in the other principal cities, for instance at Van, showed no goodwill towards the English.

In the course of this narrative I have had occasion from time to time to remark on the condition of the subject population in Armenia and Asia Minor; and in order to show that I have rather understated than overstated the case, it may be well for me, now that we are about to leave the last great city that we visited in Armenia, to corroborate my statements by further evidence. During the summer of 1879 a Blue-book was published (Turkey, No. 10) entitled, 'Correspondence respecting the Condition of the Population in Asia Minor and Syria,' which is mainly composed of consular reports relating to those countries. In this Major Trotter writes to Lord Salisbury with reference to the ill-treatment of the Armenians by the Kurds (p. 15) : ' It is useless entering into details of the thousand and one modes in which the Beys can, and generally do, oppress the rayahs of their villages—forced labour and heavy and unlawful exactions of many kinds, both in money and produce, contemptuous and insulting language, often accompanied by blows to the males, and too often by violation of honour to the females.[1] It can easily be understood that in a country where no law exists, where the feudal chiefs are possessed of almost absolute power over a race of people whom they both dislike and despise, the state of the subject race is truly miserable.' On the same point Sir A. H. Layard addresses a *Note Verbale* to the Porte, in which he says (pp. 106–7) : ' Her Majesty's Ambas-

---

[1] In this respect I am sorry to see that the Kurds are painted in darker colours than what I had been led to believe was the case.

sador desires to submit to the Sublime Porte a statement relating to the oppression and outrages to which the Armenians of the village of Ognoa, in the district of Gönig, in Kurdistan, are subjected by Kurdish chiefs. . . . The state of things existing in this village unhappily appears to prevail over a great part of the east of Anatolia, comprised in what is called Kurdistan.' With regard to the zaptiehs Major Trotter writes (pp. 28, 29): 'Your Excellency is probably aware that the monthly pay of a zaptieh, in addition to a bread ration, is 70 piastres a month, paid, if at all, in caïmé—*i.e.* at present rates, about 3*s.* a month. Even assuming them to be regularly paid, which they are not, how is it possible for a man to exist and provide for his family on this miserable pittance ? . . . As it is, they are generally believed, in order to obtain a living, to get their share of almost every robbery that occurs, if, indeed, they are not in many instances the actual criminals.'

With regard to the Circassians in Asia Minor, Colonel Wilson writes (p. 126): 'The Circassians came into the country with nothing but their arms ; now every Circassian has a horse, some two or three. They receive an allowance raised by a tax upon the community amongst which they live ; but, not content with this, take what they please from the people. They follow no pursuits save those of highway robbery and petty pilfering, and being well armed with rifles, revolvers, and swords, whilst the zaptiehs have often nothing better than flint-lock guns, they place the local government at defiance ; the people who suffer have no redress.' With regard to the courts of justice the same writer says

(p. 127): 'The state of the courts leaves much to be desired; the councils, though in theory elected by the people, are really nominated by the local government, or the seats on them are sold; bribery and corruption are the rule, not the exception; retention in or escape from prison is frequently a matter of bribery; there is a general complaint that justice is rarely executed on behalf of a Christian or against a Moslem; and that, though Christian evidence is nominally received, little or no weight is attached to it in the courts. The cost of litigation is so great that the villagers when robbed often refrain from bringing the robbery to the notice of the local authorities; the uncertainty of obtaining a verdict, the loss of time involved by compulsory attendance at the chief town of the kaimakamlik, and the expense of the trial, sufficiently account for this.' On the subject of the condition of the country generally, and the prevailing disorganisation, no language could well be stronger than that of Sir Henry Layard (see especially pp. 93 and 100), both to the Porte and the Home Government.

It is my object rather to state facts than to draw conclusions, but perhaps it may not be out of place to consider for a moment, with regard to Armenia, what possible remedy can be found for this state of things. It is hardly necessary at present to consider whether that country can be constituted an independent state. There is a *primâ facie* objection to this on the ground that the Armenians do not form an absolute majority of the population; but to this no great weight need be attached, because they are the original inhabitants, and possess almost all the intelligence and capacity for progress that exists in the country, and it is bad government that has caused the emigration by which their number has been reduced. Besides this, the nomad Kurds are hardly an element that need be taken into consideration in determining the question. The opinion of residents in the country, however, was not in favour of its being governed by the Armenians; though, if other expedients fail, this can at least be tried, and some persons who have a right to judge believe that they would succeed. But three reforms may at least be demanded, the concession of which would soon ameliorate the condition of the people, viz. the appointment of a Christian governor with large powers, the permission to form a local militia, and the right of spending the greater part of the revenue of the province on local objects. The first of these reforms would secure the country against the peculation and misgovernment of Turkish officials; the second would soon establish order, for that the Kurds are no formidable enemies if any serious resistance is offered to them, was amply proved in the late war; and the third would tend rapidly to develop the resources of the land and the industry of the people. It is greatly to the interest of England to see that these changes are introduced, and in other ways to uphold the cause of the Armenians, because of the importance of interposing a people that is animated with a strong feeling of national life, and indisposed to be absorbed by any other empire, between the Russian dominions and Asia Minor. But of one thing we may feel certain—that these concessions will not be made by the Porte except under severe pressure, and perhaps only as the result of a violent struggle.

On September 18 we commenced the last stage of our journey, and leaving Erzeroum, rode westwards across the plain. The road which we followed was solidly built, but we had not gone far before, to our astonishment, we found it cut through from side to side by a deep dike, by which all passengers, and still more all vehicles, were forced to turn aside into the neighbouring fields. The explanation of this seemed to be that, when the road was constructed, no provision was made for the passage of the surface-water underneath it, and in order to remedy this it was afterwards spoiled. Some way further on the causeway, though still solid, became so rough, that travellers avoided it, and followed an easier track along the roadside. At the end of three hours we reached the foot of the hills which project from the southern side of the plain; here is the village of Ilidja ('Warm Spring'), in the midst of which the copious sources from which it takes its name issue from the rock. There can be little doubt that this was the site of the warm baths which Anatolius, the founder of Theodosiopolis, is stated to have constructed in the neighbourhood of that place.[1] We now began to approach the Frat, or western Euphrates, the reedy winding stream of which is somewhat wider than that of the Murad at the point where we first saw its upper course. The source of the Frat lies amongst the mountains to the north of Erzeroum, about six hours distant from that city. We had thus visited the head waters of the four great rivers that rise in Armenia, to explore which had been one object of our journey—those of the western

[1] Moses of Chorene, iii. 50. See Saint-Martin, *Mémoires*, i. 67.

branch of the Tigris near Kharput, those of the eastern branch of that river above Bitlis, the upper stream of the eastern Euphrates at Diyadin, and here that of the western confluent which still retains its name. We followed the slopes of the hills overlooking the course of the river, about which numerous water birds were to be seen, until after seven hours we reached a khan, newly built and in nice order, where we determined to pass the night. A khan was a novelty to us, owing to the absence of such places of accommodation in the country through which we had lately been travelling, and proved to us that we were now on a more frequented road. The newness of its construction, and its name Yeni Khan, *i.e.* 'the new khan,' were accounted for by its having been erected to replace a similar building at some little distance off, which had been ruined by the Russians during the war. Throughout this day the temperature had been decidedly chilly, and the nights from this time onward were so cold that we were glad to use all the coverings that we had brought with us.

In the course of the following day we crossed the Frat by a wooden bridge supported on stone piers. Its surroundings were picturesque, for just above this point the river is joined by a tributary, and between the two a steep mass of rock rises with a village nestling at its foot. The road now begins to ascend, and follows the line of the hills on the opposite side of the stream, which here wanders hither and thither through a wide valley; afterwards we penetrated into the mountains, and passing through a narrow gorge, reached the commencement of the ascent of the lofty Kop Dagh, which is the great barrier between Erzeroum and Baiburt on the road to Trebizond, and forms the watershed between the valley of the Euphrates and the Black Sea. Here there was a khan, but it appeared such an uninviting resting-place for the night, that we determined to cross the pass at once, though the afternoon was already far advanced. The road in this part has been finely engineered, and rises in a gentle gradient, though, as the native rock protrudes here and there in rough masses, it would appear either that it was never completed, or that the macadamised part has all been worn away; the smaller bridges, too, have mostly been allowed to fall out of repair, so that many of them are all but impassable. The higher we rose the finer the views became over successive mountain ranges towards the south and the long depression which marks the course of the Frat, and the wild storms which were sweeping over the sky in that direction added to the grandeur of the effect. The sun set just as we reached the summit, the height of which is 7,600 feet, and we had a longer descent than we expected before reaching a halting-place. Fortunately we had been joined on the way from Erzeroum by an Armenian merchant—a *chasseur de loupes*, or collector of, and dealer in, the excrescences of walnut trees—who at this time was coming from Van, and seemed to be familiar with every step of the road. Both in his general appearance and the vivacity of his manner, this gentleman resembled a Frenchman much more than an Armenian. He carried an opera-glass slung over one shoulder, but in other respects was very sportingly attired; he was an ardent lover of *le sport*, and amused us by the way in which he would at a moment's notice leave his horse in the road, and rush about over the rocks and watercourses to get a shot at a partridge or wild duck. Under his guidance we left the main road, and leading our horses, scrambled down by steep descents in the midst of aromatic shrubs, which emitted scents such as we had rarely smelt on the plateaux of Armenia. By this means we saved an hour in time, but it was quite dark when we found ourselves at a large khan, which from the mountain is called Kop Khané, and is the natural starting-point or resting-place for those who cross the pass.

The river which we followed downwards the next morning through a wide valley between lofty mountains, is the Tchoruk, the ancient Acampsis, which flows towards the Black Sea, reaching it near Batoum. The clouds, which for some time had been threatening, now broke in heavy rain; but the previous part of our journey had been so fortunate in this respect, that this was only the second occasion on which we had been met by unfavourable weather. It was not long past noon when we reached our immediate destination, the town of Baiburt, but we determined to spend the rest of the day there, in order to examine carefully the ruins of its castle, the magnificent appearance of which we were not prepared for. The town is hardly visible from this side until you enter it, for the valley here makes an excessively sharp turn, and on passing this you suddenly see the buildings rising up the hills on both sides of the river, which has now become a considerable stream. The river bank itself is flanked by extensive vegetable gardens and poplar plantations, while directly opposite stands the lofty castle-hill, crowned with a long and varied line of fortifications. Baiburt is a considerable town of 2,000 houses, 300 of which are inhabited by Christians.

At Erzeroum we had been told that on our journey we should probably fall in with Samih Pasha, who was on his way from Constantinople to Van, on a mission to re-establish order among the Kurds; for there were strong suspicions at this time, as I have already intimated, of a general rising among that people, the tribes of the Julamerk being in open hostility to the Government, and it being shrewdly suspected that the movements among the Haideranlis and others had a political significance. Samih is considered a capable man, but has been regarded with some suspicion on account of his Russian proclivities. It happened that his arrival at Baiburt was expected just as we entered the public square, where a squadron of cavalry was drawn up to receive him, and shortly afterwards his portly form appeared, drawn in a two-horsed carriage, which was followed by a not very imposing retinue. The moment was an unfortunate one for us, for the authorities to whom we applied for a lodging were too much occupied with the great man's arrival to think of anything else, and with less than the usual courtesy we were sent to a very uninviting khan. The difficulty was solved in a similar way to what had occurred on one or two former occasions, for when my companion was returning to complain of this, he was met by a hospitable Armenian, who offered to entertain us in his house, which was situated on the slopes of the castle-hill; this proposal we gladly accepted.

The castle is built upon an isolated mass of rock,

running from east to west, and steep on every side, but especially at the eastern end, where it descends precipitously to the river. The Tchoruk here makes another sudden bend, so as to flow round two sides of the hill, after which it may be seen from above winding away in the direction of Batoum. The principal line of walls follows the crest throughout its whole length, and there is also a lower wall on the southern side, some way down the hill overlooking the town. At intervals in the walls there are towers, some round and some square, and the whole is composed of a yellowish brown stone. We entered the fortifications by a gateway near the south-eastern angle, and then descending the steep slopes on the further side, reached the entrance to two covered staircases, which lead down to the level of the stream, and were no doubt intended to secure a supply of water. Mounting again from these along the northern side, we found a vaulted chamber, now ruined, which probably served for a cistern; and still higher up there were remains of the apse of a Christian church, and some insignificant ruins of a mosque. The highest fortifications are at the western extremity, where the towers rise to a great elevation above the ground below, and the masonry is very massive. The views of the town and river, with the plantations and gardens, as seen through the openings in the walls, are extremely pretty. The principal entrance is towards the south-west; near this there is an Arabic inscription in large letters high up on the wall, and there is another by the gateway; a third was pointed out to us at the east end by the zaptieh who accompanied us. As we descended towards the town, he also showed us, just below the castle walls, a small inclosure containing the tomb of a Turkish saint, which was an object of pilgrimage. An Armenian priest, who visited us in the course of the evening, said that he had copied and translated all the inscriptions, and that they referred to the reconstruction of the building by the Seljouks. It was originally built, he said, by the Armenians, to whose time the passages leading to the water belonged, but by far the greater part was Seljoukian. In many respects it reminded us of the architecture of the castle of Bitlis. This priest had once lived in Manchester, which place he had left five years before. He spoke English, but very slowly, like one who was trying to recollect it. He told us he had only spoken it about six times since he had returned from England.

There are two routes which lead from Baiburt to Trebizond, one of which is taken by the main road, and follows the course of the river valleys, while the other strikes across the intervening mountains. The former of these is the easier of the two, but much more circuitous, and accordingly at Erzeroum we were recommended to take the mountain road; but here the Turkish authorities, when we applied to them, appeared to know but little about the latter way, and discouraged us from following it, saying that in bad weather if clouds came over it was easy to miss the track, and recommending us at the same time to take five zaptiehs as a protection—a proposal which we at once declined as unnecessary. We determined to follow this route, though there seemed to be some slight risk attending it, for we had heard of people being robbed in those parts, and possibly at this time there was an additional element of insecurity owing to the Mussulman emigrants from Lazistan, many of whom had passed through this country, when they left their homes in order to avoid becoming Russian subjects; but it was at once shorter, and likely to prove the more interesting. The two roads diverge at the village of Varzahan, about two hours distant from Baiburt, and here we made our first halt, when we resumed our journey on the following day, in order to visit the remarkable architectural remains at that place.

The ancient buildings at Varzahan occupy a rising ground above the modern village. From a distance they might easily be mistaken for towers; but as you approach, you find that they are mediaeval Armenian edifices of very elaborate design. The best preserved of these is a small octagonal chapel or tomb, the outer wall of which is standing, though the roof and most of the interior is destroyed. A single column, however, remains upright within, and this formed one of a circle of similar shafts, between which and the wall a sort of aisle or passage must have run round, and which would seem to have supported a cupola. On the western, northern, and southern sides are entrance doors, and in a corresponding position towards the east is a small apse. Over the west door there is a large window, but the others throughout the building are mere slits, the lights being usually double with a small pier dividing them, while above these again is another opening equally narrow. All the arches are round, and here and there in the openings of the windows are the remains of rude patterns in fresco. Close by this stands another building, so ruined that its plan can hardly be made out, but on the eastern side a pointed arch remains, and over it a fragment of a blind arcade, with niches on its external face, which seems to have formed part of the drum or lantern of a cupola. In both these the ornamentation was careful and delicate, the cable or twisted moulding prevailing. In the neighbourhood was an ancient cemetery, in one part of which, side by side, were three tombs cut into the shape of rams, the carving of the limbs and tails being in very low relief. At a little distance from this group, and on higher ground, is another church, which appears to have been in the form of a Greek cross, with a central cupola; a large part of the drum of the cupola remains, with numerous small round-headed windows, but it was impossible to visit the interior of the building, as all the entrances had been blocked up.

The architects of these edifices were no despicable artists, but neither inscriptions nor other sources of evidence remain to show at what period they lived. In their architectural features, the buildings show many points of resemblance to those of Ani in Russian Armenia, and from this we may conclude that they are of the eleventh or twelfth century. But they possess very few features in common with the other remarkable churches which we have noticed in this country, such as that of Utch Keliseh, near Diyadin, or that of the monastery of Surp Garabed, near Mush. Indeed, it seems almost impossible to trace any consecutive development in the styles of Armenian architecture, though the influence both of Persian and Byzantine art may be visible in them. With regard to the forms of these edifices, Mr. Fergusson remarks in his 'History of Architecture:' 'The plans of Armenian churches defy classification; some are square, or rectangles of every conceivable proportion of length to breadth, some octagons or hexagons, and some of the most indescribable irregularity.'[1]

At Varzahan we noticed for the first time that there was freshly fallen snow on the neighbouring mountain tops, and this seemed to be a warning to us that we ought soon to be leaving the country. The plentiful rain which subsequently fell during our stay at Trebizond and our voyage along the coast of the Black Sea, fully confirmed this, and showed that the season for travelling in Armenia was past. During the afternoon of the same day we reached a khan, where the intricate passes begin that lead to Trebizond; here we stopped for the night, and commenced the ascent the following morning. Our way now lay over granite mountains, wild and bare, though with some elements of grandeur, such as are found in the inferior passes of the Alps. The path was a mere mountain track, far less well marked than we had expected to find it; and in the winter-time it can hardly be passable, for the steep slopes which it frequently traverses must at that time of year be covered with ice or frozen snow. At this season large flocks of broad-tailed sheep were feeding in the valleys or along the declivities. The pass consists of a succession of *cols*, on the first of which is a small cemetery, containing the tomb of a Turkish saint, whence the whole pass gets the name of Hadji Vali Mezari, or 'the tomb of Hadji Vali.' All round this numerous white crocuses were springing from the ground. Then followed an extensive space of upland pasture, in the midst of

[1] Vol. ii. p. 473 (2nd ed.).

which is a small fountain with a Turkish inscription—a friendly object in so desolate a spot. Once more we ascended to a higher *col*, and on the further side of this rested awhile by a spring in a regular Alpine meadow covered with short green turf. At last a steep descent of 1,600 feet, down which we had to lead our horses, brought us to the entrance of a narrow gorge between steep and lofty granite cliffs, the scenery of which was not unworthy of the St. Gothard pass. A stream flows through this, and when we emerged at the further end we might have hoped to follow its course downwards, but the mountain ranges in this part are far too much jumbled together to allow of so simple an outlet, and we were forced to diverge from it through a side valley in which a tributary flows. Thus far the day had been fine, and in this we were fortunate, for in bad weather the path might have been difficult to find; but now the clouds which had added to the grandeur of the gorge by drifting through it and trailing about its precipices, closed in around us, and in the midst of these we mounted once more to a great height, until at last a short descent brought us to our resting-place, the village of Tasch Kiupri, which is so called from a stone bridge in its neighbourhood. The whole of this day's ride had been strangely solitary, and it is evident that very few travellers pass by this way. The *khanji* here was a Greek, and spoke Greek as his native language—not Turkish, as is the case with the Greeks in the interior of Asia Minor; this was our first evidence that we were approaching a district inhabited by that people.

On resuming our journey the next day (September 23) we quitted the direct road to Trebizond, as it was now our object to visit the famous Greek monastery of Sumelas, which is situated in one of the lateral valleys a little distance off. At first our track once more ascended, but we had not proceeded far before our eyes were gladdened by a most welcome sight. 'Thalatta! Thalatta!' we both exclaimed, for it was indeed the sea; and it must have been from a point somewhat corresponding to this that Xenophon and his soldiers first saw it. Their exclamation has become a household word, and only those who have fought their way for months through an enemy's country, and have often passed the night on fields of snow, as they did, could realise what it meant to them. But even an ordinary traveller, who has journeyed, first along the arid, uniform levels between Ararat and Erzeroum, among villages either ruined or at the best resembling mud-heaps, and afterwards over the chill bleak mountains which separate Armenia from the coast, could feel the inspiring effect of this view. And such a view! we had seen nothing equal to it in our whole tour. From our elevated position, between 7,000 and 8,000 feet above the sea, we looked down into a deep valley, in which were cheerful well-built villages, with walls of stone and red-tiled roofs; beyond this rose forest-clad mountains, separated from one another by ravines; then followed a succession of delicately cut ridges, gradually descending towards Trebizond; further still, away to the north-east, cape after cape was seen extending into the sea, while the ranges behind them ran up towards the snow-topped mountains of Lazistan; and, completing all, the expanse of the soft-blue

Euxine. The whole scene, from its delicacy and multiplicity of form, and the combination of sea and mountains, was wonderfully like the coasts of Greece; it seemed natural, from its mere aspect, that such a region should have been inhabited by the Greeks in ancient times.

Let us return for a moment to the Ten Thousand, to whom we must now say farewell. We left them on the plain of Pasin to the eastward of Erzeroum.[1] As I have already remarked, the probabilities are in favour of their having followed very nearly the same route which we have taken, though the spot from which they first saw the sea, and the pass by which they descended from the highlands to the coast, appear to have lain somewhat further to the east. This would be the natural direction for them to take, and the account which Xenophon has given seems to be less difficult to reconcile with this than with any other. When they reached the head waters of the Frat, as it would have defeated their object to follow that stream, they would be almost forced to make their way over the mountains to the north-west. The two principal points which are mentioned in their route are a large river called Harpasus, and an important town called Gymnias. The former of these is probably to be identified with the Tchoruk, and the site of the latter (though this is purely a matter of conjecture) may have been at no great distance from Baiburt. It will have been seen from the intricacy and steepness of the mountain paths which I have described in our last day's journey, that the ranges between that place and the sea may almost as well

[1] See above, p. 407.

be crossed at one point as at another, and it seems probable that the Greeks at last descended by a river-valley, which reaches the coast some way to the east of Trebizond.[1]

[1] See Bunbury's *History of Ancient Geography*, i. 375-378.

CHAPTER XVI.

SUMELAS AND TREBIZOND.

Valley of Sumelas—Extraordinary position of the monastery—Rich vegetation—Approach to Sumelas—The interior—Its foundation—Story of Sultan Murad IV.—The church—Bull of Alexius III.—Firman of Mahomet II.—The refectory and library—Rhododendrons and azaleas—Exquisite scenery—Greek characteristics among the people—First view of Trebizond—Position of the mediæval city: its history—Court of the Grand Comneni—Antiquities of Trebizond —The great siege—Mediæval game of polo—Church of Haghia Sophia —Destruction of ancient monuments—Conclusion of the journey.

AFTER we had taken our fill of gazing at the sea, we once more turned our steps inland in the direction of the monastery of Sumelas. The path now rose to a considerably greater height than before, and from the elevation we had attained we could judge of the lofty barrier which the mountains form between the district of Trebizond and the neighbouring parts of Armenia and Asia Minor. So complete is the watershed that no streams whatsoever pass through these ranges from the interior to the sea, and with Asia Minor in particular there is hardly any communication from the coast. These geographical features explain the mediaeval history of Trebizond, and its existence for so long a period as an independent kingdom, for it was thus isolated from the adjoining continent and defended against attacks from that quarter, whilst at the same time it was forced to depend on its own narrow, though productive, territory, and on the sea. As we proceeded,

THE MONASTERY OF SUMELAS.

the track became so slight as to be hardly traceable, and at length we reached a steep declivity, where we made our way on foot down the rough mountain sides, until we reached a spot overlooking a deep valley, in the midst of rhododendron bushes mingled with fern. Here we rested by a stream, and our horses tasted such grass as they had not met with for many a long day.

What followed appeared to us like a fairy scene, coming as we did from a barren and desolate land. We soon arrived at a point where the object of our search was visible, occupying a most extraordinary position on the opposite side of the valley. Here a perpendicular cliff rises to the height of nearly a thousand feet, and in the very middle of the face of this, in the hollow of a cavern, stands the monastery, its white buildings offering a marked contrast to the brown rock, which seems to form their setting. The first feeling of the beholder is one of amazement that any human beings should have established themselves in a place apparently so inaccessible. In many respects it resembles the convent of Megaspelaeon in the Morea, which also occupies a large cave, as its name implies; but in that case the cavern stands at the foot of the cliff, and consequently is easy of access, whereas here it is impossible at first sight to discover any means of approach. Not the least conspicuous object in the neighbourhood of the building is a long line of arches attached to the rock, which support a watercourse that supplies the monastery. But the surroundings of this strange picture are a mass of luxuriance. The valley below, as it winds away towards the north in the midst of numerous folds of the hills, is full of the richest vegetation, and the sides and summits of the great cliff itself are clothed with trees, wherever these can take root. The winding path by which we now descended led through a forest of firs, interspersed with the brighter foliage of the beech, the sycamore, the alder, and the hazel, together with the scarlet berries of the mountain ash, and a tall undergrowth of rhododendrons and azaleas; and notwithstanding the lateness of the season many flowering-plants were still in blossom. These were mostly familiar friends from the *flora* of the lower Alps. There was the *Impatiens noli-me-tangere* with its pendent golden cornucopias, the yellow salvia, the tall blue spikes of the *Gentiana asclepiadea*, and here and there a belated primrose; and some of the slopes were quite coloured by the autumnal crocus, the flowers of which far exceeded in size any that I had ever seen in Switzerland. There too I found the *Saxifraga cymbalaria*, one of the rarest of all the saxifrages, a delicate plant with ivy-shaped leaf and yellow flower, which I had once before met with, close to the snow among the summits of Mount Parnassus, but which is not found, I believe, in other European floras.[1] Add to all this ferns and grass and trickling rills, and then judge whether, after having hardly seen during two months either a wild flower or a full-grown forest tree, we were not justified in thinking that we had entered an earthly Paradise.

At the bottom of the valley we reached the stream, which resembles a clear Devonshire brook, falling

[1] See Mr. Ball's paper on 'The Origin of the Flora of the European Alps' in the *Geographical Society's Proceedings* for Sept. 1870, p. 577.

from rock to rock in steep rapids; this we crossed by a small covered wooden bridge, of singularly Tyrolese aspect, the roofing of which was intended, no doubt, like those in the Alps, to cast off the weight of snow in winter. From this a very steep zigzag path, embowered in trees, mounts upward to a number of curious cones of rock, which stand at a somewhat lower elevation than the monastery, by the side of the great cliff on which it is built. In the neighbourhood of these are a number of cottages, from which a comparatively level track leads to the point whence the approach is made. This is not the least wonderful feature of the place, and an inspection of it proves both the original inaccessibility of the cavern, and the persevering ingenuity of those who first occupied it. On this side of the cliff there is a slight projection in the rock at a somewhat higher level than the cave, and the opportunity thus afforded has been improved so as to render an entrance practicable. From the spot where we were now standing fifty stone steps have been constructed, reaching to the summit of this buttress, and thence again a wooden staircase descends an equal distance on the further side into the monastery. The actual gateway is at the top of the flight of steps; here we found the hegumen awaiting us, and as it was a narrow portal, and he was a very corpulent man—a rare thing amongst Greek monks, whose meagre diet usually produces a spare habit of body—he nearly occupied the whole space. He addressed us in Greek with the usual words of welcome (καλῶς ὡρίσατε), and we were delighted to feel that we were once more among a Greek-speaking people. We were then conducted down the staircase, and through intricate passages to the further end of the building, where we were established in a comfortable room overlooking the valley. The height of the monastery above the stream is 400 feet, and notwithstanding that we had descended so far in the course of the day, it is still 4,000 feet above the sea-level. When evening came, we were glad of a fire, and piled the logs of resinous pinewood on our hearth.

To describe the appearance of the interior of the monastery is an almost impossible task, owing to the absence of uniformity in the buildings, some being of wood and some of stone, and the closeness with which they are packed away within a confined space, standing at every conceivable angle to one another, and connected by staircases leading up and down, and bridges thrown across, in all directions. As seen from opposite, the cave appears to be somewhat shallow, but when you are inside, it proves to be deeper from front to back than you would have imagined; and it is wonderful to stand at any point in the midst of the buildings, and see its dark masses towering above. So solid is the rock in its composition, that no detached pieces ever fall into the monastery. Here you may wander about through tiny courts and confined passages, from which you emerge from time to time on to small balconies that overhang the precipice. The most massive part of the structure is that which we inhabited; this was built fifteen years ago, probably in the place of some older buildings, and is composed of three storeys, which are supported by a substantial wall. The chambers in this are principally reserved for visitors.

On the fifteenth of August, the great festival of the Virgin, the monastery, we were told, is resorted to by crowds of pilgrims. The view which its windows command is hardly less wonderful than that of the place itself from without. Immediately beneath is the stream, which gradually descends in its brawling course until at some distance off it reaches a depth of 700 feet below the building; and in the other direction the eye ranges up the valley until it meets the bare crests of the peaks; while on the opposite side a lofty wooded mountain rises steeply with broken ridges. The depth of the gorge affords infinite opportunity for picturesque contrasts, an effect which is especially striking after nightfall, when the moonlight throws the rocky buttresses alternately into light and shade.

The monastery of Sumelas is dedicated to the Blessed Virgin (Παναγία), and now contains twelve monks, who are all priests. It was founded, according to the hegumen, fifteen hundred years ago, by Barnabas, a priest, and Sophronios a deacon, natives of Athens. But whatever may be the true history of its foundation, it is certain that the first person who raised it to importance was the Emperor Alexius Comnenus III. of Trebizond; he rebuilt it in the year 1360, and richly endowed it, and guaranteed it certain rights and privileges. The successors of that prince also patronised it, and when their dynasty was brought to an end by Mahomet II., subsequently to the capture of Constantinople, it was treated with marked favour by the conqueror. But the most curious legend of the monastery relates to a successor of that sultan, Murad IV. This was narrated to me the morning after our arrival by the man who had accompanied our horses from Erzeroum, and who had often visited this place; but it seemed all the more quaint when coming from his lips, as he was a Mahometan. It ran as follows. When Sultan Murad was on his way to Bagdad with his army, he passed over the mountains that rise opposite the monastery; and on seeing the building in the gorge below him, he gave orders to one of his generals to fire down upon it and destroy it. Be it remarked in passing, that the region here spoken of is rather difficult ground for artillery to traverse, but this circumstance need not be allowed to interfere with the story. The Sultan's orders were obeyed, but, wonderful to relate, all the cannons refused to go off. The general to whom the command was given then proposed to his master that they should make the attempt from a height somewhat further on; but when this was tried, the result was no more successful than on the former occasion. Then the Sultan perceived that it was a miracle, and exclaimed with enthusiasm, 'If I return from Bagdad, I will ornament this monastery with silver!' The conclusion of the story, to say the truth, is somewhat shabby. Murad returned, and ornamented the church of the monastery—not however with silver, as he had vowed, but with copper, as may be seen at the present day.

Let me now describe the principal buildings, and first of all the church. The body of this, which forms a rude square, is not visible from outside, since it occupies the innermost part of the cavern; all that is seen is the chancel and apse, which project at the eastern end. The outer wall of these is covered with frescoes of scriptural and religious subjects, but they have been sadly defaced—not by Mahometans, as has sometimes happened in other convents—but by Greeks who have written their names over them. The roof of this part is covered with copper, as related in the legend. In front of the church hangs a large wooden *semantron* or sounding board, and close by is a newly-built and painted bell-tower, with a dome, containing five bells. One of these we had heard sounded for service on two occasions during the night. The two keys, with which the church-door was opened, were linked together by a number of long fine silver chains of exquisite workmanship. The interior is unavoidably very dark, and the numerous glass chandeliers that are suspended from the roof, together with some beautiful silver lamps, must often be needed. The roof itself presents a peculiar appearance owing to its irregularity, for it is nothing else than the roof of the cavern plastered over. Numerous small Byzantine pictures are hung about in various places, and parts of the walls are covered with frescoes, among which may be seen portraits—imaginary, of course—of SS. Barnabas and Sophronios. At the west end stands an elaborately carved and gilt pulpit, from which the Gospel is read, and the *iconostasis* or altar-screen, which faces it, is also richly decorated. Within this, in the sanctuary, is kept the great object of veneration for which the monastery is famous—a small picture of the Virgin, said to be by the hand of St. Luke. In consequence of its age, and the smoke from the tapers of innumerable devotees, hardly anything more than the old wood on which it is painted is visible; but it is in great reputation amongst Mahometans as well as Christians, for this Madonna delivers her votaries without respect of creed from plagues of locusts, and Turkish women are accustomed to visit her shrine in order to obtain relief from sickness and barrenness.[1]

We were next allowed to inspect the relics and other valuable objects which are kept within the church. First were produced the heads of SS. Barnabas and Sophronios, which are kept in separate cases. These, we observed, were not treated with any very great amount of respect, for the monks did not assume their vestments before handling them, nor were tapers lighted in their honour, as would have been the case on Mount Athos. Then came a piece of the true cross, very beautifully mounted, and ornamented with silver and jewels. It was kept in a silver-gilt casket, and was the gift of the Emperor Manuel III. of Trebizond. There was also a Byzantine manuscript of the Gospels in its original metal binding, in shape a small quarto, and semiuncial in writing, illuminated with full-page figures of the Evangelists, which were well executed. The real treasure of this convent, however, which I had looked forward to seeing with great anxiety, is the famous golden bull of the Emperor Alexius III., which became thenceforth the charter of its foundation, and is one of the finest specimens of such documents. It is a paper scroll backed with silk, about thirteen inches wide, and fifteen feet long, and at its head are two portraits of Alexius himself and his queen, clad in robes of crimson and gold, and holding between them a church, which symbolises the monastery. The like-

---

[1] Fallmerayer, *Fragmente aus dem Orient*, i. 179.

nesses are evidently originals, for there is nothing conventional about the faces. Underneath these was originally the golden seal, but this, as might be expected, has not been spared. The heading, which is written in gold letters, contains the emperor's titles— 'Alexius, Faithful in Christ our God, King and Emperor of all the East, of the Iberians, and of Perateia,[1] the Grand Comnenus.' The rest of the document is written in black ink, with numerous contractions; but wherever the name of king ($\beta\alpha\sigma\iota\lambda\epsilon\acute{u}s$) occurs, it is in red, and so is the signature at the end, which repeats the title given above, and is subscribed in a large bold hand. The scroll is cracked in several places, and in one the crack extends right across the paper. It is lamentable to think that so valuable a document should be in the keeping of such ignorant and careless people as the monks appeared to be.[2]

Another manuscript of considerable interest, which is also preserved within the church, is the firman of Mahomet II., by which he granted his protection to the monastery. This is a fine specimen of Turkish calligraphy, and with it are a number of similar firmans of later sultans, granting to the monks immunity from taxation. In the present evil days of Ottoman bankruptcy no such privileges are allowed, and consequently the present occupants of the convent have received no document of the kind from the reigning Sultan, and have to pay taxes like other subjects

---

[1] By Perateia, or 'the province beyond the sea,' is meant the possessions of the emperors in the Tauric Chersonese (Crimea).

[2] The original text of the bull of Sumelas, which was copied by Prof. Fallmerayer, is given by him in his *Original-Fragmenta*, in the *Transactions of the Academy of Munich* for 1843, *Hist. Class.* vol. iii. pp. 92 foll., and a German translation of the same, ibid. pp. 58 foll.

of the Porte. While we were inspecting these manuscripts, we had an astonishing instance of the ignorance of which I have just spoken. My companion was anxious to make certain that the sultan who issued the first firman was the conqueror of Constantinople, and accordingly asked the hegumen which Mahomet he meant. To this the hegumen replied, 'Why, the *prophet* Mahomet.' When we looked up in blank amazement, thinking our ears had deceived us, another of the monks, who noticed our perplexity, reassured us by saying, 'That's quite right; it was the *great* Mahomet—the *prophet*' (μάλιστα· ὁ μέγας, ὁ προφήτης). After hearing that, we asked no more questions.

As this monastery is a Coenobia—that is to say, the monks do not live separately, as is the case in some of these communities, but take their meals in common—it possesses a refectory (τράπεζα). This, however, is the rudest chamber of the kind that I have ever seen, small and low, and provided only with two rough wooden tables and benches. So ill-cared for was it, that I should have supposed it to be disused; but the hegumen assured us that the brethren met there twice a day. Not the least curious of the buildings is the kitchen, a small square structure of great antiquity, with a domed stone roof, black with the smoke of ages. The interior was extremely dark, for there are few windows, and these face inwards towards the cavern. There is also a sacred spring (ἁγίασμα), such as is often found in Greek monasteries; but here, instead of being a well or source, it is formed by the water that drips from the roof of the cavern into a square cistern inclosed by masonry, which stands on the opposite side of the church to the bell-tower. From this, no doubt, the inmates were originally provided with water; but as the amount proved after a time to be insufficient for their use, an additional supply was afterwards introduced from without by means of the aqueduct, which is carried along the face of the rock near the flight of steps by which the monastery is entered.

It remains to speak of the library. When I inquired for this, the hegumen pointed to a stone chamber built high up against the face of the rock, with no means of access to the door. On our expressing a wish to visit it, a ladder was sent for, and when this had been brought, and the key had been obtained, we mounted, the hegumen preceding us and displaying greater powers of climbing than we had anticipated from the portliness of his person. We found, alas! a small dark chamber with one unglazed window, so that, what with the humid atmosphere without, and the cold rock behind, the place could not fail to be damp; and the books were piled on one another in the utmost confusion. It was almost impossible to examine them, but I met with three manuscripts of the Gospels, of good execution, but not illuminated. The hegumen informed us that they had built a new library, but that the books had not yet been removed thither. I am afraid, however, that they stand but a poor chance of careful treatment at the hands of such unintelligent owners.

During the afternoon of the day following our arrival, we sauntered down the zigzag path that leads to the foot of the great cliff, and thence through delightful glades to the valley far below, where walnuts and chestnuts were added to the vegetation I have already described. It appeared to us one of the loveliest spots we had ever seen, and an ideal resting-place for tired wanderers. Wherever the eye turns, new delights meet it. What must it be in spring, when the rhododendrons and azaleas are in blossom, and the ground is starred with primroses and Alpine flowers! How a landscape-painter would rejoice in rocky boulders rising by the side of crystal streams, and crowned, not with heather and bilberry, but with this luxuriant undergrowth! The rhododendron here, be it understood, is not the little alpenrose, but of the same species as that which grows in our gardens; and the azalea is the famous kind which, in consequence of its flourishing in this neighbourhood, is called *Azalea pontica*. The moisture which distils from its yellow blossoms is poisonous, and affects the honey of the bees that feed upon it. This fact corroborates the curious statement in Xenophon's narrative, where he mentions that his soldiers, after eating of the honey of this country, were attacked by vomiting, and displayed all the symptoms of intoxication and frenzy.[1] A similar circumstance is related by Strabo with regard to Pompey's forces, only in that case the honey seems to have been obtained immediately from the trees.[2]

The next morning we started early, for we had a long ride before us to reach Trebizond. We also anticipated a change of weather, for the air was soft and warm, forming a strong contrast to the temperature of the two last days, which had made a fire so welcome. We descended by the same path as before,

[1] Xen. *Anab.* iv. 8, § 20, 21. [2] Strabo, xii. p. 549.

until we reached a covered bridge, resembling that by which we had approached, but considerably lower down the course of the stream ; here we turned to take a last look at the monastery in its wonderful position, now towering high above us. The ride down the valley for several hours from this point was one of those experiences, the delights of which it is hopeless to endeavour to communicate in words. There is nothing in the Alps to which one can compare it, owing to the clearness of the water and the variety of the vegetation. To Fallmerayer it recalled the approach to the Grande Chartreuse, but even that glorious valley lacks the luxuriant undergrowths of this southern region. The beautiful ride from Cauterets to the Pont d'Espagne in the Pyrenees resembles it perhaps more nearly, but there too the views are more confined and less varied. Here you ride along terrace paths cut through the forest, sometimes following a level high above the river, and sometimes descending in zigzags towards it, but everywhere embowered in trees, while all around you on the steep banks the rhododendrons and azaleas rise to the height of fifteen or twenty feet, and the large spreading leaves of the hellebore thrust themselves through the ground, which is already carpeted with wood-sorrel and other tender plants. Then at every turn of the road new views open in different directions of the folds of the valley, with peeps of the stream far below, and the fir-clad mountains rising to a great elevation above ; and as we look back, the gorge seems to be closed by the great rock, on the face of which, now averted from us, the monastery stands. At last we reach a point where the river has to be recrossed, for below this the ravine becomes so narrow as not to admit of the passage of a path, and we now ascend for several hundred feet on the opposite side, until we arrive at a projecting rock, crowned with a little chapel. This marks the highest point of the road, and after passing it we wind downwards, skirting the face of the cliffs, and following the sinuosities of the hillsides, until we join another valley, wider and barer, where the palluria and sarsaparilla grow over the walls, and the heat-loving fig-tree has fixed itself in the rocks. Throughout the whole route we were struck by the excellence of the path, by the good repair of the neighbouring farms and homesteads, and by the careful weeding that was going on in the clearings. The land in this part belongs to the monks, and it was evident that, if they are no scholars, they at all events pay attention to their property.

At a distance of four hours from the monastery the village of Djevislik is reached, where we once more meet the main road from Erzeroum, which here crosses the river by a new two-arched bridge. At this point the stream of Sumelas is joined by another of equal size, and their combined waters form the river that flows to Trebizond, which in ancient times was called the Pyxites, and is now the Surmel. The road in this part has been very carefully constructed, and now the country began to show signs of civilisation, such as we had not seen in any previous part of our journey, from the well-built stone houses with roofs of slate or shingle ; and the Greek villages on the hillsides presented a prosperous appearance and an aspect of comfort. The faces, too, that we saw along the road wore the quick bright look which everywhere accompanies the Greek race; for the Greeks of this district are true Greeks, and not merely—like those whom we had met with elsewhere in Asia Minor —the original inhabitants of the country, who are reckoned as Greeks from having belonged to the Greek church since the days of the Byzantine empire. The scenery of the long valley that here leads down to the sea forcibly recalled to us that of the Bavarian highlands, from the broad open hillsides, the bright vegetation, and the forests that rose above. At last a number of spiry cypresses appeared—a tree which we had not seen since leaving Constantinople—betokening a warmer and more kindly climate; and at the same time other features contributed to the same impression of geniality. In Armenia we had been especially struck with the careworn look of the people; even the children had none of the brightness of other children: the life seemed too hard, and the surroundings too dull, to encourage them to mirth. But here smiles and laughter were in abundance on the faces of the peasants, groups of whom we met returning from the city. A heavy thunderstorm had preceded us, and the rain that had fallen contributed an additional freshnes so the maize-fields and other clearings on the hillsides; and thus it appeared to us indeed a Happy Valley, which conducted us to Trebizond. We soon arrived at the seashore, and came in sight of the city, which was the term of our wanderings. We thus concluded a ride of fifteen hundred miles, which had been accomplished without illness or accident of any kind.

The aspect of Trebizond, as you approach it from the east, is singularly pretty. About two miles to the west of the mouth of the stream, a low promontory juts northward into the sea, forming a graceful bay; and the eastern side of this headland, except the extremity, which remains a bare rock, is sprinkled with well-built houses, gay with tiled roofs, and painted in different colours, white, yellow, red, and green; all round which are the freshest of gardens, while the summit is crowned by a long line of tall cypresses, which mark the site of an old Turkish cemetery. These buildings belong to a suburb, for the main part of the city is not visible from this side. When we entered, we took up our abode at a comfortable little hotel, one of the very few decent ones that are to be met with in Turkey, which commands a view over the bay, with the successive ranges of the coast of Lazistan in the distance towards the east. It was a lively neighbourhood from the number of caravans that might be seen starting for the interior, especially for Persia, for the landing-place from the steamers is hard by; and a motley effect was produced by the dresses of the various nationalities, among whom the Persians were conspicuous by their high black caps or round brown ones of mushroom shape, and by their long robes reaching to the ankles, sometimes entirely of spotless white, sometimes of green, which seems to be a favourite colour with them. To the west of this suburb stretches the extensive Christian quarter, and beyond this again is the Kaleh, or walled town, inhabited by the Turks, which was the site of the ancient city. The total population of the place is estimated at 32,000, of whom 2,000 are Armenians, 7,000 or 8,000 Greeks, and the rest Turks.

The last day of our stay in Asia Minor was

devoted to the city and its antiquities, which we visited under the escort of a *yuzbashi* (captain) and two zaptiehs; the company of these authorities was needed in order to enable us to see the mosques and the castle. The position which was occupied by the Hellenic and mediaeval city is a very remarkable one. At first sight it seems strange that the original settlers should not have chosen the promontory itself for their site, as it commands the harbour, and is well suited for purposes of defence; but a nearer acquaintance with the locality at once justifies their preference. Here two deep valleys, descending from the interior, run parallel at no great distance from one another down to the sea, inclosing between them a sloping table of ground—whence the original name of the place, Trapezus, or the 'Table-land'—which falls in steep rocky precipices on the two sides. The whole is still inclosed by the Byzantine walls, which follow the line of the cliffs, and are carried along the sea-face;[1] and the upper part of the level, which is separated from the lower by an inner cross wall, forms the castle, while at the highest point, where a sort of neck is formed between the two valleys, is the keep which crowns the whole. On either side, about half-way between this keep and the sea, the valleys are crossed by massive bridges, and on the further side of the westernmost of these, away from the city, a large tower and other fortifications remain, which must have served to defend the approach from this quarter.

[1] The sea-wall, we should remark, does not belong to the earliest period, but was built at the beginning of the fourteenth century by the Emperor Alexius II., who thus added a third quarter to the city. Before that time the northern wall ran parallel to the shore at some little distance inland. Fallmerayer, *Fragmente aus dem Orient*, i. 82.

It is difficult to conceive anything more picturesque than these fortifications and their surroundings. They have not indeed the triple line which renders the old walls on the land side of Constantinople so striking, but the irregularity of the cliffs which they follow, and the towers, some round, some angular, which project from them, offer far greater variety to the eye; and many of these towers are themselves covered with creepers, while the gardens that occupy the two narrow valleys teem with luxuriant vegetation, and the eye wanders through them, on the one side up to the gracefully shaped mountains, and on the other down to the blue Euxine.

The city of Trapezus was a colony of Sinope, but it first comes into notice at the time of the Retreat of the Ten Thousand, who found repose in this place, and were hospitably treated by the inhabitants. Its remote situation caused it to be of small importance in Greek history, but its position relatively to the interior of Asia rendered it then, as it has done ever since, a flourishing commercial emporium. Its real greatness, however, dates from a much later period, and may be said to have been almost the result of accident. At the time of that disgraceful buccaneering expedition which is dignified with the name of the Fourth Crusade (A.D. 1204), when the Byzantine empire was dismembered and its capital occupied by the Latins, a scion of the family of the Comneni, called Alexius, escaped into Asia, and having collected an army of Iberian mercenaries entered Trebizond, where he was acknowledged as the legitimate sovereign, and assumed the title of Grand-Comnenos. Though only twenty-two years of age, Alexius was a man of ability and resolute will, and since at this period of anarchy a vigorous ruler was what everyone was desiring, he succeeded without difficulty in making himself master of the greater part of the southern coast of the Black Sea. The empire that was thus founded continued to exist for two centuries and a half, until it was brought to an end by the great destroyer, Mahomet II., eight years after he had captured Constantinople. Its isolated position, defended on the one side by the sea, and on the other by the lofty chains which intervene between it and Asia Minor, was at once the cause of its duration and the secret of its history. By this means it was able to defy both the Seljouks and the Ottomans, and to maintain its independence against the emperors of Nicaea and Constantinople. But for the same reason its policy was always narrow, and it never attained to real greatness, or exercised any beneficial influence on the world at large. It reflected most of the features of the great Byzantine empire of which it was a miniature copy, with the exception of those which imparted to it its real power and grandeur. The palace of Trebizond was famed for its magnificence, the court for its luxury and its elaborate ceremonial, while at the same time it was frequently a hotbed of intrigue and immorality. The inhabitants of the country, whether Greeks or Lazes, were vigorous races, and the land itself was salubrious and productive; the best that could be said for the government was that it preserved the people from anarchy, and thus enabled them to enjoy these advantages. To do this was necessary to its existence, but of any further improvement or development of its subjects it took but little heed.

At the same time there is a strong element of romance in the history of this remote empire, and in the existence of so much refinement in the neighbourhood of so wild a region. The imperial family, both men and women, were renowned for their beauty—a characteristic which is noticeable in the portrait of Alexius III. on the bull of Sumelas; and the princesses of this race were sought as brides by kings and chieftains of widely distant countries. We find them married, not only to Byzantine emperors of the dynasty of the Palaeologi, to Genoese nobles, and to Crusaders, but to Mahometan princes—to the rulers of Persia and of the Mongols and Turcomans, and to the sons of Turkish emirs; and the connections thus formed not only originated a variety of diplomatic relations, and friendly or offensive alliances, but furnished the material for numerous stories of chivalry and adventure.[1] The Grand Comneni were also patrons of art and learning, and in consequence of this their court was resorted to by many eminent men, by whose agency the library of the palace was provided with valuable manuscripts, and the city was adorned with splendid buildings. The appearance of the place, indeed, when at the height of its prosperity, must have been truly enchanting. The writers of that time speak with enthusiasm of its lofty towers, of the churches and monasteries in the suburbs, and especially of the gardens, orchards, and olive-groves, which the delightful, but humid, climate was so well qualified to foster. It excited the admiration of Gonzales Clavijo, the Spanish envoy, when he passed through it on his way to visit the court of Timour

---

[1] Fallmerayer, *Geschichte des Kaiserthums Trapezunt*, p. 313.

at Samaracand;[1] and Cardinal Bessarion, who was a native of the place, in the latter part of his life, when the city had passed into the hands of the Mahometans, and he was himself a dignitary of the Roman church, so little forgot the impression it had made upon him, that he wrote a work entitled, 'The Praises of Trebizond.'[2]

Only one of the principal antiquities lies within the area of the old city. This is the Orta-hissar mosque, which was once a Christian church, dedicated to the Panaghia Chrysokephalos, or Virgin of the Golden Head, and is a well-preserved specimen of a Byzantine edifice, since, except for the ordinary arrangements necessary to adapt it to the Mahometan worship, the original structure has been hardly at all interfered with. It is a large and massive building, with two narthexes or antechapels at the west end, while the nave has two bays, both to the east and west of the central cupola, exclusive of the apse. At the sides are low aisles, also ending in apses, and supporting galleries. It is excessively plain, there being hardly any ornament throughout. On the other side of the eastern ravine, occupying a striking position opposite the castle, is another mosque, the Yeni Djuma djami, or New Friday mosque, formerly the church of St. Eugenius, the patron saint of Trebizond, who was said to have received martyrdom on this spot during Diocletian's persecution. This is a much smaller building, and perfectly plain, but excellent in its proportions, forming a complete Greek

---

[1] Clavijo, *Historia del gran Tamorlan*, p. 84.
[2] 'Εγκώμιον Τραπεζοῦντος. It exists in manuscript at Venice, and is quoted by Fallmerayer, *Original-Fragmenta*, Pt. i. p. 130.

cross, with a fine cupola, which is pierced with numerous small windows. A tall minaret has now been added to it on the north side.

Owing to its commanding situation, this church, to which a monastery was originally attached, played an important part in the history of the city, and was the scene of the crisis of the greatest siege which it had to undergo. This was in the reign of the second emperor, Andronicus I., and the attacking force was the army of the Seljouks, commanded by Melik, the son of the great Sultan Alaeddin. After an ineffectual assault on the northern wall in the direction of the sea, it was determined to attack it from the opposite quarter. The history of what followed is thus given by Finlay.

'The next attempt to storm Trebizond was made from the south. Melik occupied the narrow platform between the two great ravines before the wall of the upper citadel with a division of his army. His own head-quarters were in the monastery of St. Eugenius, the church itself serving as the residence of his harem. It was resolved to surprise the upper citadel by a night attack; but the darkness which was to aid the success of the operation proved the ruin of the Turkish army. The three divisions of the besiegers, occupying the eastern suburb, the hill of St. Eugenius, and the platform above the citadel, were separated from one another by deep ravines, yet they were destined to act in concert. As the troops were moving forward to support the storming party, a dreadful tempest, accompanied by a hail-storm and a deluge of rain, suddenly swelled the torrents in the ravines. The troops from St. Eugenius and the eastern suburb were unable to mount the rocky ascent to the platform, and some were carried away by the flood as they were crossing the ravine. The feint attack from the north was repulsed, and the whole assault failed. The defeated troops were everywhere driven back on those destined to support them. The cavalry, horse and man, was forced over the precipices; the infantry was driven back into the torrents which poured down from the mountains, and the confusion was soon inextricable. When the fury of the storm abated, and it became possible to render the local knowledge of the garrison of some avail, a sortie was directed against the head-quarters of Melik from the northern gates. The whole Seljouk army then fled in confusion, abandoning its camp and leaving everything to the enemy. Melik himself joined the fugitives, and was made prisoner at Kouration by a party of mountaineers from Matzouka. The glory of the victory was attributed to St. Eugenius, whose history it enriched with many a legend!'[1]

After visiting these buildings within the modern city, we proceeded to the most important of all the ancient churches, that of Haghia Sophia, which lies about two miles off to the west, in a conspicuous position overlooking the sea. On our way thither we passed the Kabak-meidan, or 'Pumpkin Square,' an extensive space of open ground, where now stand the low wooden one-storeyed buildings of a hospital, which was erected during the late war. An Italian doctor in the Turkish service, who took his meals in our hotel, told us that twelve or fourteen doctors, of

[1] Finlay, *History of Greece*, iv. 335, 336 (new ed.)

whom he was one, were constantly at work there at that time, the wounded being brought from Batoum, Erzeroum, and elsewhere. He spoke of the admirable patience of the Turkish soldiers, and also of their fatalism, which constantly caused them to prefer to die rather than undergo an operation. It has been conjectured that this space was the site of the mediaeval tzukanisterion or polo-ground of Trebizond, for which amusement it would be excellently suited. This game was a favourite one with the nobles both of Trebizond and Constantinople, and was played on horseback much in the same way as the modern polo. The excitement it caused among the spectators almost rivalled that of the hippodrome, and it appears to have been as dangerous as it was fashionable. It caused the death of one Emperor of Trebizond, John I., through a fall from his horse, and the more famous Manuel I. of Constantinople was nearly killed in the same manner.

Unfortunately for us, the church of Haghia Sophia had been appropriated to military purposes, and at this time was full of stores, while in the open ground about it a barrack had been built, which was still occupied by soldiers; this erection with its red roofs gave the whole place from a distance the appearance of a monastery. Our obliging companion, the *yuzbashi*, had warned us beforehand that there might be some difficulty about getting admittance into the building, but we trusted to his presence and the authority of our firman to facilitate matters. Our experience of Turkey, however, ought to have taught us better. The key was not there, and the people in charge sent hither and thither to find it, until after about half an hour it was discovered that the functionary who kept it lived somewhere very near our hotel—that is to say, about three miles off. On hearing this, though they offered to send for it with the utmost speed, we gave up the matter as hopeless. Through a window of one of the transepts, however, we were able to obtain a sufficiently good idea of the interior, which in most respects resembles that of the church first described, only its architecture is lighter from the cupola being supported on detached pillars, as is the case with many of the churches in the monasteries of Athos. At the west end, beyond the narthex, is a *proaulion*, or outer porch, running the whole width of the building; and the triple arches through which this was entered are supported on capitals elaborately carved in incised ornament, with honeycomb work above. About a hundred feet off from the west end of the church rises a tall and massive campanile, the windows of which are very small until near the top, where it is pierced with pointed arches; a wooden staircase inside leads to the summit, from which there is a fine view over the mountains and the wide sweep of the bay. Some part of the inner walls has been covered with frescoes of religious subjects, the colours of which are still fresh, but they have been dreadfully defaced. Until lately the church also contained some interesting mural paintings, and among them a likeness of the Emperor Manuel I. of Trebizond, by whom it was built; but these must now have disappeared, as the whole of the interior has been covered with a coat of whitewash.

The destruction of ancient monuments that is

going on in Turkey is lamentable to think of, and Trebizond especially has suffered in this way. In Texier and Pullan's great work on Byzantine architecture are represented the life-sized figures of the Emperor Alexius III., his mother Irene, and the Empress Theodora, clad in their imperial robes, as they were painted on the walls of the vestibule of the church in the nunnery of the Panaghia Theotocos or Theoskepastos, which stands in a steep position on the face of the Boz-tepé ('Grey Hill'), as the mountain is called which rises behind the Christian quarter of the town. This piece of antiquity, which an archæologist might regard as the greatest glory of Trebizond, has now disappeared. In 1843 the church was repaired and the vestibule replastered by the liberality of an ignorant abbess, and some modern figures were daubed over the surface of the ancient paintings.[1] But, if our *yuzbashi* was to be trusted, another monument of still greater antiquity has also lately perished. This is the inscription over the entrance to the castle, which commemorated the restoration of the public buildings of the city by Justinian.[2] We inquired carefully for this, but the only information we could obtain was, that an inscription over a gateway corresponding to the one we mentioned had been removed some time ago. Some persons said that a Mouaveen (Christian assistant-governor) had carried it away with him, while others thought that it was somewhere in the precincts of the pasha's serai, but no further intelligence respecting it was to be obtained. Perhaps, after all, these statements may have been

[1] Finlay, *History of Greece*, iv. p. 383 *note* 2.
[2] The inscription is given in Texier and Pullan, p. 190.

extemporised, and the inscription may be standing over some gateway which we did not see, though it certainly is not over that by which we entered the castle ; but if it really has been destroyed, this is the worst act of vandalism that has been perpetrated for many years.

We had now accomplished the object of our journey, and on September 27 we left Trebizond by the French steamer, and returned to Constantinople.

INDEX.

ACA

ACAMPSIS, river, 423
Adeljivas, 325
Aghir Gheul, 330, 339
Agriculture in Turkey, 18, 133, 200, 313
Ak Dagh, 25, 51
Akhlat, 315; castle of, 317; history of, 319 foll.; battle of, 321
Akhtamar, 350
Ala Dagh, 385
Aladjah, 53
Alashgerd, plain of, 386
Alexander the Great, reputed founder of Bitlis Castle, 306, 318
Alexius Comnenus I., founds empire of Trebizond, 452
Alexius Comnenus III., handsome in person, 454; rebuilds Sumelas, 439; bull of, 442
Ali Dagh, 105, 113
Aljike, 336
Allah Dagh, 125
Allaja Khan, 201
Alp Arslan, 319
Alphabet, Armenian, invented by St. Mezrop, 252
Amasia, position of, 26 foll.; antiquities of, 32 foll.; sieges of, 38; 'Tombs of the Kings' at, 33 foll.
American missions, at Marsovan, 39; at Kaiserieh, 110; at Sivas, 181; at Kharput, 226; at Bitlis, 302;

ARM

at Van, 348; at Erzeroum, 411; general estimate of, 236
Amrakom, 405
Anabad, island, 340
Aneroid, effects of low pressure on, 332
Angora goats, 57, 84
Anti-Taurus, 125, 174, 231; pass over, 197; character of, 203
Aqueduct, ancient, near Amasia, 44
Arabgir, 213, 231
Ararat, seen from Sipan, 331; views of, 369, 375, 380; remarks on, 382
Araxes, course of, 387; bridge over, 405
Architecture—Byzantine, 143, 455, 459; Seljoukian, 35, 111, 160, 316; Armenian, 164, 273, 393, 428
Ardjish, lake, 370
Argaeus, Mt., views of, 94, 105, 119, 153, 165, 170; retains its ancient name, 94; ascent of, 119 foll.; view from the summit, 125; height of, 126; former ascents, 128
Armenia, geographical position of, 187, 188; climate of, 159, 188, 314, 411
Armenia College, 226 foll.; studies pursued in, 229
Armenia Minor, province of, 176
Armenian Church, the oldest national Church, 191; its tenets, 191, 192

ARM

Armenian language, ancient and modern, 228
Armenians, characteristics of, 97, 193; their history, 188 foll.; migrate into Asia Minor, 176; their dispersion, 193; their numbers, 194; their grievances, 232, 233, 234, 416; their hopes fixed on England, 162, 275
Artshag, lake, 368
Asia Minor, climate of, 17, 57, 80, 89, 98, 140, 149, 172, 180; geographical features of, 21; fertility of, 41, 183; causes of depopulation of, 85
Assyrian art, in Asia Minor, 62, 63, 72, 73, 78; influence on Armenia, 362, 363
Assyrians, attack Armenia, 180, 363
Atmosphere, clearness of, in Asia Minor, 169; in Armenia, 215
Avanz, landing-place of Van, 341
Azalea pontica, 436; its poisonous qualities, 446

BAGRATIDAE, 190
Baiburt, 423
Baldwin II., king of Jerusalem, 220
Baptist, St. John, a popular saint in Armenia, 163; his relics, 163, 272; legends concerning him, 272
Basch-keui, 134
Basil, St., Bishop of Caesareia, 145; founder of the coenobite system, 145, 146; his retreat in Pontus, 147
Bas-reliefs on rocks at Boghaz-keui, 66 foll.; meaning of, 73 foll.; monuments similar to, 76
Bayazid, ruinous state of, 384; captured by Russians, 389; invested by Turks, 390; restored by Berlin Treaty, 385
Bells, rarely heard in Turkey, 276
Bende-Mahi-su, 372

CHA

Bessarion, Cardinal, a native of Trebizond, 455
Beys, Kurdish, 307
Bingheul Dagh, 387
Birds in Armenia, 241, 265, 329, 399, 400
Bitlis, 301; its climate, 302; castle of, 306
Bitlis-chai (Eastern Tigris), 301
Boats on Lake Van, 335, 338, 341
Boghaz-keui, 64; inscribed rocks near, 66; ancient palace at, 71
Bread, different kinds of, 87; mode of baking, 88
Bull of Alexius III., 442
Butter, mode of making, 257
Byzantine architecture, in caves of Gueremeh, 143; at Trebizond, 455, 459

CABAK TEPE, 80
Caesareia (Kaiserieh), 107; besieged by Sapor, 108; St. Basil, bishop of, 145
Campaign of Russians in Armenia, 388 foll.
Cappadocia, plateaux of, 98, 99; absence of trees in, 121 a land of rock-dwellings, 127; its theologians, 146
Caravan route to Persia, 384, 399, 400, 404; increasing traffic, 404
Carcathiocerta, 222
Carduchi, 258
Castles—at Amasia, 33; at Kaiserieh, 111; at Sivas, 177; at Kharput, 218; at Palu, 250; at Bitlis, 306; at Akhlat, 317; at Adeljivas, 325; at Van, 343, 349 foll.; at Erzeroum, 414; at Baiburt, 425; at Trebizond, 451
Cataracts of the Euphrates, 208
Centrites, river, 299
Chambers in the rocks—at Amasia, 33; at Palu, 252; at Van, 351; their object, 355

CHA

Changeli, monastery of, 268, 276
Chevli, 264
Church, Armenian, position of in Turkey, 161, 192; tenets of, 191; rival patriarchates in, 192, 350
Churches, rock-hewn, at Gueremeh, 143 foll.
Circassians, 13, 136, 170, 174, 337, 417
Clavijo, Gonzales, visits Trebizond, 454
Climate of Asia Minor, 17, 57, 80, 89, 98, 140, 149, 172, 180; of Armenia, 159, 188, 320, 411
Consular reports on the country, 416
Consuls, the English military, 30, 108, 179, 345, 401, 408
Crater of Mt. Sipan, 329
Crusaders, confined at Kharput, 220; at Palu, 251
Cuneiform inscriptions, at Palu, 251; at Van, 344, 352, 353; first copied by Schulz, 354; not Assyrian, 354
Currency, abolition of copper, 184, 397; depreciation of metallic, 398
Customs—blessing the harvest, 24; escorting the traveller, 98, 160, 166

DARON, district of, 276; history of, 276
Delibaba pass, 387, 400 foll.; village, 403
Delik Tasch, pass of, 197, 389
Dere-beys, or 'lords of the valleys,' 82, 91, 175, 199
Dersim, Kurds of the, 234, 255, 261
Deveh Boyoun, pass, 387, 391, 407
Diarbekir, head-quarters of the Jacobites, 225; road to, 243, 247
Diglito, another form of Tigris, 294, 296
Distances, difficulty in exactly computing, 169
Diyadin, 383
Dung-fuel (see Tezek)
Dust-storm, 318

GAR

EAGLES, 400
Earthquakes, at Kaiserieh, 131
Eden, position of the Garden of, 210
Egin, 227, 231
Elevation of Asia Minor, 98, 169, 170; of Armenia, 187, 385
Encampments, Kurdish, 376 foll.
England favourably regarded in Asia Minor, 42, 57, 136; the hope of the Armenians, 162, 275
Erzeroum, plain of, 408, 420; city of, 408 foll.; history of, 410; siege of, 414
Eshek Elias, battle of, 389, 402
Etchmiadzin, patriarch of, 161; patriarchs buried at Utch Kelisch, 394
Eugenius, St., patron saint of Trebizond, 455
Euphrates, first view of, 204; ferry across at Keban Maden, 205, 206; two streams of in Armenia, 207; cataracts of, 208; lower course of, 208; historical notice of, 209. (See Frat, Murad)
Euyuk, antiquities at, 55 foll.
Everek, village of, 115

FAMINE in Asia Minor, 89; its disastrous results, 90, 110, 181; its causes, 91, 92; prospect of in Armenia, 415
Fish in Lake Van, 339
Fountain of St. Gregory, 275
Frat, river (Western Euphrates), 207, 420, 422; source of, 420
French language spoken in Armenia, 288, 347
Frescoes, ancient, at Amasia, 36; at Gueremeh, 143 foll.
Furniture, Oriental, 173

GALATIA, 80
Garabed, Surp, meaning of the name, 163; monastery of, near

GEL

Kaiserieh, 160 foll.; near Mush, 270 foll.
Gelaleddin, besieges Akhlat, 320
Geography of Asia Minor, 21; of Armenia, 187, 188; of the highest uplands, 385 foll.
Gheuljik, lake, 240, 247; a source of the Tigris, 241
Grand Comneni of Trebizond, their luxurious court, 454
Greek language in Asia Minor, 117, 152; in Armenia, 339; in the district of Trebizond, 430, 437
Greeks, of Asia Minor, 41, 117, 138, 154; in Armenia, 212; of Trebizond, 430, 449
Gregory the Illuminator, 163, 191, 272, 279, 281; his fountain, 275
Grolla, Kurdish village of, 256
Gueremeh, valley of, 140 foll.; ancient monastic community at, 141; rock-hewn churches at, 143 foll.; severe climate of, 149
Gum tragacanth, 120, 305

HAIDERANLI Kurds, 366, 373 foll.
Halys, delta of, 8; stream of, 57; bridges over, 100, 174, 196; name of, 167; at Sivas, 173, 174
Harpasus, 432
Harvest, custom of blessing the, 24
Has-keui, 287
Hassan-kaleh, 387, 406
Hatoum, manuscript of King, 274
Hekim-khan, 202
Hindoos, colony of, in Armenia, 276; their origin and history, 277 foll.; their conversion, 281
Hittites, the, in Asia Minor, 77
Horses in Asia Minor, 84; in Armenia, 366
Horse-shoe arch, 111, 143; not invented by the Arabs, 151; its early use in Asia Minor, 151, 152

KAR

Hospitality in the East, 116, 138, 214, 290, 377, 424
Houen, mosque of, at Kaiserieh, 110 foll.
Houses, excavated from tufa, 134; mode of building in Asia Minor, 172; in Armenia, 395
Houshousi, river, 243

ICONOSTASIS, not found in Armenian churches, 165, 274; found in Greek churches, 143, 441
Ignatius, name of Jacobite patriarchs, 226
Hidja, baths of, 420
Indje-su, 154; stream of, 155
Innaknian, convent of, 276
Inscriptions—Greek, at Amasia, 36; hieroglyphic, on rocks at Boghazkeui, 77; Roman, at Kharput, 222; cuneiform, at Palu, 251; at Van, 344, 352, 353, 354
Iris, delta of, 9; at Amasia, 26; name Yeshil Irmak, 27; flood of, 30; upper valley of, 44; St. Basil's retreat near, 147

JACOBITES, sect of, 224; at Kharput, 218; at Bitlis, 307
Jacobus Baradaeus, 225
Jocelyn of Courtnay, confined at Kharput, 220
Julamerk district, 374
Justice, administration of, 41, 96, 136, 233, 290, 418
Justinian, fortified Caesareia, 108; restored buildings at Trebizond, 460

KAISERIEH, plain of, 103; city of, 106 foll.; exposed to earthquakes, 131
Kalender, 263
Kara Dagh, 21

KAR

Kara Keliseh, 398
Karakenduz, 368
Kara-su, 288, 289; identified with the Teleboas, 299
Keban Maden, Euphrates at, 205; village of, 211; mine of, 212
Keuseh Dagh, 399
Kharput, 217 foll.; history of, 222 foll.; castle of, 218; its history, 219 foll.
Khelat (see Akhlat)
Khorkhor, caves of, 352
Kiupri-keui, 391
Kizilbashes, 259 foll., 378
Kizil Irmak (see Halys), origin of name, 101
Kop Dagh, 422
Kurdish language, 257; dialects of, 229
Kurdistan, mountains of, 303, 330, 341
Kurds, their history, 257, 258; their religion, 259; their physiognomy, 228, 267, 308; nomad Kurds, 375; points of resemblance to Arabs, 376

L ADIK, 23
Language, Kurdish, 257
Lazes, 13, 427, 453
Lazistan, mountains of, 431, 450
Legends—about Argaeus, 128; about the Tigris, 293 foll.; about Sipan, 333; about Aghir Gheul, 330; about St. John the Baptist, 272; about Semiramis, 359; about Murad IV. at Sumelas, 440; of the Armenian nation, 382
'Loupes,' trade in, 304, 422

M AHMOUD, Sultan, centralising policy of, 91, 175, 307
Mahomet II., conquers Trebizond, 453; protects Sumelas, 443

MUR

Mahometans, their relation to the Christians, 181, 232, 418; deplorable condition of, in Asia Minor, 184
Male population of Asia Minor decimated by the war, 135, 171
Manna, 263, 269, 304
Manuscripts, rare in Armenia, 286; manuscript of King Hatoum, 274; manuscripts at Sumelas, 442
Manzikert, battle of, 100; position of, 386
Marsovan, plain of, 25
Massis, name of Ararat, 382
Mazaca, 107
Melas, river, 103
Melik, besieges Trebizond, 456
Mezireh, 215; plain of, 219, 239
Mezrop, St., invents the Armenian alphabet, 191; his reputed dwelling-place at Palu, 252; born near Mush, 286
Mine at Keban Maden, 212
Mineral waters, 304
Missions, the American, 236
Mollah Suleiman, 399
Moltke, Count von, his visit to Delik Tasch, 198; passes rapids of Euphrates, 208
Monasteries — Surp Garabed of Kaiserieh, 160 foll.; Surp Garabed of Mush, 270 foll.; Utch Keliseh, 392; Sumelas, 435
Monastic community at Gueremeh, 141
Moses of Chorene, born near Mush, 286; account of Van, 359 foll.
Mouaveen, or Christian assistant-governor, 347, 460
Muharram, spectacle of, 411
Mukhtar Pasha, commander in Asia, 388 foll., 402; retreat of, 405
Murad IV., Sultan, 168, 386, 440
Murad, river (Eastern Euphrates), 207, 248, 264, 269, 282; its source,

MUS

385; upper course, 386, 391; origin of name, 386

Mush, plain of, 269, 282, 287; town of, 283

NAPHTHA well, 349
Niches carved in the rocks, 137, 141, 165; intended for sepulture, 150

Nimrud Dagh, 280, 309, 313, 340; called Nemrut Tagh, 291

Niphates, mountains, 306

Norshunjuk, 327

Nose-rings, 271, 308

Nurshin, 289

OBSIDIAN, 263

PAGHESH, 307
Palace, ancient, at Euyuk, 58; at Boghaz-keui, 71

Palu, 250; castle-rock of, 251

Pasin, plain of, 406

Passes—over Anti-Taurus, 197; from Armenia into Kurdistan, 292; of Delibaba, 400; over the Kop Dagh, 422; behind Trebizond, 429 foll.

Pergri, 371; fortress of, 371

Persians, at Van, 344; in the plain of Alashgerd, 395; at Erzeroum, 411; at Trebizond, 450

Phrygians, their mode of building, 149

Pilgrimages, Christian, 164, 253, 271, 439, 442; Mahometan, 426

Pliny, on the Tigris and Arsanias, 244, 297; on the source of the Tigris, 294

Polo ground at Trebizond, 458

Pontus, kings of, 37; Amasia and Sinope capitals of, 37; St. Basil's retreat in, 147

Poplars, why grown in Armenia, 396

Posting in Turkey, 12, 16

SAM

Protestants, Armenian, 39, 95, 104, 111, 118; number of, in Armenia, 348

Provisions, cheapness of, in Asia Minor, 84

Pterium, site of, 72

Pyxites, river, 448

QUARTERING of Kurds on Armenians, 285

RAMAZAN fast, effects of, 254, 284, 372; observance of, 255; disadvantage to travellers, 308

Refectory, rock-hewn, 142; at Sumelas, 444

Refuges, 300

Repose of the Virgin, festival of, 271, 439

Rhododendrons, 436, 446

Ritter's 'Erdkunde,' the best guide to Armenia, 194

Rivers passing through lakes, 294

Rock-dwellings, near the Halys, 101; on the summit of Argaeus, 127; at Basch-keui, 134; at Urgub, 137; at Gueremeh, 141 foll.; at Surp Garabed of Kaiserieh, 165; at Akhlat, 316, 318; their object, 355

Roof of Western Asia, 385

Rupenian dynasty, 190

Russel Baliol, at Akhlat, 320

Russian campaign in Armenia, 388 foll.

Russians, their popularity in Asia Minor, 42; unpopularity in Armenia, 415

SAILORS, Armenian, 338, 341
Saladin, a Kurd by birth, 258, 320

Salt-lakes, 125, 133, 167, 197, 368

Samsoun, 9

INDEX.

SAP

Sapor, besieged Caesareia, 108
Sarikamis, 248
Schools, American, in Turkey, 237
Sebastoia (Sivas) 176
Seljouk Turks, invade Armenia, 190; their ravages in Asia Minor, 86; besiege Trebizond, 456
Seljouk architecture, 35, 111, 160, 316
Semiramis, at Van, 349; Moses of Chorene's account of, 359
Sempad, king, buried at Changeli, 274
Sheep, broad-tailed breed of, 156, 429
Shemiramagerd, old name of Van, 349
Shepherds, Turkish, 114
Shiites, 259
Sieges—of Amasia, 33; of Caesareia, 108; of Sivas, 177; of Kharput, 221; of Akhlat, 320; of Van, 365; of Erzeroum, 414; of Trebizond, 456
Singing, Armenian, 235, 274
Sinope, position of, 7
Sipan, Mount, 292, 309, 330, 399; ascent of, 326 foll.; height of, 332; legends concerning, 333
Sivas, important position of, 176; history of, 176 foll.; unhealthiness of, 178
Sivli Tasch, 137
Soghanli Dagh, 387, 390, 403
Soldiers, absence of, in Asia Minor and Armenia, 180, 348
Solomon, his fame in Asia, 318
Sophene, boundaries of, 208
Sphinxes, at Euyuk, 55, 61; origin of, 62, 63
Spring, sacred, at Sumelas, 444
Strabo, born at Amasia, 37, 38; excellence of his description of Amasia, 38; his account of the Tigris, 293
Student-interpreters, 179
Sultan-khané, 168

TIR

Sumelas, monastery, 435 foll.; valley of, 435, 446; bull of, 442
Sunnites, 250, 308
Surp Garabed (see Garabed)
Suzerainty of Kurds over Armenians, 232
Syrian Church, 224

TACHTALI-CHAI, 206
Tadvan, 310, 312
Tahir-keui — in the Anti-Taurus, 204; in Armenia, 380; battle at, 402
Takht-i-Soliman, 318
Talas, village of, 100
Taron (see Daron)
Taurus, range of, 215, 219, 230, 251
Taxation, 91, 170, 171, 184, 196
Tchapan Oglou, family of, at Yeuzgatt, 82
Tchekarek, river, 46, 51
Tchifteh Minareh, 412
Tchoruk, river, 423, 425
Teftik, or Angora goat, 84
Tekieh of Osman Pasha, 87
Telegrams in Turkey, 345
Ten Thousand, retreat of the (see Xenophon)
Tents, Kurdish, their construction, 378
Tergukassoff, Russian commander in Armenia, 389
Tezek, 88, 135, 257; not mentioned by Xenophon, 287
Threshing, mode of, 133
Tigris, western source of, 241-3; not connected with Euphrates, 244; eastern source, 292; connected with a tributary of the Euphrates, 292, 297; ancient legends about it, 292 foll.
Timour, besieges Amasia, 33; Sivas, 177; Van, 365
Tiridates, embraces Christianity, 180, 191

Tobacco, monopoly of, 290
Togarmah, 189, 366
Tombs, Seljouk, 111, 160, 316, 408
Tombs of the kings at Amasia, 33 foll. ; date of, 37
Tourbillons of dust, 104 ; formation of, 154
Trebizond, geographical position of, 434 ; appearance of, 450 ; origin of the name, 451 ; the mediaeval city, 451; history of, 452 foll. ; antiquities of, 455; siege of, 456
Trees, absence of, 53, 85, 99, 121, 370
Troglodytes, in Cappadocia, 145, 150
Tufa, houses excavated in, 134; obelisks of, 135, 140
Turkish cookery, 65
Turkish language, spoken by Greeks and Armenians, 107, 177 ; pronunciation of, 291, 371
Turkish peasantry in Asia Minor, 48, 171

UNDERGROUND houses, 256, 396
Urarti, name of Ararat, 363
Urgub, 137 foll.
Utch Keliseh, monastery, 392

VAN, city of, 344 ; unhealthiness of, 357 ; history of, 359 foll. ; castle of, 343, 349 foll.; Moses of Chorene's description of, 361
Van, lake of—called 'the sea,' 292 Strabo and Pliny upon it, 293 foll. ; not noticed by Xenophon, 299; first view of, 310 ; its characteristics, 311 foll.; saltness of, 324, 335; head of, 369

Vandalism in Turkey, 460
Varak Dagh, 342, 349
Vartabeds, 118, 166
Varzahan, ancient buildings at, 427
Vaspourakan, 364
Vegetables, cultivation of, 305
Villages, in Asia Minor, 52 ; in Armenia, 287
Vineyards, in Asia Minor, 52, 83; in Armenia, 283
Volcanoes, 130; Argaeus, 125, 130; Nimrud Dagh, 313; Sipan, 329, 330; Ararat, 381
Vultures, 29, 219

WATERSHEDS — between the Halys and Euphrates, 107 ; between the Tigris and Euphrates, 292 ; between the Eastern Euphrates and Araxes, 387, 400; between the Western Euphrates and Araxes, 387, 408 ; between the Western Euphrates and Acampsis, 422
Wine, rarely met with in Armenia, 215

XENOPHON, march of, 287, 298, 406, 432, 446
Xerxes, inscription of, at Van, 345

YAILA, or Turkish shepherds' encampment, 114
Yazili Kaya, or 'Inscribed Rock,' at Boghaz-keui, 66 foll.
Yeuzgatt, 80 foll. ; height of, 83

ZENOBIUS, bishop, 272, 276
Ziaret, 275

Spottiswoode & Co., Printers, New-street Square, and Parliament-street.

39 Paternoster Row, E.C.
London, *April* 1880.

GENERAL LISTS OF WORKS

PUBLISHED BY

Messrs. Longmans, Green & Co.

HISTORY, POLITICS, HISTORICAL MEMOIRS, &c.

Russia Before and After the War. By the Author of 'Society in St. Petersburg' &c. Translated from the German (with later Additions by the Author) by EDWARD FAIRFAX TAYLOR. Second Edition. 8vo. 14*s.*

Russia and England from 1876 to 1880; a Protest and an Appeal. By O. K. Author of 'Is Russia Wrong?' With a Preface by J. A. FROUDE, M.A. Portrait and Maps. 8vo. 14*s.*

History of England from the Conclusion of the Great War in 1815. By SPENCER WALPOLE. 8vo. VOLS. I. & II. 1815-1832 (Second Edition, revised) price 36*s.* VOL. III. 1832-1841, price 18*s.*

History of England in the 18th Century. By W. E. H. LECKY, M.A VOLS. I. & II. 1700-1760. Second Edition. 2 vols. 8vo. 36*s.*

The History of England from the Accession of James II. By the Right Hon. Lord MACAULAY.
STUDENT'S EDITION, 2 vols. cr. 8vo. 12*s.*
PEOPLE'S EDITION, 4 vols. cr. 8vo. 16*s.*
CABINET EDITION, 8 vols. post 8vo. 48*s.*
LIBRARY EDITION, 5 vols. 8vo. £4.

Lord Macaulay's Works. Complete and uniform Library Edition. Edited by his Sister, Lady TREVELYAN. 8 vols. 8vo. with Portrait, £5. 5*s.*

Critical and Historical Essays contributed to the Edinburgh Review. By the Right Hon. Lord MACAULAY.
CHEAP EDITION, crown 8vo. 3*s.* 6*d.*
STUDENT'S EDITION, crown 8vo. 6*s.*
PEOPLE'S EDITION, 2 vols. crown 8vo. 8*s.*
CABINET EDITION, 4 vols. 24*s.*
LIBRARY EDITION, 3 vols. 8vo. 36*s.*

The History of England from the Fall of Wolsey to the Defeat of the Spanish Armada. By J. A. FROUDE, M.A.
CABINET EDITION, 12 vols. crown, £3. 12*s.*
LIBRARY EDITION, 12 vols. demy, £8. 18*s.*

The English in Ireland in the Eighteenth Century. By J. A. FROUDE, M.A. 3 vols. 8vo. £2. 8*s.*

Journal of the Reigns of King George IV. and King William IV. By the late C. C. F. GREVILLE, Esq. Edited by H. REEVE, Esq. Fifth Edition. 3 vols. 8vo. price 36*s.*

The Life of Napoleon III. derived from State Records, Unpublished Family Correspondence, and Personal Testimony. By BLANCHARD JERROLD. In Four Volumes, 8vo. with numerous Portraits and Facsimiles. VOLS. I. to III. price 18*s.* each.

A

The Constitutional History of England since the Accession of George III. 1760-1870. By Sir THOMAS ERSKINE MAY, K.C.B. D.C.L. Sixth Edition. 3 vols. crown 8vo. 18s.

Democracy in Europe; a History. By Sir THOMAS ERSKINE MAY, K.C.B. D.C.L. 2 vols. 8vo. 32s.

Introductory Lectures on Modern History delivered in 1841 and 1842. By the late THOMAS ARNOLD, D.D. 8vo. 7s. 6d.

On Parliamentary Government in England; its Origin, Development, and Practical Operation. By ALPHEUS TODD. 2 vols. 8vo. 37s.

History of Civilisation in England and France, Spain and Scotland. By HENRY THOMAS BUCKLE. 3 vols. crown 8vo. 24s.

Lectures on the History of England from the Earliest Times to the Death of King Edward II. By W. LONGMAN, F.S.A. Maps and Illustrations. 8vo. 15s.

History of the Life & Times of Edward III. By W. LONGMAN, F.S.A. With 9 Maps, 8 Plates, and 16 Woodcuts. 2 vols. 8vo. 28s.

History of the Life and Reign of Richard III. Including the Story of PERKIN WARBECK. By JAMES GAIRDNER. Second Edition, Portrait and Map. Crown 8vo. 10s. 6d.

Memoirs of the Civil War in Wales and the Marches, 1642-1649. By JOHN ROLAND PHILLIPS, of Lincoln's Inn, Barrister-at-Law. 8vo. 16s.

History of England under the Duke of Buckingham and Charles I. 1624-1628. By S. R. GARDINER. 2 vols. 8vo. Maps, 24s.

The Personal Government of Charles I. from the Death of Buckingham to the Declaration in favour of Ship Money, 1628-1637. By S. R. GARDINER. 2 vols. 8vo. 24s.

Memorials of the Civil War between King Charles I. and the Parliament of England as it affected Herefordshire and the Adjacent Counties. By the Rev. J. WEBB, M.A. Edited and completed by the Rev. T. W. WEBB, M.A. 2 vols. 8vo. Illustrations, 42s.

Popular History of France, from the Earliest Times to the Death of Louis XIV. By Miss SEWELL. Crown 8vo. Maps, 7s. 6d.

A Student's Manual of the History of India from the Earliest Period to the Present. By Col. MEADOWS TAYLOR, M.R.A.S. Third Thousand. Crown 8vo. Maps, 7s. 6d.

Lord Minto in India; Correspondence of the First Earl of Minto, while Governor-General of India, from 1807 to 1814. Edited by his Great-Niece, the COUNTESS of MINTO. Completing Lord Minto's Life and Letters published in 1874 by the Countess of Minto, in Three Volumes. Post 8vo. Maps, 12s.

Indian Polity; a View of the System of Administration in India. By Lieut.-Col. G. CHESNEY. 8vo. 21s.

Waterloo Lectures; a Study of the Campaign of 1815. By Col. C. C. CHESNEY, R.E. 8vo. 10s. 6d.

The Oxford Reformers— John Colet, Erasmus, and Thomas More; a History of their Fellow-Work. By F. SEEBOHM. 8vo. 14s.

History of the Romans under the Empire. By Dean MERIVALE, D.D. 8 vols. post 8vo. 48s.

General History of Rome from B.C. 753 to A.D. 476. By Dean MERIVALE, D.D. Crown 8vo. Maps, price 7s. 6d.

The Fall of the Roman Republic; a Short History of the Last Century of the Commonwealth. By Dean MERIVALE, D.D. 12mo. 7s. 6d.

The History of Rome.
By WILHELM IHNE. VOLS. I. to III. 8vo, price 45s.

Carthage and the Carthaginians.
By R. BOSWORTH SMITH, M.A. Second Edition. Maps, Plans, &c. Crown 8vo. 10s. 6d.

The Sixth Oriental Monarchy;
or, the Geography, History, and Antiquities of Parthia. By G. RAWLINSON, M.A. With Maps and Illustrations. 8vo. 16s.

The Seventh Great Oriental Monarchy;
or, a History of the Sassanians. By G. RAWLINSON, M.A. With Map and 95 Illustrations. 8vo. 28s.

The History of European Morals
from Augustus to Charlemagne. By W. E. H. LECKY, M.A. 2 vols. crown 8vo. 16s.

History of the Rise and Influence of the Spirit of Rationalism in Europe.
By W. E. H. LECKY, M.A. 2 vols. crown 8vo. 16s.

The History of Philosophy,
from Thales to Comte. By GEORGE HENRY LEWES. Fifth Edition. 2 vols. 8vo. 32s.

A History of Classical Greek Literature.
By the Rev. J. P. MAHAFFY, M.A. Trin. Coll. Dublin. 2 vols. crown 8vo. price 7s. 6d. each.

Zeller's Stoics, Epicureans, and Sceptics.
Translated by the Rev. O. J. REICHEL, M.A. New Edition revised. Crown 8vo. 15s.

Zeller's Socrates & the Socratic Schools.
Translated by the Rev. O. J. REICHEL, M.A. Second Edition. Crown 8vo. 10s. 6d.

Zeller's Plato & the Older Academy.
Translated by S. FRANCES ALLEYNE and ALFRED GOODWIN, B.A. Crown 8vo. 18s.

'Aristotle and the Elder Peripatetics' and 'The Pre-Socratic Schools,' completing the English Edition of ZELLER's Work on Ancient Greek Philosophy, are preparing for publication.

Epochs of Modern History.
Edited by C. COLBECK, M.A.

Church's Beginning of the Middle Ages, 2s. 6d.
Cox's Crusades, 2s. 6d.
Creighton's Age of Elizabeth, 2s. 6d.
Gairdner's Houses of Lancaster and York, 2s. 6d.
Gardiner's Puritan Revolution, 2s. 6d.
———— Thirty Years' War, 2s. 6d.
Hale's Fall of the Stuarts, 2s. 6d.
Johnson's Normans in Europe, 2s. 6d.
Ludlow's War of American Independence, 2s. 6d.
Morris's Age of Anne, 2s. 6d.
Seebohm's Protestant Revolution, 2/6.
Stubbs's Early Plantagenets, 2s. 6d.
Warburton's Edward III. 2s. 6d.

Epochs of Ancient History.
Edited by the Rev. Sir G. W. COX, Bart. M.A. & C. SANKEY, M.A.

Beesly's Gracchi, Marius & Sulla, 2s. 6d.
Capes's Age of the Antonines, 2s. 6d.
———— Early Roman Empire, 2s. 6d.
Cox's Athenian Empire, 2s. 6d.
———— Greeks & Persians, 2s. 6d.
Curteis's Macedonian Empire, 2s. 6d.
Ihne's Rome to its Capture by the Gauls, 2s. 6d.
Merivale's Roman Triumvirates, 2s. 6d.
Sankey's Spartan & Theban Supremacies, 2s. 6d.

Creighton's Shilling History
of England, introductory to 'Epochs of English History.' Fcp. 8vo. 1s.

Epochs of English History.
Edited by the Rev. MANDELL CREIGHTON, M.A. Fcp. 8vo. 5s.

Browning's Modern England, 1820-1874, 9d.
Cordery's Struggle against Absolute Monarchy, 1603-1688, 9d.
Creighton's (Mrs.) England a Continental Power, 1066-1216, 9d.
Creighton's (Rev. M.) Tudors and the Reformation, 1485-1603, 9d.
Rowley's Rise of the People, 1215-1485, price 9d.
Rowley's Settlement of the Constitution, 1688-1778, 9d.
Tancock's England during the American & European Wars, 1778-1820, 9d.
York-Powell's Early England to the Conquest, 1s.

The Student's Manual of Ancient History; the Political History, Geography and Social State of the Principal Nations of Antiquity. By W. COOKE TAYLOR, LL.D. Cr. 8vo. 7s. 6d.

The Student's Manual of Modern History; the Rise and Progress of the Principal European Nations. By W. COOKE TAYLOR, LL.D. Crown 8vo. 7s. 6d.

BIOGRAPHICAL WORKS.

The Life of Henry Venn, B.D. Prebendary of St. Paul's, and Hon. Sec. of the Church Missionary Society; with Extracts from his Letters and Papers. By the Rev. W. KNIGHT, M.A. With an Introduction by the Rev. J. VENN, M.A. [*Just ready.*

Memoirs of the Life of Anna Jameson, Author of 'Sacred and Legendary Art' &c. By her Niece, GERARDINE MACPHERSON. 8vo. with Portrait, 12s. 6d.

Isaac Casaubon, 1559-1614. By MARK PATTISON, Rector of Lincoln College, Oxford. 8vo. 18s.

The Life and Letters of Lord Macaulay. By his Nephew, G. OTTO TREVELYAN, M.P.
CABINET EDITION, 2 vols. crown 8vo. 12s.
LIBRARY EDITION, 2 vols. 8vo. 36s.

The Life of Sir Martin Frobisher, Knt. containing a Narrative of the Spanish Armada. By the Rev. FRANK JONES, B.A. Portrait, Maps, and Facsimile. Crown 8vo. 6s.

The Life, Works, and Opinions of Heinrich Heine. By WILLIAM STIGAND. 2 vols. 8vo. Portrait, 28s.

The Life of Mozart. Translated from the German Work of Dr. LUDWIG NOHL by Lady WALLACE. 2 vols. crown 8vo. Portraits, 21s.

The Life of Simon de Montfort, Earl of Leicester, with special reference to the Parliamentary History of his time. By G. W. PROTHERO. Crown 8vo. Maps, 9s.

Felix Mendelssohn's Letters, translated by Lady WALLACE. 2 vols. crown 8vo. 5s. each.

Autobiography. By JOHN STUART MILL. 8vo. 7s. 6d.

Apologia pro Vitâ Suâ; Being a History of his Religious Opinions by JOHN HENRY NEWMAN, D.D. Crown 8vo. 6s.

Leaders of Public Opinion in Ireland; Swift, Flood, Grattan, O'Connell. By W. E. H. LECKY, M.A. Crown 8vo. 7s. 6d.

Essays in Ecclesiastical Biography. By the Right Hon. Sir J. STEPHEN, LL.D. Crown 8vo. 7s. 6d.

Cæsar; a Sketch. By JAMES ANTHONY FROUDE, M.A. formerly Fellow of Exeter College, Oxford. With Portrait and Map. 8vo. 16s.

Life of the Duke of Wellington. By the Rev. G. R. GLEIG, M.A. Crown 8vo. Portrait, 6s.

Memoirs of Sir Henry Havelock, K.C.B. By JOHN CLARK MARSHMAN. Crown 8vo. 3s. 6d.

Vicissitudes of Families. By Sir BERNARD BURKE, C.B. Two vols. crown 8vo. 21s.

Maunder's Treasury of Biography, reconstructed and in great part re-written, with above 1,600 additional Memoirs by W. L. R. CATES. Fcp. 8vo. 6s.

MENTAL and POLITICAL PHILOSOPHY.

Comte's System of Positive Polity, or Treatise upon Sociology :—
VOL. I. **General View of Positivism** and Introductory Principles. Translated by J. H. BRIDGES, M.B. 8vo. 21*s*.
VOL. II. **The Social Statics,** or the Abstract Laws of Human Order. Translated by F. HARRISON, M.A. 8vo. 14*s*.
VOL. III. **The Social Dynamics,** or the General Laws of Human Progress (the Philosophy of History). Translated by E. S. BEESLY, M.A. 8vo. 21*s*.
VOL. IV. **The Theory of the Future of Man**; with COMTE'S Early Essays on Social Philosophy. Translated by R. CONGREVE, M.D. and H. D. HUTTON, B.A. 8vo. 24*s*.

De Tocqueville's Democracy in America, translated by H. REEVE. 2 vols. crown 8vo. 16*s*.

Analysis of the Phenomena of the Human Mind. By JAMES MILL. With Notes, Illustrative and Critical. 2 vols. 8vo. 28*s*.

On Representative Government. By JOHN STUART MILL. Crown 8vo. 2*s*.

On Liberty. By JOHN STUART MILL. Post 8vo. 7*s*. 6*d*. crown 8vo. 1*s*. 4*d*.

Principles of Political Economy. By JOHN STUART MILL. 2 vols. 8vo. 30*s*. or 1 vol. crown 8vo. 5*s*.

Essays on some Unsettled Questions of Political Economy. By JOHN STUART MILL. 8vo. 6*s*. 6*d*.

Utilitarianism. By JOHN STUART MILL. 8vo. 5*s*.

The Subjection of Women. By JOHN STUART MILL. Fourth Edition. Crown 8vo. 6*s*.

Examination of Sir William Hamilton's Philosophy. By JOHN STUART MILL. 8vo. 16*s*.

A System of Logic, Ratiocinative and Inductive. By JOHN STUART MILL. 2 vols. 8vo. 25*s*.

Dissertations and Discussions. By JOHN STUART MILL. 4 vols. 8vo. £2. 7*s*.

The A B C of Philosophy; a Text-Book for Students. By the Rev. T. GRIFFITH, M.A. Prebendary of St. Paul's. Crown 8vo. 5*s*.

Philosophical Fragments written during intervals of Business. By J. D. MORELL, LL.D. Crown 8vo. 5*s*.

Path and Goal; a Discussion on the Elements of Civilisation and the Conditions of Happiness. By M. M. KALISCH, Ph.D. M.A. 8vo. price 12*s*. 6*d*.

The Law of Nations considered as Independent Political Communities. By Sir TRAVERS TWISS, D.C.L. 2 vols. 8vo. £1. 13*s*.

A Systematic View of the Science of Jurisprudence. By SHELDON AMOS, M.A. 8vo. 18*s*.

A Primer of the English Constitution and Government. By S. AMOS, M.A. Crown 8vo. 6*s*.

Fifty Years of the English Constitution, 1830-1880. By SHELDON AMOS, M.A. Crown 8vo. 10*s*. 6*d*.

Principles of Economical Philosophy. By H. D. MACLEOD, M.A. Second Edition in 2 vols. VOL. I. 8vo. 15*s*. VOL. II. PART I. 12*s*.

Lord Bacon's Works, collected & edited by R. L. ELLIS, M.A. J. SPEDDING, M.A. and D. D. HEATH. 7 vols. 8vo. £3. 13*s*. 6*d*.

Letters and Life of Francis Bacon, including all his Occasional Works. Collected and edited, with a Commentary, by J. SPEDDING. 7 vols. 8vo. £4. 4*s*.

The Institutes of Justinian; with English Introduction, Translation, and Notes. By T. C. SANDARS, M.A. 8vo. 18s.

The Nicomachean Ethics of Aristotle, translated into English by R. WILLIAMS, B.A. Crown 8vo. price 7s. 6d.

Aristotle's Politics, Books I. III. IV. (VII.) Greek Text, with an English Translation by W. E. BOLLAND, M.A. and Short Essays by A. LANG, M.A. Crown 8vo. 7s. 6d.

The Politics of Aristotle; Greek Text, with English Notes. By RICHARD CONGREVE, M.A. 8vo. 18s.

The Ethics of Aristotle; with Essays and Notes. By Sir A. GRANT, Bart. LL.D. 2 vols. 8vo. 32s.

Bacon's Essays, with Annotations. By R. WHATELY, D.D. 8vo. 10s. 6d.

Picture Logic; an Attempt to Popularise the Science of Reasoning. By A. SWINBOURNE, B.A. Post 8vo. 5s.

Elements of Logic. By R. WHATELY, D.D. 8vo. 10s. 6d. Crown 8vo. 4s. 6d.

Elements of Rhetoric. By R. WHATELY, D.D. 8vo. 10s. 6d. Crown 8vo. 4s. 6d.

On the Influence of Authority in Matters of Opinion. By the late Sir. G. C. LEWIS, Bart. 8vo. 14s.

The Senses and the Intellect. By A. BAIN, LL.D. 8vo. 15s.

The Emotions and the Will. By A. BAIN, LL.D. 8vo. 15s.

Mental and Moral Science; a Compendium of Psychology and Ethics. By A. BAIN, LL.D. Crown 8vo. 10s. 6d.

An Outline of the Necessary Laws of Thought; a Treatise on Pure and Applied Logic. By W. THOMSON, D.D. Crown 8vo. 6s.

Essays in Political and Moral Philosophy. By T. E. CLIFFE LESLIE, Hon. LL.D. Dubl. of Lincoln's Inn, Barrister-at-Law. 8vo. 10s. 6d.

Hume's Philosophical Works. Edited, with Notes, &c. by T. H. GREEN, M.A. and the Rev. T. H. GROSE, M.A. 4 vols. 8vo. 56s. Or separately, Essays, 2 vols. 28s. Treatise on Human Nature, 2 vols. 28s.

Lectures on German Thought. Six Lectures on the History and Prominent Features of German Thought during the last Two Hundred Years, delivered at the Royal Institution of Great Britain. By KARL HILLEBRAND. Rewritten and enlarged. Crown 8vo. 7s. 6d.

MISCELLANEOUS & CRITICAL WORKS.

Selected Essays, chiefly from Contributions to the Edinburgh and Quarterly Reviews. By A. HAYWARD, Q.C. 2 vols. crown 8vo. 12s.

Miscellaneous Writings of J. Conington, M.A. Edited by J. A. SYMONDS, M.A. 2 vols. 8vo. 28s.

Short Studies on Great Subjects. By J. A. FROUDE, M.A. 3 vols. crown 8vo. 18s.

Literary Studies. By the late WALTER BAGEHOT, M.A. Fellow of University College, London. Edited, with a Prefatory Memoir, by R. H. HUTTON. Second Edition. 2 vols. 8vo. with Portrait, 28s.

Manual of English Literature, Historical and Critical. By T. ARNOLD, M.A. Crown 8vo. 7s. 6d.

The Wit and Wisdom of the Rev. Sydney Smith. Crown 8vo. 3s. 6d.

Lord Macaulay's Miscellaneous Writings :—
LIBRARY EDITION, 2 vols. 8vo. 21s.
PEOPLE'S EDITION, 1 vol. cr. 8vo. 4s. 6d.

Lord Macaulay's Miscellaneous Writings and Speeches.
Student's Edition. Crown 8vo. 6s.

Speeches of the Right
Hon. Lord Macaulay, corrected by Himself. Crown 8vo. 3s. 6d.

Selections from the Writings of Lord Macaulay.
Edited, with Notes, by G. O. TREVELYAN, M.P. Crown. 8vo. 6s.

Miscellaneous and Posthumous Works of the late Henry Thomas Buckle.
Edited by HELEN TAYLOR. 3 vols. 8vo. 52s. 6d.

Miscellaneous Works of
Thomas Arnold, D.D. late Head Master of Rugby School. 8vo. 7s. 6d.

The Pastor's Narrative;
or, before and after the Battle of Wörth, 1870. By Pastor KLEIN. Translated by Mrs. F. E. MARSHALL. Crown 8vo. Map, 6s.

German Home Life;
a Series of Essays on the Domestic Life of Germany. Crown 8vo. 6s.

Realities of Irish Life.
By W. STEUART TRENCH. Crown 8vo. 2s. 6d. boards, or 3s. 6d. cloth.

Two Lectures on South
Africa delivered before the Philosophical Institute, Edinburgh, Jan. 6 & 9, 1880. By JAMES ANTHONY FROUDE, M.A. 8vo. 5s.

Cetshwayo's Dutchman;
the Private Journal of a White Trader in Zululand during the British Invasion. By CORNELIUS VIJN. Translated and edited with Preface and Notes by the Right Rev. J. W. COLENSO, D.D. Bishop of Natal. Crown 8vo. Portrait. 5s.

Apparitions; a Narrative
of Facts. By the Rev. B. W. SAVILE, M.A. Second Edition. Crown 8vo. price 5s.

Max Müller and the
Philosophy of Language. By LUDWIG NOIRÉ. 8vo. 6s.

Lectures on the Science
of Language. By F. MAX MÜLLER, M.A. 2 vols. crown 8vo. 16s.

Chips from a German
Workshop; Essays on the Science of Religion, and on Mythology, Traditions & Customs. By F. MAX MÜLLER, M.A. 4 vols. 8vo. £2. 18s.

Language & Languages.
A Revised Edition of Chapters on Language and Families of Speech. By F. W. FARRAR, D.D. F.R.S. Crown 8vo. 6s.

The Essays and Contributions of A. K. H. B.
Uniform Cabinet Editions in crown 8vo.

Recreations of a Country Parson, Three Series, 3s. 6d. each.

Landscapes, Churches, and Moralities, price 3s. 6d.

Seaside Musings, 3s. 6d.

Changed Aspects of Unchanged Truths, 3s. 6d.

Counsel and Comfort from a City Pulpit, 3s. 6d.

Lessons of Middle Age, 3s. 6d.

Leisure Hours in Town, 3s. 6d.

Autumn Holidays of a Country Parson, price 3s. 6d.

Sunday Afternoons at the Parish Church of a University City, 3s. 6d.

The Commonplace Philosopher in Town and Country, 3s. 6d.

Present-Day Thoughts, 3s. 6d.

Critical Essays of a Country Parson, price 3s. 6d.

The Graver Thoughts of a Country Parson, Three Series, 3s. 6d. each.

DICTIONARIES and OTHER BOOKS of REFERENCE.

One-Volume Dictionary of the English Language. By R. G. LATHAM, M.A. M.D. Medium 8vo. 24s.

Larger Dictionary of the English Language. By R. G. LATHAM, M.A. M.D. Founded on Johnson's English Dictionary as edited by the Rev. H. J. TODD. 4 vols. 4to. £7.

Roget's Thesaurus of English Words and Phrases, classified and arranged so as to facilitate the expression of Ideas, and assist in Literary Composition. Revised and enlarged by the Author's Son, J. L. ROGET. Crown 8vo. 10s. 6d.

English Synonymes. By E. J. WHATELY. Edited by R. WHATELY, D.D. Fcp. 8vo. 3s.

Handbook of the English Language. By R. G. LATHAM, M.A. M.D. Crown 8vo. 6s.

Contanseau's Practical Dictionary of the French and English Languages. Post 8vo. price 7s. 6d.

Contanseau's Pocket Dictionary, French and English, abridged from the Practical Dictionary by the Author. Square 18mo. 3s. 6d.

A Practical Dictionary of the German and English Languages. By Rev. W. L. BLACKLEY, M.A. & Dr. C. M. FRIEDLÄNDER. Post 8vo. 7s. 6d.

A New Pocket Dictionary of the German and English Languages. By F. W. LONGMAN, Ball. Coll. Oxford. Square 18mo. 5s.

Becker's Gallus ; Roman Scenes of the Time of Augustus. Translated by the Rev. F. METCALFE, M.A. Post 8vo. 7s. 6d.

Becker's Charicles; Illustrations of the Private Life of the Ancient Greeks. Translated by the Rev. F. METCALFE, M.A. Post 8vo. 7s. 6d.

A Dictionary of Roman and Greek Antiquities. With 2,000 Woodcuts illustrative of the Arts and Life of the Greeks and Romans. By A. RICH, B.A. Crown 8vo. 7s. 6d.

A Greek-English Lexicon. By H. G. LIDDELL, D.D. Dean of Christchurch, and R. SCOTT, D.D. Dean of Rochester. Crown 4to. 36s.

Liddell & Scott's Lexicon, Greek and English, abridged for Schools. Square 12mo. 7s. 6d.

An English-Greek Lexicon, containing all the Greek Words used by Writers of good authority. By C. D. YONGE, M.A. 4to. 21s. School Abridgment, square 12mo. 8s. 6d.

A Latin-English Dictionary. By JOHN T. WHITE, D.D. Oxon. and J. E. RIDDLE, M.A. Oxon. Sixth Edition, revised. Quarto 21s.

White's College Latin-English Dictionary, for the use of University Students. Royal 8vo. 12s.

M'Culloch's Dictionary of Commerce and Commercial Navigation. Re-edited, with a Supplement shewing the Progress of British Commercial Legislation to the Year 1880, by HUGH G. REID. With 11 Maps and 30 Charts. 8vo. 63s. The SUPPLEMENT separately, price 5s.

Keith Johnston's General Dictionary of Geography, Descriptive, Physical, Statistical, and Historical ; a complete Gazetteer of the World. Medium 8vo. 42s.

The Public Schools Atlas of Ancient Geography, in 28 entirely new Coloured Maps. Edited by the Rev. G. BUTLER, M.A. Imperial 8vo. or imperial 4to. 7s. 6d.

The Public Schools Atlas of Modern Geography, in 31 entirely new Coloured Maps. Edited by the Rev. G. BUTLER, M.A. Uniform, 5s.

ASTRONOMY and METEOROLOGY.

Outlines of Astronomy.
By Sir J. F. W. HERSCHEL, Bart. M.A. Latest Edition, with Plates and Diagrams. Square crown 8vo. 12s.

Essays on Astronomy.
A Series of Papers on Planets and Meteors, the Sun and Sun-surrounding Space, Stars and Star Cloudlets. By R. A. PROCTOR, B.A. With 10 Plates and 24 Woodcuts. 8vo. 12s.

The Moon; her Motions, Aspects, Scenery, and Physical Condition. By R. A. PROCTOR, B.A. With Plates, Charts, Woodcuts, and Lunar Photographs. Crown 8vo. 10s. 6d.

The Sun; Ruler, Light, Fire, and Life of the Planetary System. By R. A. PROCTOR, B.A. With Plates & Woodcuts. Crown 8vo. 14s.

The Orbs Around Us;
a Series of Essays on the Moon & Planets, Meteors & Comets, the Sun & Coloured Pairs of Suns. By R. A. PROCTOR, B.A. With Chart and Diagrams. Crown 8vo. 7s. 6d.

Other Worlds than Ours;
The Plurality of Worlds Studied under the Light of Recent Scientific Researches. By R. A. PROCTOR, B.A. With 14 Illustrations. Cr. 8vo. 10s. 6d.

The Universe of Stars;
Presenting Researches into and New Views respecting the Constitution of the Heavens. By R. A. PROCTOR, B.A. Second Edition, with 22 Charts (4 Coloured) and 22 Diagrams. 8vo. price 10s. 6d.

The Transits of Venus;
A Popular Account of Past and Coming Transits. By R. A. PROCTOR, B.A. 20 Plates (12 Coloured) and 27 Woodcuts. Crown 8vo. 8s. 6d.

Saturn and its System.
By R. A. PROCTOR, B.A. 8vo. with 14 Plates, 14s.

The Moon, and the Condition and Configurations of its Surface. By E. NEISON, F.R.A.S. With 26 Maps & 5 Plates. Medium 8vo. 31s. 6d.

A New Star Atlas, for the Library, the School, and the Observatory, in 12 Circular Maps (with 2 Index Plates). By R. A. PROCTOR, B.A. Crown 8vo. 5s.

Larger Star Atlas, for the Library, in Twelve Circular Maps, with Introduction and 2 Index Plates. By R. A. PROCTOR, B.A. Folio, 15s. or Maps only, 12s. 6d.

A Treatise on the Cy-cloid, and on all forms of Cycloidal Curves, and on the use of Cycloidal Curves in dealing with the Motions of Planets, Comets, &c. and of Matter projected from the Sun. By R. A. PROCTOR, B.A. With 161 Diagrams. Crown 8vo. 10s. 6d.

Dove's Law of Storms,
considered in connexion with the Ordinary Movements of the Atmosphere. Translated by R. H. SCOTT, M.A. 8vo. 10s. 6d.

Air and Rain; the Beginnings of a Chemical Climatology. By R. A. SMITH, F.R.S. 8vo. 24s.

Schellen's Spectrum Analysis, in its Application to Terrestrial Substances and the Physical Constitution of the Heavenly Bodies. Translated by JANE and C. LASSELL, with Notes by W. HUGGINS, LL.D. F.R.S. 8vo. Plates and Woodcuts, 28s.

NATURAL HISTORY and PHYSICAL SCIENCE.

Professor Helmholtz' Popular Lectures on Scientific Subjects. Translated by E. ATKINSON, F.C.S. With numerous Wood Engravings. 8vo. 12s. 6d.

Professor Helmholtz on the Sensations of Tone, as a Physiological Basis for the Theory of Music. Translated by A. J. ELLIS, F.R.S. 8vo. 36s.

Ganot's Natural Philosophy for General Readers and Young Persons; a Course of Physics divested of Mathematical Formulæ and expressed in the language of daily life. Translated by E. ATKINSON, F.C.S. Third Edition. Plates and Woodcuts. Crown 8vo. 7s. 6d.

Ganot's Elementary Treatise on Physics, Experimental and Applied, for the use of Colleges and Schools. Translated by E. ATKINSON, F.C.S. Ninth Edition. Plates and Woodcuts. Large crown 8vo. 15s.

Arnott's Elements of Physics or Natural Philosophy. Seventh Edition, edited by A. BAIN, LL.D. and A. S. TAYLOR, M.D. F.R.S. Crown 8vo. Woodcuts, 12s. 6d.

The Correlation of Physical Forces. By the Hon. Sir W. R. GROVE, F.R.S. &c. Sixth Edition, revised and augmented. 8vo. 15s.

Weinhold's Introduction to Experimental Physics; including Directions for Constructing Physical Apparatus and for Making Experiments. Translated by B. LOEWY, F.R.A.S. 8vo. Plates & Woodcuts 31s. 6d.

A Treatise on Magnetism, General and Terrestrial. By H. LLOYD, D.D. D.C.L. 8vo. 10s. 6d.

Elementary Treatise on the Wave-Theory of Light. By H. LLOYD, D.D. D.C.L. 8vo. 10s. 6d.

Fragments of Science. By JOHN TYNDALL, F.R.S. Sixth Edition, revised and augmented. 2 vols. crown 8vo. 16s.

Heat a Mode of Motion. By JOHN TYNDALL, F.R.S. Fifth Edition in preparation.

Sound. By JOHN TYNDALL, F.R.S. Third Edition, including Recent Researches on Fog-Signalling. Crown 8vo. price 10s. 6d.

Contributions to Molecular Physics in the domain of Radiant Heat. By JOHN TYNDALL, F.R.S. Plates and Woodcuts. 8vo. 16s.

Professor Tyndall's Researches on Diamagnetism and Magne-Crystallic Action; including Diamagnetic Polarity. New Edition in preparation.

Professor Tyndall's Lectures on Light, delivered in America in 1872 and 1873. With Portrait, Plate & Diagrams. Crown 8vo. 7s. 6d.

Professor Tyndall's Lessons in Electricity at the Royal Institution, 1875-6. With 58 Woodcuts. Crown 8vo. 2s. 6d.

Professor Tyndall's Notes of a Course of Seven Lectures on Electrical Phenomena and Theories, delivered at the Royal Institution. Crown 8vo. 1s. sewed, 1s. 6d. cloth.

Professor Tyndall's Notes of a Course of Nine Lectures on Light, delivered at the Royal Institution. Crown 8vo. 1s. swd., 1s. 6d. cloth.

Principles of Animal Mechanics. By the Rev. S. HAUGHTON, F.R.S. Second Edition. 8vo. 21s.

Text-Books of Science,

Mechanical and Physical, adapted for the use of Artisans and of Students in Public and Science Schools. Small 8vo. with Woodcuts, &c.

Abney's Photography, 3s. 6d.
Anderson's (Sir John) Strength of Materials, 3s. 6d.
Armstrong's Organic Chemistry, 3s. 6d.
Barry's Railway Appliances, 3s. 6d.
Bloxam's Metals, 3s. 6d.
Goodeve's Mechanics, 3s. 6d.
——— Mechanism, 3s. 6d.
Gore's Electro-Metallurgy, 6s.
Griffin's Algebra & Trigonometry, 3/6.
Jenkin's Electricity & Magnetism, 3/6.
Maxwell's Theory of Heat, 3s. 6d.
Merrifield's Technical Arithmetic, 3s. 6d.
Miller's Inorganic Chemistry, 3s. 6d.
Preece & Sivewright's Telegraphy, 3/6.
Rutley's Study of Rocks, 4s. 6d.
Shelley's Workshop Appliances, 3s. 6d.
Thomé's Structural and Physiological Botany, 6s.
Thorpe's Quantitative Analysis, 4s. 6d.
Thorpe & Muir's Qualitative Analysis, price 3s. 6d.
Tilden's Chemical Philosophy, 3s. 6d.
Unwin's Machine Design, 3s. 6d.
Watson's Plane & Solid Geometry, 3/6.

Light Science for Leisure

Hours; Familiar Essays on Scientific Subjects, Natural Phenomena, &c. By R. A. PROCTOR, B.A. 2 vols. crown 8vo. 7s. 6d. each.

An Introduction to the

Systematic Zoology and Morphology of Vertebrate Animals. By A. MACALISTER, M.D. With 28 Diagrams. 8vo. 10s. 6d.

The Comparative Anatomy and Physiology of the Vertebrate Animals. By RICHARD OWEN, F.R.S. With 1,472 Woodcuts. 3 vols. 8vo. £3. 13s. 6d.

Homes without Hands;

a Description of the Habitations of Animals, classed according to their Principle of Construction. By the Rev. J. G. WOOD, M.A. With about 140 Vignettes on Wood. 8vo. 14s.

Wood's Strange Dwellings; a Description of the Habitations of Animals, abridged from 'Homes without Hands.' With Frontispiece and 60 Woodcuts. Crown 8vo. 7s. 6d.

Wood's Insects at Home;

a Popular Account of British Insects, their Structure, Habits, and Transformations. 8vo. Woodcuts, 14s.

Wood's Insects Abroad;

a Popular Account of Foreign Insects, their Structure, Habits, and Transformations. 8vo. Woodcuts, 14s.

Wood's Out of Doors; a Selection of Original Articles on Practical Natural History. With 6 Illustrations. Crown 8vo. 7s. 6d.

Wood's Bible Animals; a description of every Living Creature mentioned in the Scriptures, from the Ape to the Coral. With 112 Vignettes. 8vo. 14s.

The Sea and its Living

Wonders. By Dr. G. HARTWIG. 8vo. with many Illustrations, 10s. 6d.

Hartwig's Tropical

World. With about 200 Illustrations. 8vo. 10s. 6d.

Hartwig's Polar World;

a Description of Man and Nature in the Arctic and Antarctic Regions of the Globe. Maps, Plates & Woodcuts. 8vo. 10s. 6d.

Hartwig's Subterranean

World. With Maps and Woodcuts. 8vo. 10s. 6d.

Hartwig's Aerial World;

a Popular Account of the Phenomena and Life of the Atmosphere. Map, Plates, Woodcuts. 8vo. 10s. 6d.

Kirby and Spence's Introduction to Entomology, or Elements of the Natural History of Insects. Crown 8vo. 5s.

A Familiar History of Birds. By E. STANLEY, D.D. Fcp. 8vo. with Woodcuts, 3s. 6d.

Rural Bird Life; Essays on Ornithology, with Instructions for Preserving Objects relating to that Science. By CHARLES DIXON. With Coloured Frontispiece and 44 Woodcuts by G. Pearson. Crown 8vo. 7s. 6d. cloth extra, gilt edges.

Rocks Classified and Described. By BERNHARD VON COTTA. An English Translation, by P. H. LAWRENCE, with English, German, and French Synonyms. Post 8vo. 14s.

The Geology of England and Wales; a Concise Account of the Lithological Characters, Leading Fossils, and Economic Products of the Rocks. By H. B. WOODWARD, F.G.S. Crown 8vo. Map & Woodcuts, 14s.

Keller's Lake Dwellings of Switzerland, and other Parts of Europe. Translated by JOHN E. LEE, F.S.A. F.G.S. With 206 Illustrations. 2 vols. royal 8vo. 42s.

Heer's Primæval World of Switzerland. Edited by JAMES HEYWOOD, M.A. F.R.S. With Map, 19 Plates, & 372 Woodcuts. 2 vols. 8vo. 16s.

The Puzzle of Life and How it Has Been Put Together; a Short History of Praehistoric Vegetable and Animal Life on the Earth. By A. NICOLS, F.R.G.S. With 12 Illustrations. Crown 8vo. 3s. 6d.

The Origin of Civilisation, and the Primitive Condition of Man; Mental and Social Condition of Savages. By Sir J. LUBBOCK, Bart. M.P. F.R.S. 8vo. Woodcuts, 18s.

A Dictionary of Science, Literature, and Art. Re-edited by the late W. T. BRANDE (the Author) and the Rev. Sir G. W. COX, Bart. M.A. 3 vols. medium 8vo. 63s.

Hullah's Course of Lectures on the History of Modern Music. 8vo. 8s. 6d.

Hullah's Second Course of Lectures on the Transition Period of Musical History. 8vo. 10s. 6d.

Loudon's Encyclopædia of Plants; comprising the Specific Character, Description, Culture, History, &c. of all the Plants found in Great Britain. With upwards of 12,000 Woodcuts. 8vo. 42s.

De Caisne & Le Maout's Descriptive and Analytical Botany. Translated by Mrs. HOOKER; edited and arranged by J. D. HOOKER, M.D. With 5,500 Woodcuts. Imperial 8vo. price 31s. 6d.

Rivers's Orchard-House; or, the Cultivation of Fruit Trees under Glass. Sixteenth Edition, re-edited by T. F. RIVERS. Crown 8vo. with 25 Woodcuts, 5s.

The Rose Amateur's Guide. By THOMAS RIVERS. Latest Edition. Fcp. 8vo. 4s. 6d.

Town and Window Gardening, including the Structure, Habits and Uses of Plants. By Mrs. BUCKTON With 127 Woodcuts. Crown 8vo. 2s.

CHEMISTRY and PHYSIOLOGY.

Practical Chemistry; the Principles of Qualitative Analysis. By W. A. TILDEN, D.Sc. Lond. F.C.S. Professor of Chemistry in Mason's College, Birmingham. Fcp. 8vo. 1s. 6d.

Miller's Elements of Chemistry, Theoretical and Practical. Re-edited, with Additions, by H. MACLEOD, F.C.S. 3 vols. 8vo.
PART I. CHEMICAL PHYSICS. 16s.
PART II. INORGANIC CHEMISTRY, 24s.
PART III. ORGANIC CHEMISTRY, 31s. 6d.

Annals of Chemical Medicine; including the Application of Chemistry to Physiology, Pathology, Therapeutics, Pharmacy, Toxicology, and Hygiene. Edited by J. L. W. THUDICHUM, M.D. VOL. I. 8vo. 14s.

Health in the House: Twenty-five Lectures on Elementary Physiology in its Application to the Daily Wants of Man and Animals. By Mrs. BUCKTON. Crown 8vo. Woodcuts, 2s.

A Dictionary of Chemistry and the Allied Branches of other Sciences. By HENRY WATTS, F.C.S. assisted by eminent Scientific and Practical Chemists. 7 vols. medium 8vo. £10. 16s. 6d.

Third **Supplement,** completing the Record of Chemical Discovery to the year 1877. PART I. 8vo. 36s. PART II. completion, in the press.

Select Methods in Chemical Analysis, chiefly Inorganic. By WM. CROOKES, F.R.S. With 22 Woodcuts. Crown 8vo. 12s. 6d.

The History, Products, and Processes of the Alkali Trade, including the most recent Improvements. By CHARLES T. KINGZETT, F.C.S. With 32 Woodcuts. 8vo. 12s.

Animal Chemistry, or the Relations of Chemistry to Physiology and Pathology: a Manual for Medical Men and Scientific Chemists. By CHARLES T. KINGZETT, F.C.S. 8vo. price 18s.

The FINE ARTS and ILLUSTRATED EDITIONS.

In Fairyland; Pictures from the Elf-World. By RICHARD DOYLE. With 16 coloured Plates, containing 36 Designs. Folio, 15s.

Lord Macaulay's Lays of Ancient Rome. With Ninety Illustrations on Wood from Drawings by G. SCHARF. Fcp. 4to. 21s.

Miniature Edition of Macaulay's Lays of Ancient Rome, with Scharf's 90 Illustrations reduced in Lithography. Imp. 16mo. 10s. 6d.

Moore's Lalla Rookh. TENNIEL'S Edition, with 68 Woodcut Illustrations. Crown 8vo. 10s. 6d.

Moore's Irish Melodies, MACLISE'S Edition, with 161 Steel Plates. Super-royal 8vo. 21s.

Lectures on Harmony, delivered at the Royal Institution. By G. A. MACFARREN. 8vo. 12s.

Sacred and Legendary Art. By Mrs. JAMESON. 6 vols. square crown 8vo. £5. 15s. 6d.

Jameson's Legends of the Saints and Martyrs. With 19 Etchings and 187 Woodcuts. 2 vols. 31s. 6d.

Jameson's Legends of the Monastic Orders. With 11 Etchings and 88 Woodcuts. 1 vol. 21s.

Jameson's Legends of the Madonna. With 27 Etchings and 165 Woodcuts. 1 vol. 21s.

Jameson's History of the Saviour, His Types and Precursors. Completed by Lady EASTLAKE. With 13 Etchings and 281 Woodcuts. 2 vols. 42s.

The Three Cathedrals dedicated to St. Paul in London. By W. LONGMAN, F.S.A. With numerous Illustrations. Square crown 8vo. 21s.

The USEFUL ARTS, MANUFACTURES, &c.

The Art of Scientific Discovery. By G. GORE, LL.D. F.R.S. Crown 8vo. 15s.

The Amateur Mechanics' Practical Handbook; describing the different Tools required in the Workshop. By A. H. G. HOBSON. With 33 Woodcuts. Crown 8vo. 2s. 6d.

The Engineer's Valuing Assistant. By H. D. HOSKOLD, Civil and Mining Engineer. 8vo. price 31s. 6d.

Industrial Chemistry; a Manual for Manufacturers and for Colleges or Technical Schools; a Translation (by Dr. T. H. BARRY) of Stohmann and Engler's German Edition of PAYEN's 'Précis de Chimie Industrielle;' with Chapters on the Chemistry of the Metals, &c. by B. H. PAUL, Ph.D. With 698 Woodcuts. Medium 8vo. 42s.

Gwilt's Encyclopædia of Architecture, with above 1,600 Woodcuts. Revised and extended by W. PAPWORTH. 8vo. 52s. 6d.

Lathes and Turning, Simple, Mechanical, and Ornamental. By W. H. NORTHCOTT. Second Edition, with 338 Illustrations. 8vo. 18s.

The Theory of Strains in Girders and similar Structures, with Observations on the application of Theory to Practice, and Tables of the Strength and other Properties of Materials. By B. B. STONEY, M.A. M. Inst. C.E. Royal 8vo. with 5 Plates and 123 Woodcuts, 36s.

A Treatise on Mills and Millwork. By the late Sir W. FAIRBAIRN, Bart. C.E. Fourth Edition, with 18 Plates and 333 Woodcuts. 1 vol. 8vo. 25s.

Useful Information for Engineers. By the late Sir W. FAIRBAIRN, Bart. C.E. With many Plates and Woodcuts. 3 vols. crown 8vo. 31s. 6d.

The Application of Cast and Wrought Iron to Building Purposes. By the late Sir W. FAIRBAIRN, Bart. C.E. With 6 Plates and 118 Woodcuts. 8vo. 16s.

Hints on Household Taste in Furniture, Upholstery, and other Details. By C. L. EASTLAKE. Fourth Edition, with 100 Illustrations. Square crown 8vo. 14s.

Handbook of Practical Telegraphy. By R. S. CULLEY, Memb. Inst. C.E. Seventh Edition. Plates & Woodcuts. 8vo. 16s.

A Treatise on the Steam Engine, in its various applications to Mines, Mills, Steam Navigation, Railways and Agriculture. By J. BOURNE, C.E. With Portrait, 37 Plates, and 546 Woodcuts. 4to. 42s.

Recent Improvements in the Steam Engine. By J. BOURNE, C.E. Fcp. 8vo. Woodcuts, 6s.

Catechism of the Steam Engine, in its various Applications. By JOHN BOURNE, C.E. Fcp. 8vo. Woodcuts, 6s.

Handbook of the Steam Engine, a Key to the Author's Catechism of the Steam Engine. By J. BOURNE, C.E. Fcp. 8vo. Woodcuts, 9s.

Examples of Steam and Gas Engines of the most recent Approved Types as employed in Mines, Factories, Steam Navigation, Railways and Agriculture, practically described. By JOHN BOURNE, C.E. With 54 Plates and 356 Woodcuts. 4to. 70s.

Cresy's Encyclopædia of Civil Engineering, Historical, Theoretical, and Practical. With above 3,000 Woodcuts. 8vo. 42s.

Ure's Dictionary of Arts, Manufactures, and Mines. Seventh Edition, re-written and enlarged by R. HUNT, F.R.S. assisted by numerous contributors. With 2,604 Woodcuts. 4 vols. medium 8vo. £7. 7s.

Practical Treatise on Metallurgy. Adapted from the last German Edition of Professor KERL'S Metallurgy by W. CROOKES, F.R.S. &c. and E. RÖHRIG, Ph.D. 3 vols. 8vo. with 625 Woodcuts. £4. 19s.

Anthracen; its Constitution, Properties, Manufacture, and Derivatives, including Artificial Alizarin, Anthrapurpurin, &c. with their Applications in Dyeing and Printing. By G. AUERBACH. Translated by W. CROOKES, F.R.S. 8vo. 12s.

On Artificial Manures, their Chemical Selection and Scientific Application to Agriculture; a Series of Lectures given at the Experimental Farm at Vincennes in 1867 and 1874-75. By M. GEORGES VILLE. Translated and edited by W. CROOKES, F.R.S. With 31 Plates. 8vo. 21s.

Practical Handbook of Dyeing and Calico-Printing. By W. CROOKES, F.R.S. &c. With numerous Illustrations and specimens of Dyed Textile Fabrics. 8vo. 42s.

The Art of Perfumery, and the Methods of Obtaining the Odours of Plants; the Growth and general Flower Farm System of Raising Fragrant Herbs; with Instructions for the Manufacture of Perfumes for the Handkerchief, Scented Powders, Odorous Vinegars and Salts, Snuff, Dentifrices, Cosmetics, Perfumed Soap, &c. By G. W. S. PIESSE, Ph.D. F.C.S. Fourth Edition, with 96 Woodcuts. Square crown 8vo. 21s.

Mitchell's Manual of Practical Assaying. Fourth Edition, revised, with the Recent Discoveries incorporated, by W. CROOKES, F.R.S. Crown 8vo. Woodcuts, 31s. 6d.

Loudon's Encyclopædia of Gardening; the Theory and Practice of Horticulture, Floriculture, Arboriculture & Landscape Gardening. With 1,000 Woodcuts. 8vo. 21s.

Loudon's Encyclopædia of Agriculture; the Laying-out, Improvement, and Management of Landed Property; the Cultivation and Economy of the Productions of Agriculture. With 1,100 Woodcuts. 8vo. 21s.

RELIGIOUS and MORAL WORKS.

A Handbook to the Bible, or, Guide to the Study of the Holy Scriptures derived from Ancient Monuments and Modern Exploration. By F. R. CONDER, and Lieut. C. R. CONDER, R.E. late Commanding the Survey of Palestine. Second Edition; Maps, Plates of Coins, &c. Post 8vo. price 7s. 6d.

Four Lectures on some Epochs of Early Church History. By the Very Rev. C. MERIVALE, D.D. Dean of Ely. Crown 8vo. 5s.

A History of the Church of England; Pre-Reformation Period. By the Rev. T. P. BOULTBEE, LL.D. 8vo. 15s.

Sketch of the History of the Church of England to the Revolution of 1688. By T. V. SHORT, D.D. Crown 8vo. 7s. 6d.

The English Church in the Eighteenth Century. By CHARLES J. ABBEY, late Fellow of University College, Oxford; and JOHN H. OVERTON, late Scholar of Lincoln College, Oxford. 2 vols. 8vo. 36s.

An Exposition of the 39 Articles, Historical and Doctrinal. By E. H. BROWNE, D.D. Bishop of Winchester. Eleventh Edition. 8vo. 16s.

A Commentary on the 39 Articles, forming an Introduction to the Theology of the Church of England. By the Rev. T. P. BOULTBEE, LL.D. New Edition. Crown 8vo. 6s.

Sermons preached mostly in the Chapel of Rugby School by the late T. ARNOLD, D.D. Collective Edition, revised by the Author's Daughter, Mrs. W. E. FORSTER. 6 vols. crown 8vo. 30s. or separately, 5s. each.

Historical Lectures on the Life of Our Lord Jesus Christ. By C. J. ELLICOTT, D.D. 8vo. 12s.

The Eclipse of Faith; or a Visit to a Religious Sceptic. By HENRY ROGERS. Fcp. 8vo. 5s.

Defence of the Eclipse of Faith. By H. ROGERS. Fcp. 8vo. 3s. 6d.

Nature, the Utility of Religion and Theism. Three Essays by JOHN STUART MILL. 8vo. 10s. 6d.

A Critical and Grammatical Commentary on St. Paul's Epistles. By C. J. ELLICOTT, D.D. 8vo. Galatians, 8s. 6d. Ephesians, 8s. 6d. Pastoral Epistles, 10s. 6d. Philippians, Colossians, & Philemon, 10s. 6d. Thessalonians, 7s. 6d.

Conybeare & Howson's Life and Epistles of St. Paul. Three Editions, copiously illustrated.
Library Edition, with all the Original Illustrations, Maps, Landscapes on Steel, Woodcuts, &c. 2 vols. 4to. 42s.
Intermediate Edition, with a Selection of Maps, Plates, and Woodcuts. 2 vols. square crown 8vo. 21s.
Student's Edition, revised and condensed, with 46 Illustrations and Maps. 1 vol. crown 8vo. 9s.

The Jewish Messiah; Critical History of the Messianic Idea among the Jews, from the Rise of the Maccabees to the Closing of the Talmud. By J. DRUMMOND, B.A. 8vo. 15s.

Bible Studies. By M. M. KALISCH, Ph.D. PART I. *The Prophecies of Balaam.* 8vo. 10s. 6d. PART II. *The Book of Jonah.* 8vo. price 10s. 6d.

Historical and Critical Commentary on the Old Testament; with a New Translation. By M. M. KALISCH, Ph.D. Vol. I. Genesis, 8vo. 18s. or adapted for the General Reader, 12s. Vol. II. Exodus, 15s. or adapted for the General Reader, 12s. Vol. III. Leviticus, Part I. 15s. or adapted for the General Reader, 8s. Vol. IV. Leviticus, Part II. 15s. or adapted for the General Reader, 8s.

Ewald's History of Israel. Translated from the German by J. E. CARPENTER, M.A. with Preface by R. MARTINEAU, M.A. 5 vols. 8vo. 63s.

Ewald's Antiquities of Israel. Translated from the German by H. S. SOLLY, M.A. 8vo. 12s. 6d.

The Types of Genesis, briefly considered as revealing the Development of Human Nature. By A. JUKES. Crown 8vo. 7s. 6d.

The Second Death and the Restitution of all Things; with some Preliminary Remarks on the Nature and Inspiration of Holy Scripture. By A. JUKES. Crown 8vo. 3s. 6d.

The Gospel for the Nineteenth Century. Third Edition. 8vo. price 10s. 6d.

Supernatural Religion; an Inquiry into the Reality of Divine Revelation. Complete Edition, thoroughly revised. 3 vols. 8vo. 36s.

Lectures on the Origin and Growth of Religion, as illustrated by the Religions of India; being the Hibbert Lectures, delivered at the Chapter House, Westminster Abbey, in 1878, by F. MAX MÜLLER, M.A. 8vo. 10s. 6d.

Introduction to the Science of Religion, Four Lectures delivered at the Royal Institution; with Essays on False Analogies and the Philosophy of Mythology. By F. MAX MÜLLER, M.A. Crown 8vo. 10s. 6d.

The Four Gospels in Greek, with Greek-English Lexicon. By JOHN T. WHITE, D.D. Oxon. Square 32mo. 5s.

Passing Thoughts on Religion. By Miss SEWELL. Fcp. 8vo. price 3s. 6d.

Thoughts for the Age. By Miss SEWELL. Fcp. 8vo. 3s. 6d.

Preparation for the Holy Communion; the Devotions chiefly from the works of Jeremy Taylor. By Miss SEWELL. 32mo. 3s.

Bishop Jeremy Taylor's
Entire Works; with Life by Bishop Heber. Revised and corrected by the Rev. C. P. EDEN. 10 vols. £5. 5s.

Hymns of Praise and
Prayer. Corrected and edited by Rev. JOHN MARTINEAU, LL.D. Crown 8vo. 4s. 6d. 32mo. 1s. 6d.

Spiritual Songs for the
Sundays and Holidays throughout the Year. By J. S. B. MONSELL, LL.D. Fcp. 8vo. 5s. 18mo. 2s.

Christ the Consoler;
a Book of Comfort for the Sick. By ELLICE HOPKINS. Second Edition. Fcp. 8vo. 2s. 6d.

Lyra Germanica; Hymns
translated from the German by Miss C. WINKWORTH. Fcp. 8vo. 5s.

The Temporal Mission
of the Holy Ghost; or, Reason and Revelation. By HENRY EDWARD MANNING, D.D. Crown 8vo. 8s. 6d.

Hours of Thought on
Sacred Things; Two Volumes of Sermons. By JAMES MARTINEAU, D.D. LL.D. 2 vols. crown 8vo. 7s. 6d. each.

Endeavours after the
Christian Life; Discourses. By JAMES MARTINEAU, D.D. LL.D. Fifth Edition. Crown 8vo. 7s. 6d.

The Pentateuch & Book
of Joshua Critically Examined. By J. W. COLENSO, D.D. Bishop of Natal. Crown 8vo. 6s.

Lectures on the Pentateuch
and the Moabite Stone; with Appendices. By J. W. COLENSO, D.D. Bishop of Natal. 8vo. 12s.

TRAVELS, VOYAGES, &c.

Sunshine and Storm in
the East, or Cruises to Cyprus and Constantinople. By Mrs. BRASSEY. With 2 Maps and 114 Illustrations engraved on Wood by G. Pearson, chiefly from Drawings by the Hon. A. Y. Bingham; the Cover from an Original Design by Gustave Doré. 8vo. 21s.

A Voyage in the 'Sunbeam,'
our Home on the Ocean for Eleven Months. By Mrs. BRASSEY. Cheaper Edition, with Map and 65 Wood Engravings. Crown 8vo. 7s. 6d.

One Thousand Miles up
the Nile; a Journey through Egypt and Nubia to the Second Cataract. By Miss AMELIA B. EDWARDS, Author of 'Untrodden Peaks and Unfrequented Valleys,' 'Barbara's History,' &c. With Facsimiles of Inscriptions, Ground Plans, Two Coloured Maps of the Nile from Alexandria to Dongola, and 80 Illustrations engraved on Wood from Drawings by the Author; bound in ornamental covers designed also by the Author. Imperial 8vo. 42s.

Wintering in the Riviera;
with Notes of Travel in Italy and France, and Practical Hints to Travellers. By WILLIAM MILLER, S.S.C. Edinburgh. With 12 Illustrations. Post 8vo. 12s. 6d.

San Remo and the Western Riviera;
comprising Bordighera, Mentone, Monaco, Beaulieu, Villefranche, Nice, Cannes, Porto Maurizio, Marina, Alassio, Verezzi, Noli, Monte Grosso, Pegli, Cornigliano, Genoa, and other Towns—climatically and medically considered. By A. HILL HASSALL, M.D. Map and Woodcuts. Crown 8vo. 10s. 6d.

Eight Years in Ceylon.
By Sir SAMUEL W. BAKER, M.A. Crown 8vo. Woodcuts, 7s. 6d.

The Rifle and the Hound
in Ceylon. By Sir SAMUEL W. BAKER, M.A. Crown 8vo. Woodcuts, 7s. 6d.

Himalayan and Sub-Himalayan Districts of British India, their Climate, Medical Topography, and Disease Distribution; with reasons for assigning a Malarious Origin to Goître and some other Diseases. By F. N. MACNAMARA, M.D. F.R.G.S. Surgeon-Major (retired) Indian Medical Service, late Professor of Chemistry, Calcutta Medical College, and Medical Inspector of Inland Labour Transport, Calcutta. 8vo. [*In the press.*]

The Alpine Club Map of Switzerland, with parts of the Neighbouring Countries, on the scale of Four Miles to an Inch. Edited by R. C. NICHOLS, F.R.G.S. 4 Sheets in Portfolio, 42s. coloured, or 34s. uncoloured.

The Alpine Guide. By JOHN BALL, M.R.I.A. Post 8vo. with Maps and other Illustrations :—

The Eastern Alps, 10s. 6d.

Central Alps, including all the Oberland District, 7s. 6d.

Western Alps, including Mont Blanc, Monte Rosa, Zermatt, &c. Price 6s. 6d.

On Alpine Travelling and the Geology of the Alps. Price 1s. Either of the Three Volumes or Parts of the 'Alpine Guide' may be had with this Introduction prefixed, 1s. extra.

WORKS of FICTION.

Novels and Tales. By the Right Hon. the EARL of BEACONSFIELD, K.G. Cabinet Editions, complete in Ten Volumes, crown 8vo. 6s. each.

Lothair, 6s.	Venetia, 6s.
Coningsby, 6s.	Alroy, Ixion, &c. 6s.
Sybil, 6s.	Young Duke &c. 6s.
Tancred, 6s.	Vivian Grey, 6s.

    Henrietta Temple, 6s.
    Contarini Fleming, &c. 6s.

Tales from Euripides; Iphigenia, Alcestis, Hecuba, Helen, Medea. By VINCENT K. COOPER, M.A. late Scholar of Brasenose College, Oxford. Fcp. 8vo. 3s. 6d.

Whispers from Fairyland. By the Right Hon. E. H. KNATCHBULL-HUGESSEN, M.P. With 9 Illustrations. Crown 8vo. 3s. 6d.

Higgledy-Piggledy; or, Stories for Everybody and Everybody's Children. By the Right Hon. E. H. KNATCHBULL-HUGESSEN, M.P. With 9 Illustrations. Cr. 8vo. 3s. 6d.

Stories and Tales. By ELIZABETH M. SEWELL. Cabinet Edition, in Ten Volumes, each containing a complete Tale or Story :—
Amy Herbert, 2s. 6d. Gertrude, 2s. 6d. The Earl's Daughter, 2s. 6d. The Experience of Life, 2s. 6d. Cleve Hall, 2s. 6d. Ivors, 2s. 6d. Katharine Ashton, 2s. 6d. Margaret Percival, 3s. 6d. Laneton Parsonage, 3s. 6d. Ursula, 3s. 6d.

The Modern Novelist's Library. Each work complete in itself, price 2s. boards, or 2s. 6d. cloth :—

By Lord BEACONSFIELD.

Lothair.	Henrietta Temple.
Coningsby.	Contarini Fleming.
Sybil.	Alroy, Ixion, &c.
Tancred.	The Young Duke, &c.
Venetia.	Vivian Grey.

By ANTHONY TROLLOPE.
    Barchester Towers.
    The Warden.

THE MODERN NOVELIST'S LIBRARY—*continued*.

By Major WHYTE-MELVILLE.
  Digby Grand. | Good for Nothing.
  General Bounce. | Holmby House.
  Kate Coventry. | The Interpreter.
  The Gladiators. | Queen's Maries.

By the Author of 'The Rose Garden.'
  Unawares.

By the Author of 'Mlle. Mori.'
  The Atelier du Lys.
  Mademoiselle Mori.

By Various Writers.
  Atherstone Priory.
  The Burgomaster's Family.
  Elsa and her Vulture.
  The Six Sisters of the Valleys.

The Novels and Tales of the Right Honourable the Earl of Beaconsfield, K.G. Complete in Ten Volumes, crown 8vo. cloth extra, gilt edges, 30s.

POETRY and THE DRAMA.

Lays of Ancient Rome; with Ivry and the Armada. By LORD MACAULAY. 16mo. 3s. 6d.

Horatii Opera. Library Edition, with English Notes, Marginal References & various Readings. Edited by Rev. J. E. YONGE, M.A. 8vo. 21s.

Poetical Works of Jean Ingelow. New Edition, reprinted, with Additional Matter, from the 23rd and 6th Editions of the two volumes respectively; with 2 Vignettes. 2 vols. fcp. 8vo. 12s.

Poems by Jean Ingelow. FIRST SERIES, with nearly 100 Woodcut Illustrations. Fcp. 4to. 21s.

The Poem of the Cid: a Translation from the Spanish, with Introduction and Notes. By JOHN ORMSBY. Crown 8vo. 5s.

Festus, a Poem. By PHILIP JAMES BAILEY. 10th Edition, enlarged & revised. Crown 8vo. 12s. 6d.

The Iliad of Homer, Homometrically translated by C. B. CAYLEY. 8vo. 12s. 6d.

The Æneid of Virgil. Translated into English Verse. By J. CONINGTON, M.A. Crown 8vo. 9s.

Bowdler's Family Shakspeare. Genuine Edition, in 1 vol. medium 8vo. large type, with 36 Woodcuts, 14s. or in 6 vols. fcp. 8vo. 21s.

Southey's Poetical Works, with the Author's last Corrections and Additions. Medium 8vo. with Portrait, 14s.

RURAL SPORTS, HORSE and CATTLE MANAGEMENT, &c.

Annals of the Road; or, Notes on Mail and Stage-Coaching in Great Britain. By Captain MALET. With 3 Woodcuts and 10 Coloured Illustrations. Medium 8vo. 21s.

Down the Road; or, Reminiscences of a Gentleman Coachman. By C. T. S. BIRCH REYNARDSON. Second Edition, with 12 Coloured Illustrations. Medium 8vo. 21s.

Blaine's Encyclopædia of Rural Sports; Complete Accounts, Historical, Practical, and Descriptive, of Hunting, Shooting, Fishing, Racing, &c. With 600 Woodcuts. 8vo. 21s.

A Book on Angling; or, Treatise on the Art of Fishing in every branch; including full Illustrated Lists of Salmon Flies. By FRANCIS FRANCIS. Post 8vo. Portrait and Plates, 15s.

Wilcocks's Sea-Fisherman: comprising the Chief Methods of Hook and Line Fishing, a glance at Nets, and remarks on Boats and Boating. Post 8vo. Woodcuts, 12s. 6d.

The Fly-Fisher's Entomology. By ALFRED RONALDS. With 20 Coloured Plates. 8vo. 14s.

Horses and Riding. By GEORGE NEVILE, M.A. With 31 Illustrations. Crown 8vo. 6s.

Youatt on the Horse. Revised and enlarged by W. WATSON, M.R.C.V.S. 8vo. Woodcuts, 12s. 6d.

Youatt's Work on the Dog. Revised and enlarged. 8vo. Woodcuts, 6s.

The Dog in Health and Disease. By STONEHENGE. Third Edition, with 78 Wood Engravings. Square crown 8vo. 7s. 6d.

The Greyhound. By STONEHENGE. Revised Edition, with 25 Portraits of Greyhounds, &c. Square crown 8vo. 15s.

Stables and Stable Fittings. By W. MILES. Imp. 8vo. with 13 Plates, 15s.

The Horse's Foot, and How to keep it Sound. By W. MILES. Imp. 8vo. Woodcuts, 12s. 6d.

A Plain Treatise on Horse-shoeing. By W. MILES. Post 8vo. Woodcuts, 2s. 6d.

Remarks on Horses' Teeth, addressed to Purchasers. By W. MILES. Post 8vo. 1s. 6d.

The Ox, his Diseases and their Treatment; with an Essay on Parturition in the Cow. By J. R. DOBSON, M.R.C.V.S. Crown 8vo. Illustrations, 7s. 6d.

WORKS of UTILITY and GENERAL INFORMATION.

Maunder's Treasury of Knowledge and Library of Reference; comprising an English Dictionary and Grammar, Universal Gazetteer, Classical Dictionary, Chronology, Law Dictionary, Synopsis of the Peerage, Useful Tables, &c. Fcp. 8vo. 6s.

Maunder's Biographical Treasury. Latest Edition, reconstructed and partly re-written, with above 1,600 additional Memoirs, by W. L. R. CATES. Fcp. 8vo. 6s.

Maunder's Treasury of Natural History; or, Popular Dictionary of Zoology. Revised and corrected Edition. Fcp. 8vo. with 900 Woodcuts, 6s.

Maunder's Scientific and Literary Treasury; a Popular Encyclopædia of Science, Literature, and Art. Latest Edition, partly re-written, with above 1,000 New Articles, by J. Y. JOHNSON. Fcp. 8vo. 6s.

Maunder's Treasury of Geography, Physical, Historical, Descriptive, and Political. Edited by W. HUGHES, F.R.G.S. With 7 Maps and 16 Plates. Fcp. 8vo. 6s.

Maunder's Historical Treasury; Introductory Outlines of Universal History, and Separate Histories of all Nations. Revised by the Rev. Sir G. W. COX, Bart. M.A. Fcp. 8vo. 6s.

WORKS published by **LONGMANS & CO.** 21

The Treasury of Botany, or Popular Dictionary of the Vegetable Kingdom; with which is incorporated a Glossary of Botanical Terms. Edited by J. LINDLEY, F.R.S. and T. MOORE, F.L.S. With 274 Woodcuts and 20 Steel Plates. Two Parts, fcp. 8vo. 12s.

The Treasury of Bible Knowledge; being a Dictionary of the Books, Persons, Places, Events, and other Matters of which mention is made in Holy Scripture. By the Rev. J. AYRE, M.A. Maps, Plates & Woodcuts. Fcp. 8vo. 6s.

A Practical Treatise on Brewing; with Formulæ for Public Brewers & Instructions for Private Families. By W. BLACK. 8vo. 10s. 6d.

The Theory of the Modern Scientific Game of Whist. By W. POLE, F.R.S. Tenth Edition. Fcp. 8vo. 2s. 6d.

The Correct Card; or, How to Play at Whist; a Whist Catechism. By Major A. CAMPBELL-WALKER, F.R.G.S. Latest Edition. Fcp. 8vo. 2s. 6d.

The Cabinet Lawyer; a Popular Digest of the Laws of England, Civil, Criminal, and Constitutional. Twenty-Fifth Edition, corrected and extended. Fcp. 8vo. 9s.

Chess Openings. By F.W. LONGMAN, Balliol College, Oxford. New Edition. Fcp. 8vo. 2s. 6d.

Pewtner's Comprehensive Specifier; a Guide to the Practical Specification of every kind of Building-Artificer's Work. Edited by W. YOUNG. Crown 8vo. 6s.

Modern Cookery for Private Families, reduced to a System of Easy Practice in a Series of carefully-tested Receipts. By ELIZA ACTON. With 8 Plates and 150 Woodcuts. Fcp. 8vo. 6s.

Food and Home Cookery. A Course of Instruction in Practical Cookery and Cleaning, for Children in Elementary Schools. By Mrs. BUCKTON. Woodcuts. Crown 8vo. 2s.

Hints to Mothers on the Management of their Health during the Period of Pregnancy and in the Lying-in Room. By THOMAS BULL, M.D. Fcp. 8vo. 2s. 6d.

The Maternal Management of Children in Health and Disease. By THOMAS BULL, M.D. Fcp. 8vo. 2s. 6d.

The Farm Valuer. By JOHN SCOTT, Land Valuer. Crown 8vo. 5s.

Rents and Purchases; or, the Valuation of Landed Property, Woods, Minerals, Buildings, &c. By JOHN SCOTT. Crown 8vo. 6s.

Economic Studies. By the late WALTER BAGEHOT, M.A. Fellow of University College, London. Edited by RICHARD HOLT HUTTON. 8vo. 10s. 6d.

Economics for Beginners By H. D. MACLEOD, M.A. Small crown 8vo. 2s. 6d.

The Elements of Banking. By H. D. MACLEOD, M.A. Fourth Edition. Crown 8vo. 5s.

The Theory and Practice of Banking. By H. D. MACLEOD, M.A. 2 vols. 8vo. 26s.

The Resources of Modern Countries; Essays towards an Estimate of the Economic Position of Nations and British Trade Prospects. By ALEX. WILSON. 2 vols. 8vo. 24s.

The Patentee's Manual; a Treatise on the Law and Practice of Letters Patent, for the use of Patentees and Inventors. By J. JOHNSON, Barrister-at-Law; and J. H. JOHNSON, Assoc. Inst. C.E. Solicitor and Patent Agent, Lincoln's Inn Fields and Glasgow. Fourth Edition, enlarged. 8vo. price 10s. 6d.

INDEX.

Abbey & Overton's English Church History   15
———'s Photography   11
Acton's Modern Cookery   21
Alpine Club Map of Switzerland   18
Alpine Guide (The)   18
Amos's Jurisprudence   5
——— Primer of the Constitution   5
——— Fifty Years of the English Constitution   5
Anderson's Strength of Materials   11
Armstrong's Organic Chemistry   11
Arnold's (Dr.) Lectures on Modern History   2
——————— Miscellaneous Works   7
——————— Sermons   15
——— (T.) English Literature   6
Arnott's Elements of Physics   10
Atelier (The) du Lys   19
Atherstone Priory   19
Autumn Holidays of a Country Parson   7
Ayre's Treasury of Bible Knowledge   21
Bacon's Essays, by Whately   6
——— Life and Letters, by Spedding   5
——— Works   5
Bagehot's Economic Studies   21
——— Literary Studies   6
Bailey's Festus, a Poem   19
Bain's Mental and Moral Science   6
——— on the Senses and Intellect   6
——— Emotions and Will   6
Baker's Two Works on Ceylon   17
Ball's Alpine Guides   18
Barry on Railway Appliances   11
Beaconsfield's (Lord) Novels and Tales   18 & 19
Becker's Charicles and Gallus   8
Beesly's Gracchi, Marius, and Sulla   3
Black's Treatise on Brewing   21
Blackley's German-English Dictionary   8
Blaine's Rural Sports   20
Bloxam's Metals   11
Bolland and Lang's Aristotle's Politics   6
Boultbee on 39 Articles   15
———'s History of the English Church   15
Bourne's Works on the Steam Engine   14
Bowdler's Family Shakespeare   19
Bramley-Moore's Six Sisters of the Valleys   19
Brande's Dictionary of Science, Literature, and Art   12
Brassey's Sunshine and Storm in the East   17
——— Voyage of the Sunbeam   17
Browne's Exposition of the 39 Articles   15
Browning's Modern England   3
Buckle's History of Civilisation   2
——— Posthumous Remains   7
Buckton's Food and Home Cookery   21
——— Health in the House   13
——— Town and Window Gardening   12
Bull's Hints to Mothers   21
——— Maternal Management of Children   21
Burgomaster's Family (The)   19
Burke's Vicissitudes of Families   4
Cabinet Lawyer   21
Capes's Age of the Antonines   3
——— Early Roman Empire   3
Cayley's Iliad of Homer   19
Cetshwayo's Dutchman, translated by Bishop Colenso   7

Changed Aspects of Unchanged Truths ...
Chesney's Indian Polity
——— Waterloo Campaign
Church's Beginning of the Middle Ages
Colenso on Moabite Stone &c.
———'s Pentateuch and Book of Joshua.
Commonplace Philosopher
Comte's Positive Polity
Conder's Handbook to the Bible
Congreve's Politics of Aristotle
Conington's Translation of Virgil's Æneid
——————— Miscellaneous Writings
Contanseau's Two French Dictionaries
Conybeare and Howson's St. Paul
Cooper's Tales from Euripides
Cordery's Struggle against Absolute Monarchy
Cotta on Rocks, by Lawrence
Counsel and Comfort from a City Pulpit
Cox's (G. W.) Athenian Empire
——————— Crusades
——————— Greeks and Persians
Creighton's Age of Elizabeth
——————— England a Continental Power
——————— Shilling History of England
——————— Tudors and the Reformation
Cresy's Encyclopædia of Civil Engineering
Critical Essays of a Country Parson
Crookes's Anthracen
——————— Chemical Analyses
——————— Dyeing and Calico-printing
Culley's Handbook of Telegraphy
Curteis's Macedonian Empire
De Caisne and Le Maout's Botany
De Tocqueville's Democracy in America
Dixon's Rural Bird Life
Dobson on the Ox
Dove's Law of Storms
Doyle's (R.) Fairyland
Drummond's Jewish Messiah
Eastlake's Hints on Household Taste
Edwards's Nile
Ellicott's Scripture Commentaries
——————— Lectures on Life of Christ
Elsa and her Vulture
Epochs of Ancient History
——————— English History
——————— Modern History
Ewald's History of Israel
——— Antiquities of Israel
Fairbairn's Applications of Iron
——— Information for Engineers
——— Mills and Millwork
Farrar's Language and Languages
Francis's Fishing Book
Frobisher's Life by Jones
Froude's Cæsar
——— English in Ireland
——— History of England
——— Lectures on South Africa
——— Short Studies
Gairdner's Houses of Lancaster and York
——— Richard III. & Perkin Warbeck
Ganot's Elementary Physics
——— Natural Philosophy
Gardiner's Buckingham and Charles

WORKS published by LONGMANS & CO. 23

rdiner's Personal Government of Charles I. 2
—— First Two Stuarts 3
—— Thirty Years' War 3
rman Home Life 7
oodeve's Mechanics 11
—— Mechanism 11
~'s Art of Scientific Discovery 14
—— Electro-Metallurgy 11
Gospel (The) for the Nineteenth Century . 16
Grant's Ethics of Aristotle 6
Graver Thoughts of a Country Parson...... 7
Greville's Journal 1
Griffin's Algebra and Trigonometry.......... 11
Griffith's A B C of Philosophy 5
Grove on Correlation of Physical Forces... 10
Gwilt's Encyclopædia of Architecture...... 14
Hale's Fall of the Stuarts...................... 3
Hartwig's Works on Natural History and Popular Science 11
Jassall's Climate of San Remo................ 17
Haughton's Animal Mechanics 10
Hayward's Selected Essays 6
Heer's Primeval World of Switzerland...... 12
Heine's Life and Works, by Stigand 4
Helmholtz on Tone 10
Helmholtz's Scientific Lectures 10
Herschel's Outlines of Astronomy 9
Hillebrand's Lectures on German Thought 6
Hobson's Amateur Mechanic.................... 14
Hopkins's Christ the Consoler 17
Hoskold's Engineer's Valuing Assistant ... 14
Hullah's History of Modern Music 12
—— Transition Period 12
Hume's Essays 6
—— Treatise on Human Nature......... 6
~'s Rome to its Capture by the Gauls... 3
—— History of Rome 3
.low's Poems 19
.meson's Sacred and Legendary Art...... 13
—— Memoirs by Macpherson 4
Jenkin's Electricity and Magnetism.......... 11
Jerrold's Life of Napoleon 1
Johnson's Normans in Europe 3
—— Patentee's Manual 21
Johnston's Geographical Dictionary.......... 8
Jukes's Types of Genesis 16
Jukes on Second Death 16
Kalisch's Bible Studies 16
—— Commentary on the Bible.......... 16
—— Path and Goal....................... 5
Keller's Lake Dwellings of Switzerland..... 12
Kerl's Metallurgy, by *Crookes* and *Röhrig*. 15
Kingzett's Alkali Trade 13
—— Animal Chemistry 13
Kirby and *Spence's* Entomology 12
Klein's Pastor's Narrative 7
Knatchbull-Hugessen's Fairy-Land 18
—— Higgledy-Piggledy 18
Landscapes, Churches, &c..................... 7
Latham's English Dictionaries 8
—— Handbook of English Language 8
Lecky's History of England..................... 1
—— European Morals.......... 3
—— Rationalism 3
—— Leaders of Public Opinion............. 4
Leisure Hours in Town 7
Leslie's Essays in Political and Moral Philosophy 6
Lessons of Middle Age 7

Lewes's Biographical History of Philosophy 3
Lewis on Authority 6
Liddell and *Scott's* Greek-English Lexicons 8
Lindley and *Moore's* Treasury of Botany ... 21
Lloyd's Magnetism 10
—— Wave-Theory of Light.............. 10
Longman's (F. W.) Chess Openings......... 21
—— German Dictionary ... 8
—— (W.) Edward the Third......... 2
—— Lectures on History of England 2
—— Old and New St. Paul's 13
Loudon's Encyclopædia of Agriculture 15
—— Gardening 15
—— Plants............ 12
Lubbock's Origin of Civilisation 12
Ludlow's American War of Independence 3
Lyra Germanica 17
Macalister's Vertebrate Animals 11
Macaulay's (Lord) Essays 1
—— History of England ... 1
—— Lays, Illustrated......... 13
—— Cheap Edition... 19
—— Life and Letters........ 4
—— Miscellaneous Writings 7
—— Speeches 7
—— Works 1
—— Writings, Selections from 7
McCulloch's Dictionary of Commerce 8
Macfarren on Musical Harmony 13
Macleod's Economical Philosophy............ 5
—— Economics for Beginners 21
—— Theory and Practice of Banking 21
—— Elements of Banking............ 21
Macnamara's Himalayan Districts of British India 18
Mademoiselle Mori 19
Mahaffy's Classical Greek Literature 3
Malet's Annals of the Road 19
Manning's Mission of the Holy Spirit 17
Marshman's Life of Havelock 4
Martineau's Christian Life..................... 17
—— Hours of Thought............. 17
—— Hymns....................... 17
Maunder's Popular Treasuries................. 20
Maxwell's Theory of Heat 11
May's History of Democracy 2
—— History of England 2
Melville's (Whyte) Novels and Tales 19
Mendelssohn's Letters 4
Merivale's Early Church History 15
—— Fall of the Roman Republic ... 3
—— General History of Rome 3
—— Roman Triumvirates............. 3
—— Romans under the Empire 3
Merrifield's Arithmetic and Mensuration... 11
Miles on Horse's Foot and Horse Shoeing 20
—— on Horse's Teeth and Stables......... 20
Mill (J.) on the Mind 5
Mill's (J. S.) Autobiography 4
—— Dissertations & Discussions 5
—— Essays on Religion............ 16
—— Hamilton's Philosophy 5
—— Liberty 5
—— Political Economy 5
—— Representative Government 5
—— Subjection of Women......... 5
—— System of Logic 5
—— Unsettled Questions 5
—— Utilitarianism 5

Miller's Elements of Chemistry	13
—— Inorganic Chemistry	11
—— Wintering in the Riviera	17
Minto (Lord) in India	2
Mitchell's Manual of Assaying	15
Modern Novelist's Library	18 & 19
Monsell's Spiritual Songs	17
Moore's Irish Melodies, Illustrated Edition	13
—— Lalla Rookh, Illustrated Edition	13
Morell's Philosophical Fragments	5
Morris's Age of Anne	3
Mozart's Life, by Nohl	4
Müller's Chips from a German Workshop	7
—— Hibbert Lectures on Religion	16
—— Science of Language	7
—— Science of Religion	16
Neison on the Moon	9
Nevile's Horses and Riding	20
Newman's Apologia pro Vitâ Suâ	4
Nicols's Puzzle of Life	12
Noiré's Müller & Philosophy of Language	7
Northcott's Lathes & Turning	14
Ormsby's Poem of the Cid	19
Owen's Comparative Anatomy and Physiology of Vertebrate Animals	11
Packe's Guide to the Pyrenees	18
Pattison's Casaubon	4
Payen's Industrial Chemistry	14
Pewtner's Comprehensive Specifier	21
Phillips's Civil War in Wales	2
Piesse's Art of Perfumery	15
Pole's Game of Whist	21
Powell's Early England	3
Preece & Sivewright's Telegraphy	11
Present-Day Thoughts	7
Proctor's Astronomical Works	9
—— Scientific Essays (Two Series)	11
Prothero's Life of Simon de Montfort	4
Public Schools Atlases	8
Rawlinson's Parthia	3
—— Sassanians	3
Recreations of a Country Parson	7
Reynardson's Down the Road	19
Rich's Dictionary of Antiquities	8
Rivers's Orchard House	12
—— Rose Amateur's Guide	12
Rogers's Eclipse of Faith	16
—— Defence of Eclipse of Faith	16
Roget's English Thesaurus	8
Ronalds' Fly-Fisher's Entomology	20
Rowley's Rise of the People	3
—— Settlement of the Constitution	3
Russia and England	1
Russia Before and After the War	1
Rutley's Study of Rocks	11
Sandars's Justinian's Institutes	6
Sankey's Sparta and Thebes	3
Savile on Apparitions	7
Schellen's Spectrum Analysis	9
Seaside Musings	7
Scott's Farm Valuer	21
—— Rents and Purchases	21
Seebohm's Oxford Reformers of 1498	2
—— Protestant Revolution	3
Sewell's History of France	2
Sewell's Passing Thoughts on Religion	16
—— Preparation for Communion	16
—— Stories and Tales	18
—— Thoughts for the Age	16
Shelley's Workshop Appliances	11
Short's Church History	15
Smith's (Sydney) Wit and Wisdom	6
—— (Dr. R. A.) Air and Rain	9
—— (R. B.) Carthage & the Carthaginians	3
Southey's Poetical Works	19
Stanley's History of British Birds	12
Stephen's Ecclesiastical Biography	4
Stonehenge, Dog and Greyhound	20
Stoney on Strains	14
Stubbs's Early Plantagenets	3
Sunday Afternoons, by A. K. H. B.	7
Supernatural Religion	16
Swinbourne's Picture Logic	6
Tancock's England during the Wars, 1778–1820	3
Taylor's History of India	2
—— Ancient and Modern History	4
—— (Jeremy) Works, edited by Eden	17
Text-Books of Science	1*.
Thomé's Botany	11
Thomson's Laws of Thought	6
Thorpe's Quantitative Analysis	11
Thorpe and Muir's Qualitative Analysis	11
Thudichum's Annals of Chemical Medicine	15
Tilden's Chemical Philosophy	11
—— Practical Chemistry	13
Todd on Parliamentary Government	2
Trench's Realities of Irish Life	7
Trollope's Warden and Barchester Towers	18
Twiss's Law of Nations	5
Tyndall's (Professor) Scientific Works	10
Unawares	19
Unwin's Machine Design	11
Ure's Arts, Manufactures, and Mines	14
Venn's Life, by Knight	4
Ville on Artificial Manures	15
Walker on Whist	21
Walpole's History of England	1
Warburton's Edward the Third	3
Watson's Geometery	11
Watts's Dictionary of Chemistry	13
Webb's Civil War in Herefordshire	2
Weinhold's Experimental Physics	10
Wellington's Life, by Gleig	4
Whately's English Synonymes	8
—— Logic	6
—— Rhetoric	6
White's Four Gospels in Greek	19
—— and Riddle's Latin Dictionaries	8
Wilcocks's Sea-Fisherman	2
Williams's Aristotle's Ethics	6
Wilson's Resources of Modern Countries	2
Wood's (J. G.) Popular Works on Natural History	1
Woodward's Geology	1.
Yonge's English-Greek Lexicons	
—— Horace	1.
Youatt on the Dog	2)
—— on the Horse	20
Zeller's Greek Philosophy	3.

Spottiswoode & Co. Printers, New-street Square, London.

www.ingramcontent.com/pod-product-compliance
Lightning Source LLC
Chambersburg PA
CBHW051158300426
44116CB00006B/350